ANNUAL EDITIONS

Educating Children with Exceptionalities

08/09

Nineteenth Edition

EDITOR

Karen L. Freiberg
University of Maryland, Baltimore County

Dr. Karen Freiberg has an interdisciplinary educational and employment background in nursing, education, and developmental psychology. She received her B.S. from the State University of New York at Plattsburgh, her M.S. from Cornell University, and her Ph.D. from Syracuse University. She has worked as a school nurse, a pediatric nurse, a public health nurse for the Navajo Indians, an associate project director for a child development clinic, a researcher in several areas of child development, and a university professor. Dr. Freiberg is the author of an award-winning textbook, *Human Development: A Life-Span Approach,* which is now in its fourth edition. She is currently on the faculty at the University of Maryland, Baltimore County.

Higher Education

Boston   Burr Ridge, IL   Dubuque, IA   New York   San Francisco   St. Louis
Bangkok   Bogotá   Caracas   Kuala Lumpur   Lisbon   London   Madrid   Mexico City
Milan   Montreal   New Delhi   Santiago   Seoul   Singapore   Sydney   Taipei   Toronto

Higher Education

ANNUAL EDITIONS: EDUCATING CHILDREN WITH EXCEPTIONALITIES, NINETEENTH EDITION

Annual Editions is published by the **Contemporary Learning Series** group within the McGraw-Hill Higher Education division.

 This book is printed on recycled, acid-free paper containing 10% postconsumer waste.

1 2 3 4 5 6 7 8 9 0 QPD/QPD 0 9 8

ISBN 978–0–07–339749–8
MHID 0–07–339749–0
ISSN 0198–7518

Managing Editor: *Larry Loeppke*
Production Manager: *Beth Kundert*
Developmental Editor: *Dave Welsh*
Editorial Assistant: *Nancy Meissner*
Production Service Assistant: *Rita Hingtgen*
Permissions Coordinator: *Shirley Lanners*
Senior Marketing Manager: *Julie Keck*
Marketing Communications Specialist: *Mary Klein*
Marketing Coordinator: *Alice Link*
Project Manager: *Jean Smith*
Design Specialist: *Tara McDermott*
Senior Administrative Assistant: *DeAnna Dausener*
Senior Operations Manager: *Pat Koch Krieger*
Cover Graphics: *Maggie Lytle*

Compositor: Laserwords Private Limited
Cover Image: Comstock/PictureQuest and © Digital Vision

Library in Congress Cataloging-in-Publication Data
Main entry under title: Annual Editions: Educating Children with Exceptionalities. 2008/2009.
 1. Educating Children with Exceptionalities—Periodicals. I. Freiberg, Karen L., *comp.* II. Title: Educating Children with Exceptionalities.
658'.05

www.mhhe.com

Editors/Advisory Board

Members of the Advisory Board are instrumental in the final selection of articles for each edition of ANNUAL EDITIONS. Their review of articles for content, level, currentness, and appropriateness provides critical direction to the editor and staff. We think that you will find their careful consideration well reflected in this volume.

Correlation Guide

The **Annual Editions** series provides students with convenient, inexpensive access to current, carefully selected articles from the public press. **Annual Editions: Educating Children with Exceptionalities 08/09** is an easy-to-use reader that presents articles on important topics such as large-scale assessments; building organizational skills in students with learning disabilities; and teaching students with emotional and behavioral disorders to manage their own behavior. For more information on **Annual Editions** and other **McGraw-Hill Contemporary Learning Series** titles visit **www.mhcls.com**. This convenient guide matches the units in **Annual Editions: Educating Children with Exceptionalities 08/09** with corresponding chapters in two of our McGraw-Hill Special Education texts.

Annual Editions: Educating Children with Exceptionalities 08/09	Taylor: Exceptional Students, 1/e	Lerner/Johns: Students with General Special Needs in Education, 1/e
Unit 1: Inclusive Education	**Chapter 1:** An Overview of Special Education **Chapter 2:** The Special Education Process: From Initial Identification to the Delivery of Services	**Chapter 1:** Students with Special Needs in General Education Classrooms **Chapter 4:** Understanding the Basics of the Law **Chapter 6:** Assessment **Chapter 7:** Planning for Instruction
Unit 2: Early Childhood	**Chapter 3:** School, Family, and Community Collaboration, **Chapter 13:** Students Who Are At-Risk: Early Identification and Intervention	**Chapter 2:** Students with High-Incidence Special Needs **Chapter 5:** Collaboration and Teamwork
Unit 3: Learning Disabilities	**Chapter 4:** Students with Learning Disabilities	**Chapter 2:** Students with High-Incidence Special Needs
Unit 4: Speech and Language Impairments	**Chapter 7:** Students with Communication Disorders	**Chapter 2:** Students with High-Incidence Special Needs **Chapter 10:** Adaptations for Teaching Oral Language **Chapter 11:** Adaptations for Teaching Reading
Unit 5: Developmental Disabilities/ Autistic Spectrum Disorders	**Chapter 5:** Students with Mental Retardation/ Intellectual Disabilities **Chapter 11:** Students with Autism Spectrum Disorders	**Chapter 2:** Students with High-Incidence Special Needs **Chapter 3:** Students with Low-Incidence Special Needs
Unit 6: Emotional and Behavioral Disorders	**Chapter 6:** Individuals with Emotional or Behavioral Disorders	**Chapter 2:** Students with High-Incidence Special Needs **Chapter 8:** Students with Behavioral Challenges **Chapter 9:** Students with Emotional, Social, and Mental Health Issues
Unit 7: Vision and Hearing Impairments	**Chapter 8:** Students Who Are Deaf and Hard of Hearing **Chapter 9:** Students with Blindness or Low Vision	**Chapter 3:** Students with Low-Incidence Special Needs
Unit 8: Multiple Disabilities	**Chapter 12:** Students with Severe Disabilities	**Chapter 3:** Students with Low-Incidence Special Needs
Unit 9: Orthopedic and Health Impairments	**Chapter 10:** Students with Physical or Health Impairments **Chapter 14:** Students with Attention Deficit/ Hyperactivity Disorders	**Chapter 2:** Students with High-Incidence Special Needs **Chapter 3:** Students with Low-Incidence Special Needs
Unit 10: Giftedness	**Chapter 15:** Students Who Are Gifted or Talented	**Chapter 2:** Students with High-Incidence Special Needs
Unit 11: Transition	**Chapter 1:** An Overview of Special Education **Chapter 3:** School, Family, and Community Collaboration	

Preface

The No Child Left Behind Act (NCLB) of 2001 required schools to have "highly qualified" educators in place to teach "core subjects" such as English, reading, math and science. By 2006 all states had "high stakes" testing established in grades 3–8 for reading and math. Schools that failed to make "adequate yearly progress" (AYP) for two years were mandated by NCLB to make improvements and provide supplemental services. Failure to make AYP for five years required a "restructure" of the school. Restructuring could involve school closings, changes in staffing, becoming a charter school, or having the state run the school. The education of children with exceptionalities created problems for many schools attempting to meet the accountability standards of NCLB. While the law allowed accommodations and modifications for testing of students with disabilities, individualized education plans (IEPs), were supposed to reflect appropriate achievement. Problems with how to assess achievement in special education have been enormous since 2001.

The mandate of NCLB and the 2004 Individuals with Disabilities Education Improvement Act (IDEIA), require that assessment of children with exceptionalities be specific to each individual and translate into instructional practice, "authentic assessment." This compendium of articles includes several references to authentic assessment and how to meet the legal rights of children with special needs.

The Individuals with Disabilities Education Improvement Act of 2004 (IDEIA) was amended to be aligned with NCLB. Both NCLB and IDEIA relate to two other civil rights laws of the USA, the Rehabilitation Act Amendment (Section 504), and the Americans with Disabilities ACT (ADA). The latter two laws prohibit disability discrimination while the NCLB and the IDEIA authorize funding to educate students with disabilities.

Under current U.S. law all children with disabilities are entitled to supportive educational services from diagnosis until age 21, and to reasonable accommodations and freedom from discrimination for life. Disability advocacy groups are continually alert to signs of exclusion of people with disabilities. Despite diverse attitudes, Congress set out four goals for them: equal opportunity, full participation, independent living, and economic self-sufficiency. IDEIA, as amended in 2004, stated that disability is a natural part of the human experience and in no way diminishes the right of individuals to participate in or contribute to society. IDEIA focuses on six principles of education to help achieve the congressional goals. These six fundamental legal educational policies are zero rejection from the educational system, nondiscriminatory evaluation, free and appropriate education in the public arena, the least-restrictive environment that meets the needs of the student, parental participation, and due process (right to sue if needs go unmet).

Annual Editions: Educating Children with Exceptionalities 08/09 includes multiple articles that deal with the legal rights of students with special needs, organized into categories of exceptionality. Many reports included in this compendium also discuss specific aspects of each category of exceptionality. Selections have been made with an eye to conveying information, giving personal experiences, offering suggestions for implementation, and stimulating meaningful discussions among future parents and teachers.

To help us improve future editions of this anthology, please complete and return the postage-paid article rating form on the last page. Your suggestions are valued and appreciated.

Karen Freiberg

Karen Freiberg
Editor

Contents

UNIT 1
Inclusive Education

UNIT 2
Early Childhood

The concepts in bold italics are developed in the article. For further expansion, please refer to the Topic Guide.

UNIT 3
Learning Disabilities

UNIT 4
Speech and Language Impairments

The concepts in bold italics are developed in the article. For further expansion, please refer to the Topic Guide.

UNIT 5
Developmental Disabilities/Autistic Spectrum Disorders

UNIT 6
Emotional and Behavioral Disorders

The concepts in bold italics are developed in the article. For further expansion, please refer to the Topic Guide.

UNIT 7
Vision and Hearing Impairments

UNIT 8
Multiple Disabilities

The concepts in bold italics are developed in the article. For further expansion, please refer to the Topic Guide.

UNIT 9
Orthopedic and Health Impairments

UNIT 10
Giftedness

The concepts in bold italics are developed in the article. For further expansion, please refer to the Topic Guide.

UNIT 11
Transition

The concepts in bold italics are developed in the article. For further expansion, please refer to the Topic Guide.

Topic Guide

This topic guide suggests how the selections in this book relate to the subjects covered in your course. You may want to use the topics listed on these pages to search the Web more easily.

On the following pages a number of Web sites have been gathered specifically for this book. They are arranged to reflect the units of this *Annual Edition*. You can link to these sites by going to the student online support site at *http://www.mhcls.com/online/*.

ALL THE ARTICLES THAT RELATE TO EACH TOPIC ARE LISTED BELOW THE BOLD-FACED TERM.

Attention Deficit Hyperactive Disorder
27. ADHD Among Students Receiving Special Education Services
33. Postsecondary Academies

Assessment
3. Large-Scale Assessments
4. Use Authentic Assessment Techniques to Fulfill the Promise of No Child Left Behind
5. Making the Case for Early Identification and Intervention for Young Children at Risk for Learning Disabilities
8. Build Organizational Skills in Students with Learning Disabilities
9. No More Friday Spelling Tests?
11. Assessment and Intervention for Bilingual Children with Phonological Disorders
12. A Speech-Language Approach to Early Reading Success
14. Service-Learning Opportunities That Include Students with Moderate and Severe Disabilities
16. Psychiatric Disorders and Treatments: A Primer for Teachers
18. Classroom Behavior Management
23. Classroom Interventions for Students with Traumatic Brain Injuries
29. Understanding the Young Gifted Child
30. Read All About It

Autism Spectrum Disorders
15. Fitting In
28. Finding What Works
33. Postsecondary Academies
34. What Happens When They Grow Up

Brain development
23. Classroom Interventions for Students with Traumatic Brain Injuries
34. What Happens When They Grow Up

Collaboration
1. Learn about Your New Students
2. Using Technology to Teach about Individual Differences Related to Disabilities
3. Large-Scale Assessments
6. Collaborative Steps
11. Assessment and Intervention for Bilingual Children with Phonological Disorders
15. Fitting In
16. Psychiatric Disorders and Treatments: A Primer for Teachers
21. Using Tactile Strategies with Students Who Are Blind and Have Severe Disabilities
22. Making Inclusion a Reality for Students with Severe Disabilities
23. Classroom Interventions for Students with Traumatic Brain Injuries
28. Finding What Works

Computers
2. Using Technology to Teach about Individual Differences Related to Disabilities
25. Savior Parents

Conflict resolution
7. Building Relationships with Challenging Children
16. Psychiatric Disorders and Treatments: A Primer for Teachers
18. Classroom Behavior Management
19. Students with Emotional and Behavioral Disorders *Can* Manage Their Own Behavior

Creativity
2. Using Technology to Teach about Individual Differences Related to Disabilities
29. Understanding the Young Gifted Child

Cultural diversity
2. Using Technology to Teach about Individual Differences Related to Disabilities
11. Assessment and Intervention for Bilingual Children with Phonological Disorders
17. I Want to Go Back to Jail
27. ADHD Among Students Receiving Special Education Services

Development disabilities
13. Filling the Potholes in the Road to Inclusion
14. Service-Learning Opportunities That Include Students with Moderate and Severe Disabilities
15. Fitting In
24. Empowering Students with Severe Disabilities to Actualize Communication Skills
34. What Happens When They Grow Up

Early childhood education
5. Making the Case for Early Identification and Intervention for Young Children at Risk for Learning Disabilities
6. Collaborative Steps
7. Building Relationships with Challenging Children
29. Understanding the Young Gifted Child

Elementary school
5. Making the Case for Early Identification and Intervention for Young Children at Risk for Learning Disabilities
9. No More Friday Spelling Tests?
11. Assessment and Intervention for Bilingual Children with Phonological Disorders
19. Students with Emotional and Behavioral Disorders *Can* Manage Their Own Behavior

Emotional and behavioral disorders
7. Building Relationships with Challenging Children
10. Addressing the Social and Emotional Needs of Twice-Exceptional Students
16. Psychiatric Disorders and Treatments: A Primer for Teachers
17. I Want to Go Back to Jail
18. Classroom Behavior Management
19. Students with Emotional and Behavioral Disorders *Can* Manage Their Own Behavior
27. ADHD Among Students Receiving Special Education Services
33. Postsecondary Academies

Internet References

The following Internet sites have been carefully researched and selected to support the articles found in this reader. The easiest way to access these selected sites is to go to our student online support site at *http://www.mhcls.com/online/*.

AE: Educating Children with Exceptionalities 08/09

The following sites were available at the time of publication. Visit our Web site—we update our student online support site regularly to reflect any changes.

General Sources

Consortium for Citizens With Disabilities
http://www.c-c-d.org

Included in this coalition organization is an Education Task Force that follows issues of early childhood special education, the president's commission on excellence in special education, issues of rethinking special education, 2001 IDEA principles, and many other related issues.

Family Village
http://www.familyvillage.wisc.edu/index.htmlx

Here is a global community of disability-related resources that is set up under such headings as library, shopping mall, school, community center, and others.

National Dissemination Center for Children With Disabilities (NICHCY)
http://www.nichcy.org/index.html

NICHCY provides information and makes referrals in areas related to specific disabilities, early intervention, special education and related services, individualized education programs, and much more. The site also connects to a listing of Parent's Guides to resources for children and youth with disabilities.

National Rehabilitation Information Center (NARIC)
http://www.naric.com

A series of databases that can be keyword-searched on subjects including physical, mental, and psychiatric disabilities, vocational rehabilitation, special education, assistive technology, and more can be found on this site.

President's Commission on Excellence in Special Education (PCESE)
http://www.ed.gov/inits/commissionsboards/whspecialeducation/

The report stemming from the work of the PCESE, *A New Era: Revitalizing Special Education for Children and Their Families*, can be downloaded in full at this site.

School Psychology Resources Online
http://www.schoolpsychology.net

Numerous sites on special conditions, disorders, and disabilities, as well as other data ranging from assertiveness/evaluation to research, are available on this resource page for psychologists, parents, and educators.

Special Education Exchange
http://www.spedex.com/main_graphics.htm

SpEdEx, as this site is more commonly known, offers a wealth of information, links, and resources to everyone interested in special education.

Special Education News
http://www.specialednews.com/disabilities/disabnews/ povanddisab031200.html

This particular section of this site discusses the problems of coping with both poverty and disability. Explore the rest of the site also for information for educators on behavior management, conflict resolution, early intervention, specific disabilities, and much more.

UNIT 1: Inclusive Education

Institute on Disability/University of New Hampshire
http://iod.unh.edu

This site includes Early Childhood, Inclusive Education, High School and Post-Secondary School, Community Living and Adult Life, Related Links, both state and national, and information on technology, health care, public policy, as well as leadership training and professional development.

Kids Together, Inc.
http://www.kidstogether.org

Based on the IDEA law about teaching children with disabilities in regular classrooms, this site contains all the information on inclusion you might need to know.

New Horizons for Learning
http://www.newhorizons.org

Based on the theory of inclusion, this site is filled with information on special needs inclusion, technology and learning, a brain lab, and much more, presented as floors in a building.

UNIT 2: Early Childhood

Division for Early Childhood
http://www.dec-sped.org

A division of the Council for Exceptional Children, the DEC advocates for the improvement of conditions of young children with special needs. Child development theory, programming data, parenting data, research, and links to other sites can be found on this site.

Institute on Community Integration Projects
http://ici.umn.edu/projectscenters/

Research projects related to early childhood and early intervention services for special education are described here.

National Association for Child Development (NACD)
http://www.nacd.org

The NACD, an international organization, is dedicated to helping children and adults reach their full potential. Its home page presents links to various programs, research, and resources into such topics as learning disabilities, ADD/ADHD, brain injuries, autism, accelerated and gifted, and other similar topic areas.

www.mhcls.com/online/

Special Education Resources on the Internet (SERI)
http://seriweb.com

SERI offers helpful sites in all phases of special education in early childhood, including disabilities, mental retardation, behavior disorders, and autism.

UNIT 3: Learning Disabilities

Children and Adults With Attention Deficit/Hyperactivity Disorder (CHADD)
http://www.chadd.org

CHADD works to improve the lives of people with AD/HD through education, advocacy, and support, offering information that can be trusted. The site includes fact sheets, legislative information, research studies, and links.

The Instant Access Treasure Chest
http://www.fln.vcu.edu/ld/ld.html

Billed as the Foreign Language Teacher's Guide to Learning Disabilities, this site contains a very thorough list of resources for anyone interested in LD education issues.

Learning Disabilities Association of America (LDA)
http://www.ldanatl.org

The purpose of the LDA is to advance the education and general welfare of children of normal and potentially normal intelligence who show handicaps of a perceptual, conceptual, or coordinative nature.

Learning Disabilities Online
http://www.ldonline.org

This is a good source for information about all kinds of learning disabilities with links to other related material.

Teaching Children With Attention Deficit Disorder
http://www.kidsource.com/kidsource/content2/add.html

This in-depth site defines both types of ADD and discusses establishing the proper learning environment.

UNIT 4: Speech and Language Impairments

Issues in Emergent Literacy for Children With Language Impairments
http://www.ciera.org/library/reports/inquiry-2/2-002/2-002.html

This article explores the relationship between oral language impairment and reading disabilities in children. The article suggests that language impairment may be a basic deficit that affects language function in both its oral and written forms.

UNIT 5: Developmental Disabilities/Autistic Spectrum Disorders

Arc of the United States
http://www.thearc.org

Here is the Web site of the national organization of and for people with mental retardation and related disabilities and their families. It includes governmental affairs, services, position statements, FAQs, publications, and related links.

Disability-Related Sources on the Web
http://www.arcarizona.org

This resource's many links include grant resources, federally funded projects and federal agencies, assistive technology, national and international organizations, and educational resources and directories.

Gentle Teaching
http://www.gentleteaching.nl

Maintained by the foundation for Gentle Teaching in the Netherlands, this page explains a nonviolent approach for helping children and adults with special needs.

UNIT 6: Emotional and Behavioral Disorders

Pacer Center: Emotional Behavioral Disorders
http://www.pacer.org/ebd/

Active in Minnesota for 8 years in helping parents become advocates for their EBD children, PACER has gone on to present workshops for parents on how to access aid for their child, explain what a parent should look for in a child they suspect of EBD, prepare a behavioral intervention guide, and link to resources, including IDEA's Parnership in Education site, and much more.

UNIT 7: Vision and Hearing Impairments

Info to Go: Laurent Clerc National Deaf Education Center
http://clerccenter.gallaudet.edu/InfoToGo/index.html

Important for parents and educators, this Web site from Gallaudet University offers information on audiology, communication, education, legal, and health issues of deaf people.

The New York Institute for Special Education
http://www.nyise.org/index.html

This school is an educational facility that serves children who are blind or visually impaired. The site includes program descriptions and resources for the blind.

UNIT 8: Multiple Disabilities

Activity Ideas for Students With Severe, Profound, or Multiple Disabilities
http://www.palaestra.com/featurestory.html

The Fall 1997 issue of the *Palaestra* contains this interesting article on teaching students who have multiple disabilities. The complete text is offered here online.

Severe and/or Multiple Disabilities
http://www.nichcy.org/pubs/factshe/fs10txt.htm

This fact sheet offers a definition of multiple disabilities, discusses incidence, characteristics, medical, and educational implications, and suggests resources and organizations that might be of help to parents and educators of children with severe impairments.

www.mhcls.com/online/

UNIT 9: Orthopedic and Health Impairments

Association to Benefit Children (ABC)
http://www.a-b-c.org

ABC presents a network of programs that includes child advocacy, education for disabled children, care for HIV-positive children, employment, housing, foster care, and day care.

An Idea Whose Time Has Come
http://www.boggscenter.org/mich3899.htm

The purpose of community-based education is to help students in special education to become more independent. Here is an excellent description of how it is being done in at least one community.

Resources for VE Teachers
http://www.cpt.fsu.edu/tree//ve/tofc.html

Effective practices for teachers of varying exceptionalities (VE) classes are listed here.

UNIT 10: Giftedness

The Council for Exceptional Children
http://www.cec.sped.org/index.html

This page will give you access to information on identifying and teaching gifted children, attention-deficit disorders, and other topics in gifted education.

UNIT 11: Transition

National Center on Secondary Education and Transition
http://www.ncset.org

This site coordinates national resources, offers technical assistance, and disseminates information related to secondary education and transition for youth with disabilities in order to create opportunities for youth to achieve successful futures.

We highly recommend that you review our Web site for expanded information and our other product lines. We are continually updating and adding links to our Web site in order to offer you the most usable and useful information that will support and expand the value of your Annual Editions. You can reach us at: *http://www.mhcls.com/annualeditions/.*

UNIT 1

Inclusive Education

Unit Selections

1. **Learn about Your New Students,** MaryAnn Barnes
2. **Using Technology to Teach about Individual Differences Related to Disabilities,** Spencer J. Salend
3. **Large-Scale Assessments,** Elizabeth A. Edgemon, Brian R. Jablonski, and John W. Lloyd
4. **Use Authentic Assessment Techniques to Fulfill the Promise of No Child Left Behind,** Carol A Layton and Robin H. Lock

Key Points to Consider

- How can a teacher be as prepared as possible to meet the education and social-emotional needs of a new student with a condition of exceptionality?

- How can a teacher help students accept and even celebrate the diversity of all classroom peers, especially those with conditions of exceptionality?

- How should teachers and IEP teams select the most appropriate accommodations for students with special needs?

- Can authentic assessments fulfill the promises of No Child Left Behind (NCLB) and the Individuals with Disabilities Education Improvement Act (IDEIA)?

Student Web Site

www.mhcls.com/online

Internet References

Further information regarding these Web sites may be found in this book's preface or online.

Institute on Disability/University of New Hampshire
http://iod.unh.edu
Kids Together, Inc.
http://www.kidstogether.org
New Horizons for Learning
http://www.newhorizons.org

The McGraw-Hill Companies, Inc./Christopher Kerrigan, photographer

A huge strength of American schools is the dedication and motivation of its professional teachers. These teaching responsibilities are carried out despite inadequate social, emotional and financial support; lack of sufficient inservice education; and few provisions for continuing education. Teachers need all the help they can get, to be the best they can possibly be, and to feel appreciated!

This unit on Inclusive Education highlights what's good in special education, and includes some suggestions for ways it can be improved.

Regular education teachers are expected to know how to provide special educational services to every child with an exceptional condition in their classroom, despite not having had coursework in special education. The numbers of students with exceptionalities who are being educated in regular education classes are increasing annually. The Individuals with Disabilities Education Improvement Act (IDEIA) has reduced the numbers of special needs students being educated in residential centers, hospitals, homes, or special schools to less than 5 percent. Children who once would have been turned away from public schools are now being admitted in enormous numbers. The No Child Left Behind Act (NCLB) has increased the emphases on high expectations for all students from highly qualified teachers who do frequent proficiency assessments.

The trend toward inclusive education necessitates more knowledge and expertise on the part of the regular education

teachers. Educating children with exceptionalities can no longer be viewed as the job of special-education teachers. This trend also mandates knowledge about collaboration and advisory activities on the part of all special educators. Teamwork is essential as special education and regular education are becoming more and more intertwined.

Public schools have an obligation to provide free educational services in the least restrictive environment possible to all children who have diagnosed conditions of exceptionality. Although laws in Canada and the United States differ slightly, all public schools have an obligation to serve children with exceptional conditions in as normal an educational environment as possible. Inclusive education is difficult. It works very well for some students with exceptionalities in some situations and marginally or not at all for other students with exceptionalities in other situations.

For inclusion to succeed within a school, everyone must be committed to be part of the solution: superintendent, principal, teachers, coaches, aides, ancillary staff, students, parents, and families. Special education teachers often find their jobs involving much more than instructing students with special needs. They serve as consultants to regular education teachers to assure that inclusion is meaningful for their students. They collaborate with parents, administrators, support personnel, and community agencies as well as with regular education teachers. They plan curriculum and oversee the writing of Individualized

Family Service Plans (IFSPs), Individualized Education Plans (IEPs) and Individualized Transition Plans (ITPs). They schedule and make sure that services are provided by all team-involved persons. They keep up with enormous amounts of paperwork. They update parents even when parents are too involved, or not involved enough. They keep abreast of new resources, new legal processes, and new instructional techniques. They make projections for the futures of their students and set out ways to make good things happen. They also struggle to be accountable, both educationally and financially, for all they do.

The term "least restrictive environment" is often mistakenly understood as the need for all children to be educated in a regular education classroom. If students can learn and achieve better in inclusive programs, then they belong there. If students can succeed only marginally in inclusive education classrooms, some alternate solutions are necessary. A continuum of placement options exists to maximize the goal of educating every child. For some children, a separate class, or even a separate school, is still optimal.

Every child with an exceptional condition is different from every other child in symptoms, needs, and teachability. Each child is, therefore, provided with a unique individualized education plan. This plan consists of both long- and short-term goals for education, specially designed instructional procedures with related services, and methods to evaluate the child's progress. The IEP is updated and revised annually. Special education teachers, parents, and all applicable service providers must collaborate at least this often to make recommendations for goals and teaching strategies. The IEPs should always be outcomes-oriented with functional curricula.

The first selection in this Inclusion Unit is an article by a leading expert on inclusive education for students with disabilities. Dr. MaryAnn Byrnes gives twenty pieces of advice for beginning the school year with new students; those with, and without disabilities. These twenty ounces of prevention can be worth more than twenty pounds of remediation.

The second article chosen for inclusion in this section deals with *Using Technology to Teach About Individual Differences Related to Disabilities.* In order for children with disabilities to feel included and natural in their environments it is necessary for them to fully participate in many activities with their peers. Collaborating on computer projects is an excellent avenue for both such cooperation and for more education about exceptional conditions.

The third report gives teachers a heads-up about the assessment requirements of IDEIA 2004 and how to implement accommodations for instruction and testing. It is a useful guide for all members of the IEP teams for students with special needs.

The final featured article discusses "authentic assessment" and gives twenty suggestions for making education and evaluation of achievement of children with disabilities more appropriate.

Learn about Your New Students

MARYANN BYRNES

Each September you meet new students. Knowing as much as possible about them helps the school year begin smoothly for teachers, students, and parents. Though evaluations and progress reports contain essential details, a wealth of information is waiting for you in the minds and files of last year's instructional team. Honest answers to these questions will help you build on the lessons learned last year and get this year off to a running start. My student, "Pat," stands for any student you are welcoming as your own.

1. What Supports Will Help Pat Succeed at the Beginning of this New Year?

Change is difficult for most people. After the "new" becomes familiar, we all settle down. Meanwhile, it is easy to misinterpret a new student's behavior during the first few days. What can last year's team tell you that would help? Will your new student need a visual schedule, an explanation of how this year's expectations differ from last year's, guidance traveling from room to room, encouragement to ask questions, a short-term behavior management program?

2. When Does Pat Need the Most Support?

Some students need support throughout the day. Other students experience times of particular stress. Does your new student require assistance most during independent learning times? Do unstructured activities, such as recess, passing time, or lunch, create a need for adult support?

3. What Can Pat Do Independently?

It is easy to focus on needs but equally important to know areas where a student can work without you. Acknowl-

edging competence and independence communicates confidence in your student. When can you (and your student) anticipate success?

4. How Do You and Pat's Parents Communicate Best?

Establishing communications quickly forges a strong school/home partnership. Do your new student's parents respond best to telephone calls, e-mails, notes sent home? Do they prefer to be called at home, or can they be reached best at work?

5. Where in the Room Does Pat Learn Best?

Although you may prefer clusters or individual desks, there might be one critical area that helps your new student focus. Do windows refresh or distract? Is there a need for an individual carrel? A floor pillow?

6. What Are the Biggest Motivators for Pat?

How did last year's team encourage this student to succeed? Some students crave attention and praise. Others relish earned time with a valued adult. Still others react well to a homework pass or time on the computer.

7. How Does Pat React to Guidance or Correction?

Does this student accept constructive guidance well or become upset if everything is not perfect? Are there language and/or cultural traditions that you should consider?

8. What Is Pat's Favorite Part of School?

Is there a subject area that this student favors? Is group discussion the high point of the day? Are athletics the only reason your new student stays in school? Build on these positive experiences during the tough times to provide motivation and reinforcement.

9. What Is Pat's Least Favorite Part of School?

You can be guaranteed this will be the most difficult part of the day. Knowing ahead of time which activity is least favored will help you prepare.

10. What Frustrates Pat?

What bothers your new student so much that it interferes with school? Struggles with academic work? Interpersonal difficulties? Changes in routine? Family and home issues?

11. What Are the Signs That Pat Is Beginning to Feel Frustrated?

Although it is usually easy to tell when a student is totally frustrated, ask about behavioral cues that appear before a crisis arrives. Does this student fidget more? ask questions more frequently? look distressed? twist hair? stare out the window?

12. What Helps Pat Reduce Frustration?

Different learners respond to different techniques. What works for your new student?

- Collaboration with a peer or diversion to a quiet work space?
- Solitude to concentrate independently or offers of assistance?
- Words of support or time out with a counselor?

13. Who Are Pat's Friends?

Know the classmates with whom your new student is most closely connected. Nurture those friendships, and consider them in your seating arrangements. Do these friends work well together, or do they distract each other?

14. Who Are Pat's Adversaries?

Anticipated problems can be avoided. Use this information as you plan learning groups. Incorporate the issues behind some of these struggles in your class meetings or social skills activities with the entire class.

15. What Are Pat's Strengths?

Too often, we concentrate on learning and behavior problems. Each student has strengths that provide opportunities for you to praise accomplishments and stretch your new student's thinking.

16. What Are Pat's Biggest Learning Challenges?

What is the essence of your new student's learning difficulty? Which areas of learning are the most difficult? What strategies did last year's team try? What worked? Why?

17. What Is the Most Important Skill Pat Learned Last Year?

A prized accomplishment needs to be valued and reinforced. Was self-control during discussions a hard-won success? Did your new student unlock the mysteries of regrouping? What helped your student achieve this growth? Can you use the same strategy this year?

18. What Is the Most Important Skill for Pat to Learn This Year?

Accomplishments lead to new challenges. Of all the possibilities, what is the single most important? Is it academic, behavioral, or interpersonal? Why is this the most important? Does your new student (and his or her parents) agree? This information focuses your efforts and those of your student.

19. What Does Pat Like Best Outside of School?

Knowledge of your student's outside interests generates conversation starters and points of interest on which to build. Should you bone up on Harry Potter or add some books on soccer to your reading list? Can your student serve as an in-class expert on a particular topic?

20. What Did You Know About Pat in June That You Wish You Had Known Last September?

This final, but critical, question leaves the door open for last year's team to tell you what you haven't asked. The answer may be the most important piece of information you receive.

Each September is a fresh start. Learning from last year's instructional team ensures that you and your students make the most of this new year. Now, what would you like to share with those who will teach your former students?

MARYANN BYRNES, EdD, is an assistant professor at the University of Massachusetts Boston, after having been a special education administrator for 18 years. Her research interests include effective participation in standards-based curriculum and controversial issues in special education. Address: MaryAnn Byrnes, 17 Sherbourne Place, Waltham, MA 02451; e-mail: maryann.byrnes@umb.edu

From *Intervention in School and Clinic,* by MaryAnn Barnes, Vol. 41, No. 1, September 2005, pp. 13–15. Copyright © 2005 by Pro-Ed, Inc. Reprinted by permission.

Using Technology to Teach about Individual Differences Related to Disabilities

SPENCER J. SALEND

As part of her efforts to teach her students how to interact with, understand, and accept others, Ms. Miller decided to teach her students about individual differences related to disabilities. Knowing that her students enjoyed using technology, Ms. Miller approached Ms. Tarik, the school's instructional technology technology-based unit to teach students about individual differences related to disabilities. They started to develop the unit by searching the Internet for content, online lesson plans, and Web sites and teaching resources about disabilities. They identified, reviewed, and evaluated Web sites to determine those sites that contained accurate, interesting, and relevant content as well as motivating learning activities and useful resources, and then began to create their unit.

Once they developed their unit, Ms. Miller and Ms. Tarik began by teaching students about the Internet and how to use it. They presented an overview of how to access and navigate the Internet, pairing experienced student users with novices. They reviewed with students how to use the Internet safely, responsibly, efficiently, and effectively. They brainstormed with students to frame rules for the use of the Internet. They also told students not to believe everything they read or hear through the Internet and gave students guidelines for examining sites and verifying information. Once they were convinced that students could use the technology appropriately, the teachers assigned students to work in groups. Each group selected a variety of learning activities from a menu that included the following:

- Visiting disability awareness Web sites.
- Searching the Internet for information about famous individuals with disabilities.
- Making an online visit to an exhibit at the Disabilities Rights Movement Virtual Museum.
- Viewing films about individuals with disabilities.
- Listening to online radio shows about disability-related topics.
- Participating in chat groups with individuals with disabilities.
- Playing online learning games related to disability.
- Performing online disability simulations.
- Using assistive devices to complete assignments.

As a culminating activity, Ms. Miller and Ms. Tarik had students work in collaborative groups to complete a WebQuest related to a specific disability that each group selected. The WebQuest asked the students to engage in several technology-based activities to learn information about the disability they had selected. Each group then created an accessible Web site concerning the disability condition that they studied, along with a Web log of the activities they engaged in to learn about disabilities and create their Web sites.

Ms. Miller and Ms. Tarik shared the groups' projects by posting links to them on the class's Web page. The teachers and students were pleased when they received e-mail messages from other teachers and their students' families about the students' products and requests to use activities from their unit.

Although technology is often thought of as an instructional tool for teaching academic content, teachers like Ms. Miller and Ms. Tarik realize that technology can also be an excellent resource for teaching about individual differences. Accordingly, this article provides guidelines, strategies, and resources for using technology to teach students about individual differences related to disabilities. Although these technology-based strategies are presented in the context of teaching students without disabilities about disabilities, they also can be used to foster the self-awareness and self-advocacy of students with disabilities (Pearl, 2004).

As Ms. Miller and Ms. Tarik did when using the Internet with their students, educators need to preview and carefully evaluate Web sites and provide students with links to recommended sites. They should teach their students how to evaluate Web sites and Web based information, including the identification of the individuals who created the site and why they created it, as well as the dates on which it was created and updated. Since Web-based information can reinforce existing societal inequities and stereotypic views of individuals with disabilities, any evaluation of the site should examine the accuracy of the content of the site as well as the impact of the content on individuals with disabilities and visitors to the site. Figure 1 offers guidelines that educators and students can use to evaluate Web sites and Web-based information addressing individual differences related to disability.

Like Ms. Miller and Ms. Tarik, educators need to establish and teach students rules and etiquette for using the Internet and protecting their privacy. This preparation involves teaching them about conducting searches, accessing appropriate material, interacting with others, and protecting their confidentiality. Educators also should teach their students to refrain from giving out personal information, and how to avoid advertising, offensive sites, mischief and viruses, and misuse of Internet accounts (Lever-Duffy, McDonald, Mizell, 2003). In addition, students and teachers can access sites on rules and etiquette for using the Internet, which can be identified through a search using "Netiquette for Students."

Disability Awareness Web Sites and Videos/DVDs

Accessing disability-awareness Web sites is a good way for students to learn about individual differences related to disabilities. These sites provide access to a wide range of information and resources about disabilities, as well as many exploratory and discovery-based learning and communication experiences. They also offer students options related to what and how they learn. Figure 2 offers a listing of potential disability-awareness Web sites for use with students. Information about additional disability-awareness resources for use with students is available on the Web site of the National Information Center for Children and Youth with Disabilities (www.nichcy.org/pubs/bibliog/bib13txt.htm) and on the Disability Resources Web site (www.disabilityresources.org/DIS-AWARE.html).

Disability-awareness videos and DVDs also can help students learn about disabilities. For example, KidAbility and A Video Guide to (Dis)Ability Awareness (www.pdassoc.com) are disability awareness videos that can be used to introduce students to the lifestyles of individuals with various disability conditions and assistive technology. What Do You Do When You See a Blind Person? (www.afb.org) and The Ten Commandments of Communicating with People with Disabilities (www.pdassoc.com) are video-based resources that can teach students how to communicate with individuals with disabilities.

Curriculum Guides and Learning Materials

Many curriculum guides and learning materials to teach students about individual differences related to disabilities are available through the Internet (National Information Center for Children and Youth with Disabilities, 2000; Shapiro, 1999). These curricular and teaching materials can be used to infuse content about individual differences related to disability into the regular course of study or as part of a separate unit related to disability. These materials usually include a variety of goals, learning activities, materials to implement the activities, multimedia materials, and a teacher's guide. For example, Special Olympics Get Into It (www.specialolympics.org/getintoit) is a series of free curriculum materials and activities that can be obtained online; they contain lessons designed to help preschool, elementary, and secondary students learn about developmental disabilities, and understand and accept individual differences. Similarly, on the Web site of the Boston Children's Museum (www.bostonkids.org/educators/disability_awareness.html), teachers can obtain information about Some Ways the Same, Some Ways Different, a disability awareness curriculum that includes activities, books, and videos that teach students about a variety of disability conditions and promote an acceptance of differences and similarities.

Teachers can use online learning activities to incorporate content about disability into the curriculum. The Center on Human Policy at Syracuse University's Disabilities Studies for Teachers Web site (www.disabilitystudiesforteachers.org/lessons.php) offers a series of lessons and varied resources for teaching about disabilities and integrating disability awareness and issues into Grades 6–12 classroom instruction. A historical perspective of disabilities, including current resources, can be integrated into the social studies curriculum through use of such Web sites as the Disability Social History Project (www.disabilityhistory.org), Developmental Disability History (www.nurses.info/specialty_developmental_history.htm) and the Disability Resources' History of Disabilities (www.disabilityresources.org/HISTORY.html). Students can use the Internet to search for information about the achievements of highly successful individuals with disabilities, as well as how those individuals dealt with, and compensated for, their disability (Eisenman & Tascione, 2002; Hartwell, 2001).

Content about disability can be incorporated across the curriculum by accessing Education for Disability and Gender Equity (EDGE) (www.disabilityhistory.org/dwa/edge/curriculum), a series of 1-hour lessons and Web resources incorporating disability-related topics into science (physics and biology) and humanities (government and culture). For example, the physics module allows students to use wheelchairs to learn about the laws of force and motion, and the culture module helps students develop an awareness of the disability culture movement and common stereotypes about individuals with disabilities. In addition to hands-on learning activities for students, the EDGE Web site includes teacher guides, access to information from individuals with disabilities, and additional resources to further students' learning.

Disability-Related Museums

Online visits to disability-related museums can make learning about disability more meaningful and real for students. Virtual museums can give students access to authentic and primary sources, artifacts, documents, and photographs that can add to the excitement of learning. For example, students can make online visits to the disability-related virtual museums presented in Figure 3.

Films, Books, and Magazines

Films, books, and magazines about individuals with disabilities and related issues can counter stereotypic views and can teach students about disabilities (Rohner & Rosberg, 2003; Safran, 2000). These materials are excellent ways to prompt students to reflect on their beliefs about individual differences and disabilities and to consider what strategies they can employ to support persons with individual differences (Prater, 2000).

The Internet can be an excellent resource for identifying appropriate films and books about disabilities. For example, Films Involving Disabilities (www.disabilityfilms.co.uk) lists and summarizes 2,500 films related to disabilities and offers resources for examining how disabilities are presented in films. Information concerning books about individuals with disabilities for use with students can be accessed on the Internet by contacting DisABILITIES Books (www.disabilitiesbooks.com), the Special Needs Project (www.specialneeds.com), Woodbine House (www.woodbinehouse.com), Albert Whitman and Company (www.awhitmanco.com), Magination Press (www.maginationpress.com), and Roots and Wings

Credibility	• Who developed the site? • Are the developers of the site credible? • How often is the site updated? • Are sources of information provided? • What are the stated and unstated goals and purposes of the site? • Does the site have a bias or a hidden agenda? • Does the site present information and situations related to the real-life experiences of students?
Content	• Is the content current, accurate, appropriate, and multicultural? • Is the content presented in an understandable, open, multicultural, and objective manner? • Are important issues presented realistically? • Does the site use inclusive and individuals-first language? • Does the content of the site foster inclusion and counter existing stereotypical views and societal inequities? • Is the readability of the content appropriate? • Is content properly organized?
Design and Navigability	• Is the design of the site welcoming? • Is the site motivating? • Is the site easy to use and navigate? • Are sections and resource links labeled? • Are graphics and images inclusive, accurate, and current? • Does the site contain motivating, thoughtful, relevant, and differentiated learning activities?
Accessibility for Individuals with Disabilities	• Is the site usable by individuals with disabilities?
Individual Differences	• Does the site present individuals with individual differences as multicultural, capable persons having unique personalities and qualities, likes and dislikes, and strengths and challenges? • Does the site foster an understanding of the importance of independence, dignity, and self-determination? • Are the varied experiences, perceptions, and contributions of individuals with individual differences depicted? • Are individuals with individual differences presented in a variety of settings? • Are individuals with individual differences presented in nonstereotypic ways? • Does the site foster the understanding that similarities and differences are natural and beneficial? • Does the site help students understand that individuals have more similarities than differences? • Does the site help establish equal-status relationships between individuals? • Does the site promote sensitivity and inclusion, and avoid pitying and protective responses? • Does the site suggest ways to take actions to challenge inequities and stereotypic perspectives and to support individuals with individual differences?

(Salend, Duhaney, Anderson & Gottschalk, 2004, Salend, 2005, and Shapiro, 1999)

Figure 1 Evaluating web sites and web-based information on individual differences.

(www.rootsandwingscatalog.com). In addition, many Web sites, such as TeachingBooks.net, provide theme-based book lists and resource links, teacher-developed reading guides and lesson plans, author interviews, and audio readings of books. Students also can read books online through the International Children's Digital Library (www.icdlbook.org). Guidelines to help teachers select appropriate films (Safran, 2000) and books (Salend, 2005) related to the theme of disabilities are available.

The Internet can also give students access to media and communications that focus on disability-related issues and news and on the interests and experiences of individuals with disabilities. For example, teachers can introduce and give students access to

CeDIR's Disability Awareness Site for Youth (www. iidc.indiana.edu/cedir/kidsweb): Offers a variety of activities to present information about a range of disabilities.

Disability Awareness Kit (www.openroad.net.au/ access/dakit/welcome.htm): Offers information, handouts, activities, and resources addressing a range of disability conditions.

Special Needs~Special Kids (Disability Awareness) (www.members.tripod.com/~imaware): Presents information fostering the awareness of a variety of disability conditions.

Internet Resources for Special Children (www. irsc.org): Offers information and Web sites regarding disabilities.

All Kids Can (www.allkidscan.com): Offers information and Web resources related to disabilities and diversity.

DisabilityResources.org (www.disabilityresources. org): Offers access to online disability-related information and resources.

Disability Central and The Active Teen (www.disability-central.com): Offers information, learning activities, and Web sites related to disabilities.

About Disability (www.aboutdisability.com): Pre-sents a listing of resources addressing disability.

Figure 2 Disability awareness Web sites

magazines and periodicals that publish articles, news, reviews, fiction, essays, and photographs on various issues affecting individuals with disabilities; examples include Ability Magazine (www.ability magazine.com), Ragged Edge Magazine Online www.ragged-edgemagazine.com), Disability World (www.disabilityworld.org), Mainstream Online Magazine: News and Advocacy in Disability Rights (www.mainstreammag.com), Kaleidoscope: International Magazine of Literature, Fine Arts, and Disability (www.udsakron. org/kaleidoscope.htm), and the Inclusion Daily Express (www. inclusiondaily.com).

Streaming Audio and Video

Through the Internet, students can use streaming audio and video technology to watch or hear live or prerecorded audio and video broadcasts of disability-related topics. Disability Radio Worldwide (www.independentliving.org/radio/index.html) and On a Roll (www.icanonline.net/channels/on_a_roll/index.cfm) are online radio programs that focus on issues involving individuals with disabilities, and the Beyond Affliction Radio show (www.npr.org/ programs/disability) offers a 4-hour radio documentary about the history of individuals with disabilities in the United States.

Online visits to disability-related museums can make learning about disability meaningful and real for students.

Video-based news segments and documentaries from professional organizations and television stations can be obtained or accessed online. Similarly, Web sites offer a variety of videos whose content can be integrated into classroom instruction through

technology. For example, BrainPop.com (www.Brain.Pop.com) accesses a wide range of animated educational movies and videos designed for use in K–12 classrooms and includes a health section that addresses disability-related topics.

Interactions with Individuals with Disabilities

The Internet can give students opportunities to communicate directly with, and learn about disabilities from, individuals with disabilities. Internet bulletin boards, e-mail, and chat groups offer students opportunities to "talk" to, share information and experiences with, and learn from individuals with disabilities (Tao & Boulware, 2002). For example, real-time chat groups offer students a forum to communicate with individuals with disabilities. Through the Internet, students and classes can have computer pals with disabilities from other schools in the district, geographic region, country, and world with whom they communicate and learn (Stanford & Siders, 2001).

Technology is available to help students communicate with individuals with disabilities through the Internet. Web Cameras (Web Cams) can allow students to have online "face-to-face" interactions with individuals with a range of disabilities, and software programs are available to facilitate e-mail communication (Salend, 2005). For example, RJ Cooper's IcanEmail is a talking e-mail program that uses prompts and an augmentative communication device to foster interactions with others electronically. Inter_Comm is a software program that allows students to use picture symbols when sending e-mail messages, and www.ebuddies.org can facilitate e-mail communication between individuals with and without developmental disabilities.

Learning Games

Online learning games furnish challenging and motivating ways for students to learn about individual differences related to disabilities. For example, the American Foundation for the Blind has created Braille Bug (www.afb.org/braillebug), a Web site that offers a variety of activities including online games to teach sighted students about Braille. Similarly, students can access the Activeteen game room at Disability Central (www.disabilitycentral.com/activteen/ gameroom/gameroom.htm) to play games that introduce students to famous individuals with disabilities, or visit the CeDIR's games chamber (www.iidc.indiana.edu/cedir/kidsweb/gameschamber. html) to learn about disabilities and the American Manual Alphabet. Students can go online to complete a Disability Awareness Scavenger Hunt (www.sumnerschools.org/sms/lessons/disability.html), a game that asks students to locate and visit Web sites to respond to disability-related questions and activities. They also can play the Disability Awareness game (www.parentsinc.org/game.html), a game based on the television show Jeopardy using disability-related content that can be played on a screen or LCD projector.

Disability Simulations

A popular strategy to teach students about individuals with disabilities involves the use of disability simulations, in which students perform a variety of activities under conditions that allow them to temporarily experience how it feels to have a disability (Hartwell, 2001; Salend, 2005). In addition to introducing students to the

Disability Rights Movement Virtual Museum (www.americanhistory.si.edu/disabilityrights/welcome.html): Offers online access to a virtual exhibition developed by the Smithsonian Natural Museum of American History on the Disability Rights Movement.

Disability History Museum (www.disabilitymuseum.org): Offers online access to exhibits, a library, and teacher resources course packets designed to teach about the historical experiences of individuals with disabilities.

Museum of disability History (www.people-inc.org/museum): Offers online access to exhibits and activities related to people with disabilities.

United States Holocaust Museum (www.holocaust-trc.org/hndcp.htm) Offers online access to information about Nazi treatment of individuals with disabilities from 1933 to 1945.

Figure 3   Disability-Related Virtual Museums.

Misunderstood Minds (www.pbs.org/wgbh/misunderstoodminds): Offers simulations addressing learning differences and disabilities related to attention, reading, writing, and mathematics difficulties.

Pediatric Neurology.Com (www.pediatricneurology.com/adhd2.htm): Offers simulations addressing attention disorders and Asperger's Syndrome.

National Coalition of Auditory Processing Disorders (www.ncapd.org): Offers simulations addressing auditory processing difficulties.

Mrs. Karen Lakes Home Page (www.nacs.k12.in.us/staff/lake/lake.html): Offers simulations related to learning disabilities and reading difficulties.

Figure 4   Online disability simulations Web sites.

challenges confronting individuals with disabilities, simulations can help students learn about the accommodations and assistive devices that individuals with disabilities find useful.

The Internet can give students opportunities to communicate directly with, and learn about disabilities from, individuals with disabilities.

Although disability simulations have traditionally been performed by students in their classrooms and schools, students can use technology to engage in online disability simulations (Pearl, 2004). For example, students can complete Barriers—The Awareness Challenge (www.health.uottawa.ca/vrlab), an online learning experience that introduces students to attitudinal and physical barriers that people who use wheelchairs encounter (Pivik, McComas, Macfarlane, & Laflamme, 2002). Using a virtual wheelchair to maneuver to several locations in a virtual school, students simulate reaching for out-of-reach objects, and hearing and responding to inappropriate comments from others. Students can perform online disability simulations by accessing the Web sites presented in Figure 4.

When using in-class or online simulations, teachers and students should understand the concerns associated with their use (Smart, 2001). Changes in behavior and attitudes associated with simulations are often brief. Simulations also can have several negative consequences, such as promoting feelings of pity toward individuals with disabilities, being artificial, and trivializing the disability experience (i.e., simulations do not allow individuals to fully understand the complex realities of individuals with disabilities; Pearl, 2004).

Teachers can limit the likelihood of the occurrence of these negative side effects by choosing simulations that are as realistic as possible and by establishing expectations that ensure that students take the activities seriously. Teachers need to make sure that simulations introduce students to the strategies and assistive devices individuals with disabilities use to overcome the challenges they may encounter.

Teachers can use online resources to help students understand the controversies associated with the use of disability simulations. For example, students can read articles and essays critiquing disability simulations by visiting the Web sites of Ragged Edge Magazine (www.raggededgemagazine.com/archive/aware.htm) and Disabilities Studies Online Magazine (www.disabilitystudies.com/teachingds.htm). Students can use e-mail to communicate with disability rights groups to obtain information about their activities and views of disability simulations. They also can participate in online communication with individuals with disabilities to discuss the value of simulations, ways to make them more realistic and effective, and alternatives to simulations as tools for learning about disabilities.

Assistive Technology

Since individuals with communication, physical, learning, and sensory disabilities use assistive devices to gain greater control over their lives and environment, teaching about these devices is an important aspect of understanding individuals with disabilities. Students can use the Internet to view descriptions and demonstrations of a wide range of assistive devices by visiting such Web sites as DisABILITY Information and Resources (www.makoa.org), ABLEDATA (www.abledata.com), Accent on Information (www.blvd.com/accent), and the Trace Center at the University of Wisconsin at Madison (www.trace.wisc.edu).

Students can learn about technology-based assistive devices by using them. For example, students can be asked to take notes using personal digital assistants (PDAs) and can complete an assignment using modified keyboards, talking word processors, and voice recognition systems.

Students can also be given opportunities to use software programs that help individuals with disabilities use the Internet (Salend, 2005). These programs allow individuals with visual, dexterity-based, cognitive, and reading disabilities to browse and navigate the Internet by using screen reading, audio prompting, and error-minimization strategies; reducing the visuals presented on the screen; and presenting computer text and graphics by reading them aloud or by displaying text in large type. For example, students can surf the Net (Internet) blindfolded using a screen-reading program and a special mouse that vibrates to indicate boxes and images on the screen.

Students can learn about technology-based assistive devices by using them.

Students can use the Internet to access information and resources related to evaluating the accessibility of Web sites. Students can visit such sites as the Companion Web site for Bobby (www.cast.org/bobby) and the Web Accessibility Initiative (www.w3.org/WAI) to obtain guidelines for evaluating Web sites in terms of their accessibility. They then can use these guidelines to evaluate commonly used Web sites for their accessibility to individuals with disabilities.

Web Logs (Blogs)

The value of technology-based learning activities can be enhanced by having students maintain Web logs (blogs), online diaries that are updated on a regular basis to present information about the class's activities. For example, students can create a blog of their online experiences in learning about disabilities and their reactions to these activities. They can identify and work on something that is a challenge for them and can maintain a blog of their progress, the barriers they encounter, and their reflections on what they have learned about themselves and others (Salend, 2005).

WebQuests

Another type of Internet-based instructional activity that teachers can use to teach students about disabilities is a WebQuest (Kelly, 2000). A WebQuest is an inquiry-oriented cooperatively structured group activity in which some or all of the information that students interact with comes from resources on the Internet. Often the learning product results in a Web site or a PowerPoint presentation. Like Ms. Miller and Ms. Tarik, teachers can have their students work in collaborative groups to complete WebQuests that ask them to use the Internet to gather and present information on different disability conditions. They then can have each group create an accessible Web site concerning the disability condition that they studied; group Web sites can be linked to the class's Web page.

Summary

Individual differences make all people unique and interesting. Unfortunately, because of observational learning, societal influences, and the environment in which they are raised, many students enter school holding misconceptions and stereotypic views about persons they perceive as different, including individuals with disabilities (Shapiro, 1999). As a result, educators may need to employ strategies for teaching students about individual differences related to disabilities. Technology offers teachers and students rich, challenging, varied, and motivating opportunities for learning about disabilities. Technology-based strategies can supplement other classroom and school-wide activities for addressing individual differences (Salend, 2005) and should be tailored by educators to the unique classroom circumstances of their educational settings. In using technology-based resources and strategies, educators and students should critically examine them to make sure that they convey factually correct information and portray individuals with disabilities in positive, independent, complex, and nonstereotypic ways.

References

Eisenman, L. T., & Tascione, L. (2002). "How come nobody told me?" Fostering self-realization through a high school English curriculum. *Learning Disabilities Research and Practice, 17,* 35–46.

Hartwell, R. (2001). Understanding disabilities. *Educational Leadership, 58*(7), 72–75.

Kelly, R. (2000). Working with WebQuests: Making the Web accessible to students with disabilities. *TEACHING Exceptional Children, 32*(6), 4–13.

Lever-Duffy, J., McDonald, J. B., & Mizell, A. P. (2003). *Teaching and learning with technology.* Boston: Allyn & Bacon.

National Information Center for Children and Youth with Disabilities. (2000). *Resources you can use: Disability awareness.* Washington, DC: Author.

Pearl, C. (2004). Laying the foundation for self-advocacy. *TEACHING Exceptional Children, 36*(3), 44–49.

Pivik, J. McComas, J., Macfarlane, I., & Laflamme, M. (2002). Using virtual reality to teach disability related awareness. *Educational Computing Technology, 26,* 225–240.

Prater, M. A. (2000). Using juvenile literature with portrayals of disabilities in your classroom. *Intervention in School and Clinic, 35*(3), 167–176.

Rohner, J., & Rosberg, M. (2003). Children with special needs—An update. *Book Links, 12*(4), 40–44.

Safran, S. P. (2000). Using movies to teach students about disabilities. *TEACHING Exceptional Children, 32*(3), 44–47.

Salend, S. J. (2005). *Creating inclusive classrooms: Effective and reflective practices for all students* (5th ed.). Columbus, OH: Merrill/Prentice Hall.

Salend, S. J., Duhaney, D., Anderson, D. J., & Gottschalk, C. (2004). Using the internet to improve homework communication and completion. *TEACHING Exceptional Children, 36*(3), 64–73.

Shapiro, A. (1999). *Everyone belongs: Changing negative attitudes toward classmates with disabilities.* New York: RoutledgeFalmer.

Smart, J. (2001). *Disability, society and the individual.* Gaithersburg, MD: Aspen.

Stanford, P., & Siders, J. A. (2001). E-pal writing. *TEACHING Exceptional Children, 34*(2), 21–25.

Tao, L., & Boulware, B. (2002). E-mail:Instructional potentials and learning opportunities. *Reading and Writing Quarterly: Overcoming Learning Difficulties, 18,* 285–288.

Spencer J. Salend (CEC Chapter #615), Professor, Department of Educational Studies, State University of New York, New Paltz. Correspondence can be sent to Spencer J. Salend at SUNY New Paltz, Department of Educational Studies, 75 South Manheim Blvd., New Paltz, NY 12561 (e-mail: salends@newpaltz.edu)

Large-Scale Assessments
A Teacher's Guide to Making Decisions About Accommodations

ELIZABETH A. EDGEMON, BRIAN R. JABLONSKI, AND JOHN W. LLOYD

L arge-scale assessments are an integral part of contemporary education. Such assessments raise questions about accommodations for students with disabilities. These questions may include the following:

- What types of accommodations are available for large-scale assessments?
- Who uses accommodations?
- How should teachers and IEP teams select appropriate accommodations?

This article provides recommendations and guidelines for decision making, in addition to offering a framework for special educators, especially members of individualized education program (IEP) teams, to use in selecting accommodations that permit students with disabilities to demonstrate knowledge, competence, and learning on large-scale assessments.

The purpose of accommodations is to allow students with disabilities to demonstrate their knowledge on assessments without interference from their disabilities, as their nondisabled peers are able to do, while not giving students with disabilities an unfair advantage over their peers (Elliott, McKevitt, & Kettler, 2002). Because disabilities affect students in different ways, educators must consider the appropriateness of testing accommodations for each individual and must consider the accommodations available and the potential benefits of using each accommodation.

What Types of Accommodations Are Available for Large-Scale Assessments?

Although statewide assessments allow many different accommodations, they fall into five basic categories: presentation, time, setting, response, and aids (Jablonski, Edgemon, Wiley, & Lloyd, 2005) (see box "What Does Legislation Say About High-Stakes Testing?"). Research provides guidance about using some accommodations for large-scale assessments for students with disabilities. However, researchers have ignored many accommodations, thereby failing to provide practitioners with evidencebased advice about using accommodations that intuitively seem promising. Furthermore, available evidence for many accommodations shows conflicting or equivocal results. The following is a summary of research related to the use and usefulness of the five categories of accommodations.

Presentation Accommodations

Presentation accommodations include Braille, large print, and read-aloud accommodations. A test proctor can administer read-aloud accommodations, or the student can use an audiotape, a videotape, or a computer. The use of read-aloud test items is a controversial accommodation, and the supporting evidence is conflicting and unclear. Although reading test items to students with disabilities generally improves their performance (e.g., Meloy, Deville, & Frisbie, 2002), this boost in performance may overestimate students' abilities (e.g., Fuchs, Fuchs, Eaton, Hamlett, & Karns, 2000) and change the skill that a test item is assessing. For example, when an educator reads to the student an item meant to assess reading ability, a correct answer is not an indicator of good reading skills but rather of good listening skills. Conversely, reading test items aloud can increase the difficulty of some test questions (Barton & Finch, 2004). Also, students who use an accommodation that allows them to read the test aloud to themselves benefit from controlling the pace of the reading, necessitating an additional accommodation of extra time on the assessment (Hollenbeck, Rozek-Tedesco, Tindal, & Glasgrow, 2000).

The purpose of accommodations is to allow students with disabilities to demonstrate their knowledge on assessments without interference from their disabilities.

Time Accommodations

Time accommodations extend the time allowed for time-limited tests or allow educators to break the test into several sessions. Researchers have studied the use of extended time more frequently than they have studied other accommodations, and educators therefore have a better understanding of its effects. Much of the research on extending time has examined the SAT and ACT (e.g., Cahalan, Mandinach, & Camara, 2002; Ragosta & Wendler, 1992; Ziomek & Andrews, 1996); however, researchers have also looked at extended time on such popular norm-referenced achievement tests as the Iowa Tests of Basic Skills (ITBS; e.g., Munger & Loyd, 1991; Perlman, Borger, Collins, Elenbogen, & Wood, 1996). This research has allowed the development of specific guidelines for extended time on the college placement tests, taking into consideration the realization that allowing students with disabilities to use extra time can overestimate a student's future performance in college (Ragosta & Wendler, 1992). Additionally, time accommodations are appropriate when paired with certain test accommodations (e.g., Braille and audiocassettes) that lengthen the amount of time required for students to complete assessments (Ragosta & Wendler, 1992). Studies of writing tests indicate that multiple-day formats improve results over single-day assessments for elementary students but not for middle school students (Crawford, Helwig, & Tindal, 2004).

Setting Accommodations

Setting accommodations include small-group administration and other such environmental modifications as special lighting or the presence of a familiar teacher. Although small-group administration is frequent, little research has singled out any one setting accommodation, so definitive conclusions about the effectiveness of these accommodations are not possible at the present time.

Response Accommodations

Response accommodations change how the student records answers. Students may dictate answers to a scribe, use a word processor or Brailler, or record answers in a test booklet. Responses written by using word processors improve performance over handwritten responses for some students but not for others (Hollenbeck, Tindal, Harniss, & Almond, 1999; MacArthur & Cavalier, 2004). In fact, evidence indicates that students' word-processed essays do not receive higher quality ratings than their handwritten essays, and students need more time to write them (MacArthur & Graham, 1987). One reason might be a lack of proficiency with the computer (Hollenbeck et al., 1999). Response accommodations are most useful when the student is familiar with using the technology employed in the accommodation (Hollenbeck, Linder, & Almond, 2002).

Aid Accommodations

Aid accommodations include the use of devices during assessment. Aids range from overlays that allow students to see only one problem at a time to calculators and voice-activated computers. The small amount of research related to such aids in large-scale testing has indicated that calculators are helpful

---

What Does Legislation Say about High-Stakes Testing?

Such legislation as the 2004 reauthorization of the Individuals With Disabilities Education Improvement Act (IDEIA) requires states to report the academic progress of students with disabilities, presumably through the use of high-stakes testing, as mandated by No Child Left Behind (NCLB). High-stakes testing should adequately reflect the achievement of all students, but the disabilities of special education students often make demonstrating their knowledge and learning difficult for them. IDEIA specifically states that IEPs must include a "statement of any individual appropriate accommodations that are necessary to measure the academic achievement and functional performance of the child on state and districtwide assessments" (Title I, Part B, Section 614). IDEIA, however, provides no guidelines or suggestions for deciding which accommodations are appropriate.

---

for students with disabilities but are more appropriate for tests of problem-solving than for computation and calculation tests (Fuchs, Fuchs, Eaton, Hamlett, & Karns, 2000).

Who Uses Accommodations?

Analyses of statewide assessments show patterns in the use of accommodations by age, type of accommodation, and disability. Students use accommodations more frequently in elementary school than in high school (Bielinski, Ysseldyke, Bolt, Friedebach, & Friedebach, 2001; Johnson, Kimball, Brown, & Anderson, 2001; Trimble, 1998). Two accommodations account for nearly all the difference between the frequency of accommodation use in elementary school and the frequency in high school:

- In elementary schools, 50% of students who use accommodations dictate to a scribe, but only 5% of high school students who use accommodations dictated their responses.
- Educators read tests to 72% of elementary students who use accommodations, but only 45% of high school students who use accommodations employ a read-aloud accommodation (Koretz & Hamilton, 2000).

Small-group, read-aloud, extended time, paraphrasing, and dictation to a scribe are the most commonly used accommodations for students at all grade levels (Bielinski et al., 2001; Koretz & Hamilton, 2000).

With the exception of the use of dictation for students with emotional and behavioral disorders, educators employ frequently used accommodations across categories of disabilities (Ysseldyke et al., 1999). Furthermore, students with mental retardation are more likely to use accommodations than are students with learning disabilities, who, in turn, are more likely to use accommodations than students with emotional and behavioral disorders (Ysseldyke et al.). Finally, the median number of accommodations for students who receive special education services for more than 50% of the day is three, whereas students who receive services for less than 50% of the day use a median of two accommodations (Elliott, Bielinski, Thurlow, DeVito, & Hedlund, 1999).

How Should Teachers and IEP Teams Select Appropriate Accommodations?

At present, IEP teams have little explicit guidance about choosing appropriate testing accommodations. Table 1 outlines the potential benefits of and cautions for using some of the more popular accommodations. In fact, unless IEP teams have received specific training, they often assign testing accommodations without considering the student's access to the curriculum or the instructional accommodations used in the classroom. Consequently, most students on a particular teacher's caseload frequently have the same set of accommodations or have no accommodations (Fuchs & Fuchs, 2001). Although offering a standard set of accommodations to all students with similar disabilities may be appealing, this practice does not help students as much as individualized accommodation packages designed by the teacher or IEP team to meet a student's specific needs

Table 1 Guidelines for Using Accommodations

Accommodation	Considerations	Cautions
Read-aloud administration (teacher, audiotape, computer, videotape)	• When questions contain large amounts of text • With students who have poor decoding skills but relatively high listening comprehension • When assessing skills other than decoding, e.g., solving math problems	• This accommodation can inflate test scores, especially when assessing reading skills • The difficulty of some types of test items can increase with read-aloud administration
Student read-aloud	• When assessing reading skills of students with learning disabilities	• Research has focused on individual administration, which is time-consuming
Dictated response (including use of speech-to-text software)	• When trying to measure written expression or composing skills	• This accommodation has been used more frequently with younger students • The quality of high school students' writing does not tend to improve • Dictated response may inflate test scores for spelling, usage, and grammar
Extended time	• When using special testing formats (e.g., Braille and oral administration) that require more time • When predictive validity is a consideration (e.g., college placement tests)	• Extended time can inflate scores if not carefully controlled • Students who do not manage time well do not benefit from this accommodation
Multiple testing sessions (nonwriting)	• Breaking a test into shorter sessions has been helpful with low-achieving students	• Multiple testing sessions have not been empirically tested on students with disabilities
Multiple testing sessions (writing)	• More helpful with elementary-aged students than with adolescents	• Benefits of this accommodation vary with age of student and specific instrument
Large print	• Primarily for students with visual impairments • Some students with learning disabilities may benefit	• Studies of effect for this accommodation for students with learning disabilities have been contradictory, showing both a positive effect and no effect
Change in setting	• Small-group accommodation (resource room) may actually be the most normal setting for some students. • Taking a test with a familiar teacher can have a positive effect	• Little empirical basis exists for using or not using this accommodation on large-scale assessments for students with disabilities

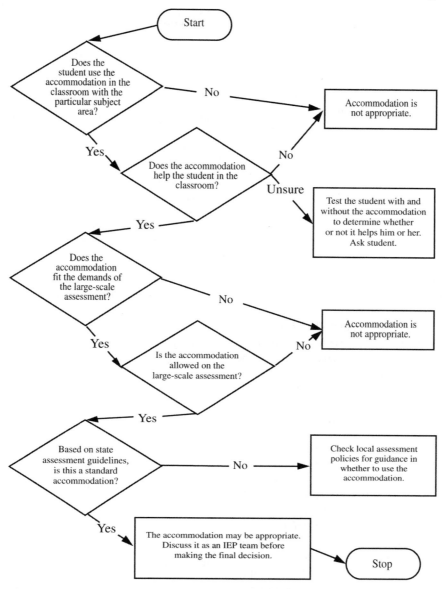

Figure 1. Decision-Making Process for Accommodations

(Elliott, Kratochwill, & McKevitt, 2001). In addition, IEP teams should have specific training, including

- Knowledge of accommodation requirements and possibilities under the Individuals with Disabilities Education Improvement Act of 2004 (IDEIA).
- Familiarization with state standards to match the students' curricular exposure and testing requirements.
- Knowledge of the process of matching accommodations with appropriate situations.
- Explanation of the roles of general and special educators in this decision-making process (Destefano, Shriner, & Lloyd, 2001).

Figure 1 shows steps that IEP teams should follow in making decisions about large-scale testing accommodations. The first step is to examine each student's individual needs, independent of his or her classmates' needs, starting with the student's

educational evaluation and paying special attention to descriptions of the student's functional skills (Ofiesh, Hughes, & Scott, 2004). The IEP team must then consider the accommodations that are necessary in the classroom to help the student access the curriculum. Assessment accommodations are only appropriate if the student's deficiencies will impair her or his ability to meet the requirements and format of the large-scale assessment in question (Ofiesh et al.) and if the student uses—and needs to use—that accommodation in the classroom.

How does the IEP team decide whether the student needs to use the accommodation in the classroom? Historically, the teacher's judgmem has served as the test for determining what a student needs if he or she is to succeed; however, this method of selecting accommodations misses a vital factor: Teachers grant accommodations to some students who do not need accommodations and who do not benefit from the altered testing conditions (Fuchs & Fuchs, 2001). To counter this tendency to overaccommodate, teachers should use empirically based decision making (Fuchs, Fuchs, Eaton, Hamlett, Binkley, et al., 2000; Fuchs, Fuchs, Eaton, Hamtett, & Karns. 2000).

When deciding whether a student needs an accommodation, the simplest question to ask is, "Does this accommodation help the student show how much he or she knows or can do?" To answer this question, IEP teams must consider the student's opportunity to use the accommodation. If a student does not use a specific accommodation in the classroom, then he or she probably will not benefit from using it on large-scale assessments. However, large-scale assessments make demands on students that they do not face in the classroom. For instance, educators may not require students with emotional and behavioral disorders to sit and work for long periods of time in the classroom, although they expect such behavior in testing situations. If the IEP team determines that an accommodation is appropriate, even though it is not a part of the student's daily requirements, educators need to teach the student to use the accommodation appropriately in the classroom and to transfer those skills to large-scale testing situations.

One way to determine whether an accommodation helps students with disabilities is to test the students with and without the accommodation on equivalent but not identical assessments and then compare the results from the assessments. Ideally, teachers would also compare the results for students with disabilities to the result that students without disabilities receive from the accommodation when they take two tests that assess similar skills (Fuchs, Fuchs, Eaton, Hamlett, Binkley, et al., 2000). Cross-referencing can increase the correlation between accommodations that an IEP team assigns and accommodations that a student needs.

Before proceeding further, the IEP team must look at the assessment itself. Different state and local education agencies allow different types of accommodations on different assessments, and educators must know the availability of accommodations, as well as any consequences of choosing to use an accommodation that is atypical or nonstandard. For example, providing a read-aloud accommodation may be permissible on a reading assessment, but the school district may consider this accommodation a nonstandard one because the assessment no longer evaluates the set of reading skills that it originally covered. In this case, the assessment results may still provide valuable information about the student's achievement—but not on the skills that the test was designed to assess—and the assessment may overestimate the student's achievement in the area that the test was designed to assess. The IEP team should consult local guidelines for assistance when making decisions about using nonstandard accommodations, because guidelines vary and because teachers may not know this information (Hollenbeck, Tindal, & Almond, 1998).

Another possibility is that an accommodation is unnecessary and inappropriate for a given assessment. For instance, an extra-time accommodation is superfluous in assessments that do not have time constraints. Even if students receive these accommodations in the classroom throughout the year, listing such accommodations as being available to the student for the large-scale assessment is inappropriate if the accommodation is part of the typical administration of the assessment.

Recommendations

With the current emphasis on high-stakes testing and with current efforts to have all students demonstrate high achievement in a wide variety of curricular areas, it is important that IEP teams provide adequate accommodations for students with disabilities. Educators should match accommodations with a student's needs and the demands of the assessment to allow students to perform to the best of their abilities without altering what the test measures, or educators must recognize that the accommodation does change what the test is measuring.

Avoiding the use of unneeded accommodations is especially important because accommodations single students out, identify them as different, and call attention to their disabilities. Therefore, IEP teams should remember the following when making decisions about testing accommodations:

- Not every accommodation is appropriate for every student or for every test. Consider accommodations for each individual student.
- Be aware of how an accommodation may change what the assessment measures.
- Match the accommodation to the testing format (e.g., extended time for timed assessments, dictation for written essays).
- Match the accommodation to individual student needs (e.g., a read-aloud accommodation in science for a student who knows the material but cannot read the test because he or she has skills that are below grade level; testing breaks for a student with ADHD who cannot concentrate for long periods of time).
- Use accommodations only if educators use them in the classroom or they are otherwise necessary.

References

Barton, K., & Finch, H. (2004). *Using DIF analysis to examine assumptions of unidimensionality across groups of students with disabilities, with accommodations, and English language learners.* Paper presented at the annual meeting of the National Council for Measurement in Education, San Diego, CA.

Bielinski, J., Ysseldyke. J., Bolt, S., Friedebach, M., & Friedebach, J. (2001). Prevalence of accommodations for students with disabilities participating in a statewide testing program. *Assessment for Effective Intervention.* 26(2), 21–28.

Cahalan, C. Mandinach, E. B., & Camara, W. J. (2002). *Predictive validity of the SAT I: Reasoning test for test-takers with learning disabilities and extended time* (College Board Research Report 2002–5). Retrieved June 21, 2004, from http://www.collegeboard.com/repository/rr20025_11437.pdf

Crawford, L., Helwig, R., & Tindal, G. (2004). Writing performance assessments: How important is extended time? *Journal of Learning Disabilities, 37,* 132–142.

Destefano, L., Shriner, J. G., & Lloyd, C. A. (2001). Teacher decision making in participation of students wiih disabilities in large-scale assessment. *Exceptional Children, 68,* 7–22.

Elliott, J., Bielinski, J., Thurlow, M., DeVito, P., & Hedlund, E. (1999). *Accommodations and the performance of all students on Rhode Island's performance assessment* (Rhode Island Assessment Report 1). Minneapolis, MN: University of

Minnesota, National Center on Educational Outcomes. (ERIC Document Reproduction Service No. ED 440 516)

Elliott, S., Kratochwill, T., & McKevitt, B. (2001). Experimental analysis of the effects of testing accommodations on the scores of students with and without disabilities. *Journal of School Psychology, 39,* 3–24.

Elliott, S. N., McKevitt, B. C, & Kettler, R. J. (2002). Testing accommodations research and decision making: The case of "good" scores being highly valued but difficult to achieve for all students. *Measurement and Evaluation in Counseling and Development, 35,* 153–166.

Fuchs, L. S., & Fuchs, D. (2001). Helping teachers formulate sound test accommodation decisions for students with learning disabilities. *Learning Disabilities Research & Practice, 16,* 174–181.

Fuchs, L. S., Fuchs, D., Eaton, S. B., Hamlett, C., Binkley, E., & Crouch, R. (2000). Using objective data sources to enhance teacher judgments aboul test accommodations. *Exceptional Children, 67,* 67–81.

Fuchs, L. S., Fuchs, D., Eaton. S. B., Hamlett, C. L., & Karns, K. M. (2000). Supplementing teacher judgments of mathematics test accommodations with objective data sources. *School Psychology Review, 29,* 65–85.

Hollenbeck, K., Linder, C., & Almond, P. (2002). *Statewide writing score comparability of various tools used by students with visual impairments* (Accommodations Research Report 8). Eugene, OR: Behavioral Research and Teaching, University of Oregon.

Hollenbeck, K., Rozek-Tedesco, M., Tindal, G., & Glasgrow, A. (2000). An exploratory study of student-paced versus teacher-paced accommodations for large-scale math tests. *Journal of Special Education Technology, I5*(2), 27–36.

Hollenbeck, K., Tindal, G., & Almond, P. (1998). Teachers' knowledge of accommodations as a validity issue in high-stakes testing. *Journal of Special Education, 32,* 175–183.

Hollenbeck, K., Tindal, G., Harniss, M., & Almond, P. (1999). *The effect of using computers as an accommodation in a statewide writing test.* Retrieved May 18, 2004, from the University of Oregon Web site: http://brt.uoregon.edu/publications_archive.htm.

Individuals With Disabilities Education Improvement Act of 2004, H. R. 1350 (2004).

Jablonski, B., Edgemon, E. A., Wiley, A. W., & Lloyd, J. W. (2005). *Large-scale testing accommodations for students with disabilities: Literature review.* Manuscript submitted for publication.

Johnson, E., Kimball, K., Brown, S. O., & Anderson, D. (2001). A statewide review of the use of accommodations in large-scale high-stakes assessments. *Exceptional Children, 67,* 251–264.

Koretz, D., & Hamilton, L. (2000). Assessment of students with disabilities in Kentucky: Inclusion, student performance, and validity. *Educational Evaluation and Policy Analysis, 22*(3), 255–272,

MacArthur, C. A., & Cavalier, A. R. (2004). Dictation and speech recognition technology as test accommodations. *Exceptional Children, 71,* 43–58.

MacAnhur, C. A., & Graham, S. (1987). Learning disabled students' composing under three methods of test production: Handwriting, word processing, and dictation. *Journal of Special Education, 21* (3), 22–42.

Meloy, L. L., Deville, C., & Frisbie, D. (2002). The effect of read aloud accommodations on test scores of students with and without a learning disability in reading. *Remedial and Special Education, 23,* 248–255.

Munger, G. F., & Loyd, B. H. (1991). The effects of speededness on test performance of handicapped and nonhandicapped examinees. *Journal of Educational Research, 85,* 53–57.

Ofiesh, N. S., Hughes, C., & Scott, S. S. (2004). Extended test time and postsecondary students with learning disabilities: A model for decision making. *Learning Disabilities Research & Practice, 19,* 57–70.

Perlman, C. L., Borger, J., Collins, C. B., Elenbogen, J. C., & Wood, J. (1996, April). *The effect of extended time limits on learning disabled students' scores on standardized reading tests.* Paper presented at the annual meeting of the National Council on Measurement in Education, New York. (ERIC Document Reproduction Service No. ED 400 316).

Ragosta, M., & Wendler, C. (1992). *Eligibility issues and comparable time limits for disabled and nondisabled SAT examinees* (College Entrance Examination Board Rep. No. 92-5). New York: Educational Testing Service. (ERIC Document Reproduction Service No. ED 349 337).

Trimble, S. (1998). *Performance trends and use of accommodations on a statewide assessment: Students with disabilities in the KIRIS on-demand assessment from 1992–93 through 1995–96* (Maryland-Kentucky Report 3). Retrieved June 16. 2004, from the National Center on Educational Outcomes, University of Minnesota. Web site: http://education.umn.edu/NCEO/OnlinePuhs/MDKY_3.html.

Ysseldyke, J., Thurlow, M., Bielinski, J., Trimble, S., Hill, K., Wickheiser, J., et al. (1999). *Characteristics of students who participate in Kentucky's testing system under various conditions* (Maryland–Kentucky Report 4). Retrieved June 16, 2004, from the National Center on Educational Outcomes, University of Minnesota, Web site: http://education.umn.edu/NCEO/OnlinePubs/MdKy_4.html.

Ziomek, R. L., & Andrews, K. M. (1996). *Predicting the college grade point averages of special tested students from their ACT assessment scores and high school grades* (Report No. ACT-RR-96-7). Iowa City, IA: American College Testing. (ERIC Document Reproduction Service No. ED 405357).

Elizabeth A. Edgemon (CEC VA Federation), Doctoral Candidate; **Brian R. Jablonski** (CEC VA Federation), Doctoral Candidate: and **John W. Lloyd** (CEC VA Federation), Professor, Curry School of Education, University of Virginia. Charlottesville. Address correspondence to Elizabeth A. Edgemon. Curry School of Education, P.O. Box 400261, University of Virginia, Charlottesville, VA 22904-4261 (e-mail: eae3j@virginia.edu).

From *Teaching Exceptional Children,* by Elizabeth A. Edgemon, Brian R. Jablonski, and John W. Lloyd, Vol. 38, No. 3, January/February 2006, pp. 6–11. Copyright © 2006 by Council for Exceptional Children. Reprinted by permission.

Use Authentic Assessment Techniques to Fulfill the Promise of No Child Left Behind

CAROL A. LAYTON AND ROBIN H. LOCK

The No Child Left Behind Act (NCLB) of 2001 mandates the nationwide development of state accountability assessment plans for all school districts and students. The bill also requires that the results of these assessments be made available in terms of individual, school, and statewide progress reports. School districts and schools failing to make adequate progress toward statewide proficiency goals must provide supplemental services for their students. These services may include free tutoring, afterschool assistance, and widespread instructional changes in the daily delivery of curriculum. In addition, each state is required to develop statewide curricular goals and objectives that are measured yearly using a state-developed achievement measure.

Progress for students with special needs is also included in this accountability system. In some states, specific guidelines for determining the use of the state-mandated assessment device contain provisions for on-grade-level assessment, below-grade-level assessment, the use of accommodations and modifications during assessment, and the need for student assessment of non-state-guided curricular expectations as delineated in the Individualized Education Program (IEP). While much attention has been given to the development of the state-mandated guidelines for determining accommodations and modifications, many states have encountered difficulty in establishing the appropriate level for assessing students with disabilities receiving special education services on the state-mandated assessment.

One state provides IEP teams with several choices when deciding upon the appropriate expected achievement level for students with disabilities receiving special education services. These choices include

- on-grade-level assessment with or without accommodations through the state-mandated assessment;
- below-grade-level assessment with or without accommodations using a state-developed alternative assessment; or

- a locally determined assessment designed by the IEP team.

IEP teams often report difficultly in pinpointing the appropriate assessment situation and indicate a need for more precise and explicit information for ascertaining the correct assessment.

Authentic assessment provides such a platform for making these types of assessment decisions on an individualized basis. Additionally, by including authentic assessment in the decision-making process, IEP teams honor both the mandates of NCLB and the Individuals with Disabilities Education Improvement Act of 2004, (IDEIA), which requires assessment practices that yield specific, individual results about student achievement that are easily translated into daily instructional practices. The following suggestions present authentic assessment techniques to validate and document the mandates of both NCLB and IDEIA.

1. Collect Daily Work Samples to Show the Student's Actual Progress

The IEP team will use this information to decide whether the student has a beginning, developing, or proficient knowledge of the particular state-mandated goal. This will help determine whether the student is performing on or below grade level on a daily basis.

2. Ensure That the IEP Reflects the Student's Instructional Level

Instructional level refers to beginning, developing, or proficient knowledge of a goal or objective. Goals and objectives should be tied to the state-mandated curriculum to ensure the student's access to the general education curriculum. This connection on the IEP is then documented through authentic assessment to provide specific examples of the student's growth from beginning mastery through proficiency.

3. Create Curriculum-based Assessments to Link Student Performance to the Curriculum

Curriculum-based assessment (CBA) examines the student's performance on the standards mandated in general education by systematically increasing the difficulty in assignments and engaging in continuous assessments (Burns, 2002). This process links high expectations concerning the student's daily learning to accepted state-mandated indicators of student proficiency.

4. Establish a Baseline Using CBA

Use CBA to establish a baseline or present level of performance (PLOP) for the development of IEPs that coordinate with state-mandated standards and support state-developed assessment. The IEP team can depend on the results of CBA to isolate the suitable assessment level for the individual student with disabilities.

5. Rely on Curriculum-based Measurement for Determining the Effectiveness of Instruction

Fuchs and Fuchs (2002) identified four factors for making data-based decisions by the IEP team to indicate progress in mastery of state-mandated standards. They are (a) shaping academic growth, (b) differentiating between unproductive instruction and undesirable student learning, (c) enlightening instructional planning, and (d) continually updating instructional effectiveness to increase student progress.

6. Use a Portfolio to Provide a Direct Bond Between Instruction and the General Education Classroom Curriculum

The portfolio provides an efficient and convenient system for logging and compiling examples of a student's comprehensive growth over time. The IEP team applies the results of the portfolio to decisions concerning the appropriate assessment based on the student instructional level. Losardo and Notari-Syverson (2001) identified the following components of portfolios, which empower the IEP team with specific information for decision making. Portfolios

- allow for ongoing assessment across environments;
- pass from teacher to teacher or grade to grade, supplying information to ease the student's transition;
- provide many ways of examining a student's performance from a variety of perspectives; and

- improve self-advocacy for students by encouraging their participation in the selection of products and communication about their work.

7. Maintain Classroom Portfolios to Create a Detailed and Complex Picture of the Student's Mastery Over Time

The IEP team will then have concrete examples of the student's actual instructional level (Stiggins, 2001) to make decisions about the student's progress from beginning to proficient mastery and to identify appropriate state-mandated assessment levels.

8. Perform Direct Observations to Record Behavior

Behavioral observations provide the IEP team with a close-up look at on-task behavior and skill performance in a variety of settings. The IEP team makes more valid instructional and assessment decisions when data confirm the results of standardized or previous test scores (Salvia and Ysseldyke, 2001).

9. Employ Direct Observations to Document the Inclusion of Research-based Strategies

In addition to observing the student's behavior, instructional delivery, classroom practices, and student response to research-based strategies can also be monitored. Details about the arrangement of the classroom, grouping for instruction, and teacher response rates and expectations, as well as other daily routines and strategies, are easily obtained through direct observations (Cohen & Spenciner, 2003).

10. Draw on Environmental Assessments to Analyze the Instructional Cycle

Environmental assessments are key elements in improving the curriculum, intervention goals, and procedures (McLean, Wolery, & Bailey, 2004). A fit between individual need and the delivery of instruction, as well as the need for and use of accommodation and modifications in the environment, aids the IEP team in selecting the appropriate state-mandated assessment.

11. Examine Environmental Assessments to Identify Staff Training Needs

Environmental assessments provide documentation of program quality and the types of improvements needed in particular settings (Salvia & Ysseldyke, 2001). Recording research-based practices and evaluating their implementation aids the IEP team in verifying their use and effectiveness in the least restrictive environment. These data direct the IEP team in determining assessment levels and the need for change in instructional practices.

12. Generate Questionnaires to Gather Different Perspectives

By having a variety of individuals complete the same questionnaire, the IEP team obtains multiple sources to document progress (Bauer & Shea, 2003). This information allows the team to become familiar with the student's generalization of the goal and achievement proficiency level.

13. Interview All Stakeholders in the Student's Academic Life

Interviews permit the teacher or examiner to gain insight into the student's life in and beyond the classroom (Spinelli, 2002). They supply the IEP team with facts concerning the use and generalization of academic skills at home and in environments beyond the classroom.

14. Explore the Results of Checklists Based on State-mandated Goals

Checklists should be used frequently to monitor the progress on state-mandated assessment goals. Checklists help determine whether the student is at risk for particular problems. They also document slow or nonexistent achievement to establish the need for changes in the instructional process.

15. Survey the Success and Use of Modifications and Accommodations in a Variety of Environments

Teacher-made checklists reveal the student's existing behaviors in the classroom setting (Gallagher, 1998). Documentation of consistent use of modifications or accommodations provides the IEP team with the rationale for including them in the state-mandated assessment process.

16. Capture Student Achievement Over Time Through Rating Scales

Rating scales portray the breadth and depth of student achievement over time (Prestidge & Williams Glaser, 2000). The IEP team evaluates readiness for a particular achievement level on the state-mandated assessment by examining both examples of

daily work and attitudinal dispositions indicating movement toward proficiency.

17. Develop Communication Notebooks to Inform Parents

The communication notebook emphasizes the dual responsibility for student learning (Williams & Cartledge, 1997) by all participants in the system including parents and teachers, students and teachers, and general and special education teachers, as well as others. Communication notebooks enable parents to make more informed decisions about their student's current programming. Frequent interaction between the home and school facilitates the understanding of a student's present level of performance. This awareness improves decision making with respect to the selection and implementation of research-based instructional strategies and determination of appropriate assessment techniques.

18. Journal to Corroborate Student Progress on IEP Goals and Objectives

By providing a connection between participants to record what is happening in the classroom, at home, and in everyday life, journals enhance the quality of the data by providing a holistic observation of the student's progress (English & Gillen, 2001). Journals present an avenue for open lines of communication.

19. Document the Correct Choice for the Level of State-mandated Assessment

Authentic assessment supplies specific examples of student achievement in a variety of settings. These data support the team's decision making concerning the level of assessment as well as appropriate modifications and accommodations for the testing environment.

20. Base Assessment Decisions on NCLB and IDEIA Mandates

NCLB and IDEIA require assessment decisions reflective of the student's strengths and needs rather than relying solely on curricular goals. Authentic assessment bridges the gap between the state-mandated assessment process and NCLB by accurately identifying strengths and needs for more individualized assessment decision making.

References

Bauer, A. M., & Shea, T. M. (2003). *Parents and schools: Creating a successful partnership for students with special needs.* Upper Saddle River, NJ: Merrill/Prentice Hall.

Burns, M. K. (2002). Comprehensive system of assessment to intervention using curriculum-based assessments. *Intervention in School and Clinic, 38*(1), 8–13.

Cohen, L. G., & Spenciner, L. J. (2003). *Assessment of children and youth with special needs.* Boston, MA: Pearson Education, Inc.

English, L. M., & Gillen, M. A. (2001). Journal writing in practice: From vision to reality. *New Directions for Adult and Continuing Education, 90,* 87–94.

Fuchs, L. S., & Fuchs, D. (2002). Curriculum-based measurement: Describing competence, enhancing outcomes, evaluating treatment, effects, and identifying treatment nonresponders. *Peabody Journal of Education, 77*(2), 64–84.

Gallagher, J. D. (1998). *Classroom assessment for teachers.* Upper Saddle River, NJ: Merrill/Prentice Hall.

Individuals with Disabilities Education Improvement Act of 2004, 20 U.S.C. § 1400 *et seq.* (2004) (reauthorization of the Individuals with Disabilities Education Act of 1990).

Losardo, A., & Notari-Syverson, A. (2001). *Alternative approaches to assessing young children.* Baltimore, MD: Paul H. Brookes.

McLean, M., Wolery, M., & Bailey, D. B., Jr. (2004). *Assessing infants and preschoolers with special needs* (3rd ed.). Upper Saddle River, NJ: Prentice Hall.

No Child Left Behind Act of 2001, 20 U.S.C. § 6301 *et seq.* (2002).

Prestidge, L. K., & Williams Glaser, C. H. (2000). Authentic assessment: Employing appropriate tools for evaluating students' work in 21st-century classrooms. *Intervention and School and Clinic, 35*(3), 178–182.

Salvia, J., & Ysseldyke, J. E. (2001). *Assessment* (8th ed.). Boston, MA: Houghton Mifflin.

Spinelli, C. G. (2002). *Classroom assessment for students with special needs in inclusive settings.* Upper Saddle River, NJ: Prentice Hall.

Stiggins, R. J. (2001). *Student-involved classroom assessment* (3rd ed.) Upper Saddle River, NJ: Prentice Hall.

Williams, V. I., & Cartledge, G. (1997). Passing notes-to parents. *Teaching Exceptional Children, 30*(1), 30–35.

CAROL A. LAYTON, EdD, associate professor, is an assessment specialist at Texas Tech University. Her interests include the authentic assessment of intrinsic processing disorders and the synthesis of evaluation results in planning successful interventions. **ROBIN H. LOCK,** PhD, is an associate professor at Texas Tech University. Her research interests include the role of intrinsic processing disorders in the diagnosis of learning disabilities and the provision of effective interventions and accommodations for students. Address: Carol A. Layton, Texas Tech University, College of Education, Box 41071, Lubbock, TX 79409-1071; e-mail: carol.layton@ttu.edu

From *Intervention in School and Clinic,* by Carol A Layton and Robin H. Lock, Vol. 42, No. 3, January 2007, pp. 169–173. Copyright © 2007 by Pro-Ed, Inc. Reprinted by permission.

UNIT 2

Early Childhood

Unit Selections

Key Points to Consider

- Can early childhood special services identify learning disabilities before public school? How?

- How can the transition to kindergarten be paved for young children with disabilities?

- Can teachers bond with sullen, angry, aggressive young children without punishing them? How?

Student Web Site

www.mhcls.com/online

Internet References

Further information regarding these Web sites may be found in this book's preface or online.

Division for Early Childhood
   http://www.dec-sped.org
Institute on Community Integration Projects
   http://ici.umn.edu/projectscenters/
National Association for Child Development (NACD)
   http://www.nacd.org
Special Education Resources on the Internet (SERI)
   http://seriweb.com

Public law 99-457 has been called one of the most important educational decisions of the United States. It was a 1986 amendment (Part H) to PL94-142 (the Education for All Handicapped Children Act), which the U.S. Congress established as a grant incentive aimed at providing services for young children at risk of disability beginning at the age of three. By 1991 this amendment to the now-renamed Individuals with Disabilities Education Improvement Act (IDEIA) was reauthorized. It operates through "Child Find," which are organizational groups that look for babies, toddlers, and preschoolers with conditions of obvious disability. These young children can receive special educational services according to IDEIA's mandate for: "a free and appropriate education for all in the least-restrictive environment." Many infants and young children are being found who are at "high risk" of developing educational disabilities (for example, low vision, hearing impairments, developmental delays) unless education begins before the age of six. This outreach is having a profound impact on the care of families and children.

The United States is faced with multiple questions about the education of its future citizens—its young children. Many American babies are born preterm, small for gestational age, or with extremely low birth weight. This is a direct result of the United States' high rate of teenage pregnancy (nearly double that of most European countries and Canada) and its low rate of providing adequate prenatal care, especially for the young, the poor, or recent immigrant mothers. These infants are at high risk for developing disabilities and conditions of educational exceptionality. Early intervention can help these babies.

All services to be provided for any infant, toddler, or preschooler with a disability, and for his or her family, are to be articulated in an individualized family service plan (IFSP). The IFSP is to be written and implemented as soon as the infant or young child is determined to be at risk. IFSPs specify what services will be provided for the parents, for the diagnosed child, for siblings, and for all significant caregivers. Children with pervasive disabilities (such as autism, traumatic brain injuries, blindness, deafness, orthopedic impairments, severe health impairments, or multiple disabilities) may require extensive and very expensive early childhood interventions.

IFSPs are written in collaboration with parents, experts in the area of the child's exceptional condition, teachers, home-service providers, and other significant providers. They are updated every 6 months until the child turns three and receives an individualized education plan (IEP). A case manager is assigned to oversee each individual child with an IFSP to ensure high-quality and continuous intervention services.

In the United States, Child Find locates and identifies infants, toddlers, and young children who qualify for early childhood special education and family services. An actual diagnosis, or label of condition of exceptionality, is not required. Assessment is usu-

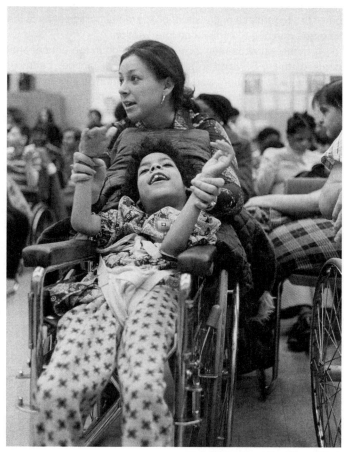

Digital Vision/PunchStock/PunchStock

ally accomplished in a multidisciplinary fashion. It can be very difficult, but as much as possible, it is conducted in the child's home in a nonthreatening fashion. Diagnosis of exceptionalities in children who cannot yet answer questions is complicated. Personal observations are used as well as parent reports. Most of the experts involved in the multidisciplinary assessment want to see the child more than once to help compensate for the fact that all children have good days and bad days. In cases where the parents are non-English speakers and a translator is required, assessment may take several days.

Despite the care taken, many children who qualify for, and would benefit from, early intervention services are missed. Child Find associations are not well funded. There are constant shortages of time, materials, and multidisciplinary professionals to do assessments. Finding translators for parents who speak uncommon foreign languages adds to the problems. Occasionally the availability of funds for early childhood interventions encourages the overdiagnosis of risk factors in infants from low-income, minority, immigrant, or rural families.

A challenge to all professionals providing early childhood special services is how to work with diverse parents. Some parents welcome any and all intervention, even if it is not merited. Other parents resist any labeling of their child as "disabled" and refuse services. Professionals must make allowances for cultural, economic, and educational diversity, multiple caregivers, and single parents. Regardless of the situation, parental participation is the sine qua non of early childhood intervention.

At-home services may include instruction in the educational goals of the IFSP, and in skills such as discipline, behavior management, nutrition, and health maintenance. At-home services also include counseling for parents, siblings, and significant others to help them deal with their fears and to help them accept, love, and challenge their special child to become all he or she is capable of being. A case manager helps ensure that there is cooperation and coordination of services by all team members.

Most children receiving early childhood services have some center-based or combined center- and home-based special education. Center care introduces children to peers and introduces the family to other families with similar concerns. It is easier to ensure quality education and evaluate progress when a child spends at least a part of his or her time in a well-equipped educational center.

The first article in Unit 2 discusses the benefits of early identification of young children with learning disabilities. The author suggests ways in which this can be accomplished. When intervention is started with IFSPs before elementary school, subsequent school progress is greatly enhanced.

The second article selected for inclusion in this unit on early childhood addresses the need for a carefully planned transition from intervention before school for children with disabilities, to public school education. Both parents and children have a degree of anxiety related to separation, and to beginning an academically focused program. The kindergarten transition sets the tone for the child's future academic success.

The last article, "Building Relationships with Challenging Children" presents positive ways to help at-risk students. The authors, Philip and Nancy Hall, eschew punishment. They recommend gentle intervention and bonding. They describe the components of these practices that help ensure that the student will become a good learner and achieve educational success.

Making the Case for Early Identification and Intervention for Young Children at Risk for Learning Disabilities

The early identification of children with learning disabilities (LD) is difficult but can be accomplished. Observation of key behaviors which are indicators of LD by preschool and kindergarten teachers can assist in this process. This early identification facilitates the use of intervention strategies to provide a positive early experience for children at risk for academic difficulties.

MARCEE M. STEELE[1,2]

Introduction

Early identification and intervention for children with special needs has been strongly recommended. Professionals in psychological, medical, scientific, and educational fields have documented the importance of the years between birth and five for learning. If there is any risk of disability, these early years become even more critical (Lerner, Lowenthal, & Egan, 2003). There is a history of research documenting the value of early identification and intervention; however, in the field of learning disabilities (LD) specifically, the literature is not as definite. There is still controversy over whether very early identification for LD is possible. A child is considered to have a LD if he/she is not working to potential in at least one academic area, has trouble processing information, and does not have any other primary disability (Lerner, 2003). The cause is generally considered neurological. The author of this article will review related literature suggesting that early LD identification is difficult but feasible, and in fact beneficial. She will make suggestions to help with early LD identification and then recommend some early intervention strategies for preschool and kindergarten teachers.

Controversy over Early Identification of Learning Disabilities

Although there is still much debate concerning the identification of LD prior to grade two, there is overwhelming research to support this timing and practice. Survey results of Snyder, Bailey, and Auer (1994), for example, reflected agreement that early LD identification is important despite confusion indicated about the LD label and diagnosis for young children.

One value of early identification and intervention is that it provides a foundation for later learning and could thereby foster later academic success experiences for children at risk (Peltzman, 1992; Soyfer, 1998). If children with LD are identified in the early childhood years, it is much more likely that they will have the opportunity to develop to potential (Peltzman, 1992).

In addition, early identification can prevent secondary problems from occurring. Unless children with potential reading and LD are identified early, they will have a greater chance of developing secondary problems such as frustration and anxiety

---

[1] University of North Carolina at Wilmington.
[2] Correspondence should be directed to Marcee M. Steele, Watson School of Education, University of North Carolina, Wilmington, NC 28403; e-mail: steelem@uncw.edu

(Catts, 1991; Lowenthal, 1998). Taylor and others, in their review of related literature, indicated that if children with LD are not identified early, the learning problems continue and could lead to more students dropping out of school, exhibiting behavior problems, and developing greater academic deficiencies. The early identification, in contrast, prevents the need for more extensive special education services in the future and leads to more inclusive programming (2000).

Reading problems, in particular, if not identified early lead to subsequent motivational problems. When children are not motivated, they have fewer opportunities to practice reading skills and therefore get even further behind academically (Catts, 1997). Vandervelden and Siegel (1997) suggest that early phonics instruction, for example, prevents later reading deficits and enhances early reading and writing experiences.

Even though these benefits support early identification of LD, there are also many concerns that should be addressed. Probably one of the biggest fears relates to the potential stigma and unnecessary labeling of young children (Snyder et al., 1994; Taylor, Anselmo, Foreman, Schatschneider, & Angelopoulos, 2000). It is not, however, necessary to use the term LD at a young age as it is for older students when determining eligibility for special education classes in public schools. Therefore, the stigma and labeling can be avoided.

In addition, there are problems with the tests that are used, especially for identification of young children with LD. The readiness tests that are normed for young children are not always accurate for prediction purposes, and they are generally very expensive (Taylor et al., 2000). A survey of states and their procedures indicated that many states are concerned with LD eligibility determination especially because of testing concerns with young children and reliability and validity issues with the tests themselves (Snyder et al., 1994). Informal assessment procedures, discussed in the next section, can be considered a viable alternative especially with young children.

Another problem with early identification is that the LD definition requires a discrepancy in an academic area, in other words, a child not working to potential. Early identification of LD is difficult with preschool children because the required underachievement does not clearly relate to young children. They would not necessarily have been exposed to academics in the formal sense so it would be difficult to determine if preschool or kindergarten children have a significant discrepancy between ability (measured by IQ tests) and achievement (based on academic test results). There are not always clear academic expectations at such an early age (Snyder et al., 1994), and therefore some schools delay the process until there is a significant discrepancy. Of course, then teachers will have wasted significant teaching time (Taylor et al., 2000). If the discrepancy cannot be determined at an early age, it is often suggested that the schools should wait until there is a discrepancy to label a child. In other words, wait until children fail and then give them the help they need! (Catts, 1991). In addition, discrepancy determination involves measures of intelligence (Lowenthal, 1998), and the intelligence tests are controversial at best. They have been highly criticized for bias, reliability, and other related issues. Instead of delaying the identification and intervention

until the child is in even more trouble, it is important to realize that the technical definition is not required for young children with LD to receive services. More general labels such as developmental delay or at risk can be used instead, avoiding some of the above concerns.

Some people even suggest that because of these difficulties and criticisms, it is not possible to identify LD at such an early age (Snyder et al., 1994). Furthermore, it is very possible that children could appear to have LD at a young age, but then the problems could disappear a little later on if it is just a lag or delay in development. (Lowenthal, 1998). Many of the LD characteristics look like typical preschool characteristics, and it is therefore difficult to make an early determination. However, if children are identified early and later outgrow their problems, there really is no harm done. The label and services can be discontinued.

Strategies for LD Identification and Intervention in Preschool and Kindergarten

In order to address many of these potential problems, early childhood teachers can implement observation strategies. Systematic observation of behaviors and search for patterns can be very useful in determining potential learning problems. Taylor et al., (2000), suggested that an alternative to discrepancy determination, teacher judgments of progress, be used especially with young children who are at risk. Mantzicopoulus and Morrison (1994) similarly concluded from their study of various prediction tools that teacher prediction is an accurate part of the process to determine early reading failure and success. Using observation as a diagnostic tool then is one way to get the benefits of early identification without the potential for stigma, unnecessary labeling, and use of questionable testing procedures. The LD label would not be necessary; instead teachers can determine that a particular child is at risk and implement appropriate interventions.

Language is one of the skill areas that teachers can observe for early identification purposes. Catts (1991), for example, suggests that it would be wise to look for some of the developmental characteristics like oral language difficulties as early as preschool to avoid some of the problems with LD identification. Because early language problems are often indicative of later reading problems, Catts (1997) suggests that observations of these language problems be used diagnostically. Difficulties with morphology, syntax, understanding words and sentences orally, awareness of speech sounds, word retrieval, verbal memory, and speech production correlate with later problems in word recognition and phonics. These problems can be observed prior to formal reading instruction and therefore are indicators of potential reading problems. He designed a list of behaviors to help with the observation of these deficits and to refer children for comprehensive evaluation. The list includes behaviors such as trouble with rhyming, difficulty remembering the alphabet, difficulty following directions, frequent mispronunciations, trouble understanding stories, small vocabulary, and short disorganized sentences when talking.

Other observable behaviors that indicate potential learning problems in preschool include hyperactivity, incoordination, perseveration, impulsivity, processing deficits, distractibility, and memory problems (Lowenthal, 1998; Peltzman, 1992). In kindergarten, readiness skills such as listening, following directions, dressing, appropriate attention span; and prerequisite academics such as alphabet skills, rhyming, colors, counting, and copying can be observed (Lowenthal, 1998).

Once identified as having possible delays and potential learning disabilities, there are several recommended strategies for early childhood teachers. The environment and focus of the program can be modified to enhance development. Peltzman (1992) recommends that the focus of an early intervention program should be to build a strong foundation rather than remediate a problem. Practice on skills in all of the developmental areas with opportunities for guidance and success is helpful. In arranging preacademic activities, Allen and Schwartz (2001) recommend short tasks with familiar materials, individual workspaces, choice of activities, clear organization and preparation, and clear transitions. In addition, consistency, repetition, and regularity in routines benefit children at risk for LD. Tasks are generally mastered more efficiently if broken down into small segments, especially for children with special needs (Klein, Cook, & Richardson-Gibbs, 2001).

In addition, early literacy interventions help prevent later reading deficits in some cases (Catts, 1996). Emerging Literacy and preacademics can be taught in a "developmentally appropriate" way. All children need to be taught skills to help them with later academic success, but if there is a disability it is even more important to start at their own level and then progress. Children's interests and related questions could be used to help guide this type of instruction. For example, oral language activities that are natural and involve typical routines and activities are most effective. Teachers can assist by expanding children's own words into complete sentences, describing their own activities, and providing models of language that describe what children are doing (Lowenthal, 1998).

Some direct teaching can also be included in the instructional plan for preschool children with potential LD. Sensory activities can be used to enhance curiosity; students at this age need freedom to explore. Some examples of activities that can be used to help prepare children for later academic learning include: writing down what children say and then reading it back, and writing their questions down and helping them find answers (Allen & Schwartz, 2001). Catts (1996) suggests including practice in sounds and words, rhyming activities, numerous experiences with books including oral reading, discussion, and vocabulary activities. Other literacy activities for kindergarten children include phonics practice to improve later reading and writing skills for children with mild disabilities. Activities such as labeling, syllable clapping, children's dictation of words, rhyming activities, and letter games all provide practice in prerequisite skills in a motivating and enjoyable way (O'Connor & others, 1996). To help prepare children for later literacy instruction, it is important that they are exposed to reading, writing, and oral language activities.

Table I   Indicators of Learning Disabilities

Difficulty with the following behaviors could indicate risk for LD if the behaviors are noticeably different from that of most peers:

Talking with words in correct order
Understanding words said aloud
Understanding sentences said aloud
Remembering specific words when talking
Remembering what they hear
Participating in rhyming games and activities
Remembering the alphabet
Following directions
Pronouncing many words correctly when speaking spontaneously
Understanding stories read aloud
Using words properly when speaking
Talking with organized sentences and thoughts
Sitting still for appropriate periods of time
Changing from one activity to another
Attending to tasks
Remembering what they see
Thinking before talking or acting
Staying focused on a topic
Listening to stories and songs for extended periods of time
Dressing
Identifying colors
Counting
Copying

Cognitive or processing skills can be practiced through directions, listening activities, games, and multisensory activities (using the sense of touch, movement, sight, and hearing), finger plays, songs, stories, puzzles, blocks, pegboards and matching games (Lowenthal, 1998). Allen and Schwartz (2001) suggest using colorful manipulatives, imitation with models and mirrors, water play, arts and crafts, housekeeping, copying patterns, memory games, following directions, coloring, cutting, counting, and grouping objects as appropriate processing and preacademic practice.

Practice developing social emotional skills, such as getting along with others and sharing, is also important for young children, especially children who are impulsive. Self-esteem needs to be addressed as well as social skills. Examples of behavioral intervention strategies for young children include taking away toys and activities for misbehavior, maintaining attention through novelty, structuring transition times, keeping consistency in routine, using short activities, structuring the environment, using token economies, shaping, timeout, and reinforcement for appropriate behaviors. It is also helpful to use group tasks and activities which integrate typically and atypically developing children (Lowenthal, 1998). In addition,

Table II Suggestions for Teachers

The following types of activities would be helpful when teaching children who are at risk for LD:
Use materials that are familiar to the children
Have individual workspaces
Allow some choice in activities
Organize and prepare tasks
Plan for clear transitions between activities
Expand children's words into sentences
Provide good language models
Teach beginning phonics skills
Label objects around the classroom
Clap out syllables
Use rhyming activities
Play alphabet and vocabulary games
Use topics of particular interest to children
Have children dictate stories and ideas
Practice with sounds
Read aloud to children from books suited to their levels and interests
Use finger plays
Incorporate songs in lessons
Use puzzles, blocks, and pegboard activities
Incorporate arts and crafts
Play memory games
Have children count objects
Develop behavior plan
Be consistent with routines and rules
Incorporate group activities
Break down tasks into small steps
Repeat new learnings frequently

References

Allen, K. E., & Schwartz, I. S. (2001). *The exceptional child: Inclusion in early childhood education.* Albany, NY: Delmar.

Catts, H. W. (1991). Early identification of reading disabilities. *Topics in Language Disorders, 12*(1), 1–16.

Catts, H. W. (1996). Defining dyslexia as a developmental language disorder: An expanded view. *Topics in Language Disorders, 16*(2), 14–29.

Catts, H. W. (1997). The early identification of language based reading disabilities. *Language, Speech, and Hearing Services in Schools, 28*(1), 86–89.

Klein, M. D., Cook, R. E., & Richardson-Gibbs, A. M. (2001). *Strategies for including children with special needs in early childhood settings.* Albany, NY: Delmar.

Lerner, J. W. (2003). *Learning disabilities: Theories, diagnosis, and teaching strategies.* Boston: Houghton Mifflin.

Lerner, J. W., Lowenthal, B., & Egan, R. W. (2003). *Preschool children with special needs.* Boston: Allyn and Bacon.

Lowenthal B. (1998). Precursors of learning disabilities in the inclusive preschool. *Learning Disabilities: A Multidisciplinary Journal, 9*(2), 25–31.

Mantzicopoulos, P. Y., & Morrison D. (1994). Early prediction of reading achievement: Exploring the relationship of cognitive and noncognitive measures to inaccurate classifications of at-risk status. *Remedial and Special Education, 15*(4), 244–251.

O'Connor, R. E., & others. (1996). The effect of kindergarten phonological intervention on the first grade reading and writing of children with mild disabilities (ERIC Document Reproduction Service No. 394129).

Peltzman, B. R. (1992). Guidelines for early identification and strategies for early intervention of at-risk learning disabled children. (ERIC Document Reproduction Service No. 351111).

Snyder, P., Bailey, D. B., & Auer, C. (1994). Preschool eligibility determination for children with known or suspected learning disabilities under IDEA. *Journal of Early Intervention, 18*(4), 380–390.

Soyfer, V. (1998) Parents promoting school success for young children with learning disabilities (ERIC Document Reproduction Service No. 428488)

Taylor, H. G., Anselmo, M., Foreman, A. L., Schatschneider, C., & Angelopoulos J. (2000). Utility of kindergarten teacher judgments in identifying early learning problems. *Journal of Learning Disabilities, 33*(2), 200–210.

Vandervelden, M. C., & Siegel, L. S. (1997). Teaching phonological processing skills in early literacy: A developmental approach. *Learning Disability Quarterly, 20*(2), 63–81.

it is important to establish clear rules, review rules frequently for prevention, and use consequences consistently (Klein et al., 2001).

Conclusion

It is clear from reviewing the related literature that early identification and intervention for young children with potential LD is valuable. A summary of key ideas for early identification and intervention by preschool and kindergarten teachers is included in Tables I and II. These suggestions can help early childhood teachers make every child's first school experience a success.

MARCEE M. STEELE, PhD, University of South Florida is a professor of special education at the University of North Carolina at Wilmington. She teaches undergraduate and graduate courses in learning disabilities, diagnostic techniques, exceptional students, and current issues in special education. She has also taught individuals with learning disabilities from pre-school to graduate school level in public and private settings for over 30 years.

From *Early Childhood Education Journal,* Vol. 32, No. 2, October 2004, pp. 75–79. Copyright © 2004 by Springer Science and Business Media. Reprinted by permission.

Collaborative Steps
Paving the Way to Kindergarten for Young Children with Disabilities

AMANDA FENLON

The night before my son was to start kindergarten, we snuggled in bed to read *Tom Goes to Kindergarten,* by Margaret Wild and David Legge, a lighthearted and humorous look at the separation anxiety felt by both children and parents. We giggled when Tom's mom and dad clung to him, not wanting to leave the classroom after being able to stay with their son on the first day. Next, we read *The Kissing Hand,* by Audrey Penn, a tender story of a mother raccoon sending her love through a kiss on her son's palm as he starts school. This time tears welled up in my eyes.

My son and I were fairly well prepared for his transition to school. As an administrator for our school district, I had taken some steps to make sure of this. The previous spring, I spoke with both the kindergarten teacher and the principal about my son's strengths and needs as a learner. As a family, we were invited to a special kindergarten orientation, and being a district employee, I had been in the school and kindergarten classroom several times before the big day. Still, I was apprehensive, excited, and honestly quite nervous about how well he would do those first few days.

Kindergarten entrance can be a joyful, although anxious time for families. Pianta and Kraft-Sayre (1999) note that a majority of parents (53 percent) included in a recent study felt positively about their child's transition to school, yet up to 35 percent of families noted some degree of anxiety about their child's entrance into school. Children's behavioral and emotional difficulties, reluctance to go to school, family adjustment problems, and unrealistic expectations from school staff were noted as parental concerns. A child's ability to separate from parents, get along with and be liked by peers and teachers, and even safety on the school bus can also cause families to worry.

Parents of children with significant disabilities share common concerns with other families. In addition, they typically have questions relating to how, when, where, and by whom their child's special services will be provided. The possibility of losing strong support systems established through preschool programs may also cause parents to worry (Wolery 1999). Thus, the entrance into school for the children with disabilities can be exceedingly complex and anxiety-laden for families. Demonstration models for transitioning children with disabilities to elementary school suggest the following best practices:

- using a collaborative team approach to involve families, both sending (preschool) and receiving (kindergarten) teachers and related services staff, and school administrators;
- setting transition goals and outlining anticipated outcomes;
- encouraging active empowerment and involvement of families in the process and enhancing communication between all involved staff; and
- focusing on the needs and strengths of individual children and the services and supports needed to be successful in kindergarten (Ross-Allen, Conn-Powers, & Fox 1991; Wolery 1999; Sandall, McLean, & Smith 2000).

Transition to kindergarten can be addressed through provisions of the Individuals with Disabilities Education Act Amendments (IDEA 1997) (determining educational placement in the least restrictive environment and special education and related services required by the child). However, the collaborative, coordinated process called for in research and best-practice publications is not clearly articulated in the federal law nor in most state agency regulations.

When young children with disabilities move from early intervention services (birth to two years) to preschool services (ages three to five years), and when youth with disabilities reach the age of 14, there are clearly articulated transition policies at federal, state, and local levels (IDEA 1997). Yet for the important step of entry into elementary school, the majority of states and local education agencies lack established guidelines or procedures governing the transition from early childhood special education programs to kindergarten (Rosenkoetter et al. 2001). Without specific protocols or regulations from state agencies, the level of communication and coordination between families and school program staff can vary greatly. Some states (Maine, Vermont, and Arkansas) have been leaders in setting up policies and procedures around this transition (Edwards 2002; Whaley, pers. comm. 2003), and this has had a significant positive impact on large numbers of families of young children with disabilities (Ross-Allen, Conn-Powers, & Fox 1991; Kohler 1994).

In addition to families' concerns, school districts may grapple with recommendations from early childhood programs that can be difficult to implement in some school settings. Schools must carefully bridge the gap between a play-based, child-centered curriculum to a kindergarten classroom with more rigorous academic standards.

In addition, the transition to kindergarten can be a time when parents of young children with disabilities pursue legal procedural safeguards such as mediation and impartial hearings to solve disagreements over services and needs (New York State Education Dept. 2003). Families of children with disabilities may disagree with a school district about the level of services to be provided or whether their child can attend a regular kindergarten class versus a self-contained classroom. They may believe the child needs more time to mature and want to delay the start of kindergarten until age six. Disputes such as these can create a strained beginning to the relationship between a family and school officials, which for children with disabilities can last until the student is age 21.

Yet for the important step of entry into elementary school, the majority of states and local education agencies lack established guidelines or procedures governing the transition from early childhood special education programs to kindergarten.

How can school districts avoid such conflicts and establish collaborative relationships with families of young children with disabilities? How can they enhance children's adjustment to and performance in kindergarten? What specific steps can staff take to be well prepared for their future students? This article describes one school district's collaborative transition process, which has been successful for many families, teachers, therapists, administrators, and especially the young children themselves.

Laying the First Stones— A Collaboration Begins

In the Baldwinsville School District in upstate New York, a collaborative step-by-step transition process guides school entrance for children with disabilities (see "Steps in the Collaborative Transition Process"). The school administrator and service providers develop and foster a supportive relationship with the family early on, beginning when a preschooler is first eligible for special education services. In Step 1 of the transition process, the district arranges for delivery of services, such as special education, speech therapy, and occupational therapy, in the child's home and within high-quality inclusive early childhood programs.

An extensive body of research tells us that children with and without disabilities learn academic, social, and communication skills, as well as character traits of empathy and appreciation of individual differences when they are educated together (Wolery & Wilbers 1994; Staub & Peck 1995; Hestenes & Carroll 2000). Our district greatly values inclusive education experiences and has facilitated the growth of several inclusive neighborhood preschools, with the belief that such programs are good preparation for entering inclusive settings in kindergarten and beyond.

Research tells us that children with and without disabilities learn academic, social, and communication skills, as well as character traits of empathy and appreciation of individual differences when they are educated together.

To prepare families for their collaborative role in the transition process (Step 2), the administrator for preschool special education introduces the process at the child's annual review meeting, roughly one-and-a-half years prior to kindergarten entry. Special educators encourage families to begin thinking about their child's entry into school and to ask any questions they may have about kindergarten. In the year prior to kindergarten entry, much collaboration takes place. The school district attempts to actively engage families in the transition process by involving them in several ways.

The parent as key decision maker is emphasized in the reauthorization of the IDEA.

The first formal contact generally comes after families receive a letter from the school district (Step 3), which serves as an invitation to join the team that will make decisions about the child as she transitions to kindergarten. Although many parents are already actively involved in their child's preschool program, this letter urges them to be even more closely involved in the planning for transition to kindergarten. The parent as key decision maker is emphasized in the reauthorization of the IDEA (1997).

Upon receipt of the letter, families frequently raise questions, such as "Will my child attend a regular kindergarten class?" "Can he receive his therapies in the classroom?" and "Can she ride the regular bus with her sister?" Such questions act as a springboard to involve parents in kindergarten observations and in collaborative teaming with preschool and school district teachers and staff. Open communication is an essential component at every step of the transition process.

Building a Foundation for the Team

In the spring prior to kindergarten entry, the school invites parents to observe kindergarten classes and meet teachers, related service staff, and the school principal (Step 4). Frequently, parents ask their child's preschool teacher or therapist to come with them when they observe and visit the school. These educators, together with parents, share child-specific, educationally relevant information with prospective teachers and therapists. This conversation sets the stage for collaborative teaming in support of the child's entrance into school. The team may discuss specific strategies or adaptive equipment to which children respond well, such as social stories (Gray & White 2002) for a child with autism; an assistive technology device for a child with emerging communication abilities; or special seating for a child who has motor impairments. School district staff listen carefully, share information about the varied ways children with disabilities can receive services once they begin school, and describe other supports that can enhance children's success in school.

The classroom observations help parents to relax because they can see firsthand the kindergarten classroom and the teacher interacting with students. Parents can ask the teacher questions about the kindergarten program and observe the level of support in the classroom. These brief and informal observations and meetings are nonthreatening and friendly. They appear to empower parents and build the relationships and trust needed for more formal decision-making meetings that come later in the transition process.

Steps in the Collaborative Transition Process

1. Children three to five years old, after being identified as needing special education, begin receiving special education, speech therapy, and occupational therapy services in inclusive early childhood settings. (year round)
2. Annual IEP (Individualized Education Program) Review meetings occur. Teams discuss each child's progress and develop an IEP for the upcoming year. If a child is entering the last year of preschool, then the team discusses kindergarten and encourages the family's involvement. (June)
3. A kindergarten transition letter (see "Dear Parents") goes out to all families of children receiving special education services who will be eligible for kindergarten the following year. (November)
4. Families respond to the letter and become part of a collaborative decision-making team. Parents and preschool staff observe kindergarten and meet kindergarten teachers, related services staff, and the school principal. Informal collaborative meetings take place. (December–April)
5. School district staff observe the children in their preschool classrooms. Both preschool and school district staffs gather and share information to prepare for each child's entrance into kindergarten. (February–April)
6. Additional collaborative meetings, if needed, occur with families and the sending and receiving school teams to discuss the proposed kindergarten recommendations and services. (April)
7. An annual IEP Review/Initial School-Age Special Education meeting occurs. All collaborating team members (parents, sending and receiving school teams, district administrator, and parent representatives) attend and participate. Each child's IEP is developed collaboratively. (April–June)
8. School district staff (teachers and related services staff) order materials and equipment needed for children entering kindergarten. (April–August)
9. Families participate in typical kindergarten orientation activities (screenings, opening picnics, and so forth). Additional observations of the children by school district staff occur, if needed, to further develop relationships and gather updated information prior to each child's first day of school. (July–August)
10. School begins. Children are included in kindergarten with proper supports and services for success. (September)

At about the same time as families and preschool staff are visiting kindergartens, the children's future teachers and related service staff visit the preschools to observe and gather educationally relevant information (Step 5). School district staff see future kindergartners engaged in activities in the preschool classroom and note how each child interacts and plays with others, follows classroom routines, and demonstrates various readiness skills. School staff say these observations are extremely valuable in predicting support needs, designing services, and planning instructional programs for children in kindergarten. Because the district values this level of planning and collaboration, they fund substitutes for staff on days when they will be out of the classroom to attend meetings or observe incoming kindergartners. Federal special education grant funds are used to support these endeavors.

Throughout the spring parents can continue to call the district administrator or other team members with questions. Frequently, when a child will need many services and supports in kindergarten, the collaborative team continues to meet on a slightly more formal basis (Step 6), prior to the initial meeting during which Individualized Education Programs (IEP) are developed (Step 7). Just discussing how, when, and where services may occur can often ease team members' anxieties.

Doors Are Open: Teams Put IEPs in Place

In the late spring the collaborative team has a formal meeting to develop the IEP (Step 7). The groundwork for this important decision-making meeting has already been laid through collaborative teaming. Parents, teachers, and related service staff have met and communicated about the child's strengths, needs, and probable services; materials and equipment can be ordered (Step 8). Because of the work that has been done to this point, this meeting is friendly and more like a coalescing and final agreement on goals and recommendations for services in kindergarten instead of a rushed and adversarial meeting between preschool providers and school district staff, with the family caught in the middle. Meetings often end with the families and kindergarten staff agreeing to get together over the summer or prior to the formalities of school start-up (Step 9).

Conclusion

The end of this process signals an important beginning to the child's formal school career and, hopefully, continued successful collaborative teaming (Step 10). Families who have participated in the collaborative transition process have indeed felt included in the making of important educational decisions about their children. Responses from parents in informal interviews include many comments:

> "Parents talking to teachers is so important, and they need to hear from us. As a parent, I know my child best, and what he needs. Getting to share that with his future teachers and therapists was necessary."

> "Seeing the classroom was fantastic. It put me at ease. I couldn't have made an intelligent decision without going to observe and talking together with everyone."

> "There's no question that I felt a big part of the process."

> "I felt comforted by us all working together on my child's behalf."

Parents of children with disabilities want to feel well connected to their school communities, just as any parent does. A child's successful transition to school helps families feel this connection. Children too know when they are part of something good.

Dear Parent(s)—

As you know, your preschool child will soon be eligible for kindergarten in the Baldwinsville School District. The transition to kindergarten from preschool is an exciting and sometimes anxious time for children and families. If your child requires special services in kindergarten, your close involvement in helping to plan the program is important to me.

I am writing this letter to you early in the year so that we might plan ahead for your child's entrance into kindergarten. Parents often have many questions about what their child's kindergarten experience will be like and how services such as special education, speech, and other therapies are delivered to the child.

This letter is my invitation to you to call me at the school district office. I can begin to answer some of the questions that might be coming to mind, and I can tell you about some of the ways we can provide services in the district. Usually in the spring, prior to your child's entering kindergarten, I take parents on visits to our elementary schools to observe classrooms and meet with school staff.

I look forward to meeting and talking with you about this important transition for your child. Working together we can plan a successful start to your child's school career.

Sincerely,
Amanda Fenlon
Administrator for Preschool Special Education

Source: Adapted by permission from A. Fenlon, "Activities to Empower Parents as Collaborators in Their Children's Education," *Literacy, Language, and Learning: Preparing Educators to Communicate and Connect with Families and Communities,* ed. P. Ruggiano Schmidt (Greenwich, CT: Information Age Publishing, 2005). www.infoagepub.com

Often, just discussing how, when, and where services may occur can ease team members' anxieties.

On a sunny, late-September day, my son hosted his sixth birthday party. Ten little boys jumped and laughed inside a large inflatable castle. Parents chatted briefly about their children's adjustment to school. Two of the boys my son had known from nursery school had become his close friends; they also happened to have disabilities, but this was irrelevant in their raucous, joyful play.

References

Edwards, V.B. 2002. Quality counts 2002: Building blocks for success. State efforts in early childhood education. *Education Week* 21(17).

Gray, C., & A.L. White. 2002. *My social stories book.* London: Jessica Kingsley.

Hestenes, L.L., & D.E. Carroll. 2000. The play interactions of young children with and without disabilities: Individual and environmental influences. *Early Childhood Research Quarterly* 15 (2): 229–46.

IDEA (Individuals with Disabilities Education Act Amendments of 1997). U.S. Code 20. 1997. S 140.

Kohler, P. 1994. Transition procedures: How Little Rock schools facilitate enrollment of kindergarten children with special needs. *Dimensions of Early Childhood* 22 (3): 26–27.

New York State Education Department 2003. *Topical Index to the State Review Officer's Decisions (2002–2003).* Albany, NY: Office of State Review.

Pianta, R.C., & M.E. Kraft-Sayre. 1999. Parents' observations about their children's transitions to kindergarten. *Young Children* 54 (3): 47–52.

Rosenkoetter, S.E., K.T. Whaley, A.H. Hains, & L. Pierce. 2001. The evolution of transition policy for young children with special needs and their families: Past, present and future. *Topics in Early Childhood Special Education* 21 (1): 3–15.

Ross-Allan, J., M. Conn-Powers, & W.L. Fox. 1991. *The TEEM manual: A manual to support the transition of young children with special needs and their families from preschool into kindergarten and other regular education environments.* Burlington, VT: Center on Disability and Community Inclusion.

Sandall, S., M.E. McLean, & B.J. Smith. 2000. *DEC recommended practices in early intervention/early childhood special education.* Denver, CO: Division for Early Childhood, Council for Exceptional Children.

Staub, D., & C. Peck. 1995. The inclusive school: What are the outcomes for nondisabled students? *Educational Leadership* 52 (4): 1–7.

Wolery, M. 1999. Children with disabilities in early elementary school. In *The transition to kindergarten,* eds. R.C. Pianta & M.J. Cox, 253–80. Baltimore, MD: Brookes.

Wolery, M., & J.S. Wilbers, eds. 1994. *Including children with special needs in early childhood programs.* Washington, DC: NAEYC.

AMANDA FENLON, EdD, is assistant professor of special education in the Curriculum and Instruction Department at State University of New York, Oswego, and chairperson for Preschool Special Education, Baldwinsville School District, New York. She has been a special education teacher, administrator, and director of an inclusive early childhood program.

From *Young Children,* March 2005, pp. 32–37. Copyright © 2005 by National Association for the Education of Young Children. Reprinted by permission. www.naeyc.org

Building Relationships with Challenging Children

Teachers who intervene gently, forego punishment, work at bonding, and ensure student success can help at-risk students make positive changes in their lives and in the classroom.

PHILIP S. HALL AND NANCY D. HALL

In their classic study, *400 Losers,* Ahlstrom and Havighurst (1971) were chagrined to discover that their six-year-long, intensive intervention program did not help a group of at-risk youth find success. But, to their surprise, a handful of the participants did turn their lives around. The adolescents who "made it" all had one experience in common: Each had developed a special relationship with either a teacher or a work supervisor during the treatment program. These adults valued the students, treated them as individuals, and expressed faith in their ability to succeed.

A strong relationship with an adult enables an at-risk youth to make life-altering changes. Educators can use specific strategies to develop these nurturing relationships, as one teacher's story demonstrates.

The Chocolate Milk Incident

When the 1st graders came into Ms. Hubble's room from recess, they were rambunctious and hard to settle. "Take your seats," Ms. Hubble told them, "and my two helpers for the week will come by with milk." That helped. At least, it helped everyone except Andreen. As the other students finished their milk and the helpers collected the empty cartons, Andreen got up from her desk. Taking her milk with her, she went to the salamander cage at the back of the room. She peered into the cage and began poking at the salamanders with her straw.

"Please take your seat, Andreen," Ms. Hubble said quietly, walking up to the girl and gently putting a hand on her shoulder. Lurching away, Andreen threw her milk carton into the air. The carton hit Ms. Hubble on the chest, and chocolate milk gushed out, staining the teacher's white blouse.

Andreen was a new student in Ms. Hubble's class. A week ago, her mother had brought her to school but stayed only long enough to complete the necessary paperwork. Officially, Ms. Hubble knew little about Andreen, but the girl's appearance and behavior told the big picture. The facts that emerged when Andreen's records arrived from her previous school only filled in the blanks.

On her first day, Andreen came into the classroom disheveled and unkempt. Her long auburn hair, tangled and unwashed, coursed down her back over her faded brown dress. Seeing Andreen's appearance and downcast demeanor, the other 1st graders instantly shunned the little girl as if her plight were contagious.

But Andreen's appearance was not her only problem. Andreen had an attitude, and that attitude was not endearing. She was a sullen, angry little girl, hypersensitive about her space and possessions. She pushed or kicked students who walked close to her desk. At recess, her classmates quickly learned to exclude her because she played to win, even if it meant bullying and inventing new rules. In the classroom, Andreen seldom complied with Ms. Hubble's requests. Just that morning, Ms. Hubble had asked Andreen to put her math paper away and finish it later, and the girl had ripped up her paper and defiantly thrown it into her desk.

For a week, Ms. Hubble had been hoping that Andreen's attitude would improve with her adjustment to the new school. But now Ms. Hubble realized that if the little girl was ever going to be successful in school, she, as her teacher, needed to immediately put time and energy into building a relationship with her.

Gentle Intervention

As chocolate milk seeped into her blouse, Ms. Hubble reminded herself that her response to this incident would set the tone for their relationship. She must let Andreen know that she was physically and emotionally safe in her teacher's presence despite this behavior. The situation required a gentle intervention.

The principle of this key relationship-building technique is that when a child engages in behavior that threatens health, safety, property, and basic rights, educators do only what is necessary to protect themselves and others (Hall, 1989). This approach reduces the number of behaviors requiring intervention, so the educator can ignore a lot of students' inappropriate behaviors for the moment and deal with them later if necessary. A gentle intervention defuses rather than detonates the situation and allows the student to maintain a sense of dignity.

After Andreen threw the milk, she turned her back on Ms. Hubble and walked quickly toward another learning center, looking as if she were about to shove the first available thing off the table. "Students," the teacher announced to the class, "it's time for reading. Everyone take out your reading book." Andreen stopped. Turning, she looked at Ms. Hubble. Stepping to her left, so as to give Andreen an unobstructed path to her desk, Ms. Hubble whispered to Andreen, "We're on page 80." For a moment, Andreen thought about what to do. Then she abruptly went to her desk and got out her reading book. As Ms. Hubble walked to the front of the room, she caught Andreen's eye and nodded her approval.

Ms. Hubble's gentle intervention had five important components:

- She unobtrusively interrupted behavior that might have resulted in property destruction.
- She preserved Andreen's dignity.
- She directed Andreen toward a positive response.
- Her directive led Andreen to an appropriate response that could be praised.
- Her directive was, at that moment, the easiest response for Andreen to make. After all, the other students were getting out their reading books, and the most unobstructed path was to her desk.

What Ms. Hubble didn't do as the chocolate milk ran down her blouse was as important as what she did. To her credit, the teacher resisted the emotion-driven impulse to reprimand Andreen. At the very least, Ms. Hubble might have said, "Look at what you've done! You've stained my blouse. You should be ashamed of yourself." That would have felt good! Certainly Andreen had it coming. And the teacher might have added, "And for that little shenanigan, Andreen, you'll stay in from recess for the rest of the week!"

In the heat of the moment, any or all of those actions would have been understandable. But what would have been their effect? In all likelihood, either the admonition or the consequence would have spurred Andreen to sweep her arm across the table, knocking something to the floor. In response, Ms. Hubble would have had to move quickly to restrain Andreen before she broke more things; and if Andreen resisted, Ms. Hubble might have had to drag her down to the principal's office where, by golly, she would have learned her lesson!

Or would she have? Actually, all Andreen would have learned is that Ms. Hubble is, in her opinion, a mean person. An hour later, Andreen would have returned to the classroom temporarily subdued but full of resentment and mistrust.

No Punishment

Had Ms. Hubble made those comments to Andreen or restricted her recess, the teacher would have punished Andreen. Punishment, we believe, is anything an educator says or does to make a student feel guilty, humiliated, or remorseful so that the student will never behave that way again (Hall & Braun, 1988).

A key to building a relationship, however, is not punishing the student—ever. Why not? Because punishment strains or even breaks the bond between teacher and student. Punishment may temporarily control behavior, but it does nothing to teach the student an appropriate response. Worse, punishing a student often instills a desire for revenge. An effective response to behavior that threatens health, safety, property, or basic rights does not include doling out punishment.

That evening, Ms. Hubble phoned Andreen's mother. She did not phone to report the chocolate milk incident. Instead, she asked permission to spend some special time with Andreen. Ms. Hubble said,

> Many of the girls in class are coming to school with their hair in braids. It's the in thing. I would love to help Andreen put her hair in braids, if she wants. Would the two of us have your permission to do that?

The mother, of course, granted permission. "Please share our conversation with Andreen," Ms. Hubble concluded.

Bonding

The next day, Ms. Hubble devoted time to another key principle of relationship building—some call it *bonding* (McGee, Menolascino, Hobbs, & Menousek, 1987). To bond, we value the student for the socially appropriate behaviors that the student can demonstrate and then provide the structure, support, and recognition that the student needs to demonstrate these behaviors. During this bonding time, the adult does not place any expectations on the student for doing the activity the "right" way.

The activity provides opportunities for the adult to value the student, which enhances the student's sense of self-worth and encourages the development of internal standards for behavior. Moreover, when a teacher values a student, the student seems to be biologically inhibited from acting aggressively against that teacher. While the student is in this zone of positive regard, she is disposed to attend to the teacher. Expanding the zone of positive regard mitigates noncompliance and defiance.

That morning, Ms. Hubble talked privately to Andreen:

> We can wash and comb your hair during the lunch break and then braid it during afternoon recess. Is that something you'd like to do?

And that is what they did. As they ate lunch privately in the classroom, the two of them chatted up a storm. They talked about anything that the little girl had on her mind, even for a fleeting instant. Ms. Hubble used the conversation not to pry, but rather to enter, by invitation only, into Andreen's world of interests, experiences, and thoughts. Some might call their student-driven conversation trite and meaningless. It wasn't. The conversation and the hair washing were a vehicle for Ms. Hubble to bond with Andreen.

The relationship that Ms. Hubble and Andreen developed that day had immediate results. When the other students saw that Ms. Hubble valued the new girl, they shifted their attitude.

Several girls complimented Andreen on her braids and slowly began to take the new girl into their fold.

Ensuring Success

Ensuring success means providing the student with the structure and support for becoming a good learner. When students, especially those with difficult temperaments, fall at learning tasks, they often explode into defiant behaviors. On the day of the chocolate milk incident, Ms. Hubble retrieved the math assignment that Andreen had torn to pieces, carefully taped the paper together, identified the specific math skill that Andreen was missing, and began to address the problem with targeted instruction.

The New Paradigm

By implementing these relationship-building principles, Ms. Hubble enabled Andreen to change her behavior and attitude. When Andreen came into the classroom each morning, she no longer hung her head and scowled. She did not push or kick students who passed by her desk; rather, she smiled at them. When Ms. Hubble made a request, Andreen usually complied. Rather than tearing up her papers, Andreen took them home to show her mother. In Ms. Hubble's classroom, the relationship building with Andreen paid dividends.

Building relationships with students who have challenging behaviors is consistent with an emerging paradigm in education. In the old paradigm, educators developed behavior programs designed to squelch students' inappropriate behaviors, a process that focused on what the student was doing wrong. Educators assumed that when they had brought the inappropriate behaviors under control, the student would automatically demonstrate socially appropriate behaviors. Behavior programming typically contained objectives like "Andrew will decrease (or increase) this behavior," an approach that put most of the

responsibility for behavior change on the student—the least capable person in the classroom.

The relationship-building approach more often leads to success.

In contrast, a relationship-building approach helps the student develop positive, socially appropriate behaviors by focusing on what the student is doing right. In the new paradigm, behavior programming puts the initial responsibility for behavior change on the teacher, the most capable and only professionally trained person in the classroom. The relationship-building approach more often leads to success.

References

Ahlstrom, W. M., & Havighurst, R. J. (1971). *400 losers.* San Francisco: Jossey-Bass.

Hall, P. S. (1989, Fall). Teaching for behavior change. *Counterpoint,* 3.

Hall, P. S., & Braun, V. R. (1988, June). Punishment: A consumer's perspective. *TASH Newsletter,* 9.

McGee, J. J., Menolascino, F. J., Hobbs, D. C., & Menousek, P. E. (1987). *Gentle teaching: A nonaversive approach for helping persons with mental retardation.* New York: Human Science Press.

PHILIP S. HALL (hallps@minotstateu.edu) is a professor in the school psychology program at Minot State University. **NANCY D. HALL** (halln@minotstateu.edu), a former elementary school principal, is Vice President for Academic Affairs at Minot State University, 500 University Ave. West, Minot, ND 58707. Their most recent book is *Educating Oppositional and Defiant Children* (ASCD, 2003).

UNIT 3
Learning Disabilities

Unit Selections

Key Points to Consider

- Can students with LDs learn better organizational skills? How?

- Can spelling rubrics replace spelling tests? What are their advantages?

- What can be done to reduce the social isolation of students with learning disabilities and giftedness?

Student Web Site

www.mhcls.com/online

Internet References

Further information regarding these Web sites may be found in this book's preface or online.

Children and Adults With Attention Deficit/Hyperactivity Disorder (CHADD)
   http://www.chadd.org

The Instant Access Treasure Chest
   http://www.fln.vcu.edu/ld/ld.html

Learning Disabilities Association of America (LDA)
   http://www.ldanatl.org

Learning Disabilities Online
   http://www.ldonline.org

Teaching Children With Attention Deficit Disorder
   http://www.kidsource.com/kidsource/content2/add.html

Digital Vision

Learning how to learn is one of life's most important tasks. For students with learning idiosyncrasies it is a most critical lesson. Today general education teachers and special educators must seriously attend to the growing numbers of students who have a wide range of different learning disabilities (LDs). LD enrollments in inclusive, regular education classes have skyrocketed. They are the fastest growing and largest category of exceptionalities in elementary, middle, and high schools. Children with LDs now make up over 50 percent of those receiving special educational services.

The ways in which students with LDs are identified and served have been radically transformed with IDEIA (Individuals with Disabilities Education Improvement Act). New assessment methods have made the identification of students with LDs easier and far more common. Many lawmakers and educators, however, feel that students who have other problems (for example, behavior disorders, poor learning histories, or dysfunctional families) are erroneously being diagnosed with LDs. IDEIA requires states to place students with disabilities in regular classrooms as much as possible or lose their federal funding. A landmark U.S. Supreme Court case in November of 1993 (*Carter v. Florence Co., S.C.*) ruled that public schools must give appropriate educational services to students with LDs or pay the tuition for private schools to do so. This ruling opened a floodgate of new litigation

by parents. IDEIA has turned out to be much more expensive than Congress envisioned when it enacted this education bill 26 years ago. The recent passage of No Child Left Behind (2001) requires that schools be held accountable for appropriate education of all students.

Is the rapid increase in students assessed as having learning disabilities an artifact of misdiagnoses, exaggeration, and a duping of the system that makes funding available for special needs? Neonatal medical technology and achievements in preventive medicine and health maintenance have greatly reduced the numbers of children who are born deaf, blind, severely physically disabled, or with multiple exceptional conditions. The very same medical technology has greatly increased the numbers of children kept alive who are born prematurely, small for gestational age, with low birth weight, and "at-risk" for less-severe disabilities such as LDs.

A learning disability is usually defined by the lay public as difficulty in reading or calculating. IDEIA defines it as a disorder in the processes involved in understanding or in using language, spoken or written, that may manifest itself in an imperfect ability to listen, speak, read, write, spell, or do mathematical calculations. Learning disabilities are identified differently outside of education. *The Diagnostic and Statistical Manual of Mental Disorders* (4th edition) divides LDs into academic skills disorders (reading, mathematics, written expression) and attention deficit hyperactive disorder (ADHD). The National Joint Committee for Learning Disabilities (NJCLD) separates LDs into specific problems related to the acquisition and use of listening, speaking, reading, writing, reasoning, or mathematical abilities. Attention deficit hyperactive disorder, if not accompanied by any specific learning problem or any specific behavioral/emotional disorder, can be assessed as a health disability by both IDEIA and NJCLD especially if it can be ameliorated with medication. Due to parental pressures, the IDEIA definition of LDs has been amended administratively to include ADHD if the deficit in attention leads to difficulty in learning. In this compendium, ADHD is treated as a health disability.

The rest of the definition of an LD is an exclusionary definition. It helps clarify the nature of LDs. They are not developmental disabilities. They are not deficiencies in any of the sensory systems (vision, hearing, taste, touch, smell, kinesthetics, vestibular sensation). They are not problems associated with health or physical mobility. They are not emotional or behavioral disorders. They are not disabilities of speech or language. They can be assessed as true LDs only if there is a discrepancy between the child's ability to learn and his or her actual learning.

IDEIA's and No Child Left Behind's strong emphases on a free and appropriate educational placement for every child with a disability has forced schools to be more cautious about all assessments and labeling. Increasing numbers of children are now being assessed as LD who once might have been labeled developmentally disabled or disabled by speech, language, emotions, behavior, or one of the senses. A child with an LD may concurrently have a disability in any of these other areas, but if this occurs, both the LD and any other disabilities must be addressed in an individualized education plan (IEP) designed especially for that unique child.

Recent research suggests that reading disabilities may affect about 15 percent of elementary school-aged children. If this is accurate, many LD children are not yet being identified and serviced. The causes of LDs are unknown. Usually some central nervous system glitches are believed to underlie the disabilities, even if their existence cannot be demonstrated. Other suspected causes include genetic inheritance, poor nutrition, or exposure to toxic agents. The NJCLD definition of LD presumes biological causation and lifetime chronicity.

This unit on learning disabilities addresses both the successes and the frustrations of educating children with LDs. The first article in the section deals with 20 ways to build better organizational skills in students with LDs. Knowing how to systematically approach assignments and how to apply methods to finish the tasks helps improve both work quality and self-esteem of the students.

In the second selection, where Kelly Loeffler asks, "No More Friday Spelling Tests?", spelling rubrics are described. These can replace spelling tests, rubrics, which teach students how to spell with knowledge of the cognitive-linguistic aspects of language. They also improve writing skills and can be used as assessment tools.

The last selection depicts the problems of social skills in students with LDs and/or giftedness. Emily Williams King suggests a variety of ways to improve these skills.

Build Organizational Skills in Students with Learning Disabilities

RITA F. FINSTEIN, FEI YAO YANG, AND RÁCHELE JONES

Organization is an essential skill for all of us. For the student who has a learning disability (LD), development of expertise may require direct instruction and guidance (Borich, 2000). The true talent of the student with LD can be masked by his inability to produce work that reflects his abilities. A student who cannot find his paper but assures you that it is finished, the one who brings a math paper that appears to be a mass of unintelligible gibberish, or the student who hands you her English paper in a crumpled wad, may simply be telling you that he or she needs help with organizational skills. Lack of organizational skills can influence the work quality, the satisfaction of turning a paper in on time, and the self-worth of any student, but it is especially significant for students with LD. This student may not turn in his science assignment because he misplaced it or forgot that he had it to do, did not take it home, and thus did not have it to turn in on time.

Good organizational skills useful throughout life can be learned through small, integrated steps practiced in and out of school. Teachers, parents, and others can foster acquisition of organizational skills. They can encourage students with LD to:

1. Believe That They Can Do What Is Asked

As the student with LD shows small increments of progress, teachers need to praise and praise often. Positive attitudes are contagious and help in learning any skill. True praise builds confidence in students with disabilities. It is not possible to say often enough "Good job. I like the way you followed the three math steps" or "Well done," when the teacher hands back the spelling test or "I like the way you are planning your day," when the student remembers to go to tutoring.

2. Work Cooperatively with Parents

Teachers should model a good relationship between home and school. A strong partnership helps the student with LD (Bryan & Burstein, 2004). Teachers can show parents how to monitor homework and to help their child follow a work schedule at home. Teachers can open communication between the parents and themselves with phone conferences and correspondence.

3. Post Needed Information on a Bulletin Board

At home, parents can help their child be organized by using a bulletin board, refrigerator door, or other convenient location to post "To Do" lists. A large metal clip can be used to collect school notices and messages that need to be returned to school. This provides a convenient place that the child will always know where to put school correspondence (Practicing Organizational Skills at Home, 2005). The parent should use guided practice, and with time, the student will be more independent in making "To Do" lists.

4. Use Checklists to Track Activities

Checklists are used frequently for school-age students. Checklists provide a way for the student to check off each task as it is finished, for example, bringing required materials to each class and returning materials to their proper place. In addition, checklists also empowers the student to feel a sense of accomplishment and self-confidence, as the marked-through or crossed-out items means that he has finished those responsibilities.

5. Make and Update a Calendar

A calendar can give an overview to an entire day, week, or school year. It helps break large tasks into sizeable, workable units. Use of different colors for various activities helps highlight the importance of due dates for projects, assignments, and exams. In addition, the calendar helps the student with LD to meet deadlines. Calendars useful for home and school can be a tool to assist students in completing tasks on time and in managing time effectively. Parents can check the calendar at home, and the teacher can monitor it at school.

6. Follow a Daily Agenda

Used with the calendar, the daily agenda breaks tasks listed on the calendar into steps for completion. The availability of commercially purchased daily agendas that provide a place to list tasks to be done or considered each day helps the student with LD meet her deadlines as marked on the calendar.

7. Use an Organizer/Planner

Organizers/planners in various formats—oral cues, charts, and diagrams (which distinguished them from the daily agenda)—are used to sketch out specific daily activities, such as homework or steps of a task or project. Parents and teachers can model the use of an organizer/planner, and with guided practice, students with LD will (a) learn the concept of preview and overview and (b) understand priorities of activities and when and how to complete the activity. They will also discover that free time can be scheduled within the daily time restraints.

8. Pair with a General Education Student

One of the most powerful influences on a student's learning is peer pressure. Teams can be formed, with one general education student who is proficient in organization skills paired with the student who needs help with such skills. The general education student acts as a role model for his partner in these teams. The organized student can mentor his buddy in organizational skills, establish appropriate attitudes for classes, and give hints on how to study for tests. The peer–buddy relationship not only fosters cooperative learning but also contributes to the success or failure of performance in school in many ways (Borich, 2000).

9. Carry Scripts/How-To Cards

Mobile remainders help students stay focused throughout the day. Students with LD can use these cards to prompt them about specific steps and remind them to complete a task. These cards are convenient to pull out of their notebook or pocket as necessary.

10. Post Reminders

Reminders provide a fast and visual communication to track task completion and can be stuck to one's notebook, inside one's locker, and so on. Students can check the reminder to know specifically what is expected. If Jim needs to be reminded of the steps to do his math problems, these can be posted inside his math book, and as he uses that book, the visual reminder is right there for him to reference. If Mary needs help remembering the "i before e" rule, the reminder is stuck on her spelling list and is visible when she begins to study.

11. Keep Everything Where It Belongs

The adage "a place for everything, and everything in its place," is true. All students misplace or lose an assignment, a book, a note to take home or return to school. These events seem to be daily happenings for the student with LD. She needs an assigned place for books, supplies, and notes traveling to and from school.

The student in elementary school with his own desk needs to put books in a specific order and a specific spot on or near his desk. To always know that the math book is directly above the language book is not only comforting but reliable. Covering each book with a different colored cover or having book titles on the spine of each book helps to identify each text with ease.

Secondary school brings use of a locker, which may exacerbate organizational challenges. The locker should have a designated place for anything that really needed and should not house unneeded articles. Textbooks can be arranged according to the class period in which they are used and should be always stored in that order. At the beginning of the year or semester, the student may have to use a posted note inside the door of his locker to remind him of this arrangement. Books should be arranged so that the spine side is out with the subject name clearly written on each spine.

At home, the student with LD needs an established place to put his books upon returning home. If he always puts his book bag in his room next to his desk, he will not have to wonder where it is. If sharpened pencils are in the well on his desk, he will always find them there. He benefits from a specific time and place to do his schoolwork, establishing a routine. It will soon become a habit if the student does his homework at 7 P.M. every evening in his room for an hour.

12. Determine What to Carry

The student who is not in a self-contained classroom and travels from room to room during the day sometimes needs help to know what and how much to take from her locker and when and how often to visit it. A counselor may be able to arrange a schedule of classes that helps with organization. For example, the counselor can arrange classes that are back to back to be on the same floor, or at least in the same part of the building, instead of having the student be on the first floor and then the third floor the next hour or in room 101, which is on the southeast end of the building, during third period, and room 163, which is on the northwest end of the building, for fourth period. However, if convenient scheduling is not possible, the student will benefit from carrying the books for first and second period with her when she leaves her locker instead of having to come back after first period to get that book for second period. This can be adjusted, depending how many books need to be carried at one time, but the object is to stress that the student should not have to return to her locker between every class.

Another situation finds the student trying to carry all that he needs for the entire day with him to every class. The student should carry only what he needs and not load himself down with books and materials he does not need to carry. This may mean he carries materials for just two classes, or it can mean that he carry more. The student may carry only the books and supplies he needs for the morning classes as he leaves for first period. At lunch he can return to his locker, put away the morning materials, and get all that is needed for the afternoon. It depends on the student's schedule. Teachers can stress the importance of this through role play, discussion, relating personal incidents, or asking students about their experiences. Essentials needed for every class should be carried at all times. This will include at least two pencils, a pen, notebook paper, and some means of storing assignments. If there are other items needed for a specific class, they can be added at the morning or afternoon stop to the locker.

An important stop at the locker is the one right before leaving school. The student with LD should check her schedule, planner, or "To Do" list—whatever she is using to document what it is she has to do—and pull from the locker those books and materials she needs to complete her homework at home. This will help eliminate not completing assignments because the materials needed to do the assignments were left at school.

13. Know Teacher Routines

Students with LD need to know the established routines for each teacher they have and follow them. Teachers at the beginning of a term hand out class requirements and expectations; the student should keep these in a notebook for reference. A good plan of action upon entering a classroom is to check to see if pencils are sharpened, look at the board to see if there is an introductory assignment to do, sit in the assigned seat, and have all books accessible for use.

14. Carry an Efficient and Orderly Notebook

A notebook with dividers separating space for each subject is a vital organizational tool. After each subject divider, a folder for assignments completed and a folder for assignments still to do not only remind the student what he must do but also secure a place for the work. Everything in the notebook should be secured either within the rings or in folders to avoid losing them if the notebook is dropped. A calendar or schedule at the front of the notebook to record daily assignments keeps the student aware of what he has done and what he still needs to do.

15. Wear a Rubber Band Bracelet

To encourage time on task and completion of work, a younger child can wear a rubber band around the wrist of her writing hand until her assignment is completed and then move the rubber band to the other wrist. The objective of this switch from the hand with which the work is done to the other, nonwriting hand,

is that it supplies a visible sign that whatever it was that had to be finished is now done.

16. Date and Title Assignments

Students can be helped in organizing their papers by dating and titling every assignment. This not only helps in keeping work in order but also gives a time frame for what needs to be studied for a test. If the test is to be over notes from February 11 to February 20, a paper dated January 30 would not be one that needs to be studied.

17. Engage in Guided Practice

Sessions to teach organizational strategies have been successful in social studies in Chicago (Fatata-Hall, 1998). Students with LD improved their grades by participating in classes that teach them good organization strategies. Teachers modeled steps and procedures, and students helped each other to improve their skills. Barry and Moore (2004) record success in giving students time to practice the steps to good organization. In another study, direct instruction in organizational strategies, such as time management, prioritizing, and study skills, increased student ability and awareness in organizing time, activities, and school work (Anday-Porter, Henne, & Horan, 2000).

18. Communicate with Teachers When Assignments Seem Overwhelming

The student should let teachers know that some assignments may be beyond her level. Lack of organizational skills is compounded when the student is also struggling with something beyond her abilities.

19. Engage in Mentoring Programs

Mentor programs are effective in assisting students with LD achieve at higher levels (Shevits, Weinfeld, Jewler, & Barnes-Robinson, 2003). A student struggling with organizational skills is teamed with an adult strong in these skills. The adult can model good skills and guide the struggling student to improve his organizational competence.

20. Have an Individualized Education Program (IEP) That Addresses Organizational Skills

The IEP lists short- and long-term goals for students. The student with LD who needs assistance in organization needs written goals to address these needs. For example, a short-term goal might be for the student to use a "To Do" list to monitor completion of math assignments for a 2-week period, with a long-term goal to complete all math assignments in the semester through use of a "To Do" list to monitor daily assignments.

References

Anday-Porter, S., Henne, K., & Horan, S. (2000). *Improving student organizational skills through the use of organizational skills in the curriculum.* Retrieved February 9, 2005, from ERIC Document Reproduction Service No. ED355616

Barry, L., & Moore, W. E., IV. (2004). Students with specific learning disabilities can pass state competency exams: Systematic strategy instruction makes a difference. *Preventing School Failure, 48*(3), 10–15.

Borich, G. D. (2000). *Effective teaching methods* (4th ed.). Upper Saddle River, NJ: Prentice Hall.

Bryan, T., & Burstein, K. (2004). Improving homework completion and academic performance: Lessons from special education. *Theory into Practice, 43*(3), 213–219.

Fatata-Hall, K. (1998). *Acquisition and application of study skills and test taking strategies with eighth grade learning disabled failing social studies.* Retrieved February 9, 2005, from ERIC Document Reproduction Service No. S0029064

Practicing organizational skills at home. (n.d.). Retrieved February 9, 2005, from http://www.hellofriend.org/parents/organizational.html

Shevits, B., Weinfeld, R., Jewler, S., & Barnes-Robinson, L. (2003). Mentoring empowers gifted/learning disabled students to soar! *Roeper Review, 26*(1), 37–40.

All three authors are doctoral students and graduate or research assistants in special education, have completed all course work, and are working on their dissertations, each concentrating on a different aspect of autism spectrum disorders and its impact. **RITA F. FINSTEIN,** MA, retired after 33 years of teaching in the public schools to pursue a doctorate. She has certification in special education, English, math, history, and early childhood and is a language retraining (for dyslexia) therapist. **FEI YAO YANG,** MEd, a Chinese student from Taiwan, graduated from Chianan Medical Junior College with a chemistry degree. Upon coming to the United States, she received a master's degree in generic special education from the University of Central Oklahoma. Her plan is to return to Taiwan to teach special education at the university level. **RÁCHELE JONES,** MA, has been studying Asperger syndrome for more than 4 years, since the diagnosis of her eldest son and, subsequently, other family members with Asperger syndrome. Currently, her primary focus is on communication issues within Asperger syndrome and how these issues affect learning. Address: Rita F. Finstein, Texas Tech University, Box 2071, Lubbock, TX 79409-1071; e-mail: ritafin@cox.net

From *Intervention in School and Clinic,* by Rita Finstein, Fei Yao Yang, and Ráchele Jones, Vol. 42, No. 3, January 2007, pp. 174–178. Copyright © 2007 by Pro-Ed, Inc. Reprinted by permission.

No More Friday Spelling Tests?
An Alternative Spelling Assessment for Students with Learning Disabilities

KELLY A. LOEFFLER

"Is it true that you do not give spelling tests?" questioned a perplexed mother at back-to-school night. I was prepared for this question and knew that parents would have difficulty accepting that their children could learn how to spell without the weekly ritual of helping their children study for the traditional spelling test. I quickly explained to her why I changed my assessment to a spelling rubric rather than a traditional spelling test.

A traditional spelling test does not provide insight into the spelling cues that the students are using, (See box, "What Cues Do Writers Use to Spell Words Accurately?") However, a spell-

What Does the Literature Say about the Need for Alternative Spelling Assessments?

Students with learning disabilities frequently misspell words. Darch, Kim, Johnson, and James (2000) explained that students with learning disabilities have difficulty spelling because they are less skilled at deducing and using spelling strategies and rules. The researchers concluded that students with learning disabilities do not use their knowledge of sound and symbol correspondences effectively. Students often substitute an incorrect vowel or leave out the vowel altogether. Jones (2001) stated that children with learning disabilities have difficulty detecting their own spelling errors. Teaching students to monitor their misspelled words is crucial to their lifelong growth as writers. A weekly test does not encourage students to monitor their spelling within the context of their writing.

In their study, Gill and Scharer (1996) developed a rubric to provide parents with ratings of their children's spelling performance without administering a spelling test. The researchers found that parents were more appreciative of this information than with obtaining the results of a weekly test.

What Cues Do Writers Use to Spell Words Accurately?

While writing, good spellers attend to one, two, or a combination of spelling cues to spell words accurately.

- One cue that a writer uses is phonics, or sounding-out the words.
- A writer also uses visual cues.
- A writer can use familiar spelling patterns and ask himself or herself whether the word looks right.
- A writer can use high-frequency words. These are words that the writer knows how to spell simply from exposure to the words through reading.

ing rubric can measure the student's ability to find misspelled words, correct them, and use an appropriate spelling strategy. Students with learning disabilities often do well on weekly spelling tests by memorizing their lists of words, rather than by internalizing spelling strategies. They are quick to forget their weekly words when given a written assignment. Assessing my students' spelling ability was more important to me than evaluating their memorization skills. Heald-Taylor (1998, p. 405) elaborates, "Learning to spell is a complex, intricate cognitive and linguistic process rather than one of rote memorization." (See box, "What Does the Literature Say?")

Developing an Alternative Spelling Assessment

For the first 2 years of my teaching career, I assigned spelling words on Monday, provided practice throughout the week, gave a pretest, and finally administered a spelling test on Friday. No undergraduate class taught me to teach spelling this way. I simply imitated the spelling methods from my own elementary school years. In grading spelling tests, I found that students with

Name: _____   Date: _____

Spelling Rubric

Title of Writing Assignment: _____   Spelling Strategy Used: _____

Criteria	5	4	3	2	1
Circles all misspelled words	Student found and circled all misspelled words.	Student circled 75%–99% of misspelled words.	Student circled 50%–74% of misspelled words.	Student circled 25%–49% of misspelled words.	Student circled 1%–24% of misspelled words.
Accurately corrects all circled misspelled words	Student accurately corrected all circled misspelled words.	Student accurately corrected 75%–99% of circled misspelled words.	Student accurately corrected 50%–74% of circled misspelled words.	Student accurately corrected 25%–49% of circled misspelled words.	Student accurately corrected 1%–24% of circled misspelled words.
Always uses sounding out, spell-checker, dictionary, or similar words to spell words without help	Student always used one of the taught spelling strategies to spell words correctly on his or her own.	Student almost always used one of the taught spelling strategies to spell words correctly on his or her own.	Student sometimes used one of the taught spelling strategies to spell words correctly on his or her own.	Student always used one of the taught spelling strategies to spell words correctly with some help from an adult.	Student sometimes used one of the taught spelling strategies to spell words correctly with some help from an adult.
Spells all words correctly in writing	Student correctly spelled all the words in his or her writing.	Student correctly spelled 74%–75% of the words in his or her writing.	Student correctly spelled 50%–74% of the words in his or her writing.	Student correctly spelled 25%–74% of the words in his or her writing.	Student correctly spelled 1%–24% of the words in his or her writing.
Grade	/20 points	% =	Letter grade =		

Comments:

Parent Signature

Figure 1   Spelling Rubric.

strong memorization ability were able to score 100% on their tests each week. Students with weaker memory skills became frustrated when they earned a poor grade. However, most of my students did not generalize their weekly spelling words to their writing. Spelling lists and tests became a waste of instructional time for my upper-elementary students. I realized that this traditional method of spelling instruction did not work for my students with learning disabilities. So I decided to try a different method.

An alternative spelling assessment was in the works. I needed a tool that promoted my instructional objectives. I wanted students to be able to find their misspellings, choose a strategy to fix them, and write legibly. From these goals I devised an original rubric (Figure 1) that grades spelling within the context of student writing.

Implementing a Spelling Rubric

I use the rubric with fifth-grade students in a resource room setting. The children are excited and pleased when I announce that I do not give spelling tests. However, winning over their parents is a little more difficult. During the first week of school, I send home a copy of the spelling rubric, along with a letter describing the rationale for its use. I encourage parents to contact me with comments and questions. Parents respond well to the rubric when it is explained clearly to them.

Assessing their spelling ability was more important to me than evaluating their memorization skills.

Explaining to the students how the new spelling "test" works is much easier. During the first month of school, I use an overhead to model finding words that "don't look right." I show students how to circle these words but continue their writing. Continuing to write is the most difficult part for the students. Students with learning disabilities usually recognize that they are not the best spellers. They want to correct their errors as quickly as possible.

To help students detect their errors. I model a spelling self-check routine to the class. The students learn to verify that each syllable has a vowel and that each syllable starts and ends with the appropriate letters. After students circle all their misspelled words, they go back and attempt to correct their spelling. The rubric requires that students use one spelling strategy on their own. The strategies can involve any of the following:

- Asking a friend.
- Sounding out the word slowly by using sound boxes or finger tapping.
- Using a dictionary.

- Using similar words to help them spell the troublesome word.
- Using a spell-checker.

Most students choose to use an electronic spell-checker. MacArthur, Graham, Haynes, and DeLaPaz (1996) found that students with learning disabilities were able to correct 37% of their errors when they used a spell-checker. Without the support of a spell-checker, students could only correct 9% of their errors. Consequently, a spell-checker can be an invaluable tool for students with learning disabilities.

Teaching students to monitor their misspelled words is crucial to their lifelong growth as writers.

To maintain a focus on writing content and creativity. I do not assess students on each composition. I alert them when I will assess their written work for spelling. When students turn in both their rough drafts and their final drafts, I use the rubric to assess their spelling. I compare the rough draft with the final draft to see the improvements that they have made. The rough drafts include their circled misspelled words with their corrections written above the word. The final drafts show their use of spelling strategies. Students are thrilled when their written pieces show few or no spelling errors. When we review their compositions, I hold a one-on-one conference with the students and use their graded rubrics. We discuss the strategies that they used to correct their misspellings. The conference also allows me to introduce new spelling strategies that are based on the errors that the students did not find. The spelling rubric helps me individualize spelling instruction and assessment for my students with learning disabilities (see box, "Steps in Using a Spelling Rubric").

After seeing my students' improvement in spelling, general and special educators in my school became interested in the rubric. They, too, were frustrated because their students were not able to generalize their weekly spelling words, (See box, "Who Benefits From a Spelling Rubric?") Even students not identified as having a learning disability have benefited from using the spelling rubric rather than a spelling test. My principal is also supportive of the alternative assessment. Because her son has a learning disability, she recognizes that not everyone ben-

Who Benefits From the Spelling Rubric?

- Upper elementary to secondary students.
- Students who have difficulty generalizing their spelling words to their writing.
- Students in general and special education settings

Steps in Using a Spelling Rubic

1. Send a letter home to parents describing the rubric. Be sure to attach a copy of the rubric to the letter.
2. Model finding words that "don't look right."
3. Model checking for a vowel in each syllable, as well as checking for appropriate beginning and ending sounds.
4. Explain strategies for correcting spelling errors.
5. Hold a conference with students about the graded spelling rubric.

efits from memorizing lists of spelling words. Her support has encouraged other teachers to undertake the challenge of alternative assessments.

Benefits of a Spelling Rubric

Using a spelling rubric has many benefits including the following:

- Students receive credit for identifying misspelled words.
- Students use an effective strategy to counteract their disability.
- Teachers identify the spelling strategies that students are using effectively.
- Spelling becomes more meaningful when it is used in context.
- Spelling rubrics allow teachers to evaluate spelling in context and provide grades that replace traditional spelling scores.
- The students' self-esteem improves.

Spelling Assessment and Instruction

Although the spelling rubric is nontraditional, spelling instruction in my classroom continues to be direct and systematic. I instruct my upper-elementary students by using the Wilson Reading System (Wilson, 1996). Within the system, students learn to tap out words to help them segment the sounds. The spelling rubric is simply another form of assessment, not to be used solely for spelling instruction. Continuing formal spelling instruction in a manner that supports each student's needs is important.

Caution

Students with learning disabilities are often very smart and tend to find the quickest way out of a writing assignment. One problem with the spelling rubric was that students would write brief compositions with words they already knew how to spell. To encourage substantial compositions, I arrange the focused correction areas to include at least five words that the students have never used. I also stipulate how many paragraphs they must write. Students are able to write substantial compositions when I give them a structural framework.

Final Thoughts

The greatest joy that came from the implementation of this spelling assessment came from Chrissy. As she was writing in her journal about her show dog, she asked me to help her spell a word. I told her to do the best she could and circle the word if it did not look right. Following this single prompt, she continued to write and diligently circled other misspelled words. She then used a spell-checker to correct those words.

This child had never received an A on a spelling test, but that day she received an A from me!

References

Darch, C., Kim, S., Johnson, S., & James, H. (2000). The strategic spelling skills of students with learning disabilities: The results of two studies [Electronic version]. *Journal of Instructional Psychology, 27*(1), 15–27.

Gill, C. H., & Scharer, P. L. (1996). "Why do they get it on Friday and misspell it on Monday?" Teachers inquiring about their students as spellers. *Language Arts, 73,* 89–96.

Heald-Taylor, B. G. (1998). Three paradigms of spelling instruction in grades 3 to 6. *The Reading Teacher, 51*(5), 404–413.

Jones, C. J. (2001). Teacher-friendly curriculum-based assessment in spelling. *TEACHING Exceptional Children, 34*(2), 32–38.

MacArthur, C. A., Graham, S., Haynes, J. B., & DeLaPaz, S. (1996). Spelling checkers and students with learning disabilities: Performance comparisons and impact on spelling. *The Journal of Special Education, 30*(1), 35–57.

Wilson, B. A. (1996). *Wilson reading system* (3rd ed.). Milbury: Barbara A. Wilson.

KELLY A. LOEFFLER, Learning Support Teacher. Cumberland Valley School District, Mechanicsburg, Pennsylvania. Address correspondence to Kelly A. Loeffler, Cumberland Valley School District, 6746 Carlisle Pike, Mechanicsburg, PA 17050. (e-mail: kloeffler@cvschools.org).

From *Teaching Exceptional Children*, by Kelly A. Loeffler, Vol. 37, No. 4, March/April 2005, pp. 24–27. Copyright © 2005 by Council for Exceptional Children. Reprinted by permission.

Addressing the Social and Emotional Needs of Twice-Exceptional Students

EMILY WILLIAMS KING

Children who are both gifted and have a learning disability (gifted/LD) face numerous challenges in the classroom and in life. These students often feel as though they are a part of two worlds, one as a student with a disability and the other as a student with outstanding abilities. Being classified as having a disability and being gifted, sometimes called twice-exceptional, can be quite confusing. These students often wonder, for example, "Why am I so good at math but need special help with reading? Where do I fit in?"

In addition to the challenge of having a disability, gifted/LD students may experience increased frustration resulting from heightened expectations and higher standards for achievement that go along with being gifted (Coleman, 2001). Because these students are labeled as "gifted," they may be expected to be strong in all areas, when in fact their strength may lie in only one or two areas (Strop, 2003).

As a result of these expectations, school can be very frustrating for a twice-exceptional student. Most curricula require students to depend on basic academic skills, such as reading, arithmetic, and writing, which can be areas of difficulty for many children who are gifted/LD. Because of their ongoing conflict between intellectual strengths and academic struggles, many students who are gifted/LD develop low self-concepts after starting school (Swesson, 1994). These students have also been shown to have difficulty with social skills and often report feelings of not fitting in with their peers (Vespi & Yewchuk, 1992). Therefore, recognizing and supporting the social and emotional needs of twice-exceptional students are just as important as addressing their academic needs. We must appropriately identify and serve students who are gifted/LD in order to maximize their potential both inside and outside the classroom.

Types of Gifted/LD Students

Students who are both gifted and have learning disabilities exhibit superior intellectual ability as well as a significant discrepancy between their level of performance in a particular area, such as reading, mathematics, spelling, or written language, as compared with their performance in areas of strength (McCoach, Kehle, Bray, & Siegle, 2001; see box, "Possible Characteristics of Twice-Exceptional Students"). The literature defines three types of students who are gifted/LD:

Many students who are gifted/LD develop low self-concepts after starting school.

1. The first group consists of students who are identified as gifted and have subtle learning disabilities (Baum, 1994). These students may have a large vocabulary and excellent verbal abilities, whereas their handwriting and spelling abilities contradict this image (Baum, 1994). Students in this category also achieve on grade level, thus causing their learning disability to be overlooked. Identification of their disabilities could offer these students an understanding of their academic difficulties (Baum, 1994).

2. The second group of students who are gifted/LD consists of those who are unidentified. In other words, their abilities and disabilities "mask" each other. These students' superior intelligence seems to compensate for their undiagnosed learning disability (Baum, 1994). They usually receive instruction in the general classroom and often perform at grade level, so no "red flags" are raised. However, these students are often functioning below their potential. The talents of students in this group often emerge in specific content areas, becoming noticed later in life. This group of students may also suffer from mild depression (Baum, 1994).

3. The third group contains those students identified as both gifted and LD. They are identified more often than those in the previous two groups because they stand out in the classroom. These bright students often fail in school and are noticed because of their disability, not because of their talents. Because little attention is given to their strengths, these students become more aware of their difficulties in learning, feeling academic failure more often than success. Over time, this negative outlook on school can lead to disruptive classroom behavior and feelings of low self-concept (Baum, 1994).

Identification of Gifted/LD Students

Identifying children who are both gifted and LD poses a challenge to teachers and school psychologists. Both teachers and parents can have difficulty associating failing grades and incomplete assignments with giftedness (Swesson, 1994). A central issue in the complexity of identifying students who are gifted/ LD is that their giftedness may mask their learning disability and that their learning disability may mask their giftedness (McCoach, et al. 2001). Although these students have varying patterns of strengths and weaknesses, they may appear to have average abilities and achievement in the classroom. This masking of abilities is also apparent in the identification of giftedness with fullscale IQ scores. These students' learning disability may in fact lower their IQ score so dramatically that they do not qualify for gifted services (Waldron & Saphire, as cited in McCoach et al., 2001). Because students who are gifted/ LD appear to have hidden gifts and at the same time have the ability to compensate for their learning disabilities, educators and psychologists must look for unique characteristics to identify this population of students.

Because many students who are gifted/LD have creative interests that may not be nurtured in the classroom, their behavior may be drastically different in their home environment. Parents should be involved in the identification process to offer insight into their child's activities outside of school (Rivera, Murdock, & Sexton, 1995). In many cases, students who are gifted/LD continually experience failure in school while successfully learning and creating at home, where they can put extended effort into their hobbies and interests (Baum,

1984). Developing a collaborative relationship between parents and teachers will also facilitate productive intervention strategies.

Emotional Concerns of Gifted/LD Students

Twice-exceptional students are often caught between two worlds. Many of these students are internally motivated and have strong beliefs in their abilities, much like gifted students, yet they repeatedly fail at certain tasks, similar to children with LD. One group of students who are gifted/LD reported having "some idea that they could not make their brain, body, or both do what they wanted each to do" (Schiff, Kaufman, & Kaufman, 1981, p. 403)

> **[Some gifted/LD] students' superior intelligence seems to compensate for their undiagnosed learning disability.**

Because of a strong belief in their abilities, gifted students also tend to have high expectations of their achievement level that are not always realistic (Vespi & Yewchuk, 1992). Therefore, a student who is gifted/LD may experience failure much more often than he or she expects, which can result in a fear of failure with future tasks. This fear can lead to frustration with, and feelings of anxiety toward, academic tasks as these students become aware of the discrepancy between their potential ability and their performance (Vespi & Yewchuk).

Students who are gifted/LD also report experiencing frustrating dichotomies of feeling both confused and bored, not understanding why they are good at some tasks and not others. The mixed messages that twice-exceptional students seem to get concerning their abilities often leave them with the feeling that they must prove they are smart (Rizza & Baum, personal communication, April 7, 2005). As a result, some students who are gifted/LD report avoiding or rushing through academic tasks in which they fear failure, often because completing the task seems more important than the quality of their work. Vespi and Yewchuk (1992) reported that not attending to a task also appears to be a way that such students cope with the anticipated frustration of a difficult task. Students who are gifted/LD often use their memory skills to hide their deficits. Hiding their deficits can develop into coping skills (Coleman, 1992).

The disappointments that twice-exceptional students experience in the classroom can often be observed in their behavior. These students may be disruptive, aggressive, and easily frustrated in the classroom environment (Fetzer, 2000). Students who are gifted/LD commonly daydream, doodle instead of listen, and may act impulsively when given directions (Fetzer). However, these students have been shown to persevere with difficult tasks when they are given encouragement and support (Vespi & Yewchuk, 1992).

Possible Characteristics of Twice-Exceptional Students

- Discrepancy between verbal and written work.
- Creativity.
- Excel on tasks requiring abstract concepts.
- Difficulty on tasks requiring memorization of isolated facts.
- Anxiety.
- Depression.
- Acting-out behavior.
- Poor organization.
- Poor motivation.
- Active problem solvers.
- Analytic thinkers.
- Strong task commitment when topic is personally meaningful.
- Withdrawal/shyness.
- Discrepancy between out-of-school talents and classroom performance.

Source: Baum, 1984 and Swesson, 1994.

Self-Concept of Gifted/LD Students

Students who are gifted/LD and who have difficulty coping with the discrepancy between their abilities and disabilities, may develop a low self-concept. Global self-concept is defined as the "general evaluation of one's self worth as a person" (Harter, Whitesell, & Junkin, 1998, p. 655). Students may also develop more specific self-concepts, such as an academic self-concept, which "refers to individuals' knowledge and perceptions about themselves in achievement situations" (Bong & Skaalvik, 2003, p. 6). Because of their experiences of failure in school, many children with learning disabilities have lower self-concepts than normally achieving students (Cooley & Ayres, 1988). Research in the area of self-concept and its relationship to LD is relatively thorough, indicating that both global and academic self-concepts affect an LD student's classroom achievement (Cooley & Ayres).

Similarly, the self-concepts of children who are both gifted and LD are lower than the self-concepts of their normally achieving peers (Waldron, Saphire, & Rosenblum, 1987). But how do students who are gifted/LD compare with those who are only LD? Children who are gifted/LD face the same academic challenges that students with LD face; however, students who are gifted/LD have additional challenges. Most children who are gifted are highly critical of themselves and tend to set extremely high goals (Waldron et al.). A student's view of his or her academic work strongly influences his or her self-concept, making students who are gifted/LD even more vulnerable (Winne, Woodlands, & Wong, 1982).

The expectations of parents and teachers further complicate students' development of self-concept. Although parents and teachers may set high standards because of the giftedness, they often lower their expectations because of the learning disability, regardless of the student's talents (Swesson, 1994). These mixed messages are hard to interpret. Therefore, students who are gifted/LD often have conflicting thoughts concerning their capabilities in the classroom and the expectations of their performance; such thoughts tend to result in a low self-concept (Waldron et al., 1987).

The expectations of parents and teachers further complicate students' development of self-concept.

Waldron and colleagues (1987) found that students who are gifted/LD had lower self-concepts than gifted students and believed that they were less intelligent than their peers. Twice-exceptional students rated themselves as more anxious and personally dissatisfied than their gifted peers, appearing to internalize their perception of academic behavior (Waldron et al.). Even when students who are gifted/LD hide their learning difficulties, they may be doing so at the expense of a lower self-concept.

Social Concerns of Gifted/LD Students

Students with LD have more social problems than their peers without LD. These problems include difficulty using appropriate social skills, generating solutions to social problems, and interpreting social cues (Stormont, Stebbins, & Holliday, 2001). In fact, students with LD are less likely to be leaders in their peer group, are less likely to be popular, and are often more rejected than their nondisabled peers (Flicek, 1992; Flicek & Landau, 1985). What about students who are both gifted and LD? Does giftedness serve as a protective factor in social situations? Actually, research has found the opposite to be true. Students who are both gifted and LD are at even more risk than their LD peers (Moon & Dillon, 1995; Vespi & Yewchuk, 1992).

Because twice-exceptional children seem to possess characteristics of both giftedness and LD, they often struggle with perceptions of being different and feeling isolated. One study that interviewed four twice-exceptional boys concluded that these children seemed to know how to make and keep friends but were often unable to put that knowledge to use in social situations (Vespi & Yewchuk, 1992). All four boys in the study reported being frustrated with their peer relationships, and three of the four appeared to relate better to adults than to their peers (Vespi & Yewchuk). Students who are gifted/LD may also experience anger, frustration, and resentment because of recognizing the discrepancy between their potential and their social and academic problems, which can further influence relations with peers (Brody & Mills, 1997; Moon & Dillon, 1995). To nurture the whole child, teachers and parents must recognize the social and emotional needs of students who are gifted/LD.

Supporting the Needs of Gifted/ LD Students

The essential element in meeting the educational needs of students who are gifted/LD is providing instruction that emphasizes these students' strengths and interests while remediating their learning deficits (Nielsen & Mortorff- Albert, 1989). However, many schools offer only remediation designed for LD only students, that is, it focuses only on improving a child's weaknesses. One study investigating the effects of special education on the global self-concept of students who are gifted/LD found that the self-concept scores of students receiving gifted services were significantly higher than those receiving services for learning disabilities only (Nielsen & Mortorff-Albert). This study concluded that the self-concepts of students who are gifted/LD appear to vary according to the type of special education services they receive. When students' services included gifted programming that focused on their strengths, the self-concepts of students who are gifted/LD matched those of their nondisabled peers (Nielsen & Mortorff-Albert).

Why is remediation alone not helpful for students who are gifted/LD? Remediation offers few opportunities for a twice-exceptional child to demonstrate his or her gifts and talents and often focuses on weaknesses at the expense of developing gifts. This set of circumstances can result in low self-esteem, a lack of motivation, depression, and stress (Baum, 1994). Therefore, students who are gifted/LD require a program designed to develop their strengths, interests, and superior intellect as well as remediate their deficits. Students who are gifted/LD need an educational environment that circumvents problematic academic areas, such as reading, arithmetic, and writing, and highlights abstract thinking and creativity (Baum, 1994).

Strategies for Supporting the Social and Emotional Needs of Gifted/LD Students

Support services for twice-exceptional children must treat the whole child—that is, must include not only academic interventions but also strategies to address these students' social and emotional needs (see box, "Guidelines for Developing Programs for Gifted/LD Students"). Following is a list of strategies that will likely benefit the students who are gifted/LD in your classroom:

1. Foster a clear understanding of their disability as well as their strengths to promote self-understanding and self-acceptance. If students are aware of their abilities, strengths, and weaknesses, they will be better prepared to make decisions about their future (Stormont et al., 2001).
2. Continually encourage gifted/LD students to succeed, and enlist the support of their parents and other teachers in this endeavor. Teach students to set realistic goals, accept their limitations, and reward their accomplishments.
3. Teach students coping strategies to use when they become frustrated. Learning ways to cope will help reinforce a student's commitment to persist with challenging tasks (Stormont et al., 2001).
4. If needed, encourage counseling to effectively monitor each student's emotions that accompany frustrations and perceived failures. Group counseling may also be beneficial, especially if students can speak with other students who are experiencing the same difficulties and frustrations (Brody & Mills, 1997).
5. Remind yourself and encourage others to recognize the unique needs of twice-exceptional students. Think of these children not only as having a disability or as being gifted but as having individual needs.
   a. Think twice about why a student may avoid a task or rush through an assignment. Does this child always avoid the same type of assignment?
   b. Offer multiple ways in which students can learn and demonstrate their knowledge in the classroom (e.g., presentations, projects, skits).

c. Encourage and positively reinforce students' efforts, especially on challenging tasks.
   d. Recognize and support the social and emotional needs of these children while also nurturing their academic strengths.
6. Provide support in establishing and maintaining social relationships by
   a. Introducing a structured learning environment that encourages positive social interactions with peers in the classroom (Vespi & Yewchuk, 1992);
   b. Increasing the opportunities for peer interactions in the classroom and supporting students in the appropriate use of social skills (Stormont et al., 2001); and
   c. Giving students who are gifted/LD opportunities to act in leadership roles with peers, especially in areas in which they excel.
7. Ensure parents' understanding of their child's giftedness and disability, emphasizing the child's potential. Build a collaborative relationship with parents to create a school–home partnership that supports the child.
8. Support students who are gifted/LD with future goals and career planning. Make sure that students are aware of their potential and do not sell themselves short.
9. Provide a mentorship with an adult who is also gifted/LD. This relationship can lend encouragement and hope to those who are frustrated with their school experiences (Swesson, 1994).

Final Thoughts

Twice-exceptional students have great potential to succeed. However, many become incredibly frustrated and have difficulty coping with the discrepancy between their giftedness and their learning disability. Their struggle to cope with frustration often leaves them feeling inadequate, disappointed, and angry, all of which negatively affect their self-concept. Many twice-exceptional students are also confused about where they fit in

Support services for twice-exceptional children must treat the whole child.

Guidelines for Developing Programs for Gifted/LD Students

- Focus attention on developing students' talents and strengthening their abilities through enrichment activities.
- Provide a nurturing environment in which students feel valued and their individual differences are respected.
- Teach compensation strategies after efforts to remediate skill deficits have helped students reach a level of proficiency.
- Encourage students' awareness of their individual strengths and weaknesses.

Source: Baum, 1990.

among their peers, and they often struggle with the social skills needed to maintain positive peer relationships.

Teachers, administrators, and parents must first acknowledge the individual gifts as well as the needs of students who are gifted/LD. These students must then be encouraged to recognize their own strengths and limitations so that they can better prepare for their future. Teachers must aim to strengthen these students' academic abilities and nurture their gifts while also supporting the social and emotional struggles that twice-exceptional students face inside and outside the classroom. By providing support that targets the whole child, we have the opportunity to tap the full potential of gifted students with learning disabilities.

References

Baum, S. M. (1984). Meeting the needs of learning disabled gifted students. *Roeper Review, 7*(1), 16–19.

Baum, S. M. (1990). *Gifted but learning disabled: A puzzling paradox.* Council for Exceptional Children: Reston, VA. ERIC Digest #E479.

Baum, S. M. (1994). Meeting the needs of gifted/learning disabled students: How far have we come? *The Journal of Secondary Gifted Education, 5*(3), 6–22.

Bong, M., & Skaalvik, E. M. (2003). Academic self-concept and self-efficacy: How different are they really? *Educational Psychology Review, 15*(1), 6.

Brody, L. E., & Mills, C. J. (1997). Gifted children with learning disabilities: A review of the issues. *Journal of Learning Disabilities, 30*(3), 282–296.

Coleman, M. R. (1992). A comparison of how gifted/LD and average/LD boys cope with school frustration. *Journal for the Education of the Gifted, 15*(3), 239–265.

Coleman, M. R. (2001). Surviving or thriving? *Gifted Child Today, 24*(3), 56–64.

Cooley, E. J., & Ayres, R. R. (1988). Self-concept and success-failure attributions of nonhandicapped students and students with learning disabilities. *Journal of Learning Disabilities, 21*(3), 174–178.

Fetzer, E. A. (2000). The gifted/learning-disabled child. *Gifted Child Today Magazine, 23*(4), 44–51.

Flicek, M. (1992). Social status of boys with both academic problems and attention-deficit hyperactivity disorder. *Journal of Clinical Child Psychology, 14,* 353–366.

Flicek, M., & Landau, S. (1985). Social status problems of learning disabled and hyperactive/learning disabled boys. *Journal of Clinical Child Psychology, 14,* 340–344.

Harter, S., Whitesell, N. R., & Junkin, L. J. (1998). Similarities and differences in domain-specific and global self-evaluations of learning-disabled, behaviorally disordered, and normally achieving adolescents. *American Educational Research Journal, 35*(4), 653–680.

McCoach, D. B., Kehle, T. J., Bray, M. A., & Siegle, D. (2001). Best practices in the identification of gifted students with learning disabilities. *Psychology in the Schools, 38*(5), 403–411.

Moon, S. M., & Dillon, D. R. (1995). Multiple exceptionalities: A case study. *Journal for the Education of the Gifted, 18*(2), 111–130.

Nielsen, M. E., & Mortorff-Albert, S. (1989). The effects of special education service on self-concept and school attitude of learning disabled/gifted students. *Roeper Review, 12*(1), 29–36.

Rivera, D. B., Murdock, J., & Sexton, D. (1995). Serving gifted/learning disabled. *Gifted Child Today Magazine, 18*(6), 34–37.

Schiff, M. M., Kaufman, A. S., & Kaufman, N. L. (1981). Scatter analysis of WISC-R profiles for learning disabled children with superior intelligence. *Journal of Learning Disabilities, 14*(7), 400–404.

Stormont, M., Stebbins, M. S., & Holliday, G. (2001). Characteristics and educational support needs of underrepresented gifted adolescents. *Psychology in the Schools, 38*(5), 413–423.

Strop, J. (2003). The affective side: Programming beyond the label. *Understanding Our Gifted, 15*(2), 27–29.

Swesson, K. (1994). Helping the gifted/learning disabled: Understanding the special needs of the "twice-exceptional." *Gifted Child Today, 17*(5), 24–26.

Vespi, L., & Yewchuk, C. (1992). A phenomological study of the social/emotional characteristics of gifted learning disabled children. *Journal for the Education of the Gifted, 16*(1), 55–72.

Waldron, K. A., Saphire, D. G., & Rosenblum, S. A. (1987). Learning disabilities and giftedness: Identification based on self-concept, behavior, and academic patterns. *Journal of Learning Disabilities, 20*(7), 422–432.

Winne, P. H., Woodlands, M. J., & Wong, B. Y. L. (1982). Comparability of self-concept among learning disabled, normal, and gifted students. *Journal of Learning Disabilities, 15*(8), 470–475.

EMILY WILLIAMS KING (CEC NC Federation), Doctoral Student, School Psychology, University of North Carolina, Chapel Hill. Address correspondence to Emily Williams King, 8 Weathergreen Court, Durham, NC 27713. (e-mail: eaw18@yahoo.com)

From *Teaching Exceptional Children,* by Emily Williams King, Vol. 38, No. 1, September/October 2005, pp. 16–20. Copyright © 2005 by Council for Exceptional Children. Reprinted by permission.

UNIT 4

Speech and Language Impairments

Unit Selections

Key Points to Consider

- How can assessment tools be selected and adapted for sensitivity to cross-cultural perspectives? What is the appropriate way to intervene when bilingual children have speech disorders?

- What can speech-language clinicians teach us about the assessment and remediation of communication and the improvement of reading skills?

Student Web Site

www.mhcls.com/online

Internet Reference

Further information regarding this Web site may be found in this book's preface or online.

Issues in Emergent Literacy for Children With Language Impairments

http://www.ciera.org/library/reports/inquiry-2/2-002/2-002.html

Speech and language impairments, although grouped together as a category of disability by the IDEIA (Individuals with Disabilities Education Improvement Act), are not synonymous. Language refers to multiple ways to communicate (for example by writing, signing, body, or voice), whereas speech refers to vocal articulation.

Many children have difficulty learning to read because of speech and/or language impairments. If they cannot receive language and/or express speech sounds correctly, the total lexicon makes less sense. Likewise, some children assessed as dyslexic (difficulty with the lexicon) are reading disabled primarily because of their disorders with speech and/or language. Telling these disorders apart can be challenging. Learning to communicate may also be difficult for children with hearing impairments, developmental disorders, some physical disorders (eg. Cerebral palsy), and some emotional disorders (e.g., elective mutism).

Speech is the vocal utterance of language. It is considered disordered in three underlying ways: voice, articulation, and fluency. Voice involves coordinated efforts by the lungs, larynx, vocal cords, and nasal passages to produce recognizable sounds. Voice can be considered disordered if it is incorrectly phonated (breathy, strained, husky, hoarse) or if it is incorrectly resonated through the nose (hyper-nasality, hypo-nasality). Articulation involves the use of the tongue, lips, teeth, and mouth to produce recognizable sounds. Articulation can be considered disordered if sounds are mispronounced, or if sounds are added, omitted, or substituted for other sounds, such as using the *z* sound for the *s* sound or *w* for *l*.

Fluency involves appropriate pauses and hesitations to keep speech sounds recognizable. Fluency can be considered disordered if sounds are very rapid with extra sounds (cluttered) or if sounds are blocked or repeated, especially at the beginning of words. Stuttering is an example of a fluency disorder of speech.

Language is the rule-based use of voice sounds, symbols, gestures, or signs to communicate. Language problems refer to the use of such devices in combinations and patterns that fail to communicate, fail to follow the arbitrary rules for that language, or lead to a delay in the use of communication devices relative to normal development in other areas (physical, cognitive, social).

The prevalence rates of speech and language disorders are higher than the rates for any other condition of disability in primary school. The exact extent of the problem, however, has been questioned because assessment of communication takes a variety of forms. Shy children may be diagnosed with delayed language. Bilingual or multilingual children are often mislabeled as having a language disorder because they come from linguistically and culturally diverse backgrounds. Many bilingual children do not need the special services provided by speech-language clinicians but do benefit from instruction in English as a second language.

All children with language or speech disorders are entitled to assessment and remediation as early in life as the problem is realized. Because children's speech is not well developed between birth and age 3, most disorders are not assessed until preschool. Students with speech-language disorders are entitled to a free and appropriate education in the least restrictive environment possible and to transitional help into the world of work, if needed, after their education is completed.

Disordered language is usually more difficult to remedy than delayed language. Disordered language may be due to a receptive problem (difficulty understanding voice sounds), an expressive problem (difficulty producing the voice sounds that follow the arbitrary rules for that language), or both. Language disorders include aphasia (no language) and dysphasia (difficulty producing language). Many language disorders are the result of a difficulty in understanding the syntactical rules and structural principles of the language (form), or they are the result of a difficulty in perceiving the semantic meanings of the words of the language (content). Many language disorders are also due to a difficulty in using the language pragmatically, in a practical context (function).

Most speech and language impairments are remediated between elementary school and high school. An exception to this is speech problems that persist due to physical impairments such as damage or dysfunction of lungs, larynx, vocal cords, or nasal passages. Another exception is language problems that persist due to concurrent disabilities such as deafness, autism, compromised mentation, traumatic brain injuries, or some emotional and behavioral disorders.

Speech-language clinicians usually provide special services to children with speech and language impairments in pull-out sessions in resource rooms. Computer technology is also frequently used to assist these children in both their regular education classes and in pull-out therapy sessions.

The first article addresses the confusion that exists over whether a child has a linguistic difference in speech/language or whether the child is, in fact, disabled in the area of communication. Students with limited English proficiency should not be labeled communication disordered unless they are significantly disabled in their mother tongue as well. However, many bilingual children do have phonological disorders in their mother tongue. Brian Goldstein and Leah Fabiano discuss their assessments and methods of remediation.

The second article discusses a two-stage program for assessment and remediation of early speech or language impairments. Working with young children in the areas of phonetic awareness, discrimination of faulty production of sounds, and listening to the sounds of language and correct articulation of sounds will not only correct communication disorders but improve reading skills.

Assessment and Intervention for Bilingual Children with Phonological Disorders

Monitoring phonological change across the two languages of bilingual children is important because it is possible that intervention provided in one language will generalize to the other language given the interdependence between the two languages.

BRIAN A. GOLDSTEIN AND LEAH FABIANO

An estimated 5.2 million bilingual children are enrolled in schools in the United States, a 61% increase since 1994 (National Center for English Language Acquisition and Language Instruction Education Programs, 2005). The increasing number of bilingual children has resulted in significant challenges to the provision of assessment and intervention services to bilingual children with phonological disorders (a term used here to apply to both segment- and pattern-based errors).

Providing assessment and intervention to children with such disorders is complicated given the lack of understanding of theories of bilingual phonological representation and the lack of knowledge of current best practices related to the assessment of and intervention for these children. The discussion below highlights theories of bilingual phonological representation and links those theories to models of assessment and intervention.

Theories of Bilingual Phonological Representation

Historically, researchers have posited two models of language representation for bilingual children. According to the Unitary System Model (e.g., Bhatia & Ritchie, 1999), bilingual children begin with a single phonological system that separates into two autonomous systems over time. In contrast, the Dual Systems Model maintains that bilingual children develop separate phonological systems for each language from birth that do not interact (e.g., Keshavarz & Ingram, 2002).

A third model, a variation of the Dual Systems Model known as the Interactional Dual Systems Model of phonological representation (Paradis, 2001), suggests that bilingual children possess two separate phonological systems with mutual influence. Various case and group studies have found support for the Interactional Dual Systems Model in that bilinguals use resources from both of their languages for efficiency in production while maintaining separation for language-specific elements (e.g., Brulard & Carr, 2003; Fabiano, 2006; Goldstein, Fabiano, & Iglesias, 2003; Johnson & Lancaster, 1998; Paradis, 2001).

Knowledge of phonological representation in bilinguals is helpful because it allows speech-language pathologists to distinguish a phonological *difference* from a *disorder*. Evidence-based assessment of phonological disorders in bilingual children should consider recent theories of bilingual phonological representation. By assessing the languages and determining how they interact, clinicians can make a valid diagnosis, determine the child's strengths and weaknesses, and plan for intervention.

Assessment of Bilingual Children

The following protocol for bilingual phonological assessment was developed based on the theoretical rationale that bilingual children maintain separation for some phonological elements while demonstrating interaction on others.

Step 1: Perform a Detailed Case History

In addition to what is normally obtained in a parent interview for a monolingual child, ask parents what a typical day is like for their child. In every situation mentioned, ask what language is typically spoken and what language the child uses during that task, or if both languages are heard/used. In addition, obtain the following information for bilingual children each time an assessment occurs: language history (when the child was exposed to and began to use each language); percent input in each language (hours per week the child *hears* each language); and percent output in each language (hours per week the child *uses* each language). It is important to remember that percent input and output are not static measures in that language environments shift over time (Pease-Alvarez, 2002).

Step 2: Obtain Speech Samples

Single-word and connected speech (conversation or narrative) samples should be obtained in both of the bilingual child's languages. It is important to collect speech samples in both languages because phonological acquisition will not be parallel across the bilingual child's two languages (Goldstein, Fabiano, & Washington, 2005). Developmental trajectories and structure of the two languages may be different for each language. As a result, the order of acquisition and phonological patterns will differ. Thus, phonological development in bilinguals is similar, but not identical, to monolinguals (e.g., Goldstein et al., 2005).

Step 3: Perform an Independent Analysis

Determine the phonetic inventory of the child in both languages using single-word and connected speech samples. Organize the inventory by place of articulation (e.g., bilabial, alveolar, etc.) and manner of articulation (e.g., stops, nasals, etc.). Obtaining a phonetic inventory in each language will aid in clinical decision-making and help to determine whether to take a phonetic or phonological approach to intervention.

Step 4: Perform a Relational Analysis

Relational analyses should be performed to examine overall consonant and vowel accuracy in each language, and accuracy of shared elements (i.e., common to both languages, such as /p/ between Spanish and English) and unshared elements (i.e., unique to each language, such as the Spanish trill). Analysis of shared and unshared elements should be examined because studies examining bilingual phonological representation have found, for example, significantly higher accuracy on shared elements compared with unshared elements, demonstrating interaction between the two languages (Fabiano, 2006; Fabiano & Goldstein 2004a, 2004b).

A phonological pattern analysis also should be included. The phonological pattern analysis should take into consideration that the type and frequency of phonological patterns vary across languages (Goldstein & Washington, 2001). For example, English allows three-member onset clusters and Spanish allows only two-member onset clusters. Because of this difference, cluster reduction is a phonological pattern that, at a given chronological age, would be developmental in English but "delayed" in Spanish.

Step 5: Perform an Error Analysis

In a substitution error analysis, one should examine targets (including phonemes that the child does not attempt to produce) and substitutes (phones the child is using in place of those target phonemes). In this analysis, one should account for cross-linguistic effects (using a phonological element specific to one language in the production of the other; for example, the Spanish trill /r/ found in an English production) and dialect features (Goldstein & Iglesias, 2001). Neither cross-linguistic effects nor dialect features should be scored as errors.

Intervention for Bilingual Children

Providing intervention to bilingual children with phonological disorders is challenging because there are relatively few research studies in this area. However, speech-language pathologists can use evidence that is known about phonological development in bilingual children, universal characteristics of phonological development, and the translation of theory into practice to guide decision-making about appropriate intervention services to bilingual children with phonological disorders. Consistent with the tenets of evidence-based practice, the process should begin with the clinical question (e.g., Justice & Fey, 2004).

> **Knowledge of phonological representation in bilinguals is helpful because it allows speech-language pathologists to distinguish a phonological *difference* from a *disorder*.**

In treating bilingual children with phonological disorders, SLPs typically ask the question, "In which language do I treat?" That question, however, is not the appropriate one, because it mistakenly assumes that phonological development in bilingual children proceeds similarly in the child's two languages. Because the structure of each language is different (e.g., different phonemes, syllable types, word shapes, etc.) and development is not the same in each language (e.g., Goldstein, 2004), intervention will need to be tailored to the construct and development of each constituent language. A more precise question is, "When do I treat in each of the two languages?" (Goldstein, 2006).

To account for the nature of bilingual language development, Kohnert and Derr (2004) and Kohnert, Yim, Nett, Fong Kan, & Duran (2005) proposed two main approaches to providing intervention to bilingual children. It should be noted that these approaches are models based on underlying research on language (including phonological) development in bilingual children, although they have yet to be tested empirically. First, the Bilingual Approach proposes that SLPs should increase language skills common to both languages. In terms of phonology, this approach would mean that clinicians would begin intervention with constructs common to both languages (e.g., CV syllables, the phoneme /s/, initial consonant clusters). Thus, the initial treatment determination is the goal and not the language of intervention.

The Bilingual Approach would support beginning with goals in which one would treat constructs common to both languages or errors or error patterns exhibited with relatively equal frequency in both languages (Yavas & Goldstein, 1998). For example, this might mean that if unstressed syllable deletion were exhibited frequently in both languages, then that pattern might be an appropriate initial intervention target. Similarly, if /s/ was frequently in error in both languages, treatment might begin targeting that phoneme.

Second, the Cross-Linguistic Approach proposes that clinicians should focus on the linguistic skills unique to each language. This approach also will be necessary (likely in conjunction with the Bilingual Approach) because of the differences in the linguistic (in this case, phonological) structures of the two languages. For example, aspirated affricates exist in Hmong, but not in English, and can only be remediated in the one language. Additionally, SLPs might use a cross-linguistic framework based on types of errors and/or error rates (Yavas & Goldstein, 1998). For example, final consonant deletion is more common in the English of Spanish-English bilingual children than in their Spanish (Goldstein et al., 2005). Thus, intervention to decrease the use of that pattern will likely occur in English but not in Spanish. Finally, errors occurring in only one language would be targets for phonological intervention (e.g., backing in Language B but not in Language A).

Language of Intervention

Once the general approach is selected, then the initial language of intervention can be determined. The initial language of intervention will depend on a variety of factors such as language history (relative experience with each language), use in each language (how frequently the child utilizes each of the languages), proficiency in each language (how well the child understands and produces each language), environment (where and with whom the child uses each language), and family considerations (the family's goals) (Goldstein, 2006).

The child's phonological skills and errors/error patterns in each of the two languages will be a factor as well. That analysis might show that the child exhibits lower accuracy, more errors, and a higher frequency-of-occurrence on phonological patterns (e.g., cluster reduction) in Language A than in Language B. Thus, intervention would begin with Language A (all other factors being relatively equal).

In working with all children (bilingual and monolingual) with phonological disorders, SLPs need to determine how their goals will be implemented. The way in which goals are implemented may conform to a number of goal attack strategies: vertical, horizontal, and cyclical approaches (Fey, 1992). A "vertical approach" is one in which one goal is taught at a time until criterion is reached. A vertical-approach analogue for bilingual children might be implemented in one of two ways.

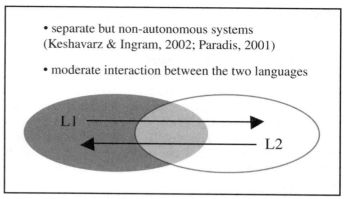

Interactional Dual Systems Model
Paradis J. *International Journal of Bilingualism*, Vol.5, no.1, March 2001, pp.19-38. Copyright © Kingston Press Ltd.

It might be used to focus on a goal that is specific to one language (e.g., trill in Spanish). Additionally, the SLP might consider how a target generalizes from one language to the other. So, remediation for /s/ occurs in English but is monitored but not targeted in Cantonese.

In a "horizontal approach," more than one goal is addressed in each session. A horizontal-approach analogue for bilingual children might be targeting one goal in Language A and one goal in Language B within the same session, although the targets would be divergent. For example, final consonants would be targeted in English, and aspirated affricates would be targeted in Hmong.

Finally, a "cyclical approach" is one in which a number of goals are addressed in a cyclical fashion, but only one goal is incorporated at a time within a session. A cyclical-approach analogue for bilingual children would be to rotate not only targets but also languages. For example, in Weeks 1–4, /s/ would be targeted in Language A and initial consonant clusters would be targeted in Language B. In Weeks 5–8, initial consonant clusters would be targeted in Language A with /s/ being the goal in Language B. (This example assumes, of course, that /s/ and clusters occur in both languages.)

Regardless of which goal attack strategy is used, patterns of phonological change should be monitored within and across the two languages (Grunwell, 1992). Monitoring these patterns serves to determine how the child's phonological system is changing during the course of intervention.

Monitoring phonological change across the two languages of bilingual children is important because it is possible that intervention provided in one language will generalize to the other language given the interdependence between the two languages (Paradis, 2001). There are a few studies that have examined this issue (Holm & Dodd, 1999; Holm, Dodd, & Ozanne, 1997; Holm, Dodd, Stow & Pert, 1998 in Holm & Dodd, 2001; Ray, 2002). Results from these studies indicate that intervention in English generally influences phonological skills in the other language. For example, Holm, Dodd, and Ozanne (1997) found that treatment of /s/ increased accuracy of that sound in both English and Cantonese. There were cases, however, in which phonological treatment in English did not affect skills in the other language. Holm, Dodd, Stow and Pert (1998 in Holm & Dodd, 2001) found that treatment of gliding did not generalize from English to Cantonese.

Unfortunately, for all these studies, intervention was provided in English only, and generalization to the other language was not always measured systematically. As a result, it is unclear if and/or how intervention in one language will generalize to the other language. It is likely, although untested, that intervention in one language will influence skills in the other language in a bi-directional manner (i.e., from Language A to Language B and vice versa). The interaction effect of providing intervention in more than one language is relatively unknown, but research on phonological development in bilingual children portends that such interaction is likely to occur.

A final consideration is the order in which goals are selected. For example, consider the targets for a monolingual English-speaking child with a severe phonological disorder. For that child, the SLP might begin intervention focusing on the inclusion of final consonants (i.e., decreasing final consonant deletion). That target would be appropriate given that, in English, final consonants are common, sounds occurring in word final position come from a large variety of sound classes, and sounds in word final position are critical for morphology.

Now consider the targets for a bilingual Spanish-English speaking child. In the child's English, focusing on final consonants still would be appropriate just as it was for the monolingual child. In Spanish, however, it would not be the most appropriate initial treatment target given that there are only five consonants

in the language that occur at the end of a word (Hammond, 2001). In Spanish, a pattern such as unstressed syllable deletion would be a more fitting initial treatment target because the majority of words in Spanish are multisyllabic (Hammond, 2001). Thus, the order in which targets are remediated will be determined, in part, by the languages spoken by the child.

Assessing and treating bilingual children with phonological disorders is neither quick nor easy. However, understanding how the phonological system is represented in bilingual children leads to a comprehensive, least-biased assessment. Information from that broad and deep assessment then can be translated into appropriate intervention goals. Those goals likely will be different at different points in time for each of the child's two languages. Thus, it is not a matter of if, but when, both languages will be used during the intervention process. Doing so will allow bilingual children with phonological disorders to attain age-appropriate phonological skills in both languages.

BRIAN A. GOLDSTEIN is an associate professor in the Department of Communication Sciences, Temple University, Philadelphia. He is the author of *Cultural and Linguistic Diversity Resource Guide for Speech-Language Pathologists* and the editor of *Bilingual Language Development and Disorders in Spanish-English Speakers.* Contact him at briang@temple.edu. **LEAH FABIANO** is a postdoctoral fellow at the Center for Research in Language at the University of California, San Diego. Her research interests include bilingual phonological representation, development, and disorders in Spanish-English speaking populations. Contact her at lfabiano@mail.sdsu.edu.

A Speech-Language Approach to Early Reading Success

ADELE GERBER AND EVELYN R. KLEIN

We are both speech-language pathologists who, in earlier periods of our careers, have served as specialists in school settings. A substantial part of our caseloads consisted of young children with articulation delays and disorders to whom we provided therapy. One of the procedures we frequently employed was intensive training in speech-sound perception that enabled the children to develop a heightened awareness of the difference between their error production and the corresponding standard sound.

On several occasions, first-grade teachers told us that children receiving articulation therapy excelled in phonics. On the basis of this information, in 1970, I (Adele Gerber) designed a program called Beginning Reading Through Speech in a format appropriate for use in kindergarten and first-grade classrooms. Recently we have revised the procedures to a format suitable for use by tutors or teachers providing individual or small-group training for children needing help mastering emergent literacy and early reading skills.

Over the past few decades, teachers have been informed about results of extensive research that has produced compelling evidence of a strong relationship between phonological awareness and the acquisition of reading awareness—that is, the perception of skills (Chaney, 1998). In particular, professional development programs have placed a heavy emphasis on phonemic awareness—that is, the perception of the speech sounds that form words—and its relevance to the mastery of letter-sound correspondences required for phonic decoding of the written word.

> **According to most theories of reading development today, phonological decoding is essential to reading.**

Having served as a consultant in the Norristown, Pennsylvania Area School District, I received a request from the reading specialist to train teachers in the area of phonemic awareness, providing assistance in understanding the process and information about procedures for its development in children engaged in early reading acquisition. A corps of elementary school teachers participated in an inservice program that presented the rationale and procedures for a speech-language approach to early reading success.

This article describes this speech-language approach, which we designed to help young children learn to associate letters with consonant sounds and to assist children who are struggling with early reading skills. Here, we also provide rationale for this innovative approach and results showing its efficacy.

Rationale for the Speech-Language Approach

According to testimony from the International Reading Association before a congressional briefing regarding effectiveness of reading instruction, "If you want to make a difference, make it different." (National Institute of Child Health and Human Development, 2000). The speech-language approach does employ procedures that differ from traditional approaches to teach letter-sound associations, one of the essential building blocks of early reading success. This approach is unique because it stems from another discipline: speech-language-hearing science.

The necessity of phoneme awareness for reading success is supported by much evidence. Poor readers have deficits in this ability when compared to normal readers of the same age and younger (Badian, 2001; Goswami & Bryant, 1994; Wagner & Torgensen, 1987). According to most theories of reading development today, phonological decoding is essential to reading. The ability to learn the sound-letter associations for decoding printed words is directly related to awareness of the sounds of speech (Kamhi & Catts, 2002).

The Speech-Language Approach

This approach consists of two stages. Stage 1 contains six steps; Stage 2 consists of four steps.

Stage 1: Training Phonemic Awareness for Consonant-Sound Perception

A phoneme is the smallest discrete speech sound in a word that has the capability to distinguish one word from another. For example, the difference between *boy* and *toy* is determined by the initial phonemes /b/ and /t/. Because the sound is embedded in the meaningful context of a word, it is difficult for some children (and some adults) to perceive it as a discrete entity.

> Failure in response to conventional phonics instruction is frequently due to attempts to match the abstract form of a letter to a sound that is not perceived.

Phonemic awareness development is critical to the speech-language pathologist's methods of treating articulation disorders. To heighten discrimination between a defective and a standard production of a speech sound, the phoneme is removed from the surrounding sounds in a word and presented in isolation (as a *phone*). Under this condition, the distinctive features of a speech sound are most apparent.

We designed the procedures in this approach to ensure success in a step-by-step progression from identification of each targeted consonant in isolation to recognition of the sound-letter correspondences in words.

According to a report from the National Reading Panel to the National Institute of Child Health and Human Development (2000), phonemic awareness training has caused reading and spelling improvement. The benefits have lasted beyond the end of training.

Step 1: Introduce the sound with a picture-sound symbol. Introduce each consonant sound with its associated picture-sound symbol. The sound picture and associated label capitalize on onomatopoeia (sounds that imitate what they denote). Cut out each of the 16 picture-sound symbols from Figure 1, and present them individually with a corresponding story that includes multiple productions of the sound in isolation. For example, a student is presented with a story (see Figure 2) about the sound of the letter. The *bubble sound,* /b/, is represented by a picture of a bubble displayed to the child (see Figure 3). We encourage teachers to develop their own stories similar in content and style to this example.

Step 2: Touch the picture of the sound symbol when hearing isolated sound. (This procedure applies to each new picture and sound.) Display a picture of the bubbles (picture-sound

Figure 1 The 16 picture-sound symbols.

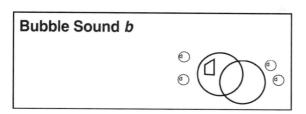

(It is recommended to have a large glass ½ full of milk or another preferred drink, a straw, and a bubble blower with soapy water or bubble solution available, if possible). The sound of 'b' is produced as an isolated sound without the vowel sound as in 'buh'.

I'm going to tell you a story about Betty. Betty was a good little girl. She helped her mother make the beds. She never talked back. But there was one thing that she did that her mother did not like. Betty loved to blow bubbles in her glass of milk. Whenever she drank milk she would blow through her straw, like this. (demonstrate) She loved to hear the bubbly sound. The bubbles seemed to say, "b b b b b," etc.

Her mother said, "Betty, why do you like to blow bubbles in your glass?"

Betty said, "Because I love to hear the bubbles say, b b b b b."

Betty's mother said, "I'll buy you a bubble blower and you can blow all the bubbles you want." So Mother bought a little bottle of liquid bubbles and a bubble blower.

Betty blew lots of pretty bubbles. But one day she said to her mother, "Mommy, these bubbles are pretty, but they don't talk."

"What do you mean, the bubbles don't talk?" asked her Mother.

"They don't say, b b b b," said Betty, "like my milky bubbles do."

"Well," said Mother, "I want you to drink your milk, not blow bubbles in it. But I want you to have fun, too. I have a good idea. I'll put the liquid bubbles in a glass and you can blow talking bubbles with your straw." So Mother put the liquid bubbles in a glass and Betty blew into it with a straw. She heard the bubbles say b b b b b any time she wanted to. But she drank her milk without blowing bubbles. So Mother was pleased, and Betty was happy with her talking bubble sound.

Can you make the bubble sound with me?

Figure 2 The bubble story for the /b/ sound.

symbol) on a workspace. Tell the child, "I will say some sounds. Some will be the bubble sound and some will be other sounds. When you hear the bubble sound, touch the bubbles." Produce a series of isolated consonant sounds; for example, "/b/, /l/, /b/, /b/, /f/, /k/, /b/," and so on.

Step 3: Touch the picture of the sound symbol when hearing the sound in syllables.
After he achieves approximately 90% correct identification, tell the child: "I'm going to talk baby talk. That means I will talk like a baby. When you hear me say the bubble sound, touch the bubble." Produce a random series of

Figure 3 Picture-Sound Symbol and Letter Cards.

consonant-vowel (CV) nonsense syllables, some starting with the bubble sound. Say, "Ba-ba, fo-fo, bi-bi, sa-sa, ta-ta, ba-ba," and so on.

Step 4: Touch the picture of the sound symbol when hearing the sound in easy words.
Following the child's approximately 90% correct identification, tell her, "I'm going to say some words. When you hear the bubble sound at the beginning of a word, touch the picture of the bubble. If it is the first word, touch this circle." Point to the circle on the left side, then continue, "And if it is the last word, touch this circle." Point to the circle on the right side. Produce a series of minimally contrastive CVC words that rhyme and include some that start with the /b/ sound. Use two drawn circles (one on the left side of page and one on the right side) to complete this step. Say, "Bat-hat; rake-bake, bin-fin; fill-bill," and so on.

Step 5: Touch the picture of the sound symbol when hearing sound in words.
Following the child's approximately 90% correct identification, say, "I'm going to say words one at a time. Touch the picture of the bubble sound when you hear a word that begins with the bubble sound." Produce a randomized list of single words, starting with one-syllable words. If the child masters the task, increase the length of the words. Say, "Bark, house, boy, paint, sing, face, book, lady, tiger, big, party, Bobby, Carlos, Kim, Felix, Billy, Keisha, Luis, Tanya," and so on.

Step 6: Match the correct sound-symbol picture with one of four sounds.
After completing Steps 1 through 5 with 4 of the 16 consonants sounds from Figure 1, display those four picture-sound symbols on the workspace. Tell the child, "I'm going to say words that start with different sounds. You point to the picture of the sound you hear at the beginning of each word." The first four

picture-sound symbols recommended are: /b/, /f/, /m/, and /t/. Say, "boy, fun, basket, money, tie, fork, talk, big, milk," and so on.

Stage 2: Matching Letter to Sound—Introductory Systematic Phonics

Step 1: Introduce letters with corresponding picture sound symbols.
Display a picture-sound symbol card and a letter card beside it. Tell the child, "This is the letter that goes with the bubble sound. Its name is 'B.' This is the letter that goes with the angry cat sound. Its name is 'F.'" We recommend continuing with the four letters previously taught.

Step 2: Match the picture-sound symbols with letters.
Display a group of letter cards and a group of picture-sound symbol cards on the workspace in random order. (The number of cards displayed depends on the level of mastery demonstrated in Step 1.) Tell the child, "We are going to play a matching game. Here are some sound pictures and some letter cards. See how many letters and sound pictures you can match."

Step 3: Identify sound-symbol pictures with various words.
If the child achieves approximately 90% accuracy at Step 2, display a group of single-syllable word cards beginning with the targeted consonants; for example: bat, fan, man, tail. Tell the child, "I will say the word. You find the picture of the sound you hear at the beginning of the word. For example, if I say 'bat,' you point to the bubble sound picture."

Step 4: Match the beginning letters with the corresponding words.
If the child achieves approximately 90% accuracy at Step 3, display a group of corresponding consonant-letter cards. Tell the child, "I will say some words that begin with these sounds. You pick up the letter that matches the first sound you hear when I say the word." Produce a list of words in random order, matching the picture-sound symbols to the letters. Say one word at a time. We recommend that initially the words consist of single-syllable rhyming groups such as pat, fat, bat, mat, and so on. When the child achieves 90% accuracy at this level, introduce more varied word patterns.

Evidence of Effectiveness

The speech-language approach to early reading success was used in the Norristown, Pennsylvania, School District to reduce the incidence of students with reading delay. In an extended-day tutorial program staffed by classroom teachers, children in first and second grades who scored at the below basic level of reading on the Houghton Mifflin Emergent Literacy Test were scheduled in groups of five per instructor for one-half hour sessions three times per week. A midyear test of progress was administered after a period extending from October, 2001 to February, 2002. Table 1 reflects the pre-and posttest results secured at the beginning of March, 2002.

Table 1   Progress of Students on Tested Emergent Literacy Skills After 5 Months of Training

Emergent Literacy Subtest	Number Students/Grade	Percentage of Students	October 2001 Skill Level	March 2002 Skill Level
Rhyme	31/1st	100%	Below Basic	Proficient
Beginning Sounds	31/1st	100%	Below Basic	Proficient
Blending Onsets/Rimes	31/1st	100%	Below Basic	Proficient
Concepts of Print	31/1st	100%	Below Basic	Proficient
Letter Naming	31/1st	100%	Below Basic	Proficient
Segmenting Onsets/Rimes	31/1st	100%	Below Basic	Basic
Phoneme Blending	31/1st	100%	Below Basic	Basic
Phoneme Segmentation	31/1st	100%	Below Basic	Basic
Word Recognition	31/1st	100%	Below Basic	Basic
Fluency	31/1st	100%	Below Basic	Basic
Word Writing	31/1st	100%	Below Basic	Basic
Sentence Dictation	31/1st	100%	Below Basic	Basic
Rhyme	7/2nd	100%	Below Basic	Proficient
Concepts of Print	7/2nd	100%	Below Basic	Proficient
Letter Naming	7/2nd	100%	Below Basic	Proficient
Fluency	7/2nd	100%	Below Basic	Proficient
Beginning Sounds	7/2nd	100%	Below Basic	Proficient
Blending Onsets/Rimes	7/2nd	100%	Below Basic	Basic
Segmenting Onsets/Rimes	7/2nd	100%	Below Basic	Basic
Phoneme Blending	7/2nd	100%	Below Basic	Basic
Phoneme Segmentation	7/2nd	100%	Below Basic	Basic
Word Recognition	7/2nd	100%	Below Basic	Basic

Of the students tested, seven second-grade students had I.Q. scores in the 60–70 range. Although prior instruction throughout the first grade had not succeeded in the development of emergent literacy skills in these students at the basic or proficient levels, 5 months of instruction in this program achieved progress—to the basic or proficient level skills for all seven students, considered to be developmentally delayed.

The data in Table 1 indicate noteworthy gains that impressed the teachers who implemented the methods. In first grade, 5 of 12 tested areas (42%) showed improvement from below basic to proficient levels and 7 of 12 of the areas (58%) improved from below basic to basic levels for all 31 first graders. In the second grade, half the tested areas showed improvement from below basic to proficient, and the other half of the tested skills areas showed improvement from below basic to basic for all 7 second graders.

The effectiveness of this step-by-step approach to reading success evidenced by the reported gains was further reflected by the reactions of teachers. The reading specialist who was the administrator of the remedial reading program stated, "The teachers loved it." She further expressed her intent to introduce the program into kindergarten classrooms at the beginning of the next school year.

The effectiveness of this step-by-step approach to reading success evidenced by the reported gains was further reflected by the reactions of teachers.

Final Thoughts

The methods used in this program emphasized the importance of connecting the auditory signal of the letter sound to the visual letter. Onomatopoeias relating common items such as the roaring sound of a lion for the sound of /r/ or the sound of a hissing snake for /s/ are used to help make an imprint to associate the concrete sound with the abstract symbol. Tying in a high-interest story that captivates the young listener by using auditory bombardment with repetitive sounds embedded in a story line keeps the children engaged and ready to learn how to associate consonant sounds with letters.

Students need to have a strong understanding of spoken language before they can understand written language. Our goal is to reduce the incidence of students with reading delay. As reading specialists in an urban-school setting where our lessskilled readers tend to have difficulty identifying, separating, and blending sound segments, we incorporated the speech/language approach in our extended day tutorial reading program. The gains have been noteworthy.

—Reported from teachers in the Norristown
School District, 2002

Studies have demonstrated that in early intervention, including phonological awareness, phonetic decoding, letter naming, sound knowledge, whole-word identification, and writing skills, along with reading connected text can be very effective (Vellutino, Scanlon, & Sipay, 1996). From an extensive review of research and practice in the area of emergent literacy, Whitehurst & Lonigan (1998) determined that well-developed language skills, letter knowledge, and some form

of phonological sensitivity are necessary for reading and writing and that the origins of these components of emergent literacy are found during the preschool years (Treiman, Tincoff, Rodruquez, Mouzaki, & Frances, 1998).

The early intervention methods used in the speech-language approach incorporate these skills and combine memory-enhancing strategies with phoneme awareness to help prevent problems during emergent literacy and the early reading period. This program approach has been found effective with beginning readers in first and second grades who were functioning at below basic level of early reading prior to instruction and at basic and proficient levels after training.

References

Badian, N. A. (2001). Phonological and orthographic processing: Their roles in reading prediction. *Annals of Dyslexia, 51,* 179–199.

Chaney, C. (1998). Preschool language and metalinguistic skills are links to reading success. *Applied Psycholinguistics, 19,* 433–446.

Goswami, U., & Bryant, P. (1994). *Phonological skills and learning to read.* Hove, UK: Lawrence Erlbaum.

Kamhi, A. G., & Catts, H. W. (2002). The language basis of reading: Implications for classification and treatment of children with reading disabilities. In K. G. Butler & E. R. Silliman (Eds.), *Speaking, reading, and writing in children with language learning disabilities* (pp. 45–72). Mahwah, NJ: Lawrence Erlbaum.

National Reading Panel. (2000). Teaching children to read: An evidence-based assessment of the scientific research literature on reading and its implications for reading instruction (NIH Publication No. 00-4769.) Report of the National Reading Panel. National Institute of Child Health and Human Development. Washington, DC.

Treiman, R., Tincoff, R., Rodriguez, K., Mouzaki, A., & Frances, D. J. (1998). The foundations of literacy: Learning the sounds of letters. *Child Development, 69*(6), 1524–1540.

Vellutino, F. R., Scanlon, D. M., & Sipay, E. R. (1996). Toward distinguishing between cognitive and experiential deficits as primary sources of difficulty in learning to read: The importance of intervention in diagnosing specific reading disability. In B. Blachman (Ed.), *Foundations of reading acquisition and dyslexia: Implications for early intervention* (pp. 347–379). Mahwah, NJ: Lawrence Erlbaum.

Wagner, R. K., & Torgensen, J. K. (1987). The nature of phonological processing and its causal role in the acquisition of reading skills. *Psychological Bulletin, 101,* 192–212.

Whitehurst, G. J., & Lonigan, C. J. (1998). Child development and emergent literacy, *Child Development, 69,* 848–872.

ADELE GERBER, Professor Emeritus, Temple University, Department of Communication Sciences, Philadelphia, Pennsylvania. **EVELYN R. KLEIN** (CEC Chapter #388), Assistant Professor, Department of Speech, Language, Hearing Science, La Salle University, Philadelphia, Pennsylvania. Address correspondence to Adele Gerber, 600 East Cathedral Road, H316, Philadelphia, PA 19128 (e-mail: adeleg410@aol.com).

UNIT 5

Developmental Disabilities/Autistic Spectrum Disorders

Unit Selections

Key Points to Consider

- What are research-based strategies that insure that students with developmental disabilities achieve in general education classrooms?

- Can service learning be used for assessment as well as education of students with developmental disabilities?

- How can teachers promote acceptance and friendships for students with autistic spectrum disorders in general education classroom?

Student Web Site

www.mhcls.com/online

Internet References

Further information regarding these Web sites may be found in this book's preface or online.

Arc of the United States
  http://www.thearc.org
Disability-Related Sources on the Web
  http://www.arcarizona.org
Gentle Teaching
  http://www.gentleteaching.nl

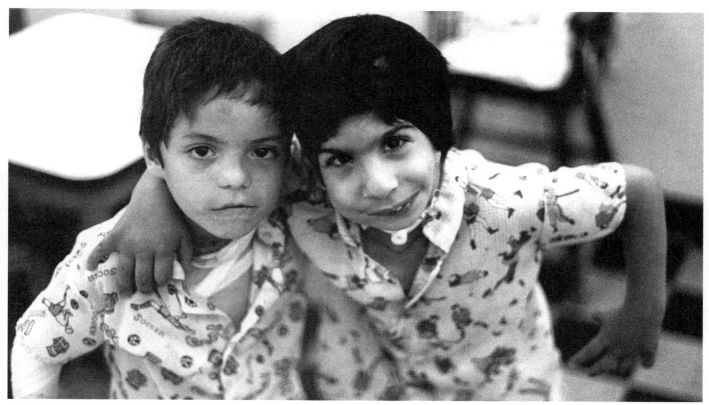

In our efforts to be more "politically correct" and to not inflict pain, we now avoid labels such as "mentally retarded." We always put the individual first and add the condition of disability second (when and if it is necessary). Students and adults who have cognitive skills falling two standard deviations below the norm for their age are now considered cognitively developmentally disabled. Children who have sustained brain damage through traumatic brain injury, even if they score two standard deviations below the intellectual norm for age, are traumatically brain injured, not developmentally disabled or intellectually impaired. Children and adults with autism or autistic spectrum disorders (such as Asperger's syndrome) are subsumed under a separate disability category by the U.S. Individuals with Disabilities Education Improvement Act (IDEIA). Three out of four individuals with classic autism score two standard deviations below the IQ mean. Nevertheless, cognitive developmental disorders, traumatic brain injuries, and autistic spectrum disorders are each recognized as separate disability categories by IDEIA.

Children with significantly subnormal intelligence were once classified as "educable," "trainable," or "custodial" for purposes of placement. These terms are strongly discouraged today. Even severely developmentally disabled children are educable and can benefit from some schooling. They must leave where they are, to be where we hope they can be. The current preferred categorical terms for children who are developmentally challenged are "intermittent," "limited," "extensive," and "pervasive." These terms refer to how much support the individuals need to function and to succeed as much as possible.

IDEIA mandates free and appropriate public school education for every child, regardless of mentation. While the legal windows on education are from ages 6 to 16 in the United States, individuals with developmental disabilities are entitled to a free and appropriate education from age of assessment (birth, early childhood) to age 21. This encompasses parent-child education programs and preschool programs early in life and transitional services into the community and world of work after the public school education is completed.

The inclusion of children with disabilities in regular education classes has been controversial (see Unit 1) throughout the time span since 1975. Some school systems have succeeded brilliantly in integrating students with cognitive developmental disabilities into their regular classes. Other schools have fought the law every step of the way. Their dark histories are full of lawsuits brought by parents to try to obtain the services to which the law entitles them. The less-than-stellar school systems, and some U.S. states that have been notorious laggards, complain that the law is too cumbersome. There have been few negative consequences for school systems or whole state education departments who have resisted placing cognitively disabled students in regular classrooms. Therefore some parents still invoke formal complaint procedures against schools to get their children out of full-time special classes or special schools.

A child with a cognitive developmental disabilities (intellectual impairment) who is in the mildest "intermittent" classification needs support at school at times when special needs arise and at times of life transitions. This terminology is generally used for children whose disabilities do not create an obvious and continual problem. These children have slower mentation but also have many abilities.

The next level of support, classified as "limited," is usually used for children whose disabilities create daily limitations on their abilities but who can achieve a degree of self-sufficiency after an appropriate education in the least restrictive environment. Limited refers to the period of time from diagnosis until adulthood (age 21). The "extensive" support classification extends the support throughout the lifespan for individuals whose developmental disabilities prohibit them from living independently. The "pervasive" support classification is used infrequently. It is only for those individuals whose disabilities prevent them from most activities of self-help. Pervasive support is intensive and life-sustaining in nature.

The majority of children with developmental disabilities (intellectual impairments) can be placed in the intermittent support classification. To casual observers, they often do not appear to have any disabilities. However, their ability to process, store, and retrieve information is limited. In the past, this group of children was given IQ measurements between two and three standard deviations below the mean (usually an IQ below 70 but above 55). Intelligence testing is an inexact science with problems of both validity and reliability. The current definition of developmental disability endorsed by the American Association on Mental Deficiency (AAMD) does not include any IQ scoring results other than to use the phrase "subaverage intellectual functioning." It emphasizes the problems that individuals with developmental disabilities have with adaptive skills such as communication, self-care, home living, social skills, community use, self-direction, health and safety, functional academics, leisure, and work.

The causes of developmental disabilities and autistic spectrum disorders are unclear. About one-half of all individuals are suspected of having sustained some brain damage prenatally, neonatally, or in childhood. Among the better-known factors that contribute to brain tissue damage are early birth or low birth weight, anoxia, malnutrition, drugs, viruses, radiation, trauma, and tumors.

The first selection chosen for this unit on developmental disabilities addresses the issue of inclusion: how can students with disabilities receive the support they need in general education classrooms? Anne Bucalos and Amy Lingo discuss strategies that have been supported by research. Both students with, and without, disabilities can have high achievement with differentiated instruction, anchored instruction, cooperative learning, peer tutoring, and strategic learning.

The second article discusses the impact of PL 107-110 (No Child Left Behind) on the education of students with developmental disabilities/cognitive impairments. The use of service-learning projects as a means of demonstrating proficiency in certain core academic subjects is explained. Service-learning has many benefits beyond assessment as well (e.g., education, peer interaction, parental involvement).

The third report, *Fitting In,* gives several tips for parents, teachers, and significant others to help students with autistic spectrum disorders (ASD) become more socially accepted in inclusive classrooms. We all need friends. Even children with ASD value acceptance by their peers. E. Amanda Boutet discusses ways to make this possible.

Filling the Potholes in the Road to Inclusion

Successful Research-Based Strategies for Intermediate and Middle School Students with Mild Disabilities

Teachers have sought appropriate strategies to ensure that students with disabilities receive the support they need within the general education classroom (Klingner, Vaughn, Hughes, Schumm, & Elbaum,1998). Paving the road to inclusion with successful academic experiences for students with mild disabilities has been especially challenging in the intermediate and middle grades, where emphasis on content mastery becomes an issue of accountability to state mandates, and many students are experiencing gaps in their content knowledge and in their knowledge of learning strategies. The good news is that the gaps are being filled with research-based strategies designed to accomplish high academic achievement of all learners. This article explores the specific characteristics among differentiated instruction, anchored instruction, cooperative learning, peer tutoring, and strategic learning that make them effective research-based strategies for repairing the potholes in the road to successful inclusion.

ANNE B. BUCALOS AND AMY S. LINGO

As the trend toward inclusive school practices has become more firmly established, teachers have sought strategies to ensure that students with disabilities receive the academic and social support they need within the general education classroom (Klingner, Vaughn, Hughes, Schumm, & Elbaum,1998). The road to "responsible inclusion" (see Vaughn & Schumm, 1995) has been rocky for administrators, teachers, and students, particularly in documenting sufficient student achievement of many students included in general education classrooms where undifferentiated, large group instruction is the norm (Baker & Zigmond, 1995). Paving the road with successful academic experiences for students with mild disabilities has been especially challenging in the intermediate and middle grades, where emphasis on content mastery becomes an issue of accountability to state mandates.

Teachers may ask if the methods they are using truly address the needs of all learners in ways that not only build content knowledge, but move students to higher levels of thinking. Some teachers remain philosophically opposed to making accommodations in the general education classroom for students with disabilities because they believe students need to learn to cope with the academic demands of middle and high school, where exceptions are unlikely to be made (Baker & Zigmond, 1995).

The need for sophisticated instruction, what Palincsar, Magnusson, Collins, and Cutter (2001) call "advanced teaching practices" is especially important in the intermediate and middle grades when pre- and early adolescents must increasingly use their foundational knowledge and basic skills in higher order thinking tasks and problem-solving. It is at this point that many marginalized students, particularly those with disabilities, are only superficially engaged in academic tasks because they have depended on others for help or they only appear to be trying to complete those tasks (Summey & Strahan, 1997). Many students with disabilities are experiencing gaps in the skills needed to gain knowledge in content and in the strategies needed to be successful in general education classrooms. Consequently, dangerous potholes await them on the road to successful learning.

The good news is that the potholes are being filled! Teachers have available to them research-based strategies that are designed to engage all learners in inclusive classrooms, and that share one or more specific characteristics that better ensure the success of all students.

What are these specific characteristics? Table 1 summarizes the characteristics of strategies that are being used successfully with intermediate and middle school students.

Each of the strategies that follow incorporates one or more of the characteristics of "advanced teaching practices" or successful research-based instruction. Teachers may find confirmation of what they use presently in their classrooms, or may add one or more of these strategies to their repertoire.

Characteristics of Successful Research-Based Strategies

- Commitment of teacher time in planning and execution of lesson(s)
- General and special education teachers available to students for **full** class period
- Clear understanding by both general and special education teachers of language and concepts central to content being covered
- Successful collaboration between teacher and student, using instructional conversation and directive questioning
- Use of conceptual anchors (video, story, problem-based scenario) to create a shared experience and framework for building on prior knowledge and to engage students in higher-order thinking skills
- Use of flexible, creative differentiated instruction *with student input*
- Use of cooperative learning with emphasis on instructional conversation and responsibility for mutual learning

What Are These Strategies and How Do They Incorporate the Characteristics?

Differentiating instruction (Tomlinson, 1999) means beginning where students are rather than beginning with the curriculum guide. Teachers in differentiated classes use time flexibly, call upon a range of instructional strategies, and create a community of learners where teachers and students are partners. Summey and Strahan (1997), using Howard Gardners's (1983) theory of multiple intelligences, created a *Mindful Learning* approach to teaching the novel, *The Outsiders,* by S. E. Hinton (1968) to seventh grade students in an inclusive language arts class. Since many of the students had severe reading disabilities, students saw the film of the novel first, then participated in activities such as making collages about the characters, designing skits with the characters, or composing songs. Differentiated instruction allowed for reading strategies to be taught using preferred intelligences and learning modalities. The students with disabilities were more engaged in the classroom activities than during more traditional instruction, and the majority consistently demonstrated the use of reading strategies.

Differentiated instruction, centered around district and state-mandated curriculum and core content assessments, permits teachers to design multi-grade level projects that evaluate progressively complex skills, with content and process differentiated for learners with diverse needs. The Pittsford Central School District in Pittsford, New York, designed a creative writing project, called "A Picture is Worth . . . Many Words," that offered different writing options to diverse students who had chosen a picture stimulus from a file of newspapers, magazines, or journal photographs, allowing each student to work on the same overall objective, but at an appropriate readiness level (Pettig, 2000). Sequentially complex tasks allow for students at different skills levels to progress while covering required content.

Table 1 contains a reference for the Pittsford creative writing project, as well as other resources on differentiated instruction.

What makes differentiated instruction an "advanced teaching practice?" What characteristics does differentiated instruction share with other successful research-based strategies? Certainly commitment of teacher time comes with the extensive planning and preparation involved in differentiating instruction. Teachers cannot adequately plan appropriate instruction without thorough background in content and a structured plan for content coverage.

Table 1   Sample Resources on Differentiated Instruction

Books:

Moll, A. (2003). *Differentiated instruction guide for inclusive teaching.* Portchester, NY: Dude Publishing.

Tomlinson, C. A. (1999). *The differentiated classroom: Responding to the needs of all learners.* Alexandria, VA: ASCD.

Winebrenner, S. (1996). *Teaching kids with learning difficulties in the regular classroom.* Minneapolis, MN: Free Spirit Publishing.

Articles:

Holloway, J. H. (2000). Preparing teachers for differentiated instruction. *Educational Leadership, 58*(1), 82–83.

Pettig, K. (2000). On the road to differentiated practice. *Educational Leadership, 58*(1), 14–18.

Tomlinson, C. A. (2000). Differentiated instruction: Can it work? *Education Digest, 65*(5), 25–32.

Web sites:

http://www.ascd.org/pdi/demo/diffinstr/differentiated1.html

ASCD site with definitions, lesson plans, demos.

http://www.cast.org/ncac/index.cfm?i=2876

National Center on Assessing the General Curriculum site with articles, lessons.

http://www.sde.com/hottopics/differentiatedinstruction.htm

Staff Development for Educators site with resources and workshops.

Suggested resources for anchored instruction and problem-based learning:

Cognition and Technology Group at Vanderbilt. (1990). Anchored instruction and its relationship to situated cognition. *Educational Researcher, 19*(6), 2–10.

Kain, D.L. (2003). *Problem-based learning for teachers, grades K–8.* Boston, MA: Allyn and Bacon.

Torp, L. & Sage, S. (1998). *Problems as possibilities: Problem-based learning for K–12 education.* Alexandria, VA: Association for Supervision and Curriculum Development.

http://www.udel.edu/pbl/
University of Delaware site for Problem-Based Learning (PBL)

http://www2.imsa.edu/programs/pbl/cpbl.html
Illinois Mathematics and Science Academy PBL site

http://www.peabody.vanderbilt.edu/projects/funded/jasper/Jasperhome.html
The Jasper Series site at Peabody (Vanderbilt University)

http://www.samford.edu/pbl/index.html
Samford University site for PBL

Suggested resources for cooperative learning:

Cohen, E. (1994). *Designing groupwork: Strategies for the heterogeneous class room* (2nd ed.). NY: Teachers College Press.

Goor, M. B. & Schwenn, J. O. (1993). Accommodating diversity and disability with cooperative learning. *Intervention in School and Clinic, 29*(1), 6–16.

http://www.clcrc.com/pages/cl.html
This site provides critical components of cooperative learning.

http://www.nerel.org/sdrs/areas/issues/content/cntareas/math/ma1group.htm
This site provides information on grouping practices.

http://www.ed.gov/databases/ERIC_Digests/ed434435.html
This is an informational site on different grouping practices.

Teachers must be available fully to students, frequently checking comprehension and allowing for student input. Last, cooperative learning activities, based on authentic problems, can be important components in differentiated instruction, particularly as tools for students to engage in instructional conversation, providing feedback to each other on comprehension and skill development.

Anchoring instruction (Hasselbring, 1994) is another strategy that is used to promote higher-order thinking among students in content area classrooms. A conceptual anchor, often video-based, is used to assist learners in forming mental models, and allows all learners within a classroom to form a common frame of reference. Combined with project-based or problem-based learning (Duch, Groh, & Allen, 2001), students are challenged to use higher-order thinking skills to solve authentic, multi-solution problems within the context of cooperative groups (see Table 2 for guidelines in using anchored instruction). Students are involved in constructing their own knowledge through disciplined inquiry, generating products of learning that have value beyond school. Eighth grade students, including several who had mild disabilities, viewed *Kim's Komet* from the Learning and Technology Center at Vanderbilt University (1996), and

then were challenged to construct graphs from tables of information related to distance, rate, and time (Bottge, Heinrichs, Chan, & Serlin, 2001). Students constructed their own derby cars and ramp to test speeds at various heights of the ramp. The remedial math students, including students with disabilities, scored as high as the prealgebra students on the posttests. Students were able to work cooperatively in small groups to problem-solve, with the teacher continually probing the students' understanding of the tasks and their thinking.

A similar format was followed with fifth-grade students with and without mild disabilities investigating 19th century westward expansion in the United States (Ferretti, MacArthur, & Okolo, 2001). Following the viewing of *The American Experience: The Donner Party* (Public Broadcasting Service, 1992), students used historical inquiry to examine primary and secondary sources to understand the experiences of emigrants and the bias with which evidence can be written. Students then designed a multimedia presentation about one of the emigrant groups to present to parents at Open House night. While students were working cooperatively in small groups, teachers used an individual interview component with the students with disabilities in order to tap their understanding of both the historical content and the process of historical inquiry. This permitted the teachers to use questioning and instructional conversation techniques to test student understanding of the concepts and strategies being used. Students with disabilities not only scored as well as non-disabled students on the posttest, but had more favorable

Table 2 Guidelines for Using Anchored Instruction and Problem-Based Learning

- Choose an appropriate anchor based on assessment of students' prior knowledge.
- Determine guidelines for group structure (heterogeneous group composition), with appropriate role assignments based on individual student needs/skills.
- Practice general problem-solving procedures, including defining the problem.
- Choose an authentic problem (one that has relevance to the students) that has a variety of possible solutions.
- Have individual as well as group accountability (within the skills levels of each group member).

Table 3 Using Cooperative Learning with Students with Mild Disabilities

- Group students heterogeneously according to individual students' needs, and assign roles based on individual student's needs and abilities.
- Prepare students by modeling appropriate behavior in a group setting.
- Monitor student learning consistently by questioning/interviewing the students.
- Make sure that group partners encourage the participation of students with disabilities, and provide needed support.
- Structure the task using clear guidelines, especially for the students with disabilities.

attitudes about their self-efficacy as learners in social studies than they did prior to the project.

In both examples of anchored instruction, students were able to establish a common frame of reference or shared experience which not only tapped into their prior knowledge, but provided a forum for instructional conversations and feedback. In both examples, teachers continuously probed students for understanding of content and strategies, and in the history unit, used an individual interview component with students with disabilities. In cooperative learning groups, students were held responsible for mutual learning, as evaluated by both products and posttests. These characteristics helped ensure student mastery of content.

Cooperative learning (Slavin, 1995) provides students with the opportunity to engage in instructional conversations that clarify, probe, and solidify learning (see Table 3 for guidelines for using cooperative learning). As students articulate their thoughts, their peers in the cooperative group can provide feedback, or ask follow-up questions to accelerate the comprehension process (Vaughn, Gersten, & Chard, 2000). Students have the opportunity to "think aloud," and teachers have a setting where they can "mini-conference" with groups, checking for understanding and elaborating on thinking and problem-solving strategies appropriate to the group task (Klingner, Vaughn, & Schumm, 1998; Vaughn et al., 2000). Using a cooperative learning format, Palincsar et al. (2001) conducted research on fourth and fifth grade students with and without disabilities who participated in guided inquiry science instruction that established the classroom as a community of inquiry. Investigations and data gathering were done in small, cooperative groups, where students first shared their interpretations of how to investigate, what sense to make of their data, and how to represent their claims to the whole classroom community. In addition to the instructional conversation occurring in each cooperative group, individual students with disabilities were briefly interviewed by the teachers every day with questions such as "What did you learn today?" or "What would have helped you learn more today?" to permit elaboration and/or clarification of content by the teachers. The majority of students with special needs showed positive changes in their understanding of scientific inquiry comparable to those of their non-disabled peers at the end of the project.

Use of cooperative learning as an effective strategy for students with and without disabilities necessitates thorough planning and execution on the parts of both general and special educators. Grouping of students, assignment of tasks, and individual and group outcomes should facilitate responsibility for mutual participation and learning. Full engagement of teachers in monitoring student understanding through questioning and clarification is essential if all students are expected to acquire and understand required content. In order to develop a community of inquiry, as in the Palincsar et al. (2001) study, teachers had to rely on instructional conversations and questioning within the cooperative groups as well as daily individual interviews with students with disabilities to permit elaboration of content and to check understanding.

Peer tutoring has been established in the literature as a successful alternative instructional method for students with disabilities (Fuchs, Fuchs, Mathes, & Simmons, 1997; Mastropieri, Scruggs, Mohler, Beranek, Spencer, Boon, & Talbott, 2001). Tutoring arrangements can be same-age or cross-age, depending on the needs of the students and availability of tutors (see Table 4 for guidelines on using classwide peer tutoring). Research on this type of instructional arrangement has been found to increase students' opportunities to respond, provide additional practice for targeted skills, and result in improvement in academic skills (Byrd, 1990; Dugan, Kamps, Leonard, Watkins, Rheinberger, & Stackhaus, 1995). Peer tutoring has been successfully used

Table 4 Guidelines for Using Classwide Peer Tutoring

- Have each member of the pair share the roles of tutor and tutee, and train them by modeling appropriate behaviors for each.
- Train each pair in giving feedback and in error correction procedures.
- Have pairs practice each role, with monitoring by the teacher.
- Begin tutoring with less complex drill and practice or vocabulary words, then transition to more challenging content when students are proficient at tutoring procedures.
- Choose materials with the appropriate difficulty level carefully, noting the skills of the tutoring pair.

Source: Fulk, B. M. & King, K. (2001). Classwide peer tutoring at work. *Teaching Exceptional Children. 34*(2), 49–52.

to improve academic skills in the areas of reading (Kamps, Barbetta, Leonard, & Delquardi, 1994) and social studies (Maheady, Harper, & Secca, 1988). Delquardi, Greenwood, Whorton, Carta, & Hall (1986) described three important principles of instruction that peer tutoring incorporates: (1) individualization of the targeted skill, (2) frequent opportunities to respond with a rapid pace of instruction, and (3) the use of immediate corrective feedback. The peer-assisted learning strategies (PALS) reading intervention program, developed by researchers at Peabody College of Vanderbilt University (Fuchs et al., 1997) has been validated as a successful reading intervention program in urban schools in grades 2–6. The PALS program consists of three critical reading strategies: (1) partner reading with the tutee receiving immediate corrective feedback for word-calling errors, (2) the reader summarizing the passage with a sequential retelling of important events and main idea, and (3) the readers predicting what will happen next in the passage, with the stronger reader reading first. Students with and without disabilities report that they enjoy playing the role of the teacher, while receiving extra help from peers with fluency and comprehension.

Classwide peer tutoring perhaps best incorporates the characteristic of instructional conversation between student pairs, with close monitoring and questioning additionally by the classroom teachers. Instruction can be differentiated to the needs of students in the pairs, using a story or passage as an anchor for common understanding. This strategy requires extensive teacher time in planning and execution, particularly in training students to give appropriate feedback. Having general and special education teachers fully available to students permits close monitoring of specific skill deficits.

Strategic learning, employing the concept of direct instruction of a specific strategy, helps students improve comprehension and mastery of content. Many students with disabilities lack the strategies for learning and comprehending contextual material, especially textbooks. Klingner et al. (1998) developed *Collaborative Strategic Reading,* which combines reading comprehension strategy instruction with heterogeneous cooperative learning, for use with fourth graders with and without disabilities in an inclusive general education classroom. The strategy included "previewing" (reading the title and headings and predicting what the passage might be about), "click and clunk" (monitoring comprehension during reading by identifying difficult words and concepts in the passage), "get the gist" (restate the most important idea in the passage), and "wrap up" (after reading, summarize what has been learned and ask questions that might occur on a test). Students were given direct instruction on how to use the strategy, an opportunity to "think aloud" about why, how, and when the techniques would be used, and then opportunity for practice. Small groups then took turns modeling the strategies for the whole class. Last, students worked in heterogeneous groups of five or six, using the strategies to learn content from a social studies text. When compared to the control group, students learning the strategies made greater gains in reading comprehension, and equal gains in content knowledge. Strategic learning incorporates responsibility for mutual learning within a cooperative learning format, using "think aloud" techniques, modeling, and practice in using the

strategies. Students are able to tackle content area reading, such as social studies, in a collaborative context, using conversation about both content and the specific strategies used to understand the content.

In summary, these research-based strategies share a number of common characteristics that promote successful learning in all students. First is the commitment of teacher time—in planning and in execution. In all of the studies cited, the special education and general education teachers were available to students for the **full** class time. Additionally, both general and special education teachers had to have a clear understanding of the language and concepts central to the study of specific topics, and to know the purposes of instruction and ways to advance student knowledge within that specific instructional content. Successful collaboration is a key element. Teachers had to be committed to engaging students as partners, continuously involving students in instructional conversation and directive questioning to ascertain student understanding and possible misconceptions.

The various studies and strategies highlighted frequently employed a conceptual anchor in the form of a video or authentic problem-based scenario that permitted the development and use of a shared experience between teacher and learners that facilitated the construction of new knowledge. Intermediate and middle school students with and without disabilities are able to more readily identify with authentic problems that challenge their higher-order thinking and problem solving skills (Levin, Hibbard, & Rock, 2002; Torp & Sage, 1998), and provide an avenue for shared decision-making. Anchored instruction using problem-based learning affords an opportunity for students to work cooperatively, satisfying social needs while facilitating social skill development, particularly in students with disabilities (Bottge et al., 2001).

Last, teachers had to be committed to facilitating the learning of *all* students through differentiating instruction when needed. Comprehensive planning, flexibility with grouping of students, willingness to creatively approach content and allowing for student input are key elements to successful differentiated instruction (Pettig, 2000). Successful differentiation requires systemic change, both in teaching practices and classroom culture (Tomlinson, 1999). Teachers must begin with small steps, such as differentiating instruction in a specific content area, and should find supportive colleagues willing to accompany them on the journey.

The Need for Continuing Research

In order for students with disabilities to be successful achievers in inclusive settings, accommodations must meet the specific needs of the learner, and must be supported by research that confirms the effectiveness of the strategies. All learners, with and without disabilities, benefit from the planning, time commitment, and teacher-student partnership that accompany appropriate methods. These "advanced teaching methods" are keys to a successful inclusion experience, and a smoother road to success for students with disabilities. It is incumbent upon teacher preparation programs and school districts mandating professional development to include instruction on these research-based strategies. Only when all educators, general and special, are able to meet the needs of all learners, will students with disabilities receive the quality of education they deserve.

References

Baker, J. M., & Zigmond, N. (1995). The meaning and practice of inclusion for students with learning disabilities: Themes and implications from the five cases. *Journal of Special Education, 29*, 163–180.

Bottge, B. A., Heinrichs, M., Chan, S., & Serlin, R. C. (2001). Anchoring adolescents' understanding of math concepts in rich problem-solving environments. *Remedial and Special Education, 22*, 299–315.

Byrd, D. E. (1990). Peer tutoring with the learning disabled: A critical review. *Journal of Educational Research, 84*, 115–118.

Cognition and Technology Group at Vanderbilt. (1990). Anchored instruction and its relationship to situated cognition. *Educational Researcher, 19*(6), 2–10.

Delquadri, J., Greenwood, C. R., Whorton, D., Carta, J. J., & Hall, R. V. (1986). Classwide peer tutoring. *Exceptional Children, 52*(6), 535–542.

Duch, B. J., Groh, S. E., & Allen, D. E. (2001). *The Power of Problem-Based Learning.* Sterling, VA: Stylus.

Dugan, E., Kamps, D., Leonard, B., Watkins, N., Rheinberger, A., & Stackhaus, J. (1995). Effects of cooperative learning groups during social studies for students with autism and fourth-grade peers. *Journal of Applied Behavior Analysis, 28*, 175–188.

Ferretti, R. P., MacArthur, C. D., & Okolo, C. M. (2001). Teaching for historical understanding in inclusive classrooms. *Learning Disability Quarterly, 24*, 59–71.

Fuchs, D., Fuchs, L. S., Mathes, P. G., & Simmons, D. C. (1997). Peer assisted learning strategies: Making classrooms more responsive to diversity. *American Educational Research Journal, 34*, 174–206.

Gardner, H. (1983). *Frames of mind: The theory of multiple intelligences.* New York: Basic Books.

Hasselbring, T. S. (1994, June). *Anchored instruction—Why are we here?* Presentation conducted at the Advanced Institute on Anchored Multimedia for Enhancing Teacher Education, Nashville, Tennessee.

Hinton, S. E. (1968). *The outsiders.* New York: Dell.

Kamps, D., Barbetta, P., Leonard, B., & Delquadri, J. (1994). Classwide peer tutoring: An integration strategy to improve reading skills and promote peer interactions among students with autism and general education peers. *Journal of Applied Behavior Analysis, 27*, 49–61.

Klingner, J. K., Vaughn, S., Hughes, M. T., Schumm, J. S., & Elbaum, B. (1998). Outcomes for students with and without learning disabilities in inclusive classrooms. *Learning Disabilities Research & Practice, 13*, 153–161.

Klingner, J. K., Vaughn, S., & Schumm, J. S. (1998). Collaborative strategic reading during social studies in heterogeneous fourth-grade classrooms. *The Elementary School Journal, 99*, 1–22.

Learning and Technology Center at Vanderbilt University. (1996). The new adventures of Jasper Woodbury [Videodisc]. Mahwah, NJ: Erlbaum.

Levin, B., Hibbard, K., & Rock, T. (2002). Using problem-based learning as a tool for learning to teach students with special needs. *Teacher Education and Special Education, 25*, 278–290.

Maheady, L., Harper, G. F., & Sacca, K. (1988). A classwide peer tutoring system in a secondary, resource room program for the mildly handicapped. *Journal of Research and Development in Education, 21*, 76–83.

Mastropieri, M. A., Scruggs, T., Mohler, L., Beranek, M., Spencer, V., Boon, R. T., & Tabott, E. (2001). Can middle school students with serious reading difficulties help each other and learn anything? *Learning Disabilities Research and Practice, 16*, 18–27.

Palincsar, A. S., Magnusson, S. J., Collins, K. M., & Cutter, J. (2001). Making science accessible to all: Results of a design experiment in inclusive classrooms. *Learning Disability Quarterly, 24*, 15–32.

Pettig, K. L. (2000). On the road to differentiated practice. *Educational Leadership, 58*(1), 14–18.

Public Broadcasting Service. (1992). *The American experience: The Donner party.* Fairfax, VA: Author.

Slavin, R. E. (1995). *Cooperative learning: Theory, research, and practice* (2nd ed.). Boston: Allyn & Bacon.

Summey, H. K., & Strahan, D. B. (1997). An exploratory study of mainstreamed seventh graders' perceptions of an inclusive approach to instruction. *Remedial and Special Education, 18*, 36–45.

Tomlinson, C. A. (1999). *The differentiated classroom: Responding to the needs of all learners.* Alexandria, VA: Association for Supervision and Curriculum Development.

Torp, L., & Sage, S. (1998). *Problems as possibilities: Problem-based learning for K–12 education.* Alexandria, VA: Association for Supervision and Curriculum Development.

Vaughn, S., Gersten, R., & Chard, D. J. (2000). The underlying message in learning disability research: Findings from research synthesis. *Exceptional Children, 67*, 99–114.

Vaughn, S., & Schumm, J. S. (1995). Responsible inclusion for students with learning disabilities. *Journal of Learning Disabilities, 28*, 264–270.

ANNE B. BUCALOS, Ed.D. is Assistant Professor and Undergraduate Chair in the School of Education, Bellarmine University, Louisville, KY. **AMY S. LINGO**, Ed.D is Assistant Professor in the School of Education, Bellarmine University.

Service-Learning Opportunities That Include Students with Moderate and Severe Disabilities

HAROLD KLEINERT, VIRGINIA MCGREGOR, MICHELLE DURBIN, TINA BLANDFORD, KAREN JONES, JOSH OWENS, BETH HARRISON, AND SALLY MIRACLE

Picture this scenario:

For Young at Heart, a monthly social and recreational event targeted specifically for senior citizens, students with moderate and severe disabilities worked with Key Club members to plan and cook a dinner for seniors, as well as plan the entertainment for the evening. During the event, students helped prepare the meal, served it, and participated in the social activities. After a successful evening, the students wrote letters to local businesses to solicit funding for the next event. Students and their peer partners composed reflections and planned a celebration. Teachers included video-taped reflections and activities into students' alternate portfolios to document their learning.

The article describes the experiences of four high schools in Kentucky that have worked to develop inclusive service-learning activities for students with moderate and severe disabilities and their peers (see box, "What Does the Literature Say?"). The students worked through the Kentucky Peer Service-Learning Project. One of the projects was the Young at Heart program, which we describe in more detail later.

Implementing a Service-Learning Project

In implementing our service-learning projects, we have used the steps developed by *Students in Service to America* (2003), with special consideration to the needs and learning characteristics of students with moderate and severe disabilities. *Students in Service to America* described a 10-step process, to which we have added an 11th step, which is to link inclusive service-learning activities to the evidence of learning required for your state's alternate educational assessment under the Individuals with Disabilities Education Act (Amendments of 1997, IDEA '97).

We illustrate each step with details of the Young at Heart program, which one of the schools conducted. We also briefly discuss other service-learning projects undertaken by various school districts.

Step 1: Assess the Resources and Needs of Your Community and School

It is essential that we include all students in locating resources and needs. Students with moderate and severe disabilities rarely have the opportunity to plan their learning activities and how they would like to contribute to their community. Students with disabilities and their peers can jointly talk with civic groups and school organizations.

Another strategy is to consider assisting in an existing service-learning activity in your school or community.

For example, in one of our schools, students with disabilities and peer tutors jointly talked with the school principal, counselors, other students in the school, and school service clubs. The students with disabilities and peer tutors found out that the school's Key Club was looking for another group to help out with Young at Heart, a monthly social and recreational event targeted specifically for senior citizens. At this monthly event, students planned and cooked a dinner for seniors, as well as planned the entertainment for the evening.

Step 2: Develop Community Partnerships

Seek out the assistance of community organizations (e.g., churches and nonprofit organizations) in identifying the needs of your community. These organizations can provide direction and consultation to your project. Students with moderate and severe disabilities, in partnership with their typical peers, can meet with these organizations. Such experiences provide valued opportunities to practice communication, social, and

What Does the Literature Say about Service Learning?

Definition. Service learning is a well-recognized strategy for enabling students to integrate and apply the knowledge and skills they learn in school to address significant needs in their schools or communities (Yoder, Retish, & Wade, 1996). Students choose to do activities to benefit their community; within those activities, teachers infuse the academic curriculum and individualized student goals.

What separates service learning from simple volunteer or community service activities is the links to *both* the curriculum *and* to the students' reflections on what they have learned as a result of that activity. Service learning is thus directly tied to the academic curriculum, and for students with disabilities, into their individualized education program (IEP) objectives.

Benefits and Results. Educators are increasingly recognizing service learning as an important learning tool for *all* students.

- In a survey of 13 special educators involved in service-learning projects with their students, Brill (1994) found increases in attendance, academic skills, and social relationships with peers for the students with disabilities.
- Yoder et al. (1996) described an inclusive service-learning program between seventh- and eighth-grade students with learning disabilities, students with limited English proficiency (LEP), and general education students. These authors noted several benefits for this heterogeneous group of students, including increased self-esteem, self-knowledge, communication, problem-solving skills, and social skills.
- The Web site for *Students in Service to America* (2003) has identified other benefits, including enhanced

student engagement in school, the opportunity to learn about new careers, and a stronger sense of being part of one's community.
- Little research exists on the use of service learning for students with moderate and severe cognitive disabilities, especially in the context of *inclusive* learning opportunities with their peers. In one such study, Burns, Storey, and Certo (1999) described an inclusive-learning project that included high school students with severe disabilities and students without disabilities. The peers who participated demonstrated significantly more positive attitudes toward people with severe disabilities than they had before their participation. In contrast, these authors found that high school students who engaged in service activities directed solely to *helping* students with severe disabilities (e.g., Special Olympics) did not evidence significant changes in attitude.
- Gent and Gurecko (1998) have also discussed the appropriateness of service learning for students with severe disabilities, and the potential benefits of creating more natural peer supports, responsible citizenship, and integrated learning and assessment strategies. These authors have noted that even students with severe disabilities can learn to reflect on the impact of what they have learned.
- A recent study described service learning as a vehicle for authentic community-referenced instruction for all students (Kluth, 2000). The study showed that the project enabled students with disabilities to practice important life skills, while providing students without disabilities opportunities to connect what they learn in class to the real world.

problem-solving skills and allows those in the community to perceive students with disabilities in a new light.

Community organizations, like churches and nonprofit agencies, can provide direction and consultation to your project.

In the Young at Heart example, the students not only met with the Key Club members, but also contacted the Center for Senior Citizens each month to let them know the time, date, and theme for each event.

Step 3: Set Clear Educational Goals and Curriculum

Make sure that targeted service-learning skills are an extension of educational goals and individualized education program (IEP) objectives. Teachers can plan to measure achievement of goals through a variety of strategies, including instructional

data on IEP objectives, student journals, peer reflections (written by collaborating peers), and letters by local civic groups or community organizations documenting the students' achievements.

In the Young at Heart example, student IEP objectives included

- Initiating and sustaining social interactions,
- Cooking and meal planning skills.
- Functional math skills (planning a budget, purchasing items, measuring, and counting items for each participant).
- Recreational skills (playing card and other table games).

Step 4: Choose Project and Begin Planning

During this step, the students and teacher should complete their evaluation of needs, as well as the extent of their own resources. In selecting the service-learning project, teams should consider community and school partnerships (what part will each play?). In addition, the planning teams should think about how the goals of the service-learning activity will be continued after the project is completed.

In the Young at Heart example, students with moderate and severe disabilities were actively involved in each stage of the planning (e.g., identifying the theme for each evening, the menu, and the recreational activities). The teacher and students have already begun planning how this service-learning project can continue beyond the current year.

In subsequent years, the teacher plans to have her students write letters to businesses to see if they can donate money, supplies, or time to Young at Heart.

Step 5: Plan Project in Detail

During this step, students should develop a specific action plan and a timeline for completing their project, determine a project budget, and assign tasks for themselves, as well as work with any community partners to identify the steps or activities the partners will undertake (*Students in Service to America,* 2003). This step provides students with disabilities and their peers with excellent opportunities to practice time, budgeting, and money management skills and to learn to divide goals into a series of smaller steps or sub-goals.

In the Young at Heart project, students were actively involved in all steps (including the budget) and the teacher carefully considered how each student with a disability could work with a peer.

Students with moderate and severe disabilities were activity involved in each stage of the planning (e.g., identifying the theme for each evening, the menu, and the recreational activities).

Step 6: Seek Necessary Funding and Resources

Some service-learning projects may require additional resources. Other school clubs, faculty, students, parents, faith-based organizations, and local businesses may be willing to help, if asked. In our Young at Heart example, the teacher was able to secure a grant from a nonprofit agency for the activity.

Step 7: Implement and Manage the Project

As students begin their project, teachers should assist them in continuously monitoring their progress. Students with disabilities might even track their own performance on key learning objectives during this step (e.g., a money management skill for a student who has that skill on his or her IEP).

In the Young at Heart program, the students were in charge of decorations, food, and entertainment for each monthly event. For the Thanksgiving event, the students decided to have formal seating for the dinner, with a peer and a student with a disability

seated at each table with several senior citizens in order to get to know the seniors better.

One student with a moderate disability, whose IEP objectives included initiating and sustaining interactions, evaluated her own performance on how well she did each time in practicing those skills. She learned not only to initiate interactions, but to even request her favorite tasks each month for Young at Heart.

Step 8: Devise Reflection Activities

Involve students, on an ongoing basis, in reflecting on what they have achieved and learned. Peers can assist students with moderate and severe disabilities in composing their reflections. Students can also document their learning by taking photographs and videotapes, or through a pictorial or photographic story. They can also integrate digital photographs into a peer service-learning project Web site. Reflections and other documentation of student learning can be excellent additions to student portfolios and can help to promote students' sense of ownership and control over their own learning (Ezell and Klein, 2003).

In the Young at Heart example, both students with disabilities and peer tutors have written reflections about their participation in Young at Heart (see boxes).

Step 9: Assess and Evaluate Your Service-Learning Program

Teachers can assist students in collecting data on their own performance. Teachers and students can also conduct interviews with others (community organization, service recipients, and other teachers) to evaluate the effect of their service-learning activity.

Peer Tutor Reflection

"Watching the students with disabilities open up and communicate with other people made me realize how much of a regular life they can live if given the opportunity to do so. I saw students in totally a new light outside of the classroom and outside of the daily math and reading work. They carried on conversations and worked at assisting everyone else just like the peer tutors did.

"Young at Heart not only helped the students with disabilities to interact with their peers and community, but it helped me to realize how incredible these students actually are. I honestly feel that I learned so much more from this experience than they did. I learned exactly how much they have to offer this world and how capable they are of doing things.

"Hopefully this event also helped to impact the community's opinions on students with disabilities. I hope the senior citizens that took part in this experience gained a better understanding for people with disabilities and realized they're people, too."

—Kali Arison, Peer, Hopkins County Central High School

For example, one strategy for evaluating the success of Young at Heart would be to survey the senior citizens about their participation at the end of the year. Such a survey would give students further opportunities for practice on IEP skills (e.g., initiating and sustaining interactions, calculating and charting the number of participants who reported that they had enjoyed the monthly activities).

Step 10: Celebrate Students' Achievements

Celebration is crucial to any service-learning project. For all students involved in the activity, it is a chance to celebrate the results of their work. For students with moderate and severe disabilities, a celebration provides the opportunity to give back to the community and to be recognized for that achievement. Participation in a service-learning project can be a great source of pride and of a sense of one's own competence.

A celebration is also a time for recognizing the contributions of one's partners. In the Young at Heart program, the teacher, students with disabilities, and peer tutors have planned a cook-out the last week of school to recognize student achievements and to celebrate their achievements. They will also recognize individual students for their participation in the program with a certificate. As they plan for next year, they are hoping to include even more students in the service-learning project.

Step 11: Include the Service-Learning Project Into Alternate Portfolio Entries, If Applicable

As we have noted, service-learning activities provide a wonderful source of evidence for student portfolios. In several states, that evidence can be used to document

- The achievement of targeted IEP objectives.
- Generalized performance across school and community settings.
- The student's ability to work toward a group goal with peers.
- Opportunities to explore a potential career option.

Portfolio evidence can include journal entries and other self-reflections, photographs, student instructional performance data, peer reflections about the student's work, and letters from participating community agencies on the success of the project (Kleinert & Kearns, 2001).

In the Young at Heart example, students with moderate and severe disabilities have had their reflections included in their alternate assessment portfolios, along with evidence of achieving their targeted skills. Peers have included their own reflections as one of the required writing pieces in Kentucky's writing portfolio required for graduation.

Young at Heart has been so successful that the students with moderate and severe disabilities and peers have decided to start their own service-learning club, *Together as Peers,* and have designed a shirt for their club with *Together as Peers* on the front and the signatures of all the club members on the back

of each shirt. The club motto is "Attitudes Are the Real Disabilities." The club now has 67 members, with students with disabilities and peers paired for each office (e.g., President, Vice-President). Each student member has to have 6 service-learning hours, and officers must complete 9 hours.

Other Examples of Service-Learning Projects

The following are other examples of service-learning projects across our participating schools.

Care Packages

Students collected nonperishable supplies for care packages for soldiers stationed overseas, and especially in war-torn areas. Students had to identify recently graduated, former students from their school who were serving overseas, determine an overall budget for their project (including the approximate cost of care packages and postage), what they could send that the soldiers would need, collect or purchase the supplies, make the care packages and take them to the post office. Students also learned a part of the history of the region in which the men and women were serving (e.g., Iraq), learned about the origins of the conflict, and followed the progress of other soldiers' efforts.

One school raised money for this project by conducting a bake sale that was promoted by the local Wal-Mart; students had to bake and sell the Items, while learning targeted IEP objectives in measuring, following directions, counting money, working in a group and on interpersonal skills.

In purchasing the items for the care packages, the students had to select the best buys for their money, learning valuable lessons in consumerism. One school also included teddy bears in care packages, so soldiers could give the bears to Iraqi children.

Reflections from Students with Disabilities

"We decorated the cafeteria and had a meal for them (Senior Citizens) and I sung for the Young at Heart. There was about 40 senior citizens there." "We wanted to help people in need." "We learned about service." "It was a lot of fun to help others."

Community Health

Students helped to plan a Community Health Fair. One of our schools has a Sports Medicine and Health Department that collaborates with a local hospital. Several of the students with disabilities take Sports Medicine classes. Together with their peers, they are planning a spring Community Health Fair open to the public.

The fair will include free blood pressure and cholesterol checks, information about preventative health care and common diseases that are especially prevalent in Kentucky (e.g., diabetes, heart disease), as well as women's and children's health issues. Students are responsible for working together to obtain the health care workers for each booth, and in the process, are learning important elements of living healthy lives themselves.

Students participating in the state alternate assessment will be able to include this activity as an important part of their Health entry for their required portfolios. These entries will document the state learner standards of "Students demonstrate the skills that they need to remain physically healthy and to accept responsibility for their own physical well-being" and "Students demonstrate the skills to evaluate and use services and resources available in their community."

Service-learning projects provide opportunities for students to practice time, budgeting, and money management skills and to learn to divide goals into a series of smaller steps.

Reading Program

Students created children's books and read those books to preschool and primary-age students. Together, students with moderate and severe disabilities and peers at three of our schools have created story books and story boards (illustrations) of children's books to read to preschool and primary-age children. Not only does this activity increase valued literacy skills for students with disabilities, but it also provides these students an added opportunity to practice those skills with students just beginning reading instruction.

Targeted skills incorporated into this service-learning activity included increased oral communication skills, sight word vocabulary, reading comprehension, and writing in complete sentences.

Toy Drive

Students conducted a drive to collect used toys in good condition to package and distribute to local facilities for Christmas. The students and peers decided where the toys would go. This activity was done as a whole school project (i.e., all students were invited to participate), to increase the number of toys brought in.

The students also held a Christmas craft sale to raise the funds needed to package and wrap the gifts, purchase batteries, and buy other accessories. During the craft sale, the students worked on IEP objectives for measuring, completion of task, following directions, handling money and making change, salesmanship, and detail to the craftsmanship of the items they were making.

Recycling

Students held a school wide recycling project in collaboration with the School Ecology Club and with a unit on recycling that

---

Teacher and Parent Reflections on Service Learning

Teacher Reflection

"The only thing I would do different is start sooner. I have been depriving my students by not giving them a way to give back to their community and feeling they have value. This project has built confidence and self-esteem for students with and without disabilities. Service learning has helped me to remember why I am a teacher!"

—Virginia McGregor, Teacher, Hopkins County Central High School

Parent Reflection

"Service learning helps students with disabilities learn about helping others. Students with disabilities often receive a great deal of help. It is so wonderful for them to help someone else. It has given Karli a great sense of awareness about how she can help others in need. This project also provided opportunities where Karli could feel that she was doing something important. I can see how gratifying it is for Karli to help someone else and make someone smile."

—Lori Edds, Parent

---

was part of Earth Science class. Students learned to weigh and calculate the amount of usable recyclables collected each week, as well as the difference between hazardous and safe materials.

Students had to do research in the library on what could be recycled, and they had to take home a survey and interview neighbors and relatives on whether they recycled, and why they did or did not do so.

Meals on Wheels

A student with a moderate to severe disability and a peer were paired for this activity. Together, they counted out what was needed for each meal (meals, utensils, drinks, desserts, etc.), and delivered the meals with staff supervision on their prescribed route. The student with a disability worked on critical communication skills (greeting each person and engaging in social conversations) and on targeted IEP math skills related to counting and addition. After graduating, the student with a disability found paid employment in a similar job delivering ink cartridges to businesses.

Clothing Drive

Students conducted a clothing drive for a garage sale to benefit Habitat for Humanity. Students were responsible for collecting, sorting, cleaning, and packing the clothes, in preparation for the Habitat for Humanity Garage Sale.

As a follow-up activity for Habitat for Humanity, students are working to construct a storage shed to house the tools used in building a Habitat house. When the house is completed, the tool shed will remain as a storage shed for the new home owners. Student learning objectives included independent living skills, math skills (measurement), and working in a group to accomplish an overall goal.

Children's Hospital

Students collected toys, books, and money for children served by the local Hospice program. Money collected was used to purchase books; students used their own knowledge of favorite children's books to make their choices. Students worked on money management (counting money, purchasing within a budget), as well as reading skills in selecting appropriate books.

Pledges for a Benefit

Students raised pledge money and volunteered at the local Down Syndrome Buddy Walk, to benefit children and adults with Down syndrome (two schools participated in this project).

Benefits of Service Learning for Students with Moderate and Severe Disabilities

Service learning provides students with moderate and severe disabilities the opportunity to give back to their communities. Too often, educators and other service providers view these students only as the recipients of services (Brill, 1994), be it through such formal services as special education, vocational rehabilitation, related services or through more informal supports, such as peer tutoring.

In addition to the benefits reported in the literature for students with and without mild disabilities (e.g., increased self-esteem, problem-solving skills, social skills), we have found that service-learning opportunities for students with moderate and severe disabilities have led to improved attitudes of peers about these students' true capabilities.

We have also found that inclusive service-learning activities allow students with disabilities who are participating in their state's alternate assessment to document increased evidence of generalization of targeted skills across multiple settings, increased use of natural supports, and document higher levels of self-direction and self-determination. Direct evidence of targeted skills, the generalization of those targeted skills, natural supports, and measures of self-determination are currently included within the scoring rubric of several states' alternate educational assessments under IDEA '97 (Browder et al., in press; Kleinert, Green, Hurte, Clayton & Oetinger, 2002). Thus service learning can provide students with an important vehicle for demonstrating what they know and are able to do.

Incorporating Student Projects into Alternate Assessments

Students have included their service-learning projects into our state's alternate assessment in a variety of ways, as follows:

- Service-learning projects provide excellent vehicles for students to demonstrate their learning in targeted

skills in such general curriculum areas as Science (the ecology service project noted previously) and Health (the Community Health Fair project noted previously). Math skills have included purchasing, choosing the best buys (comparative shopping), managing a budget, and measurement skills. Language arts skills have been incorporated through the students' own reflections on service learning, and through writing and adapting stories for young children. Targeted skills in these and related areas are included in most states' alternate assessments (Browder et al., in press), and content from the areas of Reading, Math, and Science are now a requirement for alternate assessments under No Child Left Behind.

- Through service learning, students are able to show that they can apply what they have learned in the classroom to other settings throughout their school and community. A number of states have included measures of generalization and multiple settings as part of their scoring rubrics for alternate assessments (Browder et al., in press).

- Service learning allows students to document sustained social interaction and cooperative group skills, also measured in several states' alternate assessments. Kentucky, as well as several other states, includes a measure of a student's network of social relationships as a part of its alternate assessment. Service-learning projects such as Young at Heart, in which students with and without disabilities are actively engaged with senior citizens and others in the community, provides vivid examples of such social networks.

- Service learning provides excellent ways for students to demonstrate such skills as planning a project and monitoring and evaluating its success. Choosing, planning, monitoring, and evaluating one's performance are all essential components of self-determination (Agran, King-Sears, Wehmeyer, & Copeland, 2003), an educational outcome that researchers have shown to be directly related to postschool success (Wehmeyer & Palmer, 2003).

Service learning provides students with moderate and severe disabilities the opportunity to give back to their communities.

Peer, Student, Teacher, and Parent Reflections

We collected reflections by a peer and reflections by students with disabilities about their service-learning projects, respectively (see boxes). We also noted perspectives from a teacher and a parent. In our interviews at participating schools, we found that administrators, general and special educators, students with and without disabilities, and parents of students with and without disabilities saw positive effects from these students' involvement with service learning.

For example, one administrator noted that, as a result of his school's peer tutoring and service-learning program, "students seem more enthusiastic about their school work and responsibilities and accomplishing the tasks and also the goals that they have during their high school years."

A parent of a participating peer at another of our schools echoed that theme:

He's found a purpose in life and a goal to reach. It seemed like he was just running and didn't know what he wanted to do. . . . But it seems like he has finally found something that he has found satisfaction and enjoyment out of at the same time.

Clearly the benefits of these programs go both ways—for students with and without disabilities!

References

Agran, M., King-Sears, M., Wehmeyer, M., & Copeland, S. (2003). *Teachers' guides to inclusive practices: Student-directed learning.* Baltimore: Paul H. Brookes.

Brill, C. (1994). The effects of participation in service-learning on adolescents with disabilities. *Journal of Adolescence, 17,* 369–380.

Browder, D., Ahlgrim-Delzell, L., Flowers, C., Karvonen, M., Spooner, F., Algozzine, R. (in press). How states implement alternate assessments for students with disabilities and recommendations for national policy. *Journal of Disability Policy Studies.*

Burns, M., Storey, K., & Certo, N. (1999). Effect of service learning on attitudes towards students with severe disabilities. *Education and Training in Mental Retardation and Developmental Disabilities, 34,* 58–65.

Ezell, D., & Klein, C. (2003). Impact of portfolio assessment on locus of control of students with and without disabilities. *Education and Training in Developmental Disabilities, 38,* 220–228.

Gent, P., & Gurecka, L. (1998). Service learning; A creative strategy for inclusive classrooms. *Journal of the Association of Persons with Severe Handicaps, 23,* 261–271.

Kleinert, H., Green, P., Hurte, M., Clayton, J., & Oetinger, C. (2002). Creating and using meaningful alternate assessments. *TEACHING Exceptional Children, 34*(5), 40–47.

Kleinert, H., & Kearns, J. (2001). *Alternate assessment: Measuring outcomes and supports for students with disabilities.* Baltimore: Paul H. Brookes.

Kluth, P. (2000). Community referenced learning and the inclusive classroom. *Remedial and Special Education, 21,* 19–26.

No Child Left Behind Act of 2001, Pub. L. No. 107-110, 115 Stat. 1425 (2002).

Students in Service to America. (2003). Retrieved December 10. 2003, from http://www.studentsinservicetoamerica.org/

Wehmeyer, M., & Palmer, S. (2003). Adult outcomes for students with cognitive disabilities three-years after high school: The impact of self-determination. *Education and Training in Developmental Disabilities, 38,* 131–144

Yoder, D., Relish, E., & Wade, R. (1996). Service learning: Meeting student and community needs. *TEACHING Exceptional Children, 28*(4), 14–18.

HAROLD KLEINERT (CEC Chapter #180), Executive Director, Interdisciplinary Human Development Institute, University of Kentucky, Lexington. **VIRGINIA MCGREGOR** (CEC Chapter #278), Teacher, Hopkins County Schools, Madisonville, Kentucky. **MICHELLE DURBIN,** Teacher, Jefferson County Public Schools, Louisville, Kentucky. **TINA BLANDFORD,** Teacher, Daviess County Public Schools, Owensboro, Kentucky. **KAREN JONES** (CEC Chapter #5), Teacher, Woodford County Public Schools, Versailles, Kentucky. **JOSH OWENS** (CEC Chapter #960), Teacher, Scott County Public Schools, Georgetown, Kentucky. **BETH HARRISON,** Project Director, Interdisciplinary Human Development Institute, University of Kentucky, Lexington. **SALLY MIRACLE** (CEC Chapter #180), Consultant, Central Kentucky Special Education Cooperative, University of Kentucky, Lexington.

Address correspondence to Harold Kleinert, Interdisciplinary Human Development Institute, University of Kentucky, 126 Mineral Industries Blds., Lexington, KY 40506-0051 (e-mail: hklein@uky.edu)

This article was supported, in part, by the U.S. Administration on Developmental Disabilities (Grant No. 90DN0107/01). However, the opinions expressed do not necessarily reflect the position or policy of the U.S. Administration on Developmental Disabilities, and no official endorsement should be inferred.

Fitting In

*Tips for Promoting Acceptance
and Friendships for Students with Autism
Spectrum Disorders in Inclusive Classrooms*

**In order for students with autism spectrum disorders (ASD)
to find acceptance and to develop friendships similar to those
of their typical peers, they must be provided with the opportunities
to do so. With appropriate planning and supports, inclusive
classrooms can provide such opportunities for children with ASD,
just as they do for typical children. This article provides tips that
teachers and parents can use to foster acceptance and friendships
of students with ASD in general education classrooms.**

E. AMANDA BOUTOT

We all need friends. For many children with disabilities, especially autism spectrum disorders (ASD), the development of social relationships may be difficult due to the nature of the disability. Children with ASD may have difficulty reading social cues; initiating, sustaining, or terminating a conversation; or behaving appropriately with peers. Further, many children with ASD have a restricted repertoire of interests or behaviors that limits interaction with same-aged peers. Finally, communication with peers may be further challenged due to limited speech and/or use of alternative communication devices.

How, then, do children with ASD make and keep friends? It is a challenging task for parents and teachers, but one that is necessary if children with ASD are to become socially successful. By interacting with same-aged, typical peers, children with ASD have been shown to improve their behaviors, communication and social skills, and play behaviors (Wolfberg, 1999), all of which are important to their overall development. Further, parents often report that having friendships is an important goal for their children with ASD.

Inclusive classrooms are one place where friendships between children with and without disabilities have the opportunity to develop and grow. However, just placing children with disabilities with typical peers does not necessarily ensure that friendships will occur (Boutot & Bryant, 2005). In order for friendships to blossom, there must first be an acceptance of the child with disabilities by the other children. For children with ASD, certain behaviors, the use of strange communication devices, or the reliance on a teaching assistant may limit their acceptance by the other students (Boutot & Bryant, 2005). Thus, parents and teachers need to take steps to promote acceptance of children with ASD and positive social interactions between them and typical peers. In this article, the concept and goal of promoting and maintaining acceptance and friendships for children with ASD within the general education classroom is referred to as *social inclusion*. The philosophy of social inclusion is that all students in a classroom can work together and "belong" in the class. This article provides information on what it means to be accepted (i.e., belong) in an inclusion class for children with disabilities, specifically ASD, as well as tips for teachers and parents on how to promote acceptance and friendships in inclusive environments.

Social Acceptance of Children without Disabilities

To understand what it will take to promote acceptance and friendships between students with and without disabilities, it is helpful to know something about how students without disabilities feel about each other and with whom they prefer to spend their time. For example, children prefer peers with whom they have something in common. Children also prefer peers who are more like themselves in terms of dress, language, behavior, and ability. Children tend to prefer students whom the teacher also likes. Finally, children prefer peers with whom they spend most of their time; hence, proximity is a key to preference (Adler, Kless, & Adler, 1992). Popularity is a concept that is often of utmost concern for typical children; Table 1 features an overview of popular versus unpopular characteristics. What makes a child popular or unpopular among his or her peers? Research over the last few decades has found consistently that the more popular students are those who wear current or trendy clothing, have leadership skills, have good social skills, and are good communicators. Popularity varies between the sexes, with girls who are better at academics being more popular, while more popular boys are those with high athletic ability. Less popular students, conversely, are those that play alone, are from lower socioeconomic status, have poor social skills, do not cooperate with others, are poor athletes (males) or poor students (females), and who display inappropriate or extreme behaviors (Farmer & Farer, 1996). It is not a stretch of the imagination to see that some students, by the very nature of their disability, may have difficulty meeting the required "image" of popularity and acceptance.

Social Acceptance of Students with Disabilities

Though disability is only one facet of any child's persona, the disability itself often prohibits or challenges some of the attributes related to acceptance and popularity among students without disabilities. For this reason, it is not unusual to find that in many cases, our efforts at social inclusion are met with failure or, at best, limited success. Research into the social acceptance of children with disabilities has consistently shown that students with disabilities are not as well accepted by their typical peers as are those without disabilities (Bender, Wyne, Struck, & Bailey, 1984; Sabornie & Kauffman, 1987). Table 2 features factors associated with social acceptance versus nonacceptance of students with disabilities by their typical peers (Brady, Shores, McEvor, Ellis, & Fox, 1987; Garrison-Harrell, Kamps, & Kravits, 1997; Krantz & McClannahan, 1993; Lord & Hopkins, 1986; Muncschenk

Table 1 Popular Versus Unpopular Characteristics

Popular	Unpopular
Wearing trendy clothing	Being from low socioeconomic status
Displaying leadership skills	Playing alone
Good social skills	Poor social skills
Good communication skills	Lack of cooperation
Good at academics (girls) or athletics (boys)	Poor students (girls) or athletes (boys)
Liked by the teacher	Display inappropriate or extreme behaviors

& Sasso, 1995; Nientimp & Cole, 1992; Odom, Hoyson, Jamieson, & Strain, 1985). Research has found that children with disabilities tend to spend time with those with the same abilities and disabilities as themselves. Although many studies have found a lower rate of acceptance for students with learning and behavioral differences, more recent studies have found no differences between students with disabilities and those without disabilities in terms of their acceptance (Hudson & Clunies-Ross, 1984; Sabornie & Kauffman, 1986). Although acceptance does not always mean friendships, these same studies have found that children with disabilities in inclusion classrooms were, in fact, members of a meaningful social group (Boutot & Bryant, 2005; Farmer & Farer, 1996).

Table 2 Factors Associated with Acceptance Versus Non-Acceptance of Students with Disabilities

Acceptance	Non-Acceptance
Perceived as being part of the class	Frequent removal from classroom
Peer tutors and/or independence	Presence of a one-on-one adult assistant
Limited self-abuse, aggression, or loud behaviors	Extreme or disruptive behaviors
Overall classroom culture of acceptance and tolerance	Negative attitude or treatment by teacher
Knowledge of the disability or differences as well as similarities	Lack of understanding of disability or differences
Specific training	Unusual or "scary" equipment or behaviors

Social

Lack of eye contact

Little or no recognition of others' emotions

Little or no response to nonverbal social cues

Difficulty reading social situations in a group

Difficulty controlling one's own emotions

Inappropriate or immature social skills

Communication

Limited to no speech

Odd prosody

No recognition of sarcasm, metaphors, or abstract
concepts

Literal thinking and speaking

Echolalia

Behavioral

Perseveration on certain topics or objects
of interest

Resistance to change

Preference to sameness

Stereotypical movements (flapping, rocking, etc.)

Self-abusive or aggressive behaviors

Figure 1   Characteristics of autism spectrum disorders.

Compared to typical students, students with ASD often have significant social skills deficits that may interfere with their acceptance by others. In addition, students with autism vary greatly in terms of severity of autistic characteristics that may prohibit successful social interactions (Mesibov & Shae, 1996). According to the *Diagnostic and Statistical Manual of Mental Disorders–Fourth Edition* (*DSM-IV;* American Psychiatric Association, 1994), the primary characteristics of autism fall into three categories: communication deficits or delays, stereotypic behaviors, and limited social relatedness. Sample characteristics of communication deficits include echolalic speech and a delay or failure to develop speech. The category of stereotypic behavior is characterized by insistence on sameness, preoccupation with certain objects or parts of objects, resistance to change, perseverative movements such as rocking or hand flapping, and self-injurious behaviors such as head banging. Lack of eye contact and lack of social and emotional reciprocity are examples of social relatedness deficits. Each characteristic symptom of autism on its own may not directly influence acceptance or friendships of a student with autism in general education setting; however, the severity of the characteristics could contribute to social success. See Figure 1 for a list of possible social, behavioral, and communicative characteristics of students with ASD.

To help students with ASD become more socially accepted and develop friendships among their typical peers, families and teachers must have a better understanding of the characteristics that contribute to acceptance and friendships. Teachers also need to be able to teach skills or remediate behaviors that may negatively affect a student's social acceptance. Further, planning is key to creating an environment that promotes "fitting in" of students with ASD with their typical peers.

Planning Strategies to Promote Acceptance and Friendships

Although some persons may suggest that simply educating students with disabilities alongside their typical peers will result in greater acceptance and promote friendships between the groups, this is not always the case. To better ensure that the goals of acceptance and meaningful social relationships will happen, careful and thoughtful planning is necessary. The following tips will aid in successful social inclusion for children with ASD:

- select classrooms wisely,
- schedule wisely,
- select supports wisely,
- prepare the classroom teacher,
- prepare the general education students,
- prepare the student with ASD, and
- secure and maintain family support.

Selecting a Classroom

Depending on the size of the school and its level (elementary or secondary), options as to the number of potential classrooms will vary. Try to select a classroom with a teacher who shares, or at least understands, the philosophy of social inclusion: that all students should work together and belong in the class. If the teacher believes that the student with ASD is not just a visitor in their class, but is to be a contributing member, it will support successful social inclusion for that child. Further, whenever possible, special education teachers should spend some time observing the general education classroom to assess its appropriateness for the student with ASD. Look for things such as teaching style: Does the teacher use appropriate pacing, positive reinforcement and corrective feedback, and multimodal instruction? Does he or she use cooperative student groups, or teach in mostly lecture format? Are expectations communicated effectively, and is downtime limited? Second, look at the dynamics of the class: Do the students seem to work together as a team, or in groups of teams, and is there a spirit of support and cooperation among them? Also assess the physical environment: Are there sensory distractions such as poor lighting or loud noises that may distract the student with ASD? Can the students see the board/screen/teacher from their seats? Are the acoustics appropriate? Finally, are all things easily accessible? Just as you want to select a classroom that best fits your student, you also want your student to fit into that classroom. Try to select a classroom in which bringing in a new student will cause least disruption.

Scheduling

While ideally you are placing a student into an inclusive environment for all or most of his or her education, there are times when removal from class may be necessary. Work with the classroom teacher so that disruptions are minimal when the student needs to come and go from class. Try to schedule departure and reentry times around natural transitions in the classroom so that they are less noticeable by the other students (such as coming back from lunch, etc.). Further, try to plan for related services to be provided in the natural setting as often as possible to eliminate the need for removal from class. Work with both the classroom teacher and the therapists to find times that work best and to plan ways to implement related service instruction within the typically occurring activities of the general education class.

Selecting Supports

Supports may be anything from copied notes from the board to a paraeducator. The rule of thumb is to select the least intrusive support necessary for the student to be successful. Think independence and normalcy; the other students rarely have an adult sit with them throughout a lesson to help them. Students with ASD will fit in much better with the class if the use of paraprofessionals is kept to a minimum. Ask support staff to help other students as well and to stand away from the student with ASD until assistance is needed. Modifications to the curriculum or the lesson should also not be disrupting or too noticeable to the rest of the class. Discretion is key in helping the student with ASD fit into his or her inclusion class.

Preparing the Classroom Teacher

No matter how willing a general education teacher is to have a student with ASD join his classroom, he or she may need help in making it work. It is helpful if the teacher has some background knowledge of special education and ASD, but if not, the special education teacher should plan to act as a resource for the teacher in everything from planning and implementing instruction to grading. Share resources, model appropriate instruction, assist with modifications and accommodations, and offer suggestions for management and teaching strategies that work well with a particular student. Special educators are sometimes viewed as having a "bag of tricks" that we keep hidden, locked away from the eyes of the general educator. Dispel this myth by being open and forthcoming with any and all suggestions.

Preparing the General Education Students

Many times, teachers do not think of preparing the general classroom peers for the arrival of a student with ASD in the interest of confidentiality. How much and what type of information you share will depend greatly on the grade level of the students and the nature of the disability. For example, in a high school situation, it may not be wise to draw attention to the student with ASD at all, unless the characteristics are disruptive or the student requires specialized equipment or other supports that will be noticeable. In elementary schools, various means of preparing typical peers have been noted. One common way is to have a class meeting, wherein someone (the general education teacher, the special education teacher, a peer who knows the student with ASD, a sibling, or a parent) will speak to the class regarding the student with ASD prior to his or her arrival (Boutot & Bryant, 2005). During such meetings, it is best to minimize those things that the student cannot do, or that make him or her different from the others, and instead emphasize things the student is good at, likes to do, and has interests in, as well as any hobbies, sports, and so on that may be similar to those of other students in the class. Emphasizing how much the students are alike versus how the students are different will promote acceptance of the student with the disability as someone "just like me." Teachers may read a book depicting someone who learns, acts, or moves differently from others (e.g., *Andy and His Yellow Frisbee,* Thompson, 1996) as a way to open discussion about the special needs of the student with ASD. Sometimes it is helpful to open with a discussion of the many ways that all people are alike and different. It is a good idea to make the typical students aware of any special equipment, modifications, communication aids, and so forth that the child with the ASD may bring to class. This will minimize confusion, concern, and curiosity that first day. If the child has some particular behaviors or issues that may draw attention or require special techniques, such as hand flapping or head banging, and so forth, it is best to mention these as well. The students should be encouraged to talk to, play with, and work with the student with ASD, and perhaps some time could be spent on teaching specific skills for doing so. Another possibility is to have one to three students from the inclusion class come into the special education class to meet and work with the student with ASD prior to his or her moving to the general education class. Which students should go will be up to the classroom teacher, but for best promotion of acceptance and friendships, select students whom the others look up to, that is, those who are most popular. This is a particularly good idea at secondary levels, where students move from class to class frequently and having a "class discussion" may not be feasible or appropriate. Select one or two students from each class, preferably a student or two who will share more than one class with the student with ASD, and bring them in as peer tutors before moving your student to the inclusion class. Having a "friend" already in the class will help the student with ASD look and feel more secure and fit in more quickly. When other students see a child (especially a more popular child) interacting naturally with the student with ASD, they will be more likely to accept him or her as a member of the class with whom they, too, might be friends.

Preparing the Student with ASD

The most important outcome of an inclusive education placement for a child with ASD is success, academically (in terms of Individualized Education Program [IEP] goals and objectives and/or progress toward the general education curriculum) as well as socially. Any skill deficits that may hinder social successes should be addressed prior to the move to general education. For example, if the student has a history of aggressive outbursts that have not been adequately decreased and/or prevented in the self-contained room, it is unlikely they will get better once in the inclusive one. Teaching self-management skills, coping and problem solving skills, social skills, functional and social communication, and self-advocacy will aid in the smooth transition of the student with ASD to the general education setting. The special education teacher can also prepare him or her by simulating a general education classroom environment in the special education classroom. If the general education teacher requires students to raise their hands before speaking, maintain a homework log, and come to class on time, for example, then begin by teaching the student with ASD these same skills and reinforcing their use. The more similar the two environments (special and inclusion classrooms), the less likely the student with ASD will react negatively to the change. Another option is to videotape a general education class for the student with ASD to watch prior to making the move. This will provide him or her opportunities to view expectations as well as provide opportunities for direct instruction of specific skills with typical peers as models. The use of social stories is also a good idea, both as an initial preparation for the transition as well as a daily reminder of expected social behaviors in the inclusion setting. Although this may not be their first general education class placement, there may still be some trepidation when going to a new place. Smoothing this transition will set the student with ASD up for success.

Securing and Maintaining Family Support

Family involvement and communication between home and school are vital in special education. When a student is in a general education setting, communication should also involve the general education teacher. Help to establish written communication on a regular basis. Set up face-to-face meetings prior to the child's placement in the general education class so that the parents and the general education teacher can feel more at ease with each other. Use a communication log or notebook that the inclusion teacher, the special education teacher, and the parents can send back and forth daily or weekly to help maintain communication. The student will feel more a part of the general education classroom if his or her teacher and parents are on the same page and in regular communication.

Conclusion

Everybody needs friends. Positive social relationships with peers are an essential ingredient to a good quality of life, both for children and adults. In order for students with ASD to develop friendships similar to those of their typical peers, they must have opportunities to do so. These opportunities can occur through interactions with typical peers in the community and school. Inclusive classrooms provide opportunities for friendships for children with ASD, just as they do for typical children, with appropriate supports and planning. Parents and professionals are encouraged to educate, enhance, and embrace opportunities for the social inclusion of students with ASD so that they can fit in the social network of their classrooms, community, and greater society.

References

Adler, P. A., Kless, S. J., & Adler, P. (1992). Socialization to gender roles: Popularity among elementary school boys and girls. *Sociology of Education, 65,* 169–188.

American Psychiatric Association. (1994). *Diagnostic and Statistical Manual of Mental Disorders (4th ed.).* Washington, DC: Author.

Bender, W. N., Wyne, M. D., Struck, G. B., & Bailey, D. B. (1984). Relative peer status of learning disabled, educable mentally handicapped, low achieving, and normally achieving children. *Child Study Journal, 13,* 209–216.

Boutot, E. A., & Bryant, D. P. (2005). Social integration of students with autism in inclusive settings. *Education and Training in Developmental Disabilities, 40*(1), 14–23.

Brady, M. P., Shores, R. E., McEvoy, M. A., Ellis, D., & Fox, J. (1987). Increasing social interactions of severely handicapped autistic children. *Journal of Autism and Developmental Disorders, 17,* 375–390.

Farmer, T. W., & Farer, E. M. Z. (1996). The social relationships of students with exceptionalities in mainstream classrooms: Social networks and homophily. *Exceptional Children, 62,* 431–450.

Garrison-Harrell, L., Kamps, D. M., & Kravits, T. (1997). The effects of peer networks on social-communicative behaviors for students with autism. *Focus on Autism and Other Developmental Disabilities, 12,* 241–256.

Hudson, A., & Clunies-Ross, G. (1984). A study of the integration of children with intellectual handicaps into regular schools.

Australia and New Zealand Journal of Developmental Disabilities, 10(3), 165–177.

Krantz, P. J., & McClannahan, M. E. (1993). Teaching children with autism to initiate to peers: Effects of a script-fading procedures. *Journal of Applied Behavior Analysis, 26*(1), 121–132.

Lord, C., & Hopkins, J.M. (1986). The social behavior of autistic children with younger and same-age nonhandicapped peers. *Journal of Autism and Developmental Disorders, 16*(3), 249–262.

Mesibov, G. B., & Shae, V. (1996). Full inclusion and students with autism. *Journal of Autism and Developmental Disorders, 26,* 337–346.

Muncschenk, N. A., & Sasso, G. M. (1995). Assessing sufficient social exemplars for students with autism. *Behavior Disorders, 21,* 62–78.

Nientimp, E. G., & Cole, C. L. (1992). Teaching socially valid social interaction responses to students with severe disabilities in an integrated school setting. *Journal of School Psychology, 30,* 343–354.

Odom, S. L., Hoyson, M., Jamieson, B., & Strain, P. S. (1985). Increasing preschoolers' peer social interactions: Cross-setting and component analysis. *Journal of Applied Behavior Analysis, 18*(1), 3–16.

Sabornie, E. J., & Kauffman, J. M. (1986). Social acceptance of learning disabled adolescents. *Learning Disability Quarterly, 9,* 55–60.

Sabornie, E. J., & Kauffman, J. M. (1987). Assigned, received, and reciprocal social status of EMR and nonhandicapped adolescents. *Education and Training of the Mentally Retarded, 22,* 139–149.

Thompson, M. (1996). *Andy and His Yellow Frisbee.* Bethesda, MD: Woodbine House.

Wolfberg, P. J. (1999). *Play and imagination in children with autism.* New York: Teachers College Press.

E. AMANDA BOUTOT, PhD, is an assistant professor at DePaul University on the Lincoln Park Campus in Chicago. Dr. Boutot researches and publishes in the area of autism. Specific research interests include play, social, and communication development; early identification; family issues; and inclusion. Address: E. Amanda Boutot, DePaul University, School of Education, 2320 N. Kenmore Ave., Chicago, IL 60614-3250; e-mail: eboutot@depaul.edu

From *Intervention in School and Clinic,* by E. Amanda Boutot, Vol. 42, No. 3, January 2007, pp. 156–161. Copyright © 2007 by Pro-Ed, Inc. Reprinted by permission.

UNIT 6

Emotional and Behavioral Disorders

Unit Selections

Key Points to Consider

- Which emotional and behavioral disorders should be referred for psychiatric treatment? How can teachers detect them?

- Would you want to teach emotionally and behaviorally disordered young women in jail? Find out why one teacher found it a choice assignment.

- What are the easiest ways to manage classroom behavior and positively impact student learning?

- How can students with EBD be taught to manage their own behavior? What results occur?

Student Web Site

www.mhcls.com/online

Internet Reference

Further information regarding this Web site may be found in this book's preface or online.

Pacer Center: Emotional Behavioral Disorders
http://www.pacer.org/ebd/

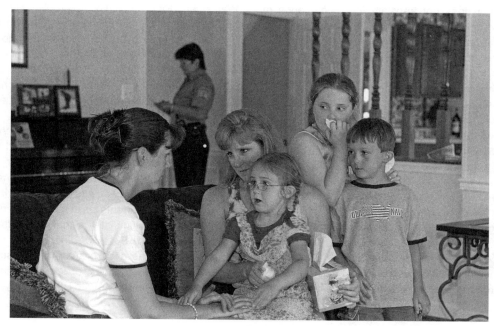

The definition of a student with emotional behavioral disorder (EBD) usually conjures up visions of the violence perpetrated by a few students who have vented their frustrations by taking guns to school. One of the hot topics in special education today is whether or not students with emotional and behavioral disorders are too dangerous to be included in regular education classes. The statistics show that students with EBDs are as likely to be the victims of violence or bullying by nondisabled classmates as to be the troublemakers. The definition of EBDs broadly includes all emotionally disordered students with subjective feelings such as sadness, fear, anger, guilt, or anxiety that give rise to altered behaviors that are outside the range of normal.

Should children with chronic and severe anger, already convicted of problem behaviors such as violent acts or threats of violence, be re-enrolled in inclusive regular education classes with individualized education plans (IEPs)? Although teachers, other pupils, and school staff may be greatly inconvenienced by the presence of one or more behaviorally disordered students in every classroom, the law is clear. The school must "show cause" if a child with EBD is to be permanently moved from the regular classroom to a more restrictive environment.

The 1994 Gun-Free Schools Act in the United States requires a one-year expulsion of a student who brings a firearm to school. The Individuals with Disabilities Education Act (IDEA) in its 1997 reauthorization made a compromise for students with EBDs or other conditions of disability. If bringing a gun to school is related to their disability (for example, as the result of being teased or bullied), they are exempt from the Gun-Free Schools Act legisla-

tion. They can be expelled, but only for 10 days while the school determines their degree of danger to others. If they are judged to really be dangerous, they can temporarily be given an alternate educational placement for 45 days, subject to reassessment. Their IEPs should not be rewritten to place them in a permanent restrictive setting unless their acts were clearly unrelated to their disabilities (hard to prove). This double standard is very controversial. Students without disabilities are expelled with no educational provisions for one full year.

For educational purposes, children with behavior disorders are usually divided into two main behavioral classifications: (1) withdrawn, shy, or anxious behaviors and (2) aggressive, acting-out behaviors. The debate about what constitutes a behavior disorder, or an emotional disorder, is not fully resolved. The Diagnostic and Statistical Manual of Mental Disorders, 4th edition (DSM-IV) sees serious behavioral disorders as a category first diagnosed in infancy, childhood, or adolescence. Among the DSM-IV disorders of childhood are eating disorders, tic disorders, elimination disorders, separation anxiety disorders, reactive attachment disorders, oppositional defiant disorder, and conduct disorder.

An alliance of educators and psychologists proposed that IDEIA remove the term "serious emotional disturbances" and instead focus on behaviors that adversely affect educational performance. Conduct usually considered a sign of emotional disorder, such as anxiety, depression, or failure of attachment, can be seen as behaviorally disordered if it interferes with academic, social, vocational, and personal accomplishment. So, also, can eating, elimination, or tic disorders and any other responses outside the range of "acceptable" for school or other settings. Such a focus on behavior can link the individualized educational plan curriculum activities to children's behavioral response styles.

Inclusive education does not translate into acceptance of disordered behaviors in the regular education classroom. Two rules of thumb for the behavior of all children, however capable or incapable, are that they conform to minimum standards of acceptable conduct and that disruptive behaviors be subject to fair and consistent disciplinary action. In order to ensure more orderly, well-regulated classroom environments, many schools are instituting conflict management courses.

What causes students to act out with hostile, aggressive behaviors directed against school personnel or other students? An easy, often-cited reason is that they are barraged with images of violence on the news, in music, on videos, on television programs, and in movies. It is too facile: Media barrage is aimed at everyone, yet only a few decide that they want to become violent and harm others. Aggressive, bullying children commonly come from homes where they see real violence, anger, and insults. They often feel disconnected, rejected, and afraid. They do not know how to communicate their distress. They may appear to be narcissistic, even as they seek attention in negative, hurtful ways. They usually have fairly easy access to weapons, alcohol, and other substances of abuse. They usually do not know any techniques of conflict management other than acting out.

The first article describes the more common psychiatric disorders that contribute to students' symptoms of EBDs. Forness, Walker, and Kavaie discuss the problems with both assessment and treatment of these disorders. Both behavioral therapy and drug therapy may be needed as well as good communication and collaboration between parents, students, and teachers.

Lynn Olcott in the second article writes "I Want to Go Back to Jail," and she did, as a teacher. She describes the rewards of helping emotionally and behaviorally disordered young women earn their general education diplomas.

The third featured article on *Classroom Behavior Management* discusses the use of a research-supported behavior modification technique known as functional behavior assessment (FBA). The authors list a dozen do's and don't's, that make it possible to reduce the negative aspects of the behaviors of students with EBD and help all students learn more efficiently.

The last exposition states that students can be taught to *Manage Their Own Behavior*. The authors present the subject Chris's behavior as a case study and describe how intervention strategies worked for him. They give detailed procedures for using this with all students with EBDs.

Psychiatric Disorders and Treatments: A Primer for Teachers

STEVEN R. FORNESS, HILL M. WALKER, AND KENNETH A. KAVALE

Children who have social or emotional problems require understanding and support from teachers and family members and may occasionally require counseling to help the child deal with his or her feelings and explore ways of coping. Psychiatric disorders, on the other hand, are generally much more disabling, more difficult to diagnose correctly, and sometimes require very specific therapeutic or medical treatments, meaning treatment with psychopharmacology (medications used to help the child control his or her emotional or behavioral symptoms).

Child psychopharmacology is a controversial field that is often sensationalized in the popular media. Coverage in the media often suggests that large numbers of children are being prescribed medication for only minor problems. Studies suggest that only a small fraction of children with serious psychiatric disorders are actually receiving such medication (Jensen et al., 1999; Zito et al., 1998). In the hands of a competent pediatrician or child psychiatrist, moreover, these medications are not only effective but an essential component of an overall treatment program for many, if not most, children with psychiatric disorders.

Psychiatric disorders are likely to be prevalent in children or adolescents receiving special education.

Careful treatment with these medications has been shown not only to effect dramatic improvement in behavioral or emotional responses of these children, but also to improve their social and academic functioning. Specific behavioral and related therapies are also critical. These may be used alone, prior to, or concurrent with psychopharmacologic treatment; and combined behavioral and psychopharmacologic treatments are often better than either used alone (Forness & Kavale, 2001; Forness, Kavale, & Davanzo, 2002).

Psychiatric disorders are classified in the fourth edition of the American Psychiatric Association's *Diagnostic and Statistical Manual (DSM IV; 1994). DSM IV* is used primarily by psychiatrists and psychologists to diagnose mental health problems in both children and adolescents. The diagnostic information contained here is taken directly from *DSM IV,* and treatment issues are referenced separately. All of these disorders were diagnosed only after a thorough evaluation that included

1. Screening for health, vision, or hearing problems.
2. Review of the child's developmental history.
3. Interviews with the parents and the child.

4. Review of information from teachers or school records.
5. Careful consideration of context and occurrence of symptoms.

Psychiatric disorders are likely to be prevalent in children or adolescents receiving special education (Garland et al., 2001). Educators working with these children should be familiar enough with such disorders so they can readily detect and refer children to mental health professionals and collaborate with these professionals in ongoing treatment. These disorders are discussed in the following paragraphs in terms of definition or diagnosis and therapeutic and psychopharmacologic treatment.

Oppositional Defiant and Conduct Disorders
Diagnosis

Both oppositional defiant and conduct disorders involve disruptive behavior. Oppositional defiant disorder often seems developmentally to precede a later diagnosis of conduct disorder. Both disorders probably occur in at least 4% of children or adolescents (Forness, Kavale, & Walker, 1999). Children with oppositional defiant disorder are those who have persistent patterns of negativistic, hostile, or defiant behavior directed primarily toward adults. Children with conduct disorder show consistent patterns of behavior in which they violate the rights of others or transgress age-appropriate social norms.

In oppositional defiant disorder, symptoms may include

- Persistent temper tantrums.
- Arguing with adults.
- Refusing to comply with reasonable adult requests.
- Annoying others.
- Vindictiveness.

The symptoms of an oppositional defiant disorder bother adults but are not considered as troublesome as conduct disorder, in which symptoms usually cluster into more serious patterns of

- Overt aggression toward people or animals.
- Destruction of property.
- Deceitfulness or theft.
- Serious violations of rules such as staying out all night and truancy from school.

As is the case with all psychiatric disorders, oppositional defiant disorder and conduct disorder are diagnosed in *DSM IV* when the child meets a set number of symptoms from among a list of several symptoms typical of the disorder. Children must have 4 from a list of 8 symptoms to be diagnosed with oppositional defiant disorder and at least 3 from a list of 15 symptoms to be diagnosed with conduct disorder. These symptoms must also meet the criteria of causing significant impairment in social, academic, or related functioning. In conduct disorder, presence of only 3 symptoms is termed *mild conduct disorder,* whereas moderate and severe conduct disorder are characterized by increasing numbers of symptoms and increasingly greater harm to others.

The symptoms of an oppositional defiant disorder bother adults but are not considered as troublesome as conduct disorder.

Treatment

The primary treatment for both oppositional defiant disorder and conduct disorder is behavioral therapy (Kavale, Forness, & Walker, 1999). Usually this takes the form of a reward or a reinforcement system in which the child earns points for appropriate behavior and is ignored or even given time-outs for inappropriate behavior. Points are usually exchanged for privileges or tangible awards at home or school. A major part of such behavioral therapy is parent or teacher consultation, so that adults can learn how to praise or reward good behavior and ignore inappropriate behavior. Social skills training is also helpful for children who do not seem to know how to behave or interact appropriately.

Unlike most psychiatric disorders, medication is not usually used to control symptoms of oppositional defiant disorder or conduct disorder directly. Both disorders, however, are very likely to co-occur or be comorbid (more than one condition existing at the same time) with a wide range of other psychiatric disorders (Forness, Kavale, & Walker, 1999). Psychopharmacology for these disorders (such as attention deficit hyperactivity disorder, depression, or anxiety disorders) may often improve symptoms of oppositional defiant disorder or conduct disorder, as well.

Attention Deficit/Hyperactivity Disorder

Diagnosis

This disorder is found in 3%–5% of children or adolescents (Forness & Kavale, 2002). It is diagnosed when a child has persistent problems in inattentive or in hyperactive-impulsive behavior. At least some of these symptoms must have appeared prior to 7 years of age. The symptoms must also persist to a degree that markedly impairs the child's functioning in two or more settings, such as home and school.

Symptoms of inattention include

- Failing to give close attention to details in school work or related activities.
- Difficulty in sustaining attention.
- Seeming not to listen.
- Difficulty in organization.
- Distractibility.

Symptoms of hyperactivity or impulsivity include

- Excessive fidgeting.
- Inability to sit still in the classroom or other situations when this is expected.

- Running about or even climbing things excessively.
- Extreme restlessness or talkativeness.
- Difficulty waiting for turn.
- Interrupting conversations.

The child must usually meet criteria in *DSM IV* for six of nine symptoms in inattention or six of nine symptoms of hyperactivity-impulsivity. Children can thus be diagnosed with three subtypes of attention deficit/hyperactivity disorder (ADHD): predominantly inattentive, predominantly hyperactive-impulsive, or combined. It is usually important to rule out other psychiatric disorders (such as depression, anxiety disorder, schizophrenia, or autism) before diagnosing ADHD, since these diagnoses may be more serious and usually take precedence. In many cases, a child may have both ADHD and one or more of these other disorders.

Treatment

The most effective treatment for ADHD generally combines both psychopharmacologic and behavioral interventions (MTA Cooperative Group, 1999a,1999b). Stimulant medications such as Ritalin, Adderall, or Dexedrine are usually the first medications considered. While it often seems paradoxical to treat an overactive child with stimulants, these drugs stimulate brain chemicals, called neurotransmitters, to work more effectively, thus allowing the child to slow down and concentrate. Children not responding to stimulant medications have sometimes been treated with other psychopharmacologic medications, such as antidepressants like Tofranil or Wellbutrin. There are other medications that can be used if the child does not respond to these drugs or when ADHD co-occurs or is comorbid with certain other psychiatric disorders.

Selecting the appropriate medication involves a process called titration (see box). Table 1 depicts some of the primary stimulants and the approximate length of time each drug lasts or has noticeable effects in the child being treated. Some of the primary side effects (see Table 1) may occur only during the titration phase of treatment and may disappear in all but a few children.

Children with ADHD may also respond to psychosocial or behavioral treatments (Forness & Kavale, 2002). Behavioral interventions include establishing predictable routines and expectations for children, both at home and at school, and reinforcing the child for meeting these expectations. By increasing goals gradually, the child does not have to be "perfect" at the outset but can accomplish small steps over a period of days or weeks. Parent education and teacher consultation can help adults in the child's life to set reasonable expectations, reinforce effective behavior, ignore hyperactive or distractible behavior, use time-out effectively, and collaborate by developing consistent expectations and reinforcers between home and school.

Research evidence on treatment of ADHDs comes both from a re-analysis of 115 recent medication studies (Forness, Kavale, Sweeney, & Crenshaw, 1999) and from a long-term nationwide study of nearly 600 children funded by the National Institute of Mental Health (NIMH; MTA Cooperative Group, 1999a, 1999b). This evidence suggests that psychopharmacologic treatment seems to be a critical factor in effective intervention for ADHD. The message from this research is also clear that best practice is a combination of medication and behavioral therapies (Swanson et al., 2001). In the NIMH study, combined treatment also tended to improve scores on reading tests and on ratings of social skills on long-term follow-up, if children remained on medication (Arnold et al., 2000).

Evidence suggests that the presence of co-occurring or comorbid psychiatric disorders in children with ADHD may influence treatment outcome (Jensen et al., 2001). Children with ADHD and no other disorders tend to respond best, sometimes with only medication. Children

Titration

The process of determining the right dose of medication, called titration, requires close collaboration between child, parents, and teachers (Wilens, 2001). The goal of titration is to use the lowest effective dose of medication while avoiding unwanted side effects.

Side effects occur because these medications, while very helpful, are still imperfect. Although stimulants target certain areas of the brain, they sometimes also spill over into other areas for which they were not intended, thus causing side effects such as loss of appetite, insomnia, dizziness, or irritability. These side effects may occur only at higher doses for some children or may occur with some children for some stimulants and not for others. At other times, these side effects may diminish as time goes by or as the child gets used to the drug. For some children, they may persist to the point where another medication or treatment must be tried instead.

In recent medication studies, researchers present side effects that occur on the drug as well as side effects that occur on placebo pills that contain no active medication. Interestingly, many children with ADHD seemed to show problems with irritability, insomnia, and poor appetite even when not on medication. Medication side effects are usually only slightly more frequent than problems that, upon careful observation, existed previously in these children before they were placed on medication.

Titration is somewhat easier with stimulants because these medications usually act within an hour or so and generally wash out of the body within a few hours or by the end of the day. The process of finding the right dose or switching to another medication may be accomplished within a few days or weeks.

Antidepressant medications, on the other hand, may take at least 3 or more weeks to obtain a full therapeutic effect.

Other medications such as antipsychotics or neuroleptics for schizophrenia or other treatment-resistant disorders may take weeks to establish the most effective regimen. Thus, effective titration for these medications may commonly take weeks or even months. The side effects of these medications are also likely to be more debilitating and may also include

- Sedation.
- Dizziness.
- Problems in heart rhythms, especially in children with a family history of heart disease.
- Tremors.
- Significant weight gain.

Prescribing physicians should warn patients and their families about what to look for in terms of both therapeutic effects and adverse side effects. Physicians should also schedule regular follow-up visits to assess and monitor both the effects and the side effects of each medication. Competent physicians do careful patient and family education to prepare the child and his or her family for the titration process. During titration, they will usually provide the family and the child's teachers with checklists of symptoms and side effects so that significant adults in the child's environment can also monitor and provide regular feedback to the physician on how the medication is working.

Certain medications require more careful screening and monitoring of health status or drug effects through blood work, electrocardiograms, and the like. Physicians should give families careful instructions for regular administration of these medications, as well as numbers to call in case of unexpected emergencies.

with ADHD and comorbid anxiety disorders seem to respond almost as well, either to medication or to behavioral therapy. Children with ADHD and comorbid oppositional defiant disorder or conduct disorder also respond relatively well but only if combined psychopharmacologic and behavioral treatments are used.

Table 1 Stimulants

Generic (and Trade) Name	Duration
Methylphenidate or MPH (Ritalin)	3–4 hours
Dextroamphetamine (Dexedrine)	6–8 hours
Amphetamine (Adderall)	7–10 hours
Sustained MPH (Concerta)	10–12 hours

Side effects: appetite loss, stomachache, headache, insomnia

Depression or Other Mood Disorders
Diagnosis

Although childhood onset of depressive or other mood disorders does not occur as frequently as ADHD, it is not uncommon and may affect more than 2% of children and at least twice that number of adolescents (Birmaher & Brent, 1998). There are essentially three major types of mood disorders: depression, dysthymia, and bipolar or manic depressive disorder. Depression is diagnosed in *DSM IV* when the child has a depressed or irritable mood or loss of interest or pleasure in most activities. Other symptoms may include

- Unexplained fluctuations in weight.
- Insomnia.
- Loss of energy.
- Diminished ability to think or concentrate.
- Feelings of excessive guilt or worthlessness.

Of nine different symptoms, at least five must occur nearly every day during a 2-week period for depression to be diagnosed.

Dysthymia is diagnosed by a depressed or irritable mood on most days for at least a year and must also be accompanied by at least two of six other symptoms. Including

- Insomnia.
- Low energy or fatigue.
- Low self-esteem.
- Poor concentration.
- Feelings of hopelessness.

The diagnosis of bipolar or manic depressive disorder depends on fluctuations in mood, from depressed episodes, as noted previously, to manic episodes. Manic episodes are characterized by distinct periods in which the child or adolescent has an abnormal and persistently elevated or expansive mood and in which three of seven other symptoms are present, such as

- Decreased need for sleep.
- Excessive talkativeness.
- Distractibility.
- Psychomotor agitation.

The most effective treatment for attention deficit hyperactivity disorder generally combines both psychopharmacologic and behavioral interventions.

All of these disorders must cause significant distress or functional impairment and require that certain other disorders, such as schizophrenia or substance abuse, be ruled out before making the diagnosis. Bipolar disorders in children are relatively rare and may be difficult to diagnose because of less distinct patterns of cycling than occur in adults; however, they become more common during adolescence and early adulthood.

Treatment

Treatment for depression usually involves cognitive behavioral therapies and psychopharmacologic treatment. Psychopharmacology for dysthymia is less predictable because symptoms may not always be consistently present, but it may be used depending on the child's or adolescent's age and presentation of symptoms (Wagner & Ambrosini, 2001).

In medicating for depression, physicians usually begin with one of the drugs known as selective serotonin reuptake inhibitors (SSRIs), such as Zoloft, Prozac, or Paxil. If the child or adolescent fails to respond to two or more of these medications, tricyclic antidepressants such as Tofranil or atypical antidepressants, such as Wellbutrin, may be tried.

In bipolar or manic depressive disorder, physicians may begin with lithium and, in some cases, attempt a trial of other mood stabilizers such as Depakote. Examples of these medications in each classification are provided in Table 2, along with the approximate time it may take to obtain a full therapeutic effect. Table 2 also lists some of the most frequently occurring side effects.

Psychopharmacologic treatment in each of these disorders, however, can be quite complex because large numbers of children or adolescents may not respond favorably enough to continue treatment or may suffer from side effects that tend to lead to discontinuation of the drug. In a significant number of cases, more than one medication may be required for effective treatment. Pediatricians usually do not have sufficient training to manage such treatment effectively, so most children with these disorders should be referred to board certified child or adolescent psychiatrists for the best outcome.

Table 2 Antidepressants/Mood Stabilizers

Class (Examples)	Full Effects
SSRI (Zoloft, Paxil, Luvox, Prozac)	2 to 4 weeks
Tricyclics (Tofranil, Elavil)	2 to 4 weeks
Atypicals (Wellbutrin, Effexor, Serzone)	2 to 4 weeks
Stabilizers (Lithium, Depakote)	7 to 10 days

Side effects: stomachache, agitation, headache, dry mouth, dizziness.

Cognitive behavioral therapies may also be effective for treatment of depressive disorders (Asarnow, Jaycox, & Tompson, 2001). Such treatment focuses on the child or adolescent monitoring his or her mood, involvement in activities, stress, or other symptomatic behaviors and is then taught to coach himself or herself through "self talk," which is designed to give a sense of control over the symptoms and negate feelings of despair, low self-esteem, helplessness, and the like. Supportive therapy and education about the nature of the child's particular disorder can help and may assist in better outcomes for psychopharmacologic treatment, if warranted.

Monitoring suicidal symptoms is especially critical in children or adolescents with these disorders. These disorders also sometimes tend to have a diagnostic progression, with dysthymia putting a child at higher risk for depression and depression putting a child at higher risk for bipolar or manic depressive disorder. Early detection and treatment is therefore very critical.

Anxiety Disorders
Diagnosis

Anxiety disorders occur in approximately 4% of children and in a slightly larger percentage of adolescents (Bernstein & Shaw, 1997). *DSM IV* lists several types of anxiety disorders, including obsessive-compulsive disorder, generalized anxiety disorder, separation anxiety disorder, and posttraumatic stress disorder. Obsessive-compulsive disorder is marked by obsessions or compulsions that cause marked distress, are excessively time consuming, or significantly interfere with the child's or adolescent's functioning or social relationships. Obsessions are recurrent and persistent thoughts or impulses that seem to have no relationship to real-life problems or that the child or adolescent seems unable to ignore or suppress, despite the fact that he or she recognizes these as merely a product of his or her own mind.

Compulsions are repetitive behaviors (such as hand washing, ordering of objects, checking on things) or mental acts (such as counting objects or repeating words silently) that, according to rigid rules, the child or adolescent feels driven to perform and are aimed at preventing or reducing some imagined distress. These behaviors or mental acts do not seem to be connected in a realistic way to this distress or are clearly excessive.

Children or adolescents may be diagnosed with generalized anxiety disorder when they demonstrate excessive worry about events or activities (such as social functioning or school performance) and find it difficult to control these responses. Worrying must cause clinically significant impairment in social or academic functioning and also be associated with at least three of six anxiety symptoms:

- Restlessness.
- Fatigue.

- Concentration problems.
- Irritability.
- Muscle tension.
- Sleep disturbance.

Separation anxiety disorder is diagnosed when a child has developmentally inappropriate and excessive anxiety concerning separation from home or family. This must cause clinically significant distress or impairment and be accompanied by at least three of eight symptoms, such as

- Excessive worrying about injury or loss of a major family member.
- Anxiety about separation from family through being kidnapped or getting lost.
- Persistent refusal or reluctance to attend school because of fear of separation.
- Sleep disturbance.
- Complaints of physical symptoms whenever separation from a major family member occurs or is anticipated.

The diagnosis of posttraumatic stress disorder is made when a child or adolescent has experienced or witnessed a traumatic event that involved intense fear, helplessness, or horror. Subsequently, following that actual event, other symptoms have to occur. The traumatic event has to be persistently re-experienced in terms of at least one of the following:

- Intrusive recollections.
- Recurrent dreams.
- Feeling that the event is actually recurring.
- Intense distress upon exposure to cues that remind the child of the event or a physiologic reaction to such cues, like shaking or sweating.

There must also be persistent avoidance of at least three things that remind the child or adolescent of the traumatic event, such as

- Avoiding thoughts or situations.
- Inability to recall important details of the trauma.
- Feeling detached from others.
- Restriction of emotional range.

Finally, the child must demonstrate at least two of five symptoms of increased arousal, such as

- Sleep disturbance.
- Irritability.
- Difficulty concentrating.
- Hypervigilance.
- Exaggerated startle response.

Community agencies and regional centers often provide education for parents in using behavioral approaches to further develop social and functional skills at home.

Treatment

Treatment for each of these anxiety disorders varies, depending on the specific diagnosis, but generally involves cognitive or behavioral therapies and possible psychopharmacologic treatment (Ollendick & King, 1998). The cognitive therapies generally focus on providing the child both with ways to monitor his or her own internal anxieties and with a sense of control through "self talk." For example, a young child with an obsessive-compulsive disorder may be taught to pretend that his or her obsessions or compulsions are like a "little monster" trying to trick him or her into performing these rituals. The child is then shown ways to make the monster less threatening or powerful.

Other cognitive or behavioral approaches focus, in similar ways, on the unreality of the anxiety and how to anticipate responding in a more adaptive way. Reinforcement schemes may also be employed to assist or motivate the child in establishing a sense of control and participating more gradually over a period of time in anxiety-provoking events.

Psychopharmacologic treatment may involve anxiolytic or antidepressant medications (Green, 2001). The anxiolytic or anxiety-breaking medications are drugs such as Klonopin, Ativan, or Buspar. These medications are relatively fast-acting and must often be taken two or three times per day. Their major side effects include sedation or drowsiness and, in a few children, may cause a sudden onset of agitation, silliness, talkativeness, or even increased anxiety, a response that usually wears off within a couple of hours.

Stopping these drugs abruptly may also lead to increased agitation or anxiety, so their use should be withdrawn gradually, as is the case with most other psychopharmacologic medications discussed. Usually anxiolytics are used in children on a short-term basis only. The antidepressants that have been found most helpful for anxiety disorders are SSRI medications (such as Paxil or Luvox) or atypical antidepressants (such as Effexor). For children and younger adolescents, SSRIs and atypical antidepressants have become the first choice for treatment of most anxiety disorders.

Schizophrenic or Other Psychotic Disorders
Diagnosis

These disorders are exceedingly rare, especially in children—the rate is probably less than a tenth of a percent (McClellan & Werry, 2000). *DSM IV* diagnoses children or adolescents with schizophrenia when at least two of the following symptoms are present:

- Delusions (such as thinking one has special powers or feeling that people are out to do one harm).
- Hallucinations (such as hearing voices or seeing things that no one else experiences).
- Disorganized speech.
- Grossly disorganized behavior.
- Certain symptoms of social withdrawal.

These symptoms must generally be present over a period of at least 6 months and must markedly affect one or more areas of functioning, like school or interpersonal relationships. Separate diagnoses exist for brief or atypical psychotic disorders, which last less than a month or do not meet full criteria.

Treatment

Treatment is usually a combination of behavioral training (including social skills training) and psychopharmacology (Vitiello, Bhatara, & Jensen, 1999). Medications for schizophrenia are currently the new or atypical neuroleptic or antipsychotic drugs such as Risperdal, Zyprexa, and Seroquel. These medications may diminish agitation almost immediately but take days to diminish hallucinations. After several weeks, these medications will improve disorganized thinking and social withdrawal. Side effects, however, can be severe, including sedation or even abnormal facial or motor movements.

These side effects tend to limit their use especially in children but, in rare cases, are seen as unavoidable or preferable in the face of full-blown psychosis, which can be devastatingly frightening to children or adolescents with the disorder and to those around them. In some instances, these newer neuroleptic drugs are also being used for treatment resistant depression and anxiety disorders.

Autistic Spectrum Disorders
Diagnosis
These disorders also occur quite infrequently but may not be as rare as childhood-onset schizophrenia (Volkmar, Cook, Pomeroy, Realmuto, & Tanguay, 1999). Autistic spectrum disorder is diagnosed by at least six symptoms across three areas:

1. Social impairment, such as
   - Lack of eye contact.
   - Failure to develop peer relationships.
   - Lack of sharing enjoyment or interests with others.
   - Lack of social or emotional give and take.

2. Communicative impairment, such as
   - Delays in spoken language.
   - Inability to initiate or sustain conversations.
   - Repetitive or odd use of phrases.
   - Lack of make-believe or social-imitative play.

3. Restrictive or repetitive behavior, such as
   - Intense preoccupations with restricted patterns of interest.
   - Inflexible routines or rituals.
   - Repetitive motor mannerisms such as hand-or finger-flapping.
   - Preoccupation only with parts of objects.

At least some of these symptoms must have occurred prior to 3 years of age. About three of every four children with autism may also have severe cognitive delays as well.

Asperger's disorder is diagnosed if at least three symptoms are present from the social impairment and restricted or repetitive behavior lists above but there are no significant delays in language or cognitive development. Pervasive developmental disorder may be diagnosed if it is not clear that symptoms were present prior to 3 years of age or if sufficient symptoms are not clearly present.

Treatment for children with autistic spectrum disorders relies primarily on developing basic language and social skills using behavioral strategies and reinforcement systems. Academic skills are taught according to the child's cognitive or intellectual levels. Community agencies and regional centers often provide education for parents in using behavioral approaches to further develop social and functional skills at home. There are as yet no recognized psychopharmacologic medications to treat autism directly. Some children with autism may also be at risk for other psychiatric disorders or symptoms, however, and they might be responsive to psychopharmacologic medications for such disorders (Sweeney, Forness, & Levitt, 1998).

Other Diagnoses in DSM IV
DSM-IV includes learning disorders, mental retardation, and communication disorders. Although they are not strictly considered mental health disorders, they are sometimes closely associated with certain psychiatric disorders. Children with these disorders are also at significantly higher risk for comorbid or co-occurring psychiatric disorders

(Beichtman, Cantwell, Forness, Kavale, & Kauffman, 1998; King, DeAntonio, McCracken, Forness, & Ackerman, 1994). Eating disorders such as anorexia nervosa are listed as psychiatric disorders in DSM IV and involve refusal to maintain normal weight for height and age (usually defined as less than 85% of expected weight), coupled with an intense fear of gaining weight and a disturbance of body image related to weight. This disorder affects primarily adolescent girls who are often apt to focus obsessively on academic achievement, in addition to their obsession with weight or diet (Lewis, 2002).

Tourettes disorder is also listed in DSM IV and involves chronic motor and sometimes vocal tics occurring many times a day, usually in bouts. This disorder is often treated by SSRI or antihypertensive medications such as Clonidine (Sweeney et al., 1998).

Substance-related disorders, such as alcohol or drug abuse are listed in DSM IV as psychiatric disorders and involve recurrent substance use that results in poor work or school performance, hazardous behavior such as impaired driving, or recurrent social or personal problems.

Final Thoughts
This is neither an exhaustive list nor a comprehensive description of childhood psychiatric disorders but, rather, an introduction for teachers and other school professionals to some of the major diagnoses that can impair school learning or classroom behavior. Detection and treatment of these disorders may sometimes greatly improve academic progress and social adjustment of children with more serious school learning or behavior problems. A behavioral checklist for teachers and parents has therefore been developed that is based on DSM IV and provides both primary and possible comorbid psychiatric diagnoses (Gadow & Sprafkin, 1994). Introductory materials to further educate teachers and parents about psychopharmacology have also been developed for those interested in particular medications (Konopasek, 2002; Wilens, 2001).

References

American Psychiatric Association. (1994). *Diagnostic and statistical manual of mental disorders* (4th ed.). Washington, DC: Author.

Arnold, L. E., Jensen, P. S., Hechtman, L., Hoagwood, K., Greenhill, L., & MTA Cooperative Group. (2000, October). *Do MTA treatment effects persist? New followup at 2 years.* Paper presented at the annual meeting of the American Academy of Child and Adolescent Psychiatry, New York.

Asarnow, J. R., Jaycox, L. H., & Tompson, M. C. (2001). Depression in youth: Psychosocial interventions. *Journal of Clinical Child Psychology, 30,* 33–47.

Beichtman, J. H., Cantwell, D. P., Forness, S. R., Kavale, K. A., & Kauffman, J. M. (1998). Practice parameters for the diagnostic assessment and treatment of children and adolescents with language and learning disorders. *Journal of the American Academy of Child and Adolescent Psychiatry, 37*(10 Supplement), 42S–62S.

Bernstein, G. A., & Shaw, K. (1997). Practice parameters for the assessment and treatment of children and adolescents with anxiety disorders. *Journal of the American Academy of Child and Adolescent Psychiatry, 36*(10 Supplement), 69–84.

Birmaher, B., & Brent, D. (1998). Practice parameters for the assessment and treatment of children and adolescents with depressive disorders. *Journal of the American Academy of Child and Adolescent Psychiatry, 37*(10 Supplement), 63–83.

Forness, S. R., & Kavale, K. A. (2001). Ignoring the odds: Hazards of not adding the medical model to special education decisions. *Behavioral Disorders, 26,* 269–281.

Forness, S. R., & Kavale, K. A. (2002). Impact of ADHD on school systems. In P. S. Jensen & J. R. Cooper (Eds.), *Attention deficit hyperactivity disorder: State of the science best practices. (pp. 1–20, 24).* Kingston, NJ: Civic Research Institute.

Forness, S. R., & Kavale, K. A., & Davanzo, P. A. (2002). Interdisciplinary treatment and the limits of behaviorism. *Behavioral Disorders, 27,* 168–178.

Forness, S. R., Kavale, K. A., Sweeney, D. P., & Crenshaw, T. M. (1999). The future of research and practice in behavioral disorders: Psychopharmacology and its school treatment implications. *Behavioral Disorders, 24,* 305–318.

Forness, S. R., Kavale, K. A., & Walker, H. M. (1999). Identifying children at risk for antisocial behavior: The case for comorbidity. In R. G. Gallimore, C. Bernheimer, D. L. MacMillan, & D. Speece (Eds.), *Developmental perspectives on children with high incidence disabilities* (pp. 135–155). Mahwah, NJ: Lawrence Erlbaum.

Gadow, K., & Sprafkin, J. (1994). Child Symptom Inventory manual. Stony Brook, NY: Checkmate Plus.

Garland, A. F., Hough, R. L., McCabe, K. M., Yeh, M., Wood, P. A., & Aarons, G. A. (2001). Prevalence of psychiatric disorders in youths across five sectors of care. *Journal of the American Academy of Child and Adolescent Psychiatry, 40,* 409–418.

Green, W. H. (2001). *Child and adolescent clinical psychopharmacology* (3rd ed.). New York: Guilford Press.

Jensen, P. S., Hinshaw, S. P., Kraemer, H. C., Lenora, N., Newcorn, J. H., Abikoff, H. B., March, J. S., Arnold, L. E., Cantwell, D. P., Conner, C. K., Elliott, G. R., Greenhill, L. L., Hechtman, L., Hoaz, B., Pelham, W. E., Severe, J. B., Swanson, J. M., Wells, K. C., Wigal, T., & Vitiello, B. (2001). ADHD comorbidity findings from the MTA study: Comparing comorbid subgroups. *Journal of the American Academy of Child and Adolescent Psychiatry, 40,* 147–158.

Jensen, P. S., Kettle, L., Roper, M. T., Sloan, M. T., Dulcan, M. K., Hoven, C., Bird, H. R., Bauermeister, J. J., & Payne, J. D. (1999). Are stimulants overprescribed? Treatment of ADHD in four U.S. communities. *Journal of the American Academy of Child and Adolescent Psychiatry, 38,* 797–804.

Kavale, K. A., Forness, S. R., & Walker, H. M. (1999). Interventions for ODD and CD in the schools. In H. Quay & A. Hogan (Eds.), *Handbook of disruptive behavior disorders* (pp. 441–454). New York: Plenum.

King, B. H., DeAntonio, C., McCracken, J. T., Forness, S. R., & Ackerman, V. (1994). Psychiatric consultation to persons with severe and profound mental retardation. *American Journal of Psychiatry, 151,* 1802–1808.

Konopasek, D. E. (2002). *Medication "Fact Sheets": A medication reference guide for the non-medical professional.* Anchorage, AK: Arctic Tern.

Lewis, M. (Ed.). (2002). *Child and adolescent psychiatry: A comprehensive textbook* (3rd ed.). New York: Guilford Press.

McClellan, J., & Werry, J. (2000). Summary of the practice parameters for the assessment and treatment of children and adolescents with schizophrenia. *Journal of the American Academy of Child and Adolescent Psychiatry, 39,* 1580–1582.

MTA Cooperative Group. (1999a). A 14-month randomized clinical trial of treatment strategies for attention deficit/hyperactivity disorder. *Archives of General Psychiatry, 56,* 1073–1086.

MTA Cooperative Group. (1999b). Moderators and mediators of treatment response for children with attention deficit/hyperactivity disorder. *Archives of General Psychiatry, 56,* 1088–1095.

Ollendick, T., & King, N. (1998). Empirically supported treatments for children with phobic and anxiety disorders: Current status. *Journal of Clinical Child Psychology, 27,* 156–167.

Swanson, J. M., Kraemer, H. C., Hinshaw, S. P., Arnold, L. E., Conners, C. K., Abikoff, H. B., Clevenger, W., Davies, M., Elliot, G. R., Greenhill, L. L., Hechtman, L., Hoza, B., Jensen, P. S., March, J. S., Newcorn, J. H., Owns, E. B., Pelham, W., Schiller, E., Severe, J. B., Simpson, S., Vitiello, B., Wells, K., Wigal, T., & Wu, M. (2001). Clinical relevance of the primary findings of the MTA: Success rates based on severity of ADHD and ODD symptoms at the end of treatment. *Journal of the American Academy of Child and Adolescent Psychiatry, 40,* 168–179.

Sweeney, D. P., Forness, S. R., & Levitt, J. G. (1998). An overview of medications commonly used to treat behavioral disorders associated with autism, Tourette's disorder, and pervasive developmental disorders. *Focus on Autism and Other Developmental Disabilities, 13,* 144–150.

Vitiello, B., Bhatara, V. S., & Jensen, P. S. (1999). Special section: Current knowledge and unmet needs in pediatric psychopharmacology. *Journal of the American Academy of Child and Adolescent Psychiatry, 38,* 501–565.

Volkmar, F., Cook, E. H., Pomeroy, J., Realmuto, G., & Tanguay, P. (1999). Practice parameters for the assessment and treatment of children, adolescents, and adults with autism and other pervasive developmental disorders. *Journal of the American Academy of Child and Adolescent Psychiatry, 38*(12 Supplement), 32–54.

Wagner, K. D., & Ambrosini, P. J. (2001). Childhood depression: Pharmacological therapy/treatment (Pharmacotherapy of childhood depression). *Journal of Clinical Child Psychology, 30,* 88–97.

Wilens, T. E. (2001). *Straight talk about psychiatric medication for kids.* New York: Guilford Press.

Zito, J. M., Safer, D. J., Riddle, M. A., Johnson, R. E., Speedie, S. M., & Fox, M. (1998). Prevalence variations in psychotropic treatment of children. *Journal of Child and Adolescent Psychopharmacology, 8,* 99–105.

STEVEN R. FORNESS, (CEC Chapter #520), Professor and Chief Educational Psychologist, UCLA Neuropsychiatric Hospital, Los Angeles, California. **HILL M. WALKER** (CEC OR Federation), Professor and Director, Institute on Violence and Destructive Behavior, University of Oregon, Eugene. **KENNETH A. KAVALE,** Professor, Division of Curriculum and Instruction, University of Iowa, Iowa City. Address correspondence to Steven R. Forness, UCLA Neuropsychiatric Hospital, 760 Westwood Plaza, Los Angeles, CA 90049.

From *Teaching Exceptional Children,* by Steven R. Forness, Hill M. Walker and Kenneth A. Kavaie, Vol. 36, no. 2, November/December 2003, pp. 42–49. Copyright © 2003 by Council for Exceptional Children. Reprinted by permission.

I Want to Go Back to Jail

At the Onondaga County Justice Center, Ms. Olcott entered the lives of the students who had disappeared from the radar screen of American education.

LYNN OLCOTT

I want to go back to jail. I'm serious. I was a more honest, more effective teacher there. I trusted my students, and they trusted me. We worked together toward the next scheduled GED (General Education Development) test and filled ourselves with as much literature as I could put in their willing hands. Every day I went deep into a maximum-security facility to the women's pod, where my students lived and ate and studied. Every day I encountered students who were eager to learn and glad for the simple materials I brought. I rediscovered pure, joyous teaching. In that stark environment, I rediscovered the educational power of kindness and respect.

Like so many of us now, I was a card-carrying member of the "sandwich generation," caregiver for my father while I still had a teenager at home. When my father died, I was exhausted, sad, and thoroughly disillusioned with long-term care, Medicare, and every other kind of care. I was eager to return to teaching, my late father's profession as well as mine. I responded to an ad in the paper looking for a teacher for an incarcerated education program, with no real idea of what that meant. My father's funeral was on a stormy Friday in January. The next week, I was thrilled to be hired as a GED teacher at the Onondaga County Justice Center. My new life had begun.

From the very beginning, I was struck by the contrast between the bleak correctional environment and the rich educational experiences offered there. The offerings were not limited to GED courses but included training in office technology, anger management, food service, and many other subjects. The Syracuse City School District, in conjunction with the Onondaga County Sheriff's Office, has operated the Incarcerated Education Program for several years. It is a "showcase program" in that it is well respected in corrections services circles. But it is practically unknown to the general public, even in the county where it exists. The Justice Center houses about 600 prisoners at any one time, and perhaps 60 or 70 of them are women. It is a non-sentenced facility, so students might be in the program for a few days or a few months before being bailed out, sentenced upstate, or transferred to other facilities. The GED test is given in-house about every two months. Pass rates, about 50%, equal and sometimes exceed those on the "outside."

In New York State, inmates aged 16 through 21 who lack a GED or high school diploma are required to attend classes. Many students over 21 attend voluntarily. Most of the girls and women I met were African American and had left school around 10th grade, usually due to pregnancy or childbirth. Most were incarcerated for economic crimes—prostitution, shoplifting, passing bad checks, selling drugs, and occasionally burglary and assault. Most scored between the fourth- and sixth-grade levels on the TABE (Test of Adult Basic Education), the test we used as a baseline. Most were involved with men who never came to see them. Most had children, whom they missed very much, being cared for by relatives.

The first student I met was Sally. She was about 40 years old, and her children were being raised by her father and stepmother. Several acts of violence had brought her here and to prison in the past. Sally instantly became my self-appointed assistant and made it her priority to have the heavy tables dragged together and the shaky whiteboard erected and ready for us every morning. She worked hard and encouraged the other students with persuasive personal lectures on the importance of education. When she left to serve time in a state prison, I missed her.

Sally's close friend Sheryl took over the role of encourager, but she left the moving of the heavy tables to the kids. I usually had eight or 10 students at a time, of different ages and working at different levels. I invented a simple, individualized system that students could enter easily and could use to track their own achievements. I taught math, science, and social studies as well as language arts. I liked the diversity of subject matter and was grateful for my own liberal arts education. Though technically I taught this medley of subjects, I was primarily a teacher of remedial reading and writing, a teacher of reading comprehension, a teacher of guerrilla English.

Teaching writing was fascinating. My students had a great deal to write about. Sheryl wrote about living in the South and about how her family had made a living picking cotton before coming north with her brave mother and cruel stepfather. Tina wrote a moving essay about wanting to gather her scattered family and cook Sunday dinner for them. A tough high school girl named Ilene wrote an amazing piece of irony about stolen watches and doing time. I was not really teaching writing at all; I was merely opening the drawstrings on bags of experiential treasure. What I was teaching—to students who had not written 250 words together in decades, if ever—was the format expected in a successful GED essay.

At the request of one of the high school girls, we read Sophocles' play *Antigone*. The students argued fiercely and eloquently over the judgment of King Creon against Antigone, who insisted on honoring her dead brother. Later we read parts of *Romeo and Juliet*. The students' soft ghetto voices gave the Elizabethan speech a powerful new music. Their favorite play was *A Raisin in the Sun*, by Lorraine Hansberry. We all knew people like Lena, the matriarch, and her weak, handsome son, from our own lives. We read excerpts from *Inside the Brain*, by Ronald Kotulak. One student traced her own learning difficulties to her mother's drug use during pregnancy. Another took heart at the awesome resilience of the adult brain, feeling that it was possible for her to master math and pass the GED, though the work was very hard for her. She had not stayed in school long enough to learn algebra, and this was a real disadvantage for GED students.

In quiet moments, I would look out on the tables of students and admit undeniably that these were the kids (whatever their ages) that we had failed to reach. These are kids we all had in our classes, kids who were often behavior problems, kids who had a hard time with learning, either because of circumstances or brain wiring or both. We passed or failed them, or we placed them elsewhere and forgot about them. They quit school, but they did not go away. I felt like Alice, stepping through the looking glass of American education and meeting firsthand these tales of almost incomprehensible woe.

Some days at the GED table were heartbreaking. There was Lily, who sometimes had to excuse herself from class, eyes brimming with tears, because the image of her teenage son, lying dead of a gunshot wound, was still too raw. Her own drug use could only intermittently obscure the pain. There was Ellie, just 18, who braided her own hair into shining French braids and who had been incarcerated one way or another since she was 10. There were girls and women with scars and burn marks and injured eyes. There were girls and women who had had their front teeth knocked out. Some were safer in jail than at home. Every day when I left the jail, I took a deep breath of fresh air, but my students were locked away, and their stories and their anguish and their unique female rage were locked away with them.

I have great respect for the deputies in the residence pods. I just came in every morning with my case of GED materials and enjoyed a few hours of pure and joyful teaching. It was the deputies who handled the round-the-clock despair of incarcerated lives.

Winter ripened into spring. My students left for prison, or for rehab, or for home, and there were new students almost every day. I could no longer support my family on the part-time salary, and we needed health insurance. Dutifully I applied for every full-time English teaching job within commuting distance from home. I am sure that I bombed more than one interview just by being too enthusiastic about jail! On the last day of summer before school started, I was hired for a long-term English substitute position in a suburban high school an hour from home. I would be able to make ends meet again, with the family insured. My father would approve. Or would he? I could not shake the feeling that, in terms of my calling as a teacher, I was selling out. I was abandoning students who needed me for students who probably didn't.

My new students are well dressed and college-bound. They have jet skis and cellphones, and if they ever get into trouble, it is unlikely that they will have to rely on a court-appointed attorney—or even need to know what one is. I do not have a classroom. But what am I complaining about? I have a cart that I take from room to room. In the jail, I lugged around a plastic case. Maybe it is the role of substitute that makes me feel tentative. Maybe it is the constant interruptions, the reminders about "crazy sock" day, the announcements about senior baby pictures, and the grade-level fund-raisers. Maybe I just want to go back to jail.

Recently I got a letter from Sally. She is doing one to three years at "Miss Betty's House," the insider's term for the Bedford Hills Correctional Facility. She tells me she is attending GED classes again, determined to pass this time. She says she will never give up, and I believe her. She thanks me for encouraging her to write. She reminds me that I always told the students that the world will be a better place when more women tell their stories. She says she plans to put her life down in a book someday, and I believe she will.

I miss the dull roar of electric doors closing behind me. I miss the courage of the students who came to the GED table ready to learn, despite broken lives, despite deep worries and uncertain futures. I miss the sense that I am somehow making it up to them for our educational failures of the past. Sure, I know it is a drop in the bucket. But I also know that each day, as I went deeper into the experiences of these women, I came closer to students who honored me with their willing minds. Each day in the jail, I was true to my calling. In jail I was a teacher.

LYNN OLCOTT is a high school teacher and freelance writer living in Homer, N.Y. She is an adjunct professor in the Foundations and Social Advocacy Department at the State University of New York, Cortland. Since writing this article, she has returned to jail.

Classroom Behavior Management
A Dozen Common Mistakes and What to Do Instead

This article presents a dozen common classroom management mistakes that teachers make, followed by suggestions as to what we should do instead. The mistakes presented are committed frequently at many grade levels and in all types of learning environments. The recommended suggestions are relatively easy to implement and useful for all types of learners.

PATRICIA M. BARBETTA, KATHLEEN LEONG NORONA, AND DAVID F. BICARD

One of our primary responsibilities as teachers is to help our students learn. It is difficult for learning to take place in chaotic environments. Subsequently, we are challenged daily to create and maintain a positive, productive classroom atmosphere conducive to learning. On any given day, this can be quite a challenge. In our attempts to face this challenge, we find ourselves making common classroom behavior management mistakes. This article is designed to presents some of these common mistakes followed by suggestions as to what we should do instead. The mistakes presented are committed frequently, at many grade levels and in all types of learning environments. Each suggestion is relatively easy to implement and useful for all types of learners.

We have based our suggestions on several assumptions and beliefs. First and foremost, teachers have considerable influence over student behavior. This is particularly true if interventions begin early and are supported at home. Next, most student misbehaviors are learned and occur for a reason. It is our job to determine those reasons and teach appropriate behaviors to replace those misbehaviors. We believe that prevention is the most effective form of behavior management. That is, the most efficient way to eliminate misbehaviors is to prevent their occurrence or escalation from the beginning. Using a proactive approach also allows us to focus more on teaching appropriate behaviors rather than eliminating negative behaviors. Our experience tells us that management systems should be flexible enough to meet the changing needs of our classrooms. Finally, students, parents, and other professionals can be effective partners in behavior management.

Mistake #1: Defining Misbehavior by How It Looks

When attempting to change misbehavior, we often describe it by only how it looks (e.g., calling out, hitting, getting out of seat). Defining misbehavior by how it looks only provides us with an incomplete picture of the behavior; it tells us little about why it occurred and doesn't help much in our behavior-change efforts. For example, a student who is off task is a common classroom problem. If two of our students are off task regularly, they may or may not be off task for the same reason. If they are off task for different reasons, our approaches to change their behaviors may need to differ. Actually, a strategy that will eliminate the off-task behavior of one student might worsen the off-task behavior of the other. Defining a misbehavior by how it looks tells us nothing about why it occurred and often doesn't help in our behavior-change efforts. Just because two behaviors look the same, doesn't mean they are the same.

Instead: Define Misbehavior by Its Function

To develop a better strategy to manage misbehaviors, we need to ask ourselves, "What was the function of this misbehavior?" Or more simply, "What did the student gain from the misbehavior?" Though our students' misbehaviors appear to occur for no reason, they do serve a purpose, otherwise they would not occur. Although some behavior problems are the result of organic issues (e.g., hyperactivity) most misbehaviors function for one of two following reasons: (a) to get something (e.g., attention from another student or teacher, gain a privilege, get a toy) or (b) to avoid something (e.g., schoolwork, teacher demands). For example, the two off-task students mentioned previously—one student might be off task to get our attention, whereas the other might be off task because his or her assignment was too difficult. For the attention-seeking student, we could ignore his or her off-task behavior and only give him our attention when he is behaving appropriately. For the academically frustrated student, a change in his or her assignment (e.g., fewer problems to solve, clearer directions) might eliminate the off-task behaviors. Clearly, these misbehaviors serve dissimilar functions and need to be solved differently.

Mistake #2: Asking, "Why Did You Do That?"

Although we are tempted, it is not a good idea to ask our students, "Why did you do that?" First, many times our students will not know the reasons why they misbehaved. Second, we often will not like their answers. For example, if Victor is playing at his desk during our lesson and we ask him why, he may very well say, "Because this lesson is so boring." We are not likely to be pleased with that response.

Instead: Assess the Behavior Directly to Determine Its Function

The function of a behavior is the purpose it serves the student (i.e., what the student gets from it). As stated previously, most misbehaviors serve a getting or an avoiding function. To determine a behavior's function, we need to study what is happening in the classroom before and after it occurs. This information-gathering procedure is called a *functional assessment.* An Antecedent-Behavior-Consequence (ABC) chart can be used as a functional assessment tool. An ABC chart has three columns on which we record the behavior and what happened before and after it. The standard way to make this chart is to separate a sheet of paper into three columns and label the first *Antecedent,* the second *Behavior,* and the third *Consequence.* When the misbehavior occurs, it is written down in the behavior column, then the observer records what happened immediately before (recorded in the antecedent column) and after its occurrence (recorded in the consequence column). To make data collection simpler, a modified ABC chart can be used that contains several predetermined categories of teacher or peer antecedent behavior, student responses, and consequential events (See Figure 1).

A functional assessment gives us a more complete picture of the misbehavior by including the environmental antecedents and consequences in its description (Alberto & Troutman, 2003). Once we determine the function of a misbehavior ("why" it occurs), we need to teach and reinforce an appropriate replacement behavior that serves the same function as the misbehavior. For instance, if a functional assessment reveals that Olivia teases her friends at recess because it is the only time that she gets their attention, we need to teach Olivia appropriate methods to get peer attention, such as sharing or asking to be invited to join in a game. A functional assessment might reveal that changes in our teaching methods are needed. For instance, if Ricardo tends to act out during math class, a change in how or what we are teaching may be in order. The problem might be that Ricardo is missing some prerequisite math skills. By reviewing those prerequisite math skills, we could reduce his frustrations and acting out, and maximize his learning.

Many times, an ABC analysis is all that is needed to determine a functional assessment. For complex behavior problems, a more detailed, multifaceted functional assessment may be needed. At those times, we should contact a behavior-management specialist, school psychologist, or other trained professional for a more thorough assessment. Conducting a functional assessment can be time consuming. However, research shows that behavior-change programs designed from this process tend to be more effective than those begun without the comprehensive information provided by this assessment (Kamps, 2002). For additional information on conducting a functional assessment, we recommend visiting the Center for Effective Collaboration and Practice Web site at http://cecp .air.org/fba/.

Mistake #3: When an Approach Isn't Working, Try Harder

When a management approach isn't working, our first tendency is to try harder. The problem is that we most often try harder negatively. We make loud, disapproving statements, increase negative consequences, or remove more privileges. This does not do anything to teach appropriate behavior. Instead, our increased negativity results in impaired student—teacher relationships and increases the likelihood of our students feeling defeated.

Instead: Try Another Way

When an approach is not working, instead of trying harder, we should try another way. Some examples include verbal redirecting, proximity control, reinforcing incompatible behaviors, changing the academic tasks and providing additional cues or prompts. These approaches are more effective, simpler to use, and create a more positive classroom climate than trying harder. If two of our students, Danny and Sara, are talking in class, instead of reprimanding them, we could walk in their direction (use proximity control), make eye contact, and provide a nonverbal cue to get on task. This approach allows Danny and Sara to save face with their peers and promotes teacher respect.

Instead of increasing negative consequences, we should increase the frequency of contingent praise for appropriate student behavior. Teacher praise is easy to deliver and is one of the most powerful tools available to us. In fact, praise (or some type of reinforcement) should be included in all approaches to behavior change. For example, when Jamal is off task, instead of reprimanding, we should find another student who is on-task and praise that student. This will reinforce the on task student and has the added benefit of notifying Jamal of his misbehavior, without singling him out. When using praise, we should remember that it is effective when it is provided immediately (minimally before the next opportunity to perform the behavior again), specifically (by identifying the behavior as we praise), and frequently.

Student's Name: _____ Date(s): _____

Check all that apply each time the student engages in the inappropriate behavior.

What Happened Before?	Behavior	What Happened After?

__ Academic Task requested
  __ Academic task too easy
  __ Academic task too hard
  __ Academic task unmotivating
  __ Academic task long
  __ Academic task unclear
__ Teacher reprimand
__ Asked to go somewhere
__ Peer teasing
__ Peer encouragement
 	
Other: _____
  _____
  _____
	__ 1. Talk-outs in class
	__ 2. Noncompliance
	__ 3. Verbal aggression
	__ 4. Inappropriate language
	__ 5. Disruptive
	__ 6. Not completing work
	__ 7. Fidgeting
	
	__ 8. _____
	
	__ 9. _____
		Get/obtain
		__ Adult attention
		__ Desired activity/item
		__ Peer attention
		
		Avoid/escape
		__ Academic task
		__ Teacher request/demands
		__ Teacher correction
		__ Classroom
		__ Peer social contact
		
		Other: _____
		  _____

Note. This is only a partial functional assessment form. The complete form would include several opportunities to record ABC assessments.

Figure 1 Antecedent-Behavior-Consequence (ABC) functional assessment form.

Our most challenging students, such as students with severe emotional and behavioral problems, often need the most reinforcement, yet they often receive the least. Descriptive research of classrooms for children with behavior disorders shows low praise rates of only 1.2 to 4.5 times per hour (Gable, Hendrickson, Young, Shores, & Stowitschek, 1983; Shores et al., 1993; Van Acker, Grant, & Henry, 1996; Wehby, Symons, & Shores, 1995). This trend needs to be changed.

Finally, when we find ourselves making more stop than start requests, we need to reverse our behavior. For example, instead of asking Sam to stop talking, ask him to work on his assignment. When he complies, provide praise. For excellent resources on practical, positive classroom management techniques, see Rhode, Jenson, and Reavis (1992) and Kerr and Nelson (2002) in the appendix.

Mistake #4: Violating the Principles of Good Classroom Rules

Classroom rules play a vital role in effective classroom management. However, rules alone exert little influence over student behavior. Too often, rules are posted at the beginning of the year, briefly reviewed once, and then attended to minimally. When this is the case, they have little to no effect on student behavior.

Instead: Follow the Guidelines for Classroom Rules

There are several rules for rule setting that, when followed, help create orderly, productive classrooms that teach appropriate social skills along with the academic curriculum. To be more effective, our classrooms should have four-to-six rules that could govern most classroom situations. Too many rules can make it difficult for students to comply and for teachers to enforce. Along with other professionals (e.g., Gathercoal, 1997; Paine, Radicchi, Rosellini, Deutchman, & Darch, 1983), we see benefits to students actively participating in rule setting. When students play an active role, they begin to learn the rules, and they are more inclined to have rule ownership. The rules become their rules, not our rules. To include students, conduct several short rule-setting meetings the first few days of school. For these meetings to be effective, we need to share with our students the rule-making guidelines (e.g., the rules need to be stated positively, they have to be observable and measurable, consequences need to be realistic). With guidelines in place, students often select rules similar to the ones we would have selected. Without guidelines, students are inclined to make too many rules, make rules that are too stringent, and make those that are not specific enough.

Classroom rules should be simple, specific, clear, and measurable. The degree of rule simplicity depends on the age and ability levels of our students. For younger students, we may want to include pictures in the rule posters. Rules are specific when they are clear and unambiguous. For example, the rule "bring books, paper, and pencils to class" is much clearer than the rule "be ready to learn." Clearly stated rules are easily observed and measured. The classroom rules should be posted.

Another characteristic of effective rules is that they are stated positively. Positively stated rules are "do" rules. Do rules provide information as to how to behave and set the occasion for teacher praise. An example is "Raise your hand for permission to talk." Conversely, negatively stated rules or "don't" rules tell students what not to do and encourage us to attend to student rule breaking. An example of a don't rule is "Don't call out."

Some teachers develop subrules that correspond with each of the major classroom rules. For example, a classroom rule might be, "Follow classroom expectations." One of the corresponding subrules for line behavior could be "Keep your hands and feet to yourself." Once the subrules are set, we need to teach or role play appropriate behavior by having mini-lessons (3–5 minutes) several times a day for the first few weeks of school. Some teachers continue to review subrules prior to each activity or periodically, depending on their students' needs. A simple, quick way to review is to have a student volunteer to read the posted subrules prior to each major activity.

We consistently need to carry out the consequences and noncompliance of our classroom rules or they will mean very little. If our students follow the rules for group work at the learning center, we should verbally praise them and provide additional reinforcement as needed (e.g., stickers, extra free time). On the other hand, if the classroom consequence for fighting with a peer is the loss of recess, then we must make certain that we follow through. We need to make clear the consequences for following and not following the rules (Babyak, Luze, & Kamps, 2000).

We often need reminders to praise our students throughout the school day. One way is to place a sign in the back of the room that says, "Have you praised your students lately?" Each time we notice the sign, we should praise a student or the group for following one of the classroom rules. Another way is to keep a running tally of our praise comments on an index card or on a card clipped to a string that hangs from our necks (similar to those used with many school identification cards).

To summarize, the guidelines for classroom rules include the following: (a) develop 4–6 measurable, observable, positive classroom rules and include students in rule development; (b) teach the rules and subrules directly; (c) post the rules and review them frequently; and, (d) be sure to carry out the consequences for rule compliance and noncompliance.

Mistake #5: Treating All Misbehaviors as "Won't Dos"

When students misbehave, it often seems as though it is exclusively a motivational issue. At times, this is true. On those occasions, we need to increase the reinforcement for appropriate behavior and eliminate it for inappropriate behavior. However, several misbehaviors are due to a lack of appropriate skills not a lack of motivation. We call these behaviors "can't dos."

Instead: Treat Some Behaviors as Can't Dos

Can't dos occur because of lack of skills not lack of motivation or reinforcement. We should deal with can't do misbehaviors the same way that we deal with student's academic mistakes. When students make repeated errors during our lessons, we make changes in how we teach (e.g., provide more examples, allow students to practice more), and provide more intensive instruction. Our improved lessons make us more proactive teachers, decreasing the likelihood of chronic, academic errors being repeated. This preventative approach is referred to as precorrection (Colvin, Sugai, & Patching, 1993). In contrast, when students chronically misbehave, we are more inclined to remain reactive, provide only correction procedures (simply tell them that they are misbehaving), and increase the intensity of our negative consequences. We would be more effective in solving chronic misbehaviors if we moved into the precorrective mode.

The following are seven major precorrection steps:

Step 1. Identify the context and the predictable behavior (where and when the misbehavior occurs);

Step 2. Specify expected behavior (what we want instead);

Step 3. Systematically modify the context (e.g., changes in instruction, tasks, schedules, seating arrangements);

Step 4. Conduct behavior rehearsals (have students practice the appropriate behavior);

Step 5. Provide strong reinforcement such as frequent and immediate teacher praise;

Step 6. Prompt expected behaviors; and

Step 7. Monitor the plan (collect data on student performance).

Let's apply this step to a traditional classroom behavior problem—calling out during teacher-led instruction. The misbehavior occurs during guided instruction (Step 1). The behavior that we want instead is for our students to raise their hands and wait to be called on (Step 2). To accomplish this goal, we could verbally remind our students to raise their hands prior to each question and no longer respond to our students' call outs. Also, we could model hand-raising as we ask the question to prompt students to do the same (Steps 3 and 6). Before our teacher-led lessons, we could have a short review of the rules for appropriate hand-raising (Step 4). When our students raise their hands appropriately, we should praise immediately and frequently and perhaps give them bonus points on the classroom management system (Step 5). Finally, to determine if our plan is effective, we should tally how often students appropriately raise their hands (Step 7).

Although initially more time consuming, precorrection procedures allow us to be more proactive than reactive and to reduce or eliminate behavior problems before they become well established. This, in turn, increases the amount of time that we have to reinforce appropriate behavior.

Mistake #6: Lack of Planning for Transition Time

When planning our teaching day, planning for transitions often gets overlooked. Yet, a significant amount of class time is spent transitioning from one subject to another or from one place to another. Without proper planning, transitioning can be one of the most frustrating times of the day for teachers. These times seem to invite behavior problems. Why? At times students are not ready for the transition. Inconsistent expectations cause transition problems. Furthermore, because we are often transitioning with the students, our attention is diverted away from them, making transitions longer and inviting even more misbehavior.

Instead: Appropriately Plan for Transition Time

Successful transitioning requires just as much planning as effective academic instruction, but the time is worth it. When transitions are done quickly and quietly, it allows lessons to start on time and can set a positive tone for the lesson, whereas unplanned, poorly done transitions can waste valuable time and cause negative student–teacher interactions.

Transition problems can be reduced significantly by following a few practical procedures. First, it is best that our transition expectations are consistent, meaning the same rules apply for each type of transition. Consistency begins by developing transition rules with our students (e.g., quietly put materials away, keep your hands and feet to yourself.)

Once we have developed our transition rules, we should teach them to our students. We can do this by having brief lessons at the beginning of the school year followed by frequent reviews. It is a good idea to post the transition rules, and have a student volunteer to read them before transitioning. We should consistently provide readiness signals or cues for pending transitions. We can do this by letting our students know that in 5 minutes the next activity will begin and that it is time to finish the task at hand. We need to follow that statement by praising students as we see them finishing their tasks. It is important not to move to the next step of the transitioning process until everyone has followed the previous steps. For example, if we ask our students to return to their seats and get out their math books, everyone needs to have followed those directions before we begin our math lesson. For groups that

have a difficult time switching gears, such as many students with learning disabilities or behavior disorders, providing a 30-second group silence at their seats prior to beginning the next activity promotes calmness before moving on. This is particularly useful when students are returning from a highly stimulating activity, such as physical education.

Many students respond positively to transition timing games. To do this, first set a time goal (e.g., everyone should be in line within 20 seconds). Using a stopwatch, time their transition and then praise individual students or the group for meeting the goal. When transitions involve leaving the classroom, prior to leaving, we should have our students take out the materials for the lesson that is going to be conducted on their return. This will facilitate getting started when they return to the classroom.

Our role as teachers during transitions should be to monitor students' performance and to praise appropriate behavior. To do this, we must have our materials prepared ahead of time. When needed, we should use students or aides to gather materials or equipment, allowing us to better attend to our students and provide praise.

Mistake #7: Ignoring All or Nothing at All

Ignoring can be a valuable tool in reducing misbehaviors when used with behavior-building strategies. However, it's difficult for many of us to determine which behaviors to ignore and which to give attention. We tend to take ignoring to extremes by ignoring almost all misbehaviors or none at all. Neither approach is effective.

Instead: Ignore Wisely

First, not all behaviors should be ignored. We should only ignore the behaviors motivated for our attention. For example, if Larry is playing his favorite computer game instead of doing math, ignoring him will not work because his behavior is not motivated by our attention. His motivation is playing on the computer. However, when behaviors are attention seeking we need to ignore continuously (every single time). As soon as we begin to ignore our student's misbehavior, he or she will seek it elsewhere, most likely from peers. It can be difficult for peers to ignore misbehaviors. Therefore, ignoring misbehavior should be a classroom rule that receives powerful reinforcement. Also, we need to plan for the misbehavior to get worse (happen more often and more intensely) before it improves. When this happens, we must continue to ignore.

Ignoring must be used in combination with behavior-building strategies, such as reinforcement of appropriate behaviors, teaching replacement behaviors, and reinforcing peers. Ignoring teaches students what not to do, but does not teach them what they should do instead. For example, a pre-school student, Monica, has a tendency to tug at our clothing or yell to get our attention. In this scenario, we should ignore these misbehaviors. In addition, we need to teach Monica appropriate ways to gain our attention (e.g., raising her hand, saying "excuse me") and praise her each time she uses these replacement behaviors. To add to the effectiveness, we could also praise peers who, in her presence, appropriately seek our attention.

There are occasions when ignoring is inappropriate. These include when there are concerns for observational learning of misbehaviors, when our students are engaging in extreme or dangerous behaviors, and, as stated earlier, when the misbehavior is not attention seeking.

Mistake #8: Overuse and Misuse of Time Out

Time out occurs when a teacher removes a student for a specific time from a chance to receive reinforcement. There are several time-out strategies ranging from brief in-class ignoring to placing a student in a secluded area. We are tempted to overuse time out because it results in a reprieve from problematic students. At times, we misuse time out by inadvertently reinforcing misbehaviors while using the procedure.

Instead: Follow the Principles of Effective Time Out

Time out can be an effective tool but only when used appropriately (Turner & Watson, 1999). First, we must remember that time out is not a place. Instead it is a process whereby all opportunities to get reinforced are withdrawn. Consequently, for it to work, the time-in area (the activity) must be more reinforcing than the time-out area. Ways to make the time-in area more reinforcing include changing the activity, our instructional techniques, and increasing our praise. For example, Trevor constantly disrupts the language arts lesson by throwing paper or talking to peers, resulting in frequent time outs in the hall. Time out would only be effective if the language-arts lesson is more stimulating than what is going on in the hall, which often is not the case. A better method would be to make the language-arts lesson highly stimulating by using cooperative learning, hands-on activities, and frequent student responding. If we still need to use time out with Trevor, we need to find a less stimulating, designated time-out area, such as a partitioned corner of the room.

For mildly disruptive misbehavior, time outs should be done in class. In-class time out involves the removal of all forms of reinforcement for a brief period of time. One type of in-class time out is *planned ignoring,* which involves the brief removal of social reinforcers, such as attention or verbal interaction. This involves looking away from the student, refraining from any interaction, or remaining quiet. A second form of in-class time out is the brief removal of the student from an activity by being placed on the outskirts (i.e., a few steps back) but still able to "look" into the more reinforcing time-in setting.

When misbehaviors are more severe, we may need to send our students to out-of-class time out. The out-of-class time out area should be a quiet, nonintimidating, reinforcement-free room with no other purpose. It should not be a highly stimulating, reinforcing place like the office area, other classrooms, or the hallway. If possible, we should use the same place for each time out. Despite our frustrations, we should administer time out with a calm, neutral tone of voice. We should also give our students a brief explanation for the time out to help build an association between the misbehavior and the time-out consequence. Time outs should last for only brief, reasonable periods of time (from a few seconds for in-class to several minutes for out-of-class time outs) and should be monitored occasionally to make certain the student is not receiving reinforcement. We should collect data to assess the overall effectiveness of time out. Finally, time out should always be used with precorrective, behavior-building strategies and reinforcement.

Mistake #9: Inconsistent Expectations and Consequences

Students are often given mixed signals as to what is expected and what will happen if they do not meet these expectations. Inconsistent expectations cause student confusion and frustration. Inconsistent consequences maintain misbehaviors and can even cause the behavior to occur more frequently or intensely. In addition, we find ourselves constantly reminding and threatening which, in turn, enhances our frustration.

Instead: Have Clear Expectations That Are Enforced and Reinforced Consistently

Expectations are clear when they are identifiable and consistent. Reviewing expectations and rehearsing rules help build routines and minimize the potential for problems. We can do this by asking our students to read the expectations prior to each activity. When we have temporary expectation changes (e.g., changes in rules due to a guest being present or special school event), we must inform our students.

Expectations are pointless if they are not backed up with reinforcement for compliance and reasonable negative consequences for noncompliance. For rule compliance, positive consequences should be applied continuously at first (every time the student is appropriate) and then intermittently (every so often). For example, if "following teacher's directions" is the classroom rule, then we should provide some form of positive consequence, perhaps praising the students for following directions quickly and appropriately. At first, praise should be delivered each time the student follows teacher directions. Once the teacher establishes the behavior (in this case, following teacher directions), we can move to an intermittent praise schedule. On the other hand, negative consequences (punishment procedures) are most effective when applied continuously. For instance, if our classroom consequence for verbal aggression toward a peer is the loss of recess privileges, then each time one of our students is verbally aggressive we should apply that negative consequence. Of course, to effectively deal with this verbal aggression, we also need to implement additional precorrective methods, such as teaching appropriate expressions of anger, peer mediation, prompting and providing praise for socially, appropriate interactions.

Mistake #10: Viewing Ourselves as the Only Classroom Manager

Managing classroom behavior may be more challenging today than ever before. Many teachers face larger class sizes, more students who come from stressful, chaotic homes, and increased diversity in students' abilities and cultures (Grossman, 2004). Yet, many of us are determined to manage classroom behavior ourselves. After all, collaborating with others takes time and energy to build rapport and come to a consensus on behavior-change priorities and strategies. It's tempting just to forge ahead. Although, going at it alone may seem like a good idea in the short-run, in the long run, we are more likely to burn out and lose our effectiveness.

Instead: Include Students, Parents, and Others in Management Efforts

Fortunately, there are many others who can assist in our behavior management efforts, including students, their peers, fellow teachers, administrators, parents, and other school personnel. One effective way to include students in their own behavior change programs is the use of self-monitoring. With self-monitoring, a student helps regulate his or her own behavior by recording its occurrence on a self-monitoring form. To help ensure accuracy of self-monitoring, we should occasionally collect the data ourselves and compare our recordings with those of our student. If our student accurately self-monitored, we should reinforce his or her accuracy. In addition, we should hold brief, occasional student–teacher conferences to review the student's progress. For more information on self-monitoring, see Alberto and Troutman (2003) or Webber, Scheuerman, McCall, and Coleman (1993). Also, go to http://www.coe.missouri.edu/~vrcbd to learn about KidTools, a computer-based program used to help students create and use a variety of self-monitoring materials. KidTools contains easy-to-use templates used to create personalized self-monitoring forms, including point cards, countoons, self management cards, make-a-plan cards, and contracts. To use this program, students enter information about target behaviors into a template and print out the card for immediate use in the classroom.

The power of the peer group can be used to produce positive changes in student behavior. Peers can serve as academic tutors and can monitor and reinforce each other's behaviors. Also, group-process, conflict resolution, or peer mediation meetings can be used in which students provide each other with behavior management suggestions (e.g., "Ignore him when he calls you names"), praise each other for behaving appropriately, and help each other resolve a current classroom behavior problem (Barbetta, 1990; Smith & Daunic, 2002). To help facilitate group cohesiveness, we can use group-oriented contingencies in which the class earns its level of privileges and reinforcers as a group.

We should also include other adults in behavior management. Fellow teachers can provide support in several ways. One way is to schedule regular meetings where we share behavior management solutions. Occasionally, we may need some extra support from a colleague, particularly if we work with students with emotional disorders. During those days, we shouldn't hesitate to ask a colleague to stop by during his or her planning period and provide us with some additional support or a short break. If we find ourselves in a teaching situation with one or more volatile students, we should develop a support plan with a teacher in a classroom nearby (Lindberg & Swick, 2002). This plan could include an agreement that our colleague will cover our room in the event we have to escort a disruptive student out of the room or contact the principal or school security. Another example of how we can support each other is by playing an active role in school-wide behavior management (Lindberg & Swick). As we move throughout the school grounds (e.g., hallway, cafeteria, auditorium, playground), we should be aware of all students' behaviors (not just our own students) and prompt and provide praise or negative consequences as appropriate.

When including administrators in behavior management, we tend to make two mistakes that are at opposite ends of the support spectrum (Lindberg & Swick, 2002). We either send students to them too frequently or we wait too long to get them involved. It is best to resolve as many behavior problems in our class and only involve administrators for more serious situations, such as physical aggression.

Parents and teachers who work actively together make a powerful team. Most parents can provide useful information about their child (i.e., medications, allergies, issues at home). Some parents can assist in our behavior management efforts at home by providing their child additional prompting and reinforcement. Although, there are many benefits to working with parents, some teachers are reluctant due to the challenges that often exist. The potential benefits, however, make it worthwhile in most situations, and there are many ways to increase parent–teacher team effectiveness (See Jones & Jones, 2002 in appendix). As teachers, it is our responsibility to build productive and positive parent–teacher partnerships. We can do this by contacting parents when their child does well, treating them with respect during conferences, maintaining positive and on-going communication, and validating any concerns they may have.

School counselors, psychologists, and other professionals can be invaluable resources. We should seek out their assistance when needed for support, guidance, and additional strategies.

Mistake #11: Missing the Link Between Instruction and Behavior

At times there is a direct link between our lessons and student misbehavior. Perhaps our lesson is too easy or difficult, ineffective, or nonstimulating, which can lead to student misbehavior (Center, Deitz, & Kaufman, 1982).

Instead: Use Academic Instruction as a Behavior Management Tool

The first line of defense in managing student behavior is effective instruction. Good teachers have always known this and research supports this notion (Evertson & Harris, 1992). Jones (1991) found that when teachers demystify learning, achievement and behavior improve dramatically. Examples of how to demystify learning include students establishing his or her learning goals, students monitoring his or her own learning, involving students in developing classroom rules and procedures, and relating lessons to students' own lives and interests.

Effective teaching practices include (but are not limited to) instruction that is fast paced, includes high rates of active student responding, involves modeling new behaviors, and provides guided practice and positive and corrective feedback (Evertson & Harris 1992; Sugai & Tindal, 1993). Effective instructional strategies include the use of response cards, guided notes, and peer tutoring (Heward, 2003; Heward et al., 1996; Miller, Barbetta, & Heron, 1994). Consistent use of these strategies, and others that share the characteristics of effective instruction, helps create highly effective learning environments, which, in turn, reduces the likelihood of behavior problems.

Mistake #12: Taking Student Behavior Too Personally

When students misbehave, it often feels like a personal attack, and for good reason. Some of our students are very good at making it feel personal. When we take students' misbehavior personally, we tend to lose our objectivity, look for quick management fixes that rarely work, and get emotionally upset, which takes time and energy away from our teaching.

Instead: Take Student Misbehavior Professionally, Not Personally

When we take misbehavior professionally, we view behavior management as our responsibility. Professionals know the importance of having a sound management system in place that deals with classwide issues and individual student problems. Professionals have realistic expectations for improvement in behavior and know that there are no quick fixes with lasting effects. Most importantly, confident professionals ask for assistance when it is needed.

Although handling misbehaviors may be more challenging than teaching academics, there are many effective strategies we can use that will make our classroom days more pleasant and less chaotic. When we are more effective, we're calmer and less likely to react personally to student misbehavior. Although some student misbehavior may appear to be targeted toward us, these behaviors may be an outcome of their own wants and needs, lack of skills, or emotional difficulties and frustrations.

The time and energy wasted being upset at our students' misbehavior is better spent celebrating our students' success.

Conclusion

This article briefly reviewed common behavior management mistakes that we make as teachers and provided numerous strategies as to what to do instead. We believe these suggestions will be useful in the context of developing and implementing a comprehensive behavior management plan. By no means do these suggestions represent a complete list of effective strategies. For more thorough information on some of the recommended strategies, refer to the reference list.

References

Alberto, P. A., & Troutman, A. C. (2003). *Applied behavior analysis for teachers.* Upper Saddle River, NJ: Pearson Prentice Hall.

Babyak, A., Luze, G., & Kamps, D. (2000). The good student game: Behavior management for diverse classrooms. *Intervention in School and Clinic, 35,* 216–223.

Barbetta, P. M. (1990). Goals: Group-oriented adapted levels system for children with behavior disorders. *Academic Therapy, 25,* 645–656.

Center, D. B., Deitz, S. M., & Kaufman, N. E. (1982). Student ability, task difficulty, and inappropriate classroom behavior: A study of children with behavioral disorders. *Behavior Modification, 6,* 355–374.

Colvin, G., Sugai, G., & Patching, B. (1993). Precorrection: An instructional approach for managing predictable problem behaviors. *Intervention in School and Clinic, 28*(3), 143–150.

Evertson, C., & Harris, A. (1992). Synthesis of research: What we know about managing classrooms. *Educational Leadership, 49,* 74–78.

Gable, R. A., Hendrickson, J. M., Young, C. C., Shores, R. E., & Stowitschek, J. J. (1983). A comparison of teacher approval and disapproval statements across categories of exceptionality. *Journal of Special Education Technology, 6,* 15–22.

Gathercoal, F. (1997). *Judicious discipline* (4th ed.). San Francisco: Caddo Gap Press.

Grossman, H. (2004). *Classroom behavior management for diverse and inclusive schools.* Lanham, MD: Rowman & Littlefield.

Heward, W. L. (2003). *Exceptional children: An introduction to special education* (7th ed.). Englewood Cliffs, NJ: Merrill/Prentice-Hall.

Heward, W. L., Gardner III, R., Cavanaugh, R. A., Courson, F. H., Grossi, T. A., & Barbetta, P. M. (1996). Everyone participates in this class. *Teaching Exceptional Children, 28,* 4–10.

Jones, V. (1991). Experienced teachers' assessment of classroom management skills presented in a summer course. *Journal of Instructional Psychology, 18,* 103–109.

Kamps, D. M. (2002). Preventing problems in improving behavior. In B. Algozzine & P. Kay (Eds.), *Preventing problem behavior* (pp. 11–36). Thousands Oaks, CA: Corwin Press.

Lindberg, J. A., & Swick, A. M. (2002). *Commonsense classroom management: Surviving September and beyond in the elementary classroom.* Thousand Oaks, CA: Corwin Press.

Miller, D. M., Barbetta, P. M., & Heron, T. E. (1994). START tutoring: Designing, training, implementing, adapting, and evaluating tutoring programs for school and home settings. In R. Gardner, D. Sianato, J. O. Cooper, W. L. Heward, T. E. Heron, J. W. Eshleman, et al. (Eds.), *Behavior analysis in education: Focus on measurably superior instruction* (pp. 265–282). Pacific Grove, CA: Brooks/Cole.

Paine, S. C., Radicchi, J., Rosellini, L. C., Deutchman, & Darch, C. B. (1983). *Structuring your classroom for academic success.* Champaign, IL: Research Press.

Shores, R. E., Jack, S. L., Gunter, P. L., Ellis, D. N., Debriere, T. J., & Wehby, J. H. (1993). Classroom interactions of children with behavior disorders. *Journal of Emotional and Behavioral Disorders, 1,* 27–39.

Smith, S. W., & Daunic, A. P. (2002). Using conflict resolution and peer mediation to support positive behavior. In B. Algozzine & P. Kay (Eds.), *Preventing problem behavior* (pp. 142–161). Thousands Oaks, CA: Corwin Press.

Sugai, G. M., & Tindel, G. A. (1993). *Effective school consultation: An interactive approach.* Pacific Grove, CA: Brooks/Cole.

Turner, H. S., & Watson, T. S. (1999). Consultant's guide for the use of time out in the preschool and elementary classroom. *Psychology in the Schools, 36*(2), 135–147.

Van Acker, R. Grant, S. H., & Henry, D. (1996). Teacher and student behavior as a function of risk for aggression. *Education and Treatment of Children, 19,* 316–334.

Webber, J., Scheuerman, B., McCall, C., & Coleman, M. (1993). Research on self-monitoring as a behavior management technique in special education classrooms: A descriptive review. *Remedial and Special Education, 14*(2), 38–56.

Wehby, J. H., Symons, F. J., & Shores, R. E. (1995). A descriptive analysis of aggressive behavior in classrooms for children with emotional and behavioral disorders. *Behavioral Disorders, 24,* 51–56.

PATRICIA M. BARBETTA is a special education associate professor and strand leader at Florida International University, Miami. **KATHLEEN LEONG NORONA** is a school psychologist in the Miami-Dade County Public Schools, Miami, Florida. **DAVID F. BICARD** is director of research and staff development at Hawthorne County Day School, New York.

From *Preventing School Failure,* Vol. 49, No. 3, Spring 2005, pp. 11–19. Reprinted by permission of the Helen Dwight Reid Educational Foundation. Published by Heldref Publications, 1319, Eighteenth St., NW, Washington, DC 20036-1802. Copyright © 2005. www.heldref.org

Students with Emotional and Behavioral Disorders *Can* Manage Their Own Behavior

BEVERLY PATTON, KRISTINE JOLIVETTE, AND MICHELLE RAMSEY

For the 5th day in a row, you arrive at school only to find your third-grade student, Chris, in the principal's office. Today, the art teacher caught Chris pushing and shoving the students around him in the breakfast line.

Three times this week, Alexa has been sent to you, her case manager, because she refused to begin her work in class. Today, the 10th grader arrived during third period with a note from the general education teacher stating she crumpled up her quiz, threw it on the floor, and refused to pick it up. You have tried everything you know to do. What now? (See box, "What Does the Literature Say About Managing Students With Emotional and Behavioral Disorders?")

Connections Between Self-Management and Students with Emotional/Behavioral Disorders (E/BD)

Students with E/BD often display one or more of the following characteristics. These characteristics must be displayed over a long period of time, to a marked degree, and adversely affect educational performance.

- An inability to learn that cannot be explained by intellectual, sensory, or health factors.
- An inability to build or maintain satisfactory interpersonal relationships with peers or teachers.
- Inappropriate types of behavior or feelings under normal circumstances.

- A general pervasive mood of unhappiness or depression.
- A tendency to develop physical symptoms or fears associated with personal or school problems. (Individuals with Disabilities Education Improvement Act, IDEA, 2004, CFR 300.7 (a) 9).

Teachers and service providers should note that displaying one or more of these characteristics could lead to failure to achieve maximum academic and/or social potential.

This article illustrates how teachers can implement self-management in the classroom. For illustration, we use two hypothetical case studies based on classroom experiences: (a) A student with E/BD and academic challenges and (b) A student with E/BD with social challenges. When teachers implement self-management with fidelity, undesirable student behaviors can be replaced with more desirable student behaviors (McQuillan & DuPaul, 1996); thus, this approach may positively affect academic and social student potential.

Chris: A Case Study

Chris is a third-grade student with E/BD who attends a small public school in a suburb of a large southeastern city. Chris's permanent records show that, since age 3, he has had a history of being aggressive towards his peers and adults. Chris is currently being served in a self-contained classroom alongside other students with E/BD, leaving the classroom only for physical education (P.E.), lunch, and art (approximately 1 hour/day). According to recent assessments, Chris has average to above-average IQ and performs on grade level. Chris currently lives with both of his parents and his older sister. He plays on the community soccer team and is involved with Cub Scouts.

Chris's Behavior

During transitions at school, Chris often kicks his peers to get items he wants, is verbally aggressive, hits or pinches them if they approach, and pushes them when the teacher is not looking. The parents of Chris's peers have called the school complaining that Chris bullies their children, and they have demanded that the school and his teacher do something about him. Suppose you are his case manager. What can you do? Chris will behave for a few minutes, but as soon as you turn your back, he is behaving inappropriately again. You are at the end of your rope. As you seek assistance from the other special education teachers at your school, a colleague suggests you try a self-management strategy with Chris.

Self-management is a practical and powerful tool for changing behavior.

Procedures for Implementing a Self-Management Plan for Chris

Here are five steps we have found useful for implementing a successful self-management plan for a student like Chris (see box, "Steps for Implementing a Self-Management Plan"). You, along with other teachers who work with Chris, can write a self-management plan and teach Chris to implement it, as follows:

1. *Identify and operationally define the behavior to be changed.* The target behavior is to decrease Chris's inappropriate aggressive behaviors during transitions. We began by stating exactly what "inappropriate" aggressive behaviors for Chris looked like. Then, we described transition times as times when the entire class is with Chris in the hallway moving between the classroom and P.E., lunch, and art. To make sure Chris understood what the appropriate behaviors were, we phrased them at his language level, as follows:

   - Keep hands and feet to yourself.
   - Talk softly or not at all.
   - Walk.
   - Stay in line with at least one arms-length from the person in front of you.
   - Speak appropriately.

What Does the Literature Say about Managing Students with Emotional and Behavioral Disorders?

New special education teachers often cite managing student behavior as the most problematic issue, especially for teachers of students with emotional and behavioral disorders (E/BD). Students with E/BD usually have difficulty managing their behavior within the context of the classroom, as well as during routine transitions. These students may display aggression, impulsivity, noncompliance, and distractibility that results in poor academic achievement (Carr & Punzo, 1993) and a disruptive learning environment.

An inexperienced teacher often spends much time focused on managing behavior of the students, rather than focused on academic instruction if effective behavior management practices are not implemented. Student self-management is a technique that has been proven effective in transferring responsibility of a student's behavior from the teacher to the student (Carr & Punzo, 1993). Likewise, research has also suggested that self-management strategies can produce improvements in academic productivity and on-task behavior, as well as a reduction of inappropriate behavior (Reid, Trout, & Schartz, 2005).

Self-management includes three components: self-monitoring, self-evaluation, and self-reinforcement (Allinder, Bolling, Oats, & Gagnon, 2000; Carr & Punzo, 1993).

- Self-monitoring refers to the process of self-observation and self-recording.
- Self-evaluation is the process of comparing the self-monitoring data to the individuals' standards for behavior.
- Self-reinforcement is the act of delivering a consequence that has reinforcing qualities.

For example, McQuillan and DuPaul (1996) found that 66% of students with E/BD in their study responded more favorably to self-management strategies than to interventions imposed and controlled by teachers. According to Schloss and Smith (1998), self-management is (a) a practical and powerful tool for changing behavior; (b) a tool that frees the teacher from primarily reacting to inappropriate student behavior to actually teaching; (c) a cost-effective tool that requires minimal energy to teach and implement; and (d) a tool that students with different abilities, grades, and disabilities can use. Because self-management techniques have been validated and have systematic implementation procedures, results from Reid et al. (2005) suggested that teachers can use self-management techniques as part of a successful behavior management plan.

This step is linked to the components of self-evaluation.

2. *Determine the criteria for mastery, using baseline data.* To determine criteria for Chris's behavioral change, we gathered baseline data. We collected these observational data before introducing the self-management plan to Chris. Chris's teachers monitored him during all hallway transitions for 3 days and noted how frequently he displayed inappropriate aggressive behaviors. On average, Chris displayed 52% inappropriate aggressive behaviors.

Self-management includes three components: self-monitoring, self-evaluation, and self-reinforcement

3. *Discuss appropriate and inappropriate behaviors with the student and reasons for the self-management plan.* Chris's appropriate and inappropriate behaviors are discussed individually with him. The baseline data that were collected are discussed with Chris and together we developed his goal (criteria for mastery). He is shown pictures of students behaving in appropriate ways and in inappropriate ways. Figure 1 provides examples of pictures shown to Chris as a reminder of appropriate versus inappropriate behaviors. This step is linked to the components of self-evaluation.

We also explained the benefits of self-management to Chris and asked that he commit to the procedure. Teachers know the reasons they believe their students can benefit from self-management, but they need to consider reasons students will perceive as beneficial (King- Sears & Bonfils, 1999). First, if Chris spends less time engaging in these inappropriate behaviors, he

Steps for Implementing a Self-Management Plan

1. Identify and operationally define the behavior to be changed.
2. Determine the criteria for mastery, using baseline data.
3. Discuss appropriate and inappropriate behaviors with the student and reasons for the self-management plan.
4. Introduce the system for self-management.
5. Provide guided practice.

would be sent to the office less. If he is in class more, he may receive better grades. Second, each time Chris engages in inappropriate behavior, the line is stopped and his peers lose time from the activities they enjoy (e.g., art, lunch, P.E.). Reducing these behaviors would decrease the teasing from his classmates. We hoped that Chris would come up with these reasons himself, but he could not, so we explained them to him. During this step, Chris signed a contract stating that he was interested in participating in a self-management plan. Figure 2 is a sample contract Chris signed.

4. *Introduce the system for self-management.*

5. *Provide guided practice.* Steps 4 and 5 occurred together. The teacher showed Chris all components of the self-management plan: self-monitoring, self-evaluation, and self-reinforcement. Chris's teacher explained to him that at the end of each transition (class to art, art to class, class to lunch, etc.),. Chris would be given his self-monitoring sheet. The sheet had a space for him to circle whether or not he displayed the five appropriate behaviors. If an appropriate behavior matched with what the teacher scored, Chris would earn a point. Even if Chris marked that he engaged in an inappropriate behavior and the teacher marked it as appropriate, Chris would not earn a point. Even though the teacher might feel Chris engaged in an appropriate behavior, we wanted to teach Chris to be aware of his own behavior and to know the difference between appropriate and inappropriate. If Chris marked that he engaged in an appropriate behavior, but the teacher marked it as inappropriate, Chris would lose a point. If Chris engaged in an inappropriate behavior and marked it correctly, his data were not changed. Figure 3 shows Chris's self-monitoring sheet for his transition from class to art.

At the end of each transition, Chris was asked to self-evaluate. He was given a sheet identical to this one, with teacher recorded behaviors. He compared his answers to his teacher's and awarded himself points based on the criteria.

If Chris earned at least four points for the transition, he could reinforce himself by selecting from a set of reinforcers he had agreed to: (a) eating with the teacher at lunch, (b) being the line leader, (c) being able to use the special paint in art, and (d) being first in line for lunch. The teacher also closely monitored the self-reinforcement plan to ensure that Chris was appropriately reinforcing himself. We decided that this reinforcement should be immediate for Chris so that he could make the connection between appropriate behavior and positive reinforcement.

Behaviors	Appropriate	Inappropriate
Keep your hands and feet to yourself		
Talk softly or not at all		
Walk		
Stay in line with at least one arms length from the person in front of you		
Speak appropriately		

Figure 1 Chart of illustrated appropriate and inappropriate behaviors.

Directions: Circle your answer.

1. I think I need to have better behavior in the halls.	Yes	No
2. I want to have better behavior.	Yes	No
3. I wish I got in trouble less.	Yes	No
4. I want to learn the self-management plan.	Yes	No

If you circled No to anything, write one sentence why: _____

_____

_____

I agree that I want to try the self-management plan.

Your signature: _____

Teacher signature: _____

Figure 2   Contract to learn and use self-management (elementary student).

As time went by and Chris became more effective at using the self-management plan, Chris's teacher allowed him to use the plan independently with periodic teacher monitoring. This self-management plan allowed Chris to take responsibility for his behavior in hope that he would become completely independent in managing his own behavior using the components of self-monitoring, self-evaluation, and self-reinforcement.

Alexa: A Case Study

Alexa is a 10th-grade student at a large inner-city high school. She receives E/BD-related services and spends the majority of her day in the general education setting. Alexa spends time in the E/BD classroom only when the general education teachers observe inappropriate behavior. Alexa lives with her mother and her mother's boyfriend. Alexa's biological father passed away 3 years ago. Recent test scores show that Alexa is performing at grade level.

Alexa's Behavior

Alexa has difficulties completing work in her general education math class. If she comes to a problem that is difficult for her, she will put her pencil down and either put her head on her desk or talk to a fellow student. When given directions by the teacher, she often is noncompliant, resulting in being sent to see her case manager or to the office. Alexa could benefit from a self-management plan centering on academic behavior to keep her on task. Her teachers hoped that the self-management plan would assist her with her on-task behaviors, increase her compliance during math class, and allow her to complete more assignments.

Procedures for Implementing a Self-Management Plan for Alexa

The procedures for implementing a self-management plan for an academic behavior for a high school student is similar to implementing the social self-management plan for an elementary student (as was the case of Chris). The five steps remain the same, and Alexa's self-management plan follows:

1. *Identify and operationally define the behavior to be changed.* In Alexa's situation, the target behavior was to increase her on-task behavior in math class. The following are descriptions of on-task behavior for Alexa:

   - Working quietly, independently, and consistently on assignments.
   - Participating in class discussions by contributing relevant (e.g., about the content) information.
   - Staying in her seat.
   - Following directions within 5 s of the direction given (King-Sears & Bonfils, 1999).
   - This step is linked to the components of self-evaluation.

2. *Determine the criteria for mastery, using baseline data.* The criteria for Alexa's mastery were determined in the same manner in which the criteria for mastery were determined for Chris. The teacher recorded baseline observational data during math class for 3 days. During the period, at 10-min intervals, the teacher recorded if Alexa was engaged in the target behaviors. The teacher calculated the percentage of time that Alexa was

Self-monitoring form for: _____Chris_____ Date: _____

Class to Art

Did I . . .

| . . . keep my hands and feet to myself? | Yes | No |

| . . . stay quiet? | Yes | No |

| . . . walk? | Yes | No |

| . . . stay in line? | Yes | No |

| . . . speak appropriately? | Yes | No |

Number **Yes** (matches teacher) _____ (one point earned)

Number **No** (matches teacher) _____ (no points earned)

Number **Yes** that teacher marked **No** _____ (minus one point)

Number **No** that teacher marked **Yes** _____ (no points earned)

Total Points: _____

Figure 3 Self-monitoring form for Chris.

engaged in the appropriate target behavior. Figure 4 shows Alexa's baseline data and the appropriate goals set for her.

3. *Discuss appropriate* and inappropri*ate behaviors with the student and reasons for the self-management plan.* Next, the teacher conferenced with Alexa to discuss her appropriate and inappropriate behaviors. She also discussed the data collected and potential goals. Alexa was an integral part of the goal-setting process; she and the teacher set a realistic yet challenging goal for the targeted behavior. The teacher showed Alexa videos of students engaging in appropriate and inappropriate behaviors related to being on task. The teacher asked Alexa to verbalize the differences between the target behaviors and inappropriate behaviors. Alexa also observed her peers (guided by the teacher) and identified differences between appropriate and inappropriate peer behavior. This step is linked to the components of self-evaluation.

The teacher elicited Alexa's motivation to learn about self-management by identifying benefits she could expect if she increased her on-task behaviors. One benefit Alexa identified was being able to finish more work in class and therefore having less homework. If she spent more time during class being on task, her class work would improve, more learning would occur, and her grades would improve. Alexa considered other benefits, such as better grades leading to more reinforcement at home, being allowed to obtain a driver's license, and having opportunities to participate in school activities.

The teacher and Alexa developed a contract indicating Alexa's interest in learning and participation with the self-management plan. The contract is similar to the contract used for Chris, but was written in more mature language for Alexa. Figure 5 is an example of Alexa's contract.

4. *Introduce the system for self-management.*
5. *Provide guided practice.* Again, Steps 4 and 5 were concurrent. The system of self-management for a high school student was somewhat different from the self-management system for an elementary-age student. For the self-monitoring aspect of self-management during math class, Alexa had an index card on her desk. She also had a small timer set at 10-min intervals. She was instructed that each time the timer reached zero, she was to self-monitor and record on her card whether she was engaged in appropriate behavior or not. The general education teacher covertly monitored this self-monitoring skill using proximity and eyegaze. On Alexa's index card, she made a check mark in the appropriate box (see Figure 6).

Behavior	Average	Goal
Working on assignment	30%	50%
Participating in class discussion	20%	40%
Staying seated	40%	60%
Following directions	20%	50%

Figure 4   Baseline data and goals for Alexa.

For the self-evaluation component of self-management, Alexa calculated the percentage of time she was on task and recorded it on her self-evaluation chart (see Figure 7). This not only gave her practice in managing her own behavior, it also gave her an opportunity to practice basic math skills.

Last, the self-reinforcement component of Alexa's self-management plan involved her being able to positively reinforce herself. At the end of the day, when Alexa met with her special education teacher, if she had met the criteria for mastery, she chose a previously agreed-on reinforcer from a list.

Implication for Practice

As is seen here, teachers can use self-management plans with students of all ages and for both social and academic behaviors. When considering using self-management techniques within the classroom, a teacher should consider the following factors:

- *Start small and think simple.* Choose a behavior that can be operationalized and easily definable by the student. The age, developmental, and maturity level of the student is an important factor when considering what behaviors can be changed with self-management techniques. Regardless, only a few behaviors should be targeted for change at a time.

- *Expect students to inaccurately report their appropriate or inappropriate behaviors at first.* The teacher will need to covertly monitor students as they reward their behaviors at the beginning of the self-management program. Students should not be reprimanded for incorrectly reporting their behaviors, but teachers can view such incidents as "teachable moments" to discuss and clarify what constitutes an appropriate behavior, the reason it is important to display appropriate behaviors, and the reasons it is important to monitor and report behaviors accurately.

- *Remember that the goal of self-management is to encourage students to become more intrinsically motivated, as opposed to extrinsically motivated.* Therefore, it is important that teachers encourage students in the beginning of self-management implementation and then fade this encouragement as the students become more successful with their individual self-management plans.

Final Thoughts

Self-management can be a successful behavior management strategy when used individually for students with E/BD (Carr & Punzo, 1993; McQuillan & DuPaul, 1996). Self-management strategies can be used with a variety

Directions: Circle your answer.		
1. I want to make better grades in math class.	Yes	No
2. I understand what on-task behavior is.	Yes	No
3. I understand that my on-task behavior influences my grades.	Yes	No
4. I will try the self-management plan to the best of my ability.	Yes	No

Write one sentence telling why you want to change your behavior: _____
_____

If you answered no to any of the questions, write one sentence telling why: _____
_____

I agree to implement the self-management as described to me.

Student signature: _____

Teacher signature: _____

Figure 5   Contract to learn and use self-management (secondary student).

Behavior	1st 10 min	2nd 10 min	3rd 10 min	4th 10 min	5th 10 min	6th 10 min
Work quietly on assignments						
Participate in class discussion						
Stay seated						
Follow directions						

Place a check mark (√) in the box if you are on task when the timer reaches zero. Place an X in the box if you are not on task when the timer reaches zero.

Don't forget to reset the timer!!   ***DO YOUR BEST!!***

Figure 6   Self-monitoring chart for Alexa.

of behaviors: writing quality and quantity, math fluency, engaged time, on-task behavior, aggressive behaviors, and social behaviors (Scholss & Smith, 1998). Self-management strategies allow students to take ownership of their behavior, involve them in the process of determining whether they are displaying appropriate behaviors, compare their behaviors to the preset criteria, and reinforce themselves appropriately.

The constant feedback enables a comparison between what the student is doing and what he or she should be doing. This, in turn, serves as a cue to maintain or increase appropriate behavior as well as change or decrease inappropriate behavior (Reid et al., 2005). As such, self-management is a viable strategy, to embed

within the positive behavioral support framework and could be used at the schoolwide, classroom, or individual level as a means to increase student ownership of their behavior. In addition, self-management can be interfaced within a student's behavior intervention plan (BIP) as the self-reinforcement can be linked directly to the function of the student's behavior.

The goal of a self-management plan is to encourage student independence in behaving more appropriately and succeeding in school.

Behavior	Monday	Tuesday	Wednesday	Thursday	Friday
Work quietly on assignments					
Participate in class discussion					
Stay seated					
Follow directions					
I met mastery today	yes no	yes no	yes no	yes no	yes no

Determine the percentage you were on task for each behavior for each day of the week and record It in the corresponding box. Circle "yes" if you met mastery for the day and "no" if you did not.

Mastery
Work quietly on assignments: 50%
Participate in class discussion: 40%
Stay seated: 60%
Follow directions: 50%

Figure 7   Self-evaluation char for Alexa.

Self-management can increase the likelihood that students will engage in more appropriate behaviors than inappropriate behaviors (Carr & Punzo, 1993). Finally, self-management is a positive and proactive strategy that can be used with students with E/BD.

References

Allinder, R. M., Bolling, R. M., Oats, R. G., & Gagnon, W. A. (2000). Effects of teacher self-monitoring on implementation of curriculum-based measurement and mathematics computation achievement of students with disabilities. *Remedial and Special Education, 21*(4), 219–226.

Carr, S. C., & Punzo, R. P. (1993). The effects of self-monitoring of academic accuracy and productivity on the performance of students with behavioral disorders. *Behavioral Disorders, 18*(4), 241–251.

Individuals With Disabilities Education Improvement Act Amendments of 2004, P.L. 108-446. 105th Congress, 1st Session.

King-Sears, M. E., & Bonfils, K. A. (1999). Self-management for middle school students with LD and ED. *Intervention in School and Clinic, 35*(2), 96–107.

McQuillan, K., & DuPaul, G. J. (1996). Classroom performance of students with serious emotional disturbance: A comparative study of evaluation methods for behavior management. *Journal of Emotional & Behavioral Disorders, 4*(3), 162–170.

Reid, R., Trout, A. L., & Schartz, M. (2005), Self-regulation interventions for children with attention deficit/hyperactivity disorder. *Exceptional Children, 71,* 361–377.

Schloss, P. J., & Smith, M. A. (1998). *Applied behavior analysis in the classroom* (2nd ed.). Needham Heights, MA: Allyn & Bacon.

Beverly Patton (CEC GA Federation) Clinical Instructor/Doctoral Student; **Kristine Jolivette** (CEC GA Federation), Assistant Professor; and **Michelle Ramsey** (CEC GA Federation), Doctoral Student Department of Educational Psychology and Special Education, Georgia State University, Atlanta. Address correspondence to Beverly Patton, Department of Educational Psychology and Special Education, Georgia State University, P.O. Box 3979, Atlanta, GA 30302-3979 (e-mail: bpatton@gsu.edu).

From *Teaching Exceptional Children,* by Beverly Patton, Kristine Jolivette, and Michelle Ramsey, Vol. 39, No. 2, November/December 2006, pp. 14–21. Copyright © 2006 by Council for Exceptional Children. Reprinted by permission.

UNIT 7

Vision and Hearing Impairments

Unit Selections

Key Points to Consider

- Should children with profound hearing loss use American Sign Language (ASL), or English, as their primary language?

- How can tactile strategies support learning for students with visual impairments and other severe disabilities?

Student Web Site

www.mhcls.com/online

Internet References

Further information regarding these Web sites may be found in this book's preface or online.

Info to Go: Laurent Clerc National Deaf Education Center
http://clerccenter.gallaudet.edu/InfoToGo/index.html
The New York Institute for Special Education
http://www.nyise.org/index.html

Earlier, more adequate prenatal care, preventive medicine, health maintenance, and medical technology have reduced the number of children born either blind or deaf. In the future, with knowledge of the human genome and with the possibility of genetic manipulation, all genetic causes of blindness and deafness may be eliminated. Now and in the future, however, environmental factors will probably still leave many children with vision and hearing impairments.

Children with visual disabilities that cannot be corrected are the smallest group of children who qualify for special educational services through the Individuals with Disabilities Education Improvement Act (IDEIA). Legally, a child is considered to have low vision if acuity in the best eye, after correction, is between 20/70 and 20/180 and if the visual field extends from 20 to 180 degrees. Legally, a child is considered blind if visual acuity in the best eye, after correction, is 20/200 or less or if the field of vision is restricted to an area of less than 20 degrees (tunnel vision). These terms do not accurately reflect a child's ability to see or read print.

The educational definition of visual impairment focuses on what experiences a child needs in order to be able to learn. One must consider the amount of visual acuity in the worst eye, the perception of light and movement, the field of vision (a person "blinded" by tunnel vision may have good visual acuity in only a very small field of vision), and the efficiency with which a person uses any residual vision.

Public Law 99-457, fully enacted by 1991, mandated early education for children with disabilities between ages three and five in the least restrictive environment. This has been reauthorized as PL102-119, which requires individualized family service plans outlining what services will be provided for parents and children, by whom, and where. These family service plans (IFSPs) are updated every six months. This early childhood extension of IDEIA has been especially important for babies born with low vision or blindness.

In infancy and early childhood, many children with low vision or blindness are given instruction in using the long cane as soon as they become mobile. Although controversial for many years, the long cane is increasingly being accepted. A long cane improves orientation and mobility and alerts persons with visual acuity that the user has a visual disability. This warning is very important for the protection of persons with blindness/low vision.

Children with visual impairments that prevent them from reading print are usually taught to read braille. Braille is a form of writing using raised dots that are "read" with the fingers. In addition to braille, children who are blind are usually taught with Optacon scanners, talking books, talking handheld calculators, closed-circuit televisions, typewriters, and special computer software.

Hearing impairments are rare, and the extreme form, legal deafness, is rarer still. A child is assessed as hard-of-hearing

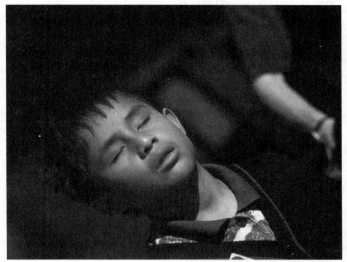

Scott T. Baxter/Getty Images

for purposes of receiving special educational services if he or she needs some form of sound amplification to comprehend oral language. A child is assessed as deaf if he or she cannot benefit from amplification. Children who are deaf are dependent on vision for language and communication.

When children are born with impaired auditory sensations, they are put into a classification of children with congenital (at or dating from birth) hearing impairments. When children acquire problems with their hearing after birth, they are put into a classification of children with adventitious hearing impairments. If the loss of hearing occurs before the child has learned speech and language, it is called a prelinguistic hearing impairment. If the loss occurs after the child has learned language, it is called a postlinguistic hearing impairment.

Children whose hearing losses involve the outer- or middle-ear structures are said to have conductive hearing losses. Conductive losses involve defects or impairments of the external auditory canal, the tympanic membrane, or the ossicles. Children whose hearing losses involve the inner ear are said to have sensorineural hearing impairments.

In 1999 The Newborn and Infant Hearing Screening and Intervention Act in the United States provided incentives for states to test the hearing of newborns before hospital discharge. Most states now offer this test for a small fee. When an infant is diagnosed with deafness or hearing loss, an appropriate early education can begin immediately under the auspices of IDEIA.

Students with vision or hearing impairments whose disabilities can be ameliorated with assistive devices can usually have their individualized needs met appropriately in inclusive classrooms. Students with visual or hearing disorders whose problems cannot be resolved with technological aids, however, need the procedural protections afforded by law. They should receive special services from age of diagnosis through age 21, in the least restrictive environment, free of charge, with semi-annually updated individualized family service plans (IFSPs) until age three and annually updated individualized education plans (IEPs) and eventually individualized transition plans (ITPs) through age 21. The numbers of children and youth who qualify for these intensive specialized educational programs are small.

Many professionals working with individuals who are deaf feel that communities of others who are deaf and who use sign language is less restrictive than a community of people who hear and who use oral speech. The debate about what has come to be known as the deaf culture has not been resolved.

The first article in this unit deals with the debate over the oral-English language approach to education of students with profound hearing loss, and the use of the alternate language, American Sign Language (ASL). Advances in medicine and technology have allowed many young children to have cochlear implants. These devices allow them to decipher some sounds and succeed with an oral education in English. Other children do better when they use ASL as their primary language and use English only as a second language, if at all. The current feeling among many educators is to try whatever works best for each individual child. Not everyone agrees with this stance. The report by Burton Bollag explains why?

The second article discusses the importance of the sense of touch for students with visual impairments. They not only need instructional materials that provide tactile information, they also need the teacher to convey expectations, mood, and other social messages through physical contact. June Downing and Deborah Chen consider many issues for educating using the sense of touch.

The Debate Over Deaf Education

Technological changes are shaking up the teaching of the hearing impaired

BURTON BOLLAG

Daniel S. Koo was born deaf. When he was 4 he started attending a public school where he spent part of each week getting intensive training in speaking and listening with the help of hearing aids.

He remembers those early years as increasingly frustrating because, try as he might, he could not understand what his teachers were saying. By fourth grade he was falling behind academically, and his parents transferred him to another public school, which practiced a little-used method, called cued speech. As teachers spoke, they would make rapid hand movements near their mouths to visually represent the sounds they were producing.

"The light bulb just went on," recalls Mr. Koo, and a world of learning opened to him. He attended the University of Maryland at College Park—attending classes with the help of an interpreter—and went on to graduate studies at Gallaudet University, in Washington, where all his classes were taught in American Sign Language. Today he is a postdoctoral fellow in neurolinguistics at Georgetown University Medical Center.

Mr. Koo's academic success is all the more remarkable when compared with the academic performance of most deaf students. According to the latest nationwide survey, the average deaf 18-year-old reads below the fourth-grade level. Despite decades of efforts, the scores have remained largely unchanged.

"Historically we have taught deaf students material way below their conceptual level since we taught them through English," says Gabriel A. Martin, chair of the communication-disorders and deaf-education department at Lamar University.

The solution, he says, is teaching deaf children through American Sign Language—their one "native" tongue. But the issue is highly controversial. Opponents say that concentrating on signing can undermine young children's acquisition of English, and largely relegates them to being able to communicate only with other deaf people.

For more than two centuries, educators of the deaf—and the college departments that train them—have debated the best way to teach deaf children. At one end of the spectrum are those who favor the "oral" method, training teachers to concentrate on developing speech and hearing skills. At the other end are those who advocate a "bilingual" approach, teaching primarily in American Sign Language and promoting English as a second language.

Scientific studies have been inconclusive in demonstrating an inherent superiority of one method over the other. But earlier detection of deafness in infants—some 45 states now require screening at birth—and recent advances in medical technology are resulting in greater hearing in a larger portion of deaf children. The development is shifting the debate in favor of the oral approach.

That is beginning to have profound effects on the work of the country's 74 academic departments of deaf education. "I know in talking to my colleagues there is a growing recognition that the kids have changed," says Harold A. Johnson, director of Kent State University's deaf-education teacher-preparation program.

Hearing More

One of the most pervasive new influences on deaf children has been the introduction of cochlear implants. The devices, first approved in 1984, bring sounds from an external hearing aid directly to the auditory nerve. The size of a needle, the devices are surgically inserted under the skin at the base of the skull, just behind the ear, where they take over the function of a damaged inner ear—the most common cause of deafness.

However, the sounds the implants produce are different, and less complete, than what is heard by people with normal hearing. People who get cochlear implants must be trained to decipher the new sounds. In addition, for the first months they must have their implants regularly "mapped"—or fine-tuned—to improve clarity and adjust volume levels.

According to the Food and Drug Administration, approximately 13,000 adults and 10,000 children had received implants by 2002, the latest year for which data are available. But the technology continues to improve, and the number of people receiving implants is increasing rapidly.

The trend is a source of anxiety to some deaf people, who feel that it may lead to an erosion of the gains they have won in recent decades in antidiscrimination legislation, and undercut their hard-won dignity. Benjamin J. Bahan, a professor of deaf studies at Gallaudet University who has been deaf since he was 4, worries that as more deaf children are given an oral education, the teaching of American Sign Language may be abandoned.

"Let those kids be bilingual," he said in an e-mail message. "After all with their implants off they are DEAF."

Yet the implants are already affecting the work of Gallaudet. With 1,900 students, it is the world's only university devoted to the deaf. Part of its mission is the development of teaching methods and materials for the more than 71,000 severely deaf children in the United States. The university runs a model elementary school and middle school on its large campus in Washington.

Up until now, Gallaudet's goal has been to make all 370 school-children it enrolls fully fluent in both English, or at least written English, and American Sign Language. But educators say they are seeing a growing number of children with implants whose improved hearing would allow them to benefit from a more oral-based education.

"Teachers come here trained in a more visual approach," says Debra B. Nussbaum, coordinator of the model schools' Cochlear Implant Education Center. But, she adds, "we've been talking about how to change our strategies."

Supporters of the oral approach say far too few teachers are being trained in that orientation. "In the last 10 to 15 years there has been a dramatic increase in demand" for oral education, says Susan T. Lenihan, director of the deaf-education program at Fontbonne University, in St. Louis. Deaf-education departments "should recognize this shift in the population," she says, and train more teachers equipped to work with deaf people with cochlear implants.

Perhaps the strongest trend in academic departments in recent years has been a growing openness to try whatever works with individual children.

Yet like many institutions, Gallaudet is moving cautiously and, so far, appears committed to maintaining a strong sign-language component in its model schools. "I do a lot of workshops across the country," says Ms. Nussbaum. "I'm hearing about kids with cochlear implants who didn't do as well as the doctors thought they would." Some children have found so little benefit from the devices that they have stopped using them, educators say.

Gallaudet wants to make sure none of the youngsters in its model schools end up like countless children in exclusively oral programs over the years: without any language—barely knowing English, but never having learned sign language. Not only are such children deprived of a developed means of communication, but with no language in the early years—the critical time for learning languages—their cognitive development may be permanently stunted, scholars say.

Communication was on the minds of many Gallaudet students when they demonstrated last week against a new president chosen by the institution's board of trustees. Protesting students accuse the new president, Jane K. Fernandes, a deaf person who only learned sign language as an adult, of having a haughty and aloof style.

While educators struggle to get the balance right between oral and visual forms of communication, perhaps the strongest trend in academic departments in recent years has been a growing openness to try whatever works with individual children. "Our students are prepared to use a wide range of teaching approaches," says T. Alan Hurwitz, vice president of the Rochester Institute of Technology and dean of its National Technical Institute for the Deaf, which enrolls approximately 60 students in a graduate education program. More important than the method used, says Mr. Hurwitz, who was born deaf and spoke through a signing interpreter, is "detecting deafness very early, getting parents involved early, and having good teachers."

Checkered History

While the popularity of different approaches has gone up and down, the root of the debate over the proper way to teach the deaf goes back more than 200 years.

In 1771 the abbé Charles-Michel de l'Epée, a young priest, founded the first public school for the deaf, in Paris. He based the language of instruction on a system of hand signs he had observed deaf French people using to communicate with one another.

During the 19th century, deaf children in America were taught mainly in sign language. But there was a competing approach, championed by, among others, Alexander Graham Bell, the inventor of the telephone, who was married to a deaf woman. The backers of this oral approach argued that sign language was a form of savagery that kept its users isolated from the rest of humanity. The oral approach won out when the International Congress of Educators of the Deaf, meeting in Milan in 1880, decreed that deaf people should be taught spoken language, not sign language.

For much of the 20th century, deaf children in America received a predominantly oral education. Sign language continued being passed down surreptitiously in the dormitories of the residential schools where most deaf children were then sent. Those caught signing were sometimes forced to sit on their hands.

The 1960s brought another shake-up, inspired by the civil-rights movement and buttressed by the work of William C. Stokoe Jr., a Chaucer scholar at Gallaudet. Mr. Stokoe published several influential works demonstrating that American Sign Language was not just a collection of gestures, but a true language with its own rules and grammatical structures. Indeed scholars, and deaf people fluent in both languages, say American Sign Language is as rich a medium as English for conveying even complex, intellectual ideas.

The development was liberating for deaf-education departments. Several new communications systems involving hand signs were developed, including cued speech, which proved so helpful to Mr. Koo.

The majority of departments moved toward an approach often referred to as "total communication," whose professed aim is to work with a variety of methods to find what works best for each child. In reality, many departments settled into a reliance on "signed English," which is not a real language like ASL, but a practice of translating spoken English, word for word. Critics say signed English is a sloppy compromise, allowing a person to speak and sign at the same time, but conveying considerably less information to a deaf listener than does ASL.

To the disappointment of many scholars, this flourishing of new methods brought virtually no improvement in the test scores of deaf schoolchildren. Some scholars have reacted, ironically, by pulling to one extreme or the other: either a bilingual approach that relies chiefly on American Sign Language, or an exclusively oral approach that excludes signing altogether.

While the bilingual approach is intellectually appealing to many academics (most agree that American Sign Language is the easiest "tongue" for deaf children to master), scholars readily acknowledge its one major drawback. About 97 percent of deaf children are born to hearing parents, and, educators say, those parents are typically unwilling or unable to master sign language. That means that children whose education is based on American Sign Language will communicate better with teachers and other deaf people than with their own parents.

"It challenges the whole notion of what it means to be a parent," says Carol J. Erting, chair of Gallaudet's education department. "Emotionally, it's just really, really hard."

More recently, the continued improvements in medical technology—digital hearing aids that work better than the traditional analog ones, and continually improving cochlear implants—have made the oral approach increasingly attractive.

While cochlear implants are bringing new hope, they are also heating up old controversies. K. Todd Houston, executive director of the Alexander Graham Bell Association for the Deaf and Hard of Hearing, the leading group promoting oral education for deaf children, asserts that "there is a window of opportunity to stimulate auditory pathways," which may be missed if a child is exposed at an early age to a signing environment. Many scholars do not agree. With bilingualism and even multilingualism common in many parts of the world, they ask, why shouldn't a deaf child be fluent in English and sign language?

Mr. Koo, the neurolinguist, says that if he and his wife have any deaf children, he will raise them bilingually, in American Sign Language and cued English, the method that involves speaking and making hand signs around the mouth to represent the sounds.

"ASL exposes children to the world's knowledge," he says, "and it incorporates self-esteem and aspects of deaf culture." Mastering English "gives them access to the richness of the English world, like Shakespeare and idioms.

"I cherish them both," he says.

Using Tactile Strategies with Students Who Are Blind and Have Severe Disabilities

JUNE E. DOWNING AND DEBORAH CHEN

Vision is a primary sense for learning. Teachers use pictures, photographs, and a variety of color-coded materials in their instruction. They also use demonstrations and considerable modeling, which requires the students' visual attention. Many students with severe and multiple disabilities have considerable difficulty understanding verbal information and so rely heavily on visual information (Alberto & Frederick, 2000; Hodgdon, 1995; Hughes, Pitkin, & Lorden, 1998).

But what about students who cannot perceive visual cues—or access verbal information? When students have severe and multiple disabilities, teachers must resort to alternative teaching strategies to provide effective and accessible instruction.

If these students are also blind or have limited vision, however, they need instructional materials that provide relevant tactile information. This article describes specific tactile strategies to support instruction of students who have severe and multiple disabilities and who do not learn visually.

When students have severe and multiple disabilities, teachers must resort to alternative teaching strategies to provide effective and accessible instruction.

Getting in Touch

A teacher's instructional style certainly influences what a student learns. Teachers engage their students by providing visual and auditory information. They convey their mood through facial expressions, body language, and tone of voice. They give directions by gestures, pointing, and spoken words. If students cannot receive or understand these modes of communication, the teacher must use alternative strategies. The primary alternatives are tactile. The teacher must convey his or her instructional expectations, mood, and information through physical and direct contact with the student. Teaching through the sense of touch may be unfamiliar and uncomfortable for most teachers, including those with training in special education. Teachers should become aware of how they interact with the student through touch. To be most effective with tactile teaching, teachers must consider many issues:

- What impressions are conveyed to a student when he or she is touched?
- Do the teacher's hands convey different information depending on their temperature, tenseness of tone, speed of movement, and degree of pressure?
- Are teachers aware of the range of emotions that they can communicate through touch?
- Where do they touch the student (e.g., palms, back of hands, arms, legs, chest)?
- Do they touch the student's bare skin or clothing over the skin?
- How do students respond to different types of tactile input?

To be maximally effective, teachers must become aware of, interpret, monitor, and modify their tactile interactions from the student's perspective.

Tactile Modeling

Sighted students learn from demonstrations and through imitation. Students who are blind or have minimal vision need opportunities to feel the demonstrator's actions by touching the parts of the body or objects involved in the actions (Smith, 1998). For example, in a cooking class, a classmate demonstrates how to make meringue by whipping egg whites. The student who is blind can feel the peer's hand holding the bowl, the other hand grasping the electric mixer. This way, the student who is blind can "see" what his or her classmate is demonstrating. Like other tactile adaptations, the use of tactile modeling requires careful planning on the part of the teacher and extra time for the student to benefit from this instructional strategy.

Tactile Mutual Attention

Sighted students visually examine and make observations about something they are looking at together. The student with minimal or no vision should have opportunities for shared exploration with classmates through tactile mutual attention (Miles, 1999). For example, during a unit of study on masks, the student and a classmate may tactilely examine an African mask, placing their hands together as they explore the relatively smooth parts of the mask and find the leather strips, beads, and decorative feathers that border the mask. This way the student has a joint focus and shares observations with a classmate. Sighted classmates will have many creative ideas of ways to use tactile modeling and tactile mutual attention with peers who are blind and have additional disabilities (see Figure 1).

Tactile Learning and Teaching

When students with severe disabilities are unable to use their vision effectively for obtaining information, they require tactile information that is accessible to their hands or other parts of their body. Tactile information, however, has different characteristics from visual.

Unlike vision, touch provides a fragment of the whole; the student must put together a series of tactile impressions to understand what other students are looking at. For example, fourth-grade students are studying different aspects of life in the desert. One student, who is deaf and blind and does not know American Sign Language, is feeling a large desert tortoise. One hand is near the tail, and the other hand is feeling one edge of the shell near the tortoise's head. It will take this student considerable time and effort to tactilely examine and discover the physical characteristics of a tortoise, while his classmates can see that it is a tortoise in one glance.

Unlike vision, touch provides a fragment of the whole; the student must put together a series of tactile impressions to understand what other students are looking at.

Certain concepts are easier to convey tactilely than others. Abstract concepts are much more difficult to adapt tactilely than more concrete facts. For instance, it is much easier to teach about helium using balloons than it is to teach historical events. The teacher must ensure that the tactile representation is truly representative of the concept and is relevant and meaningful to the student. For example, to teach that the solid state of water is ice, the use of raised (tactile) lines in waves to represent water and raised (tactile) straight lines to represent ice is not

1. Select the message that you want to communicate to the student (e.g., greeting, reassurance, encouragement, praise, redirection, demonstration).
2. Decide how best to communicate that message through the type of touch (i.e., duration, pressure, movement) and where to touch the student (e.g., back of hand, shoulder, or knee).
3. Identify how you will let the student know that you are close (e.g., by saying his name) before touching him or her (e.g., on the elbow).
4. Discuss whether and how to examine an item with the student (e.g., by having two students examine an African mask).
5. Decide whether and how to use tactile modeling (e.g., by asking a classmate to show the student how to blow up a balloon).
6. Observe the student's reactions to your tactile interactions and modify the interaction accordingly.
7. Identify how you will end the interaction (e.g., let the student know that you are leaving by giving him a double pat on the shoulder).

Figure 1 Considerations for interacting through touch.

meaningful or understandable to most students with severe and multiple disabilities. In contrast, the use of water (wet, liquid) and ice (cold, solid) would clearly represent the critical aspects of the topic of study.

The educational team must decide what aspects of a lesson can be represented tactilely to make instruction most easily understood. At times, the best tactile representation may be tangential to the specific subject. For example, for a lesson on Lewis and Clark and their exploration of the West, artifacts of the Old West (e.g., pieces of clothing, fur, leather pieces, a whip, and tools) can be used to provide a tactile experience for the student with no usable vision. Such items would also benefit the entire class. Acting out the event using objects as props also adds clarity and interest to a seemingly abstract topic.

Obviously, students with different skills and abilities will develop different concepts of the topic of study. For example, whereas fifth-grade students without disabilities in geometry class learn how to find the area of a square, a student who has severe and multiple impairments, including blindness, may just be learning to sort square shapes from round ones. General and special educators need to understand such differences and still challenge students to learn what they can.

Presenting Tactile Information

You can provide visual (e.g., pictures or sign language) and auditory (e.g., speech) information to several students at once. These so called *distance senses* are quick and efficient. In contrast, tactile information requires individual physical contact and takes more time to understand. You must allow extra time for presentation of tactile information so the student has an opportunity to touch, handle, examine, and eventually synthesize and understand information (Downing & Demchak, 2002). Here are some reminders:

- Decide how to introduce an item to the student.
- The item should be accessible so the student can detect its presence and then manipulate it to determine its identity or relationship to familiar experiences.
- Touching the item to some part of the student's body (e.g., arm or side or back of hand) is less intrusive than manipulating the student's hand to take the item and therefore, such an approach is recommended (Dote-Kwan & Chen, 1999; Miles, 1999; Smith, 1998). Some students are timid about tactile exploration because they are wary and careful about handling unfamiliar or disliked materials.

Allow extra time for presentation of tactile information so the student has an opportunity to touch, handle, examine, and eventually synthesize and understand information.

A teacher or peer may introduce a new object to the student, by holding the object, and placing the back of his or her hand under the student's hand. The student is more likely to accept the touch of a familiar hand than that of an unfamiliar object. Slowly the teacher or peer can rotate his or her hand until the student is touching the object. This way the student has physical support while deciding whether to touch and examine the object (Dote-Kwan & Chen, 1999). After the student detects the presence of the item, he or she is more likely to take the item and explore it (if physically possible).

Ideally, students will use their hands to explore; however, some students have such severe physical disabilities that they may use touch receptors in their tongue, on their cheeks, or inside of their arms. In all cases, you need to encourage the student's active participation (even if only partial) in accessing information.

Providing Effective Tactile Representation

To determine whether tactile information is truly representative of a specific concept, the representation must be tactilely salient and meaningful. Because it is natural for sighted teachers to have a visual perspective, it is difficult to make tactile adaptations that make sense tactilely. For example, tactile outlines of items (e.g., string glued to a drawing of a house) may be used to represent different concepts but may not be recognized tactilely or understood by the student. Although miniatures are

1. Identify the objective of the lesson or the instructional concept.
2. Select the materials to convey this concept.
3. Close your eyes and examine the material with your hands.
4. Take a tactile perspective, not visual, when deciding how and what to present.
5. If the entire concept (e.g., house) is too complicated to represent through a tactile adaptation, then select one aspect of the concept (e.g., key) for the tactile representation.
6. Consider the student's previous tactile experiences. What items has he or she examined?
7. How does the student examine materials through the sense of touch?
8. Decide how the item will be introduced to the student.
9. Identify what supports the student needs to tactilely examine the item.
10. Decide what language input (descriptive words) will be used to convey the student's experience of the material.

Figure 2 Considerations for developing tactile adaptions.

convenient because of their size and are easy to handle, they are based on visual characteristics of the objects they represent. For example, a small plastic dog has no tactile characteristics in common with a real dog. Similarly, a miniature of a house, while visually recognizable, does not resemble a house when examined tactilely. A key that the student has used to open the front door of his house will form a more accurate concept of "house."

Experiment with what can be perceived tactilely by blindfolding yourself and examining the adaptation using only your sense of touch. In addition, avoid misconceptions as much as possible. For example, in a kindergarten classroom, a student brought a glass paperweight with a rose in it for show and tell. He talked about the rose as he passed it around the class. When a classmate who has no vision and limited language was allowed to hold the paperweight, he was confused when told "it's a rose." More appropriate language should be used to describe what this student is experiencing (e.g., "round," "smooth," "heavy," and "glass"). If this student is to understand the meaning of "rose," then you need to provide a real rose, so the student can perceive its shape, texture, size, and scent (see Figure 2 for other considerations).

Hyperresponsivity to Touch

Some students demonstrate strong reactions to tactile information, even though this may be the best way for them to receive information. These reactions are often referred to as *tactile defensiveness* and treated as a negative characteristic of the student. Some people have a low sensory threshold and are hyperreactive or hyperresponsive to certain sensory stimulation (Williamson & Anzalone, 2001). Tactile responsivity is simply the degree to which an individual responds to tactile stimulation. Some individuals can tolerate considerable and varied amounts of tactile input without much reaction (e.g., tactile hyporesponsivity), while others are very sensitive to certain types of tactile input (tactile hyperresponsivity). These responses vary from person to person. Some people can wear certain fabrics next to their skin while others cannot.

Teachers must be aware of and respect these individual differences. Teachers should not take students' hands and physically make them touch materials if they are not willing to do so (Smith, 1998). If students are forced to have aversive tactile experiences, they are less likely to explore tactilely. The term tactile defensiveness has a negative connotation that may interfere with effective intervention. If the student has a sensory modulation problem that results in hyperresponsiveness, then the educational team should include an occupational therapist. Creative ways to bypass this problem and assist the student to handle tactile information are needed.

A Team Effort

Making appropriate tactile accommodations (instructional strategies or materials) cannot be left to one member of the team (i.e., the teacher certified in the area of visual impairment). A team effort is required, with different team members contributing their skills, knowledge, experiences, and ideas (Downing, 2002; Silberman, Sacks, & Wolfe, 1998). A special educator specifically trained in the area of visual impairments and blindness can be helpful with teaching ideas and tactile resources. Depending on this teacher's professional training and experiences, however, he or she may be unfamiliar with the types of accommodations a particular student may need. The student who is blind, has spoken language, and reads braille has very different learning needs from those of a student who does not speak, does not read braille, and has limited receptive language.

Relying on one specialist to meet the tactile needs of a student who is blind with additional severe disabilities should be avoided. The ideas of all members of the team are needed, including family members and classmates who do not have disabilities (Downing, 2002). This way tactile adaptations and strategies are more likely to be used at home and school and with peers.

Team members should consider how the student perceives information through touch, the student's best physical position, the student's ability to move different parts of his body, and past experiences with tactile information. Family members can provide insight on the student's tactile experiences and preferences. Occupational therapists can provide valuable information on the student's use of his hands, responsivity to tactile items, and strategies to decrease hyperresponsivity. Physical therapists can help with positioning considerations and adaptive equipment that support tactile exploration. In collabora-

tion with the general educator, the teacher certified in visual impairments can provide ideas for making tactile adaptations to instructional materials. Classmates can be asked for their ideas on how to use tactile modeling or to gather objects and tactile materials that can make a lesson more meaningful.

> The ideas of all members of the team are needed, including family members and classmates who do not have disabilities.

Final Thoughts

Meeting the learning needs of students who have severe disabilities and who do not have clear access to visual information is a significant instructional challenge. Teaching through touch is unfamiliar and perhaps awkward for most sighted people, but learning though touch is essential for students who are blind or have minimal vision. Effective use of tactile strategies must consider the individual student's needs and abilities, learning environment, and task. These strategies can best support students' learning when there is a concerted effort on the part of the educational team, additional time for the presentation of tactile information, and systematic evaluation of adaptations.

References

Alberto, P. A., & Frederick, L. D. (2000). Teaching picture reading as an enabling skill. *TEACHING Exceptional Children, 33*(1), 60–64.

Dote-Kwan, J., & Chen, D. (1999). Developing meaningful interventions. In D. Chen (Ed.), *Essential elements in early communication visual impairments and multiple disabilities* (pp. 287–336). New York: American Foundation for the Blind Press.

Downing, J. E. (2002). Working cooperatively: The role of team members. In J. E. Downing (Ed.), *Including students with severe and multiple disabilities in typical classrooms: Practical strategies for teachers* (2nd ed., pp. 189–210). Baltimore: Paul H. Brookes.

Downing, J. E., & Demchak, M. A. (2002). First steps: Determining individual abilities and how best to support students. In J. E. Downing (Ed.), *Including students with severe and multiple disabilities in typical classrooms: Practical strategies for teachers* (2nd ed., pp. 37–70). Baltimore: Paul H. Brookes.

Hodgdon, L. A. (1995). *Visual strategies for improving communication. Vol. 1: Practical supports for school and home.* Troy, MI: QuirkRoberts.

Hughes, C., Pitkin, S. E., & Lorden, S. W. (1998). Assessing preferences and choices of persons with severe and profound mental retardation. *Education and Training in Mental Retardation and Developmental Disabilities, 33,* 299–316.

Miles, B. (1999). *Talking the language of the hands to the hands.* Monmouth, OR: DBLINK, The National Information Clearinghouse on Children Who Are Deaf-Blind. (ERIC Document Reproduction Service No. ED 419 331)

Silberman, R. K., Sacks, S. Z., & Wolfe, J. (1998). Instructional strategies for educating students who have visual impairments with severe disabilities. In S. Z. Sacks & R. K. Silberman (Eds.), *Educating students who have visual impairments with other disabilities* (pp. 101–137). Baltimore: Paul H. Brookes.

Smith, M. (1998). Feelin' groovy: Functional tactual skills. Retrieved January 24, 2000, from http://www.tsbvi.edu/Outreach/seehear/summer98/groovy.htm

Williamson, G. G., & Anzalone, M. (2001). *Sensory integration and self regulation in infants and toddlers: Helping very young children interact with their environment.* Washington, DC: Zero to Three. (ERIC Document Reproduction Service No. ED 466 317)

JUNE E. DOWNING (CEC Chapter #29), Professor; and DEBORAH CHEN (CEC Chapter #918) Professor, Department of Special Education, California State University, Northridge. Address correspondence to June E. Downing, Department of Special Education, California State University, Northridge, 18111 Nordhoff St., Northridge, CA 91330-8265 (e-mail: june.downing@csun.edu).

The development of this article was supported by the U.S. Department of Education, Office of Special Education and Rehabilitative Services Grant # H3224T990025. The content, however, does not necessarily reflect the views of the U.S. Department of Education, and no official endorsement should be inferred.

UNIT 8
Multiple Disabilities

Unit Selections

Key Points to Consider

- What types of preplanning and planning are required to develop IEPs for students with multiple disabilities being integrated into general education settings? Why is collaboration essential?

- Can students with traumatic brain injuries benefit from reentry into general education classes? How can this be accomplished successfully?

- What types of augmentative technology can help students with multiple disabilities communicate? What other ways do they have to make their thoughts known?

Student Web Site
www.mhcls.com/online

Internet References
Further information regarding these Web sites may be found in this book's preface or online.

Activity Ideas for Students With Severe, Profound, or Multiple Disabilities
http://www.palaestra.com/featurestory.html
Severe and/or Multiple Disabilities
http://www.nichcy.org/pubs/factshe/fs10txt.htm

For most of the twentieth century, children with multiple disabilities (MD) were kept hidden in their parents' homes or put into institutions. Any father or mother presenting such a child at a public school for admission was ridiculed and turned away. The Individuals with Disabilities Education Improvement Act (IDEIA) in the United States has turned this around. Such children may now be enrolled in general education classes if that is appropriate. They are entitled to a free education in the least restrictive environment that serves their needs. IDEIA has allowed millions of students, who once would have been written off as "uneducable" to be given some form of schooling.

A child placed in the category of multiple disabilities (MD) has two or more co-occurring areas of exceptionality. Each child with MD is very special and very needy. Consider the physicist, Steven Hawking, who has a brilliant mind but cannot communicate or move without augmentative technology. While many MD students have some cognitive disabilities, many have normal or above normal intellect. Their impairments may be developmental disabilities, speech and language impairments, autism, traumatic brain injuries, emotional and behavioral disorders, visual impairments, hearing impairments, orthopedic impairments, health impairments, or any combinations of these.

The practice of deinstitutionalization (removing individuals from hospitals and large residential institutions and keeping them in their own homes) and the legal initiatives requiring free and appropriate public education in the least restrictive environment have closed some of the cracks through which these children once fell.

Schools are attempting to provide students with MD with the best education possible. Often, when schools fail, it is some condition(s) outside the school's control that share the onus of responsibility. Schools, when they fail to be effective, usually provide inadequate services due to lack of professional development. Without adequate teacher preparation, and sufficient teaching support, education of all children in inclusive classrooms becomes infeasible. Professional development must be both improved and expanded to give regularized education a leg to stand on.

The lay public is often unprepared for children with traumatic brain injuries and other forms of MD to be accepted for inclusion in public schools. Advocates for the rights of disabled individuals have used the term "handicapism" to describe this prejudice and discrimination directed at disabled students. The greater the disability, the greater the evinced prejudice. A disability (not able) is not the same as a handicap (hindrance, not at an advantage). The words should not be used interchangeably. A person who is not able to do something (walk, see, hear) has a disability but does not have to be handicapped. Schools and communities may impose handicaps (hindrances) by preventing the student with the disability from functioning in an alternative way. Thus, if

DigitalVision/PunchStock/PunchStock

a student who cannot walk can instead locomote in a wheelchair, he or she is not handicapped. If a building or classroom has no ramps, however, and is inaccessible to a wheelchair user, then the school has imposed a handicap by preventing access to that particular property of the environment. If a student cannot use vocal cords to communicate, and is provided with an augmentative and alternate communication (AAC) system, he or she is not handicapped. If a building or classroom has no power supply or other provisions for use of the AAC system, then the environment again has imposed a handicap. There are millions of ways in which properties of our environments and characteristics of our behavior prevent children with multiple disabilities from functioning up to their potentialities.

Some public schools have resisted the regular education initiative (REI) that calls for general education classes rather than special education classes to be primarily responsible for the education of students with more severe and multiple disabilities.

The inclusive school movement, which supports the REI, would have special education teachers become consultants, resource specialists, collaborative teachers, or itinerant teachers rather than full-time special education teachers. While arguments for and against the REI have not been resolved, most educators agree that an appropriate education for each child with a disability may require a continuum of services. Some children, especially those with multiple disabilities, may require an environment more restrictive than a general education classroom for at least part of the day in order to get the type of assistance they need to function up to their potentialities. Teacher education typically does not offer comprehensive preparation for working with children with MD who require extensive special educational services. In addition, children with MD often require related services (for example, chemotherapy, physical therapy, psychotherapy, transportation) to enable them to learn in a classroom environment. Hopefully, teacher preparation, in-service education and professional development sessions will address some of these concerns of service delivery in the near future.

Many children and youth with MD suffer from a lack of understanding, a lack of empathy, and handicapist attitudes that are directed at them. They present very special problems for teachers to solve. Often the message they hear is, "Just go away." The challenge of writing an appropriate individualized education plan (IEP) is enormous. Updating the IEP each year and preparing an individualized transition plan (ITP), which will allow the student with MD to function as independently as possible after age 21, is mandated by law. These students must be served. Teachers must be given the time and support needed to do so. Excuses such as no time, no money, and no personnel to provide appropriate services are unacceptable. Teachers can expect progress and good results, even with the most multiply disabled.

The first article in this unit "Making Inclusion a Reality for Students with Severe Disabilities" emphasizes the how, when, and where of inclusion. The time for debating whether to include students with MD is past. Collaborative planning is essential for appropriate integration and education of students with MD. A cascade of integration options makes it possible for students with MD to be included even during content area instruction. The authors give suggestions for designing IEPs with workable instructional objectives.

The second article in this unit suggests that students with traumatic brain injuries should be allowed to reenter public schools despite a range of cognitive, physical, and social-emotional disorders that may affect their education. The author, Julie Bowen, gives a variety of specific research-based learning strategies that aide this process. Educators who work with all students with MDs can benefit from these behavioral and instructional interventions.

The unit's final article, "Empowering Students with Severe Disabilities," discusses functional communication. Students can use gestures, sign language, and/or augmentative technological aids to express their needs and desires. Service providers can learn to translate their vocalizations, gestures, signs, and augmentative aids in order to provide more appropriate education and care.

Making Inclusion a Reality for Students with Severe Disabilities

PAMELA S. WOLFE AND TRACEY E. HALL

L et's end the debate about *whether* to include students with severe disabilities in the general education classroom (see box, "What Does the Literature Say?"). Let's focus on *how* and *when* and *where*. This article provides helpful perspectives and suggestions for teachers, students, and parents in the struggle to provide an appropriate education for all students.

Here, we provide a cascade of integration options for inclusion. These integration options are based on the work of many researchers (Bradley, King-Sears, & Tessier- Switlick, 1997; Giangreco, Cloninger, & Iverson, 1998; Janney & Snell, 2000; Stainback & Stainback, 2000).

> **The social integration focus of inclusion negates the opportunity for the student with disabilities to receive instruction in content areas.**

In these options, we have applied content area instruction to inclusive settings, using a case example. We have also outlined a system designed to facilitate collaborative planning between general and special education teachers, using a student's individualized education program (IEP) as a foundation for decision making. Use of the IEP ensures that educational programming is both individualized and integrated with the general classroom curriculum.

The Cascade of Integration Options

The Individuals with Disabilities Education Act (IDEA) promotes the concept of placement of students with disabilities into the least restrictive environment (LRE). The concept of LRE is based on the belief that educators must provide a range of placement options (Mastropieri & Scruggs, 2000; Thomas & Rapport, 1998). A cascade of placement options can range from the home-school and general education class setting to institutional placements. This cascade of services highlights the need to individualize and base decisions for placement on the student's unique needs.

As noted, schools and districts are placing more students with severe disabilities in general education settings. But placement alone is insufficient to guarantee that the student with disabilities will benefit educationally. The optimal integration option is based on two factors:

- The type of activity undertaken in the general education setting.
- The objectives stated on the student's IEP.

Decisions about including a student with severe disabilities are frequently oriented toward fitting the student into the existing general education classroom activities and focus primarily on social integration (Scruggs & Mastropieri, 1996). The social integration focus negates the opportunity for the "included" student to receive instruction in content areas. Although we acknowledge the value of social integration, we advocate that programming should emanate from the student's IEP objectives. Teachers should consider content area coursework as a means by which the student may meet his or her IEP objectives. For example, teachers can address many objectives from the IEP in the general education setting by considering a range of adaptations and accommodations.

The Cascade of Integration Options illustrates a range of accommodations for students with severe disabilities who are included in general education settings (see box, "Cascade of Integration Options"). This cascade includes the following poles:

- The least restrictive inclusion option in which no changes are made (unadapted participation in the general education curriculum).
- A more restrictive option in which students with severe disabilities are temporarily removed from the setting (functional curriculum outside the general education classroom).

The cascade also includes a series of questions designed to help educators make decisions concerning the most appropriate integration options during content area instruction.

What Does the Literature Say about Inclusion for Students with Severe Disabilities?

The inclusion of students with severe disabilities into general education classrooms has become increasingly prevalent (Katsiyannis, Conderman, & Franks, 1995; Sailor, Gee, & Karasoff, 2000; U.S. Department of Education, 2000). Although IDEA '97 does not mandate the inclusion of students with disabilities, the legislation strongly encourages consideration of appropriate placement in general education settings.

Definition. The term *inclusion* has many interpretations. We have adopted the definition of inclusion noted by Mastropieri and Scruggs (2000) in which *students with disabilities are served in the general education classroom under the instruction of the general education teacher.* Specifically it involves providing support services to the student in the general education setting versus excluding the student from the setting and their peers. Inclusion requires the provision of adaptations and accommodations to classroom curriculum to ensure that the student will benefit from the placement. The definition, however, does not require that the student with special needs perform at a level comparable to peers without disabilities.

Benefits of Inclusion. Many research studies have shown that the inclusion of students with severe disabilities into general education settings is beneficial for all students (those with and without disabilities) particularly in relation to social acceptance, self-esteem, and social skills (Kennedy, Shukla, & Fryxell, 1997; Mu, Siegel, & Allinder, 2000). Although some research has indicated academic gains, teachers are more challenged to appropriately include students with severe disabilities in the content areas (Heller, 2001). Content domain areas include social studies, sciences, health, and related academic subjects.

Role of IEP. Given that the goal of inclusion is to assure that *all* students benefit from instruction, educators must provide programming that meets the needs of *all* students including those with disabilities. For students with disabilities, the IEP serves as the document to guide program planning and instruction. Educators should use the IEP to determine *what* should be taught, *how* the content should be taught, and *who* can most appropriately provide instruction.

Roles of Professionals. There are many professions involved in providing services for students with severe disabilities in included settings. Two frequent members to this team of professionals are the general education and special education teachers. The collaboration of these teachers is essential to assure that the student with disabilities is successful in the placement both socially and academically (Jackson, Ryndak, & Billingsley, 2000; Salend, 2001; Salisbury, Evans, & Palombaro, 1997; Snell & Janney, 2000). Both teachers need to be aware of the student's IEP objectives and use this document to guide program planning decisions and data collection procedures. To meet the needs of students with disabilities in the general education classroom, changes in the curriculum may be necessary.

Collaborative Planning for Inclusion

As noted previously, the collaboration of educators involved with the student having severe disabilities is essential to ensure appropriate integration and educational programming. Special and general education teachers must share knowledge about teaching strategies when planning effective instruction. Through collaborative teaming, teachers set the stage for student achievement of goals.

We have identified two stages of planning for special and general education teachers when considering options for content area integration. Table 1 lists these stages as *preplanning* and collaborative *planning* activities.

- *In the preplanning stages,* the general education teacher reflects on the content area unit activities and conducts a task analysis to identify key components of the lessons. Once the general education teacher has identified components of the unit, the special education teacher is asked to reflect upon the individual student's IEP objectives and how those objectives can be addressed in the general education content area unit. This stage is a *thinking* or *reflection activity* before a meeting; or the teachers could hold a face-to-face meeting to think together.

- *In the collaborative planning stage,* the two teachers meet to determine the most appropriate integration options in relation to the IEP, what adaptations or accommodations will be required, what additional supports are needed, and how student progress will be monitored (see Table 1).

Case Study of Collaborative Planning

Table 2 shows a case example of the Cascade of Integration Options in operation, as educators implement accommodations for a student included in content area instruction. The example reflects the plan for a student named Billy, who is included in a sixth-grade classroom.

Billy's IEP contains instructional objectives in a variety of domain areas, including communication, functional academics, socialization, fine and gross motor skills, hygiene, and leisure and recreation. The teachers formed their instructional plan

Cascade of Integration Options

Unadapted Participation in the General Curriculum

Same activities, same objectives, same setting

- Can student complete the activities as written for the general education classroom?
- Do one or more lesson objectives match the student's IEP?

Adaptations to the General Curriculum

Same activities, different (related) objectives, same setting

- Can the student meet the lesson objectives with minor modifications (time, response mode)?

Embedded Skills within the General Curriculum

Similar activity, different (related) objectives, same setting

- Are there components of the activity that can be met by the students, even if not the central objective of the lesson but match an IEP objective?

Functional Curriculum in the General Education Classroom

Different activities, different (related) objectives, same setting

- Are the class activities greatly unrelated to the student's IEP? Are there IEP? Are there IEP objectives that could be met in the same setting?

Functional Curriculum Outside General Education Classroom

Different activities, different (unrelated) objectives, different setting

- Are the class activities greatly unrelated to the student's IEP? Are IEP objectives better met in a different setting (require equipment, repetition, etc.)?

based on Billy's IEP objectives. The teachers collaboratively determined how they could meet many of Billy's IEP objectives within the content area of social studies.

Critical to the successful application of the Cascade is a well-designed IEP with clearly stated instructional objectives

---

As Table 2 illustrates, the integration option varies across the activities and days of the instructional unit. Further, note that the teachers considered the need for additional support to implement instruction (adaptive equipment, additional personnel,

technical support). In this case Billy was able to work on nearly all of his IEP objectives in the content area unit. The one exception is Billy's IEP objective related to hygiene; for programming related to showering and shaving, Billy is temporarily removed from the general education setting (functional curriculum outside the general classroom conducted during an adapted physical education class).

As Table 2 shows, teachers used a variety of integration options. Through the use of integration options, Billy was able to obtain instruction on important IEP objectives even though he did not always work on the general education social studies outcomes. Further, by employing the Cascade of Integration Options, Billy's teachers were able to provide Billy with the following:

- Social skills practice.
- Instruction on social studies information.
- Instruction on IEP objectives that focused on Billy's needs.

Although this article focused on the case of Billy, educators can apply the Cascade of Integration Options with most students and areas of instruction, throughout the school year. Critical to the successful application of the Cascade is a well-designed IEP with clearly stated instructional objectives.

Final Thoughts

Inclusion of students with disabilities requires the provision of curriculum and classroom adaptations. But inclusion does not require that the student with special needs perform at a level comparable to peers without disabilities. Students with disabilities may be included during content area instruction if teachers consider the Cascade of Integration Options.

If teachers collaborate to employ such options through carefully planned instruction, they can include students with severe disabilities in general education settings in meaningful ways—for *all* students.

References

Bradley, D. F., King-Sears, M. E., & Tessier-Switlick, D. M. (1997). *Teaching students in inclusive settings*. Boston: Allyn & Bacon.

Heller, K. W. (2001). Adaptations and instruction in science and social studies. In J. L. Bigge, S. J. Best, & K. W. Heller (Eds.), *Teaching individuals with physical, health, or multiple disabilities* (4th ed., pp). Upper Saddle River, NJ: Merrill.

Giangreco, M. F., Cloninger, C. J., & Iverson, V. S. (1998). *Choosing outcomes and accommodations for children* (2nd ed.). Baltimore: Paul H. Brookes.

Jackson, L., Ryndak, D. L., & Billingsley, F. (2000). Useful practices in inclusive education: A preliminary view of what experts in moderate to severe disabilities are saying. *Journal of The Association for Persons with Severe Handicaps, 25*(3), 129–141.

Janney, R., & Snell, M. E. (2000). *Teachers' guide to inclusive practices: Modifying schoolwork*. Baltimore: Paul H. Brookes.

Katsiyannis, A., Conderman, G., & Franks, D. J. (1995). State practices on inclusion: A national review. *Remedial and Special Education, 16,* 279–287.

Table 1 Stages of Planning for Curriculum Adaptations for Student with Disabilities in General Education Settings

Preplanning		Planning

Preplanning

General Education Teacher Unit Plan Analysis

What are the objectives of my lessons?

- What is the purpose of the unit?
- What skills do I want students to obtain?

What are the steps students must undertake to complete the unit?

- What are the component activities within the series of lessons? (list in order)
- Do the activities directly relate to the overall objective of the unit?
- Are the steps logically sequenced?

Will the completion of the unit include individual and/or group activities?

- Cooperative Learning Groups
- Individual
- Group activities
- Individual and Group

What learner products are expected?

- Written report   • Oral Report
- Tests   • Computer Question
- Concept maps/graphic displays

What is the time frame to complete the activities for this unit?

- Single day   • Monthly
- Weekly   • Bimonthly
- Longer term

What are the required materials for the activities and/or unit?

- Resource materials   • Class text
- Computer internet
- Misc. materials (school, home)

How will student progress be as sessed throughout the unit?

- End-of-unit test
- Rubric
- Performance or subjective evaluation

Special Education Teacher

What are the IEP objectives for the in cluded student(s)?

What domain areas from the IEP can be addressed in the instructional unit?

Does this student have characteristics that will require adaptations? Have I considered:

- Cognitive skills
- Motor skills
- Communication skills
- Social skills

What levels of adaptations from the continuum are appropriate for this student for different activities within the unit?

What required unit adaptations could be made for this student in terms of the following:

- Materials
- Time requirements
- Product expectations

Planning

General and Special Education Teacher Planning Meeting

Based on the unit analysis, what IEP objectives can be worked on during content area instruction?

What adaptations or accommodations will be required to work on these objectives?

What other supports will the general education teacher need to successfully complete the activity?

- Teaching assistant present
- Adaptive equipment
- Technical support
- Materials adaptations
- Co-teach with special education teacher

Are the student's IEP objectives being addressed in this unit in a meaningful way?

How will teachers communicate about student progress throughout the unit?

- Informal discussion
- Weekly meetings
- Report from assistant
- Communication journal

How will progress toward attainment of IEP goal(s) be assessed?

Table 2 Case Example of Collaborative Planning in Content Area Instruction (Social Studies)

Preplanning

	Day 1	Day 2	Day 3	Day 4	Day 5
Activity	Assign to one of three map groups. • Political map • Geographic map • Natural resources map Start research for map information. Textbook, Encyclopedia. Newspaper, Library books, CD-ROM, Internet. 30-minute library time.	Continue research. Draw the map on 3′ × 5′ poster board, include scale, legend, major cities, and landmarks. Each student must draw and color a minimum of 10 features for specific map in appropriate location. 1-hour map making.	Continue map making: Draw the map on 3′ × 5′ poster board, include scale, leg end, major cities, and landmarks. Draw or color features for specific map in appropriate location. 1-hour map making.	Final map construction. Preparation for oral presentation. Division of speaking roles. 30-minutes map work. 30-minutes presentation work.	Three groups orally present maps to class. 30-minute presentations for each group.
IEP Objective	**Communication:** Initiate conversation about map with group members using communication device. **Functional Academics Reading:** Identify parts of newspaper for peers to find map information. **Social Skills:** Take turns interacting with peers during research; maintain appropriate personal space. **Gross Motor:** Manipulate wheelchair to and within library.	**Fine Motor:** Cut out three pictures that represent resources on the map with adaptive scissors. **Functional Academics Math:** Count the number of resource features group members made (10 each). **Communication:** Initiative with peers if ready for them to count if number of items is correct using communication device.	**Fine Motor:** Paste the three objects on the map. **Functional Academics Math:** Alert the group when time is up map making. **Communication:** Initiate communication with peers using device.	**Functional Academics Reading:** While students are completing research information for presentation, student uses newspaper to identify leisure activities (movie section, TV guide). **Leisure:** Select preferred leisure activity for the weekend. **Functional Academics Math:** Practice time-telling in preparation for group presentation, day 5.	**Communication:** Introduce members of the working group to the class using communication device. **Functional Academics Math:** Keep time for the group. Notify members when half-hour period is over.

Planning

	Day 1	Day 2	Day 3	Day 4	Day 5
Level of Adaptation	Embedded skills within the general curriculum. Similar activities, different objectives, same setting.	Adaptations to the general curriculum. Same activities, different objectives, same setting.	Adaptations to the general curriculum. Same activities, different objectives, same setting.	Functional curriculum in the general education classroom. Different activities, different objectives, same setting.	Unadapted participation in the general curriculum. Same activities, same objective, same setting.
Support from Special Education Teacher	Co-teach presentation of the map assignment to class. Needed technical support.	Provide adapted scissors to general education room. Provide enlarged pictures for student to cut. Needed technical support.	Needed technical support.	Needed technical support.	None.

Kennedy, C. H., Shukla, S., & Fryxell, D. (1997). Comparing the effects of educational placement on the social relationships of intermediate school students with severe disabilities. *Exceptional Children, 64,* 31–47.

Mastropieri, M. A., & Scruggs, T. E. (2000). *The inclusive classroom. Strategies for effective instruction.* Upper Saddle River, NJ: Merrill.

Mu, K., Siegel, E. B., & Allinder, R. M. (2000). Peer interactions and sociometric status of high school students with moderate or severe disabilities in general education classrooms. *Journal of The Association for Persons with Severe Handicaps, 25*(3), 142–152.

Sailor, W., Gee, K., & Karasoff, P. (2000). Inclusion and school restructuring. In M. E. Snell & F. Brown (Eds.), *Instruction of students with severe disabilities* (5th ed.), 31–66. Upper Saddle River, NJ: Merrill.

Salend, S. J. (2001). *Creating inclusive classrooms. Effective and reflective practices* (4th ed.). Upper Saddle River, NJ: Merrill.

Salisbury, C. L., Evans, I. M., & Palombaro, M. M. (1997). Collaborative problem-solving to promote the inclusion of young children with significant disabilities in primary grades. *Exceptional Children, 63,* 195–209.

Scruggs, T. E., & Mastropieri, M. A. (1996). Teacher perceptions of mainstreaming/inclusion 1958–1995: A research synthesis. *Exceptional Children, 63,* 59–74.

Snell, M. E., & Janney, R. (2000). *Teachers' guides to inclusive practices: Collaborative teaming.* Baltimore: Paul H. Brookes.

Stainback, S., & Stainback, W. (Eds.). (2000). *Inclusion: A guide for educators.* Baltimore: Paul H. Brookes.

Thomas, S. B., & Rapport, M. J. K. (1998). The least restrictive environment: Understanding the directions of the courts. *The Journal of Special Education, 32*(2), 66–78.

U.S. Department of Education. (2000). *Twenty-second annual report to Congress on the implementation of the Individuals with Disabilities Education Act.* Washington, DC: Author. (ERIC Document Reproduction Service No. ED 444 333)

PAMELA S. WOLFE, Associate Professor, Department of Educational and School Psychology and Special Education, The Pennsylvania State University, University Park. **TRACEY E. HALL** (CEC Chapter #18), Senior Research Scientist/Instructional Designer, Center for Applied Special Technology (CAST), Peabody, Massachusetts. Address correspondence to Pamela S. Wolfe, 212A CEDAR Building, The Pennsylvania State University, University Park, PA 16802 (e-mail: psw7@psu.edu).

From *Teaching Exceptional Children,* by Pamela S. Wolfe and Tracey E. Hall, Vol. 35, no. 4, March/April 2003, pp. 56–61. Copyright © 2003 by Council for Exceptional Children. Reprinted by permission.

Classroom Interventions for Students with Traumatic Brain Injuries

Students who have sustained a traumatic brain injury (TBI) return to the school setting with a range of cognitive, psychosocial, and physical deficits that can significantly affect their academic functioning. Successful educational reintegration for students with TBI requires careful assessment of each child's unique needs and abilities and the selection of classroom interventions designed to meet those needs. In this article, the author presents information about the range of services that are available in the school setting and discusses typical environmental and classroom accommodations that have proven effective. The author discusses a variety of specific research-based learning strategies, behavioral interventions, and instructional interventions available to educators who work with TBI students.

JULIE M. BOWEN

Most children who have sustained a traumatic brain injury (TBI), even a severe brain injury, will eventually return to a school or classroom setting following discharge from acute hospitalization (Klonoff & Paris, 1974; Rosen & Gerring, 1986). Some will return after only a brief hospitalization and others after a lengthy hospitalization and rehabilitation program. Because the recovery process can take several months or even years, many of these children continue to have rehabilitation needs and cognitive impairments and will return to school while still in the recovery stages. It often becomes the responsibility of the educational system to facilitate ongoing recovery and to provide needed services to help these children progress in their academic and social functioning. My purpose in this article is to review intervention strategies from recent research that are available to educators as they assist children with TBI when they return to the school environment. An *intervention* is defined as the systematic application of research-validated procedures to change behaviors through manipulation of antecedents and consequences or by teaching new skills (Bowen, Jenson, & Clark, 2004). Successful readjustment to school may require adaptation of the learning environment, acquisition or reacquisition of skills, provision of compensatory aids and strategies, as well as support services from special education providers.

Setting the Stage

Regardless of the severity of the injury and length of rehabilitation services, advance communication and coordination between the hospital, therapists, family, and the school system is a critical first step in student's returning to school. The goal of this communication should be to gather medical and functional information to assist the school in developing an appropriate and individualized plan for the student's reentry into school, whether it is a few accommodations in a regular class setting or an intensive special education program. This communication should be ongoing and the reentry plan determined prior to the student's return to school. Specific classroom interventions and accommodations required to optimize a successful school reintegration should be developed after careful assessment of students' needs, including medical, physical, cognitive, and social-emotional problems. Thus, the educational program and classroom interventions designed to benefit students with TBI must be based on the unique needs of each individual. Because of the rapidly changing needs and recovery of children with TBI, initial evaluations conducted while in the hospital may not be accurate descriptions of the students at the time of their reentry into school. Therefore, ongoing observation and assessment of students after their return to school is usually required to develop appropriate interventions and to evaluate the effectiveness of interventions.

The range of neurologic sequelae following TBI is too diverse to prescribe specific intervention strategies that work for all students, and there are few empirical studies that validate specific interventions for students with TBI. However, validated approaches that are effective for students with other disabilities similar to those of students with brain injury offer practical intervention choices for teachers working with students with TBI. Ylvisaker and colleagues (2001) suggest that students with TBI be identified by functional need and that teachers may then select from proven instructional interventions for a particular need. Although serving students based on functional needs is important, it is also critical for educators to have an understanding of TBI as a disability and of the commonly associated features of an acquired brain injury.

Common Sequelae of TBI

Children who have sustained a TBI may exhibit a wide range of newly acquired deficits or alterations in cognition, physical mobility, self-care skills, and communication skills as well as changes in emotional and behavioral regulation, which may significantly affect school functioning (Fletcher & Levin, 1988). The nature and severity of the injury, acute medical complications, age of the child, preinjury characteristics, and the interaction of these factors with the family system and environment will affect the course of recovery and school outcome (Wilkening, 1997). Each child will present a unique pattern of sequelae ranging from mild to severe.

Although there is considerable variability in outcome following TBI, there are also general features of acquired brain injury common to many children who sustain a brain injury, particularly when structural brain damage is present. These are related to vulnerable areas of the brain often affected during a closed head injury, including damage to the frontal lobes, and the anterior and medial temporal lobes. Children with frontal lobe injury typically experience greater difficulty with executive function, which includes attentional processes, self-regulation, goal setting, initiating, and inhibiting behavior. Many behavior and social problems observed in children with TBI are related to poor executive functioning. They may also have problems with organization—planning, prioritizing, analyzing tasks, and completing a sequence of activities. Cognitive impairments can include memory problems, slowed information processing, and language disturbances. Memory impairment (recalling and retaining information) is one of the most common deficits associated with pediatric TBI (Ewing-Cobbs & Fletcher, 1990). Physical functioning can also be markedly impaired following severe TBI. Loss of function in all or some extremities, spasticity, decreased motor speed, and poor coordination in fine or gross motor movements may require physical and environmental accommodations and/or assistance with self-care skills (feeding and toileting) in the school setting.

Assessment

In addition to formalized assessment of cognitive skills that may be conducted, the special education team at the school (i.e., school psychologist, special educator, speech language pathologist), uses a Functional Behavioral Assessment (FBA) to examine, measure, and treat many deficits associated with TBI, particularly behavioral changes related to increased

---

ABC Functional Assessment Sheet

Student's Name: _____   Date: _____

Teacher's Name: _____   Setting: _____

Antecedent—Something Before the Behavior

Time _____

People _____

Places _____

Events _____

Other Behaviors _____

Behavior—Specific, Observable, Objective

Behavior excesses (to decrease) _____

_____

Behavior deficits (to increase) _____

_____

Consequence—Something that Follows the Behavior

Punishment _____

Positive reinforcers (attention, tangibles, sensory) _____

_____

Negative Reinforcers (escape, avoidance) _____

_____

Replacement Behavior _____

Comments _____

_____

_____

_____

_____

Figure 1 Antecedent-Behavior-Consequence (ABC) form.

impulsiveness, inappropriate emotional outbursts, aggression, and inattention. An assessment of the environmental variables (immediate and distant) that contribute to the occurrence of a behavior that is negatively impacting school functioning will assist in developing effective strategies. The following are the four typical categories of behavioral function: (a) gaining attention from peers or adults, (b) escaping or avoiding a nonpreferred task or person, (c) gaining access to tangible reinforcement, and (d) gaining sensory stimulation or relief. An FBA includes a descriptive assessment based on observations of the student, structured interviews, and manipulation of variables to determine the function of problematic behaviors (Gardner, Bird, Maguire, Carreiro, & Abenaim, 2003). Studies involving use of FBA to develop effective intervention plans for individuals with TBI have been reported in the literature (e.g., Feeney & Ylvisaker, 1995).

An ABC (Antecendent-Behavior-Consequence) assessment is one simple means of conducting an FBA. In conducting an ABC Assessment, assessors record the events that occur immediately before and after the unwanted behavior (antecedents and consequences). They collect information such as time of day, with whom the behavior occurs, specific places, other events, and rate and type of reinforcers are collected to help select an appropriate replacement behavior and an effective intervention plan. Distant events and physiologic conditions (e.g., physical pain, cognitive limitations) that may be contributing to the behavior should also be considered (Bowen et al., 2004). Figure 1 provides a sample ABC form.

Following assessment of educationally relevant sequelae and determining the unique needs of a student who has sustained a TBI, the school team can design an optimal educational program based on this information. An effective intervention plan will incorporate antecedent-focused intervention procedures, including empirically proven environmental structuring and effective teaching strategies, as well as teaching students useful skills and compensatory strategies to meet their goals.

Structuring the Environment

Because a TBI involves a progressive recovery process, a student's physical and mental endurances may be limited during their initial return to school and steadily improve over time. Therefore, consideration of different schooling options may be necessary, including homebound instruction, gradual increase in school attendance, or change in class schedules to a less demanding course load. Academic programming and scheduling must be flexible and customized to fit children's changing needs. Class enrollment and expectations should be based on students' current, rather than previous, academic performances. Rather than push students quickly through classes and require them to make up missed assignments, students should be allowed additional time to relearn concepts and regain skills.

Structuring the school environment is a way to manage antecedents or consequences contributing to many problem behaviors, and to prevent the behavior from occurring. Many of the environmental strategies that will optimize success for students with TBI are effective with students with other learning problems. These strategies can be employed in general or special

education settings. If attention, sensitivity to overstimulation, disinhibition, and emotional lability are identified as problems, the classroom environment should be quiet and simplified. Noise and activity levels should be controlled and unnecessary distracters and sensory stimulation (including noise, light, and movement) should be minimized (Farmer & Peterson, 1995). This may require seating the student near the teacher or by an appropriate peer, providing a study carrel, removing extra materials (e.g., pencils, books, papers), and dividing work or task lengths into smaller sections. Students may use an FM unit or earplugs to reduce external noise. Students may need a designated space in which to rest or take time out from stimulation and be allowed to have "down time."

Special attention should be given to the physical arrangement and structure of the classroom to facilitate mobility and accommodate physical needs. A student with poor mobility may need assistance to participate in typical classroom activities. The school may need to ensure the availability of accessible bathrooms and ramps. Frequently traveled areas should be sufficiently wide for smooth transition and be free of obstacles. Students may need to be specifically taught and allowed to rehearse the routines of the learning environment, including building orientation and room design. Students in secondary schools may have a particularly difficult time navigating hallways and moving from class to class. Providing extra time for transitions and leaving class a few minutes early, before other students are in the hallways, is often recommended. A peer buddy or an adult aide may be assigned to help with hallway transitions, to provide physical assistance (e.g., in the lunchroom or bathrooms), and to ensure safety.

Classroom structure should also include a predictable and consistent routine. Consideration should also be given to the length of school day that students can tolerate, their nutritional needs, and their fatigue levels and need for rest breaks; classes should be scheduled to capitalize on optimal attention periods. For students who are easily fatigued, a schedule consisting of alternating instruction, activity, and rest periods may be needed. Students with challenging behaviors are more likely to engage in appropriate, on-task behaviors when presented with a positive, well-understood daily routine. Providing a written schedule or posting a visual chart of the daily routine will help reduce confusion. Students may need simplified instructions, written or picture checklists of task steps, maps, or strategically placed signs to carry out tasks. It is important to involve the student in reviewing the schedule at the beginning of the day or period and verbally review the steps. Transition times and out-of-classroom activities should be preplanned and structured to reduce stimulation and emotional distress. Using auditory or visual cues to signal changes in the routine and giving the student advance warning is also helpful. Teachers of the same student should agree on environmental strategies and apply them consistently throughout the school day.

Typical Classroom Accommodations

Another way of altering the environment is to provide external devices and cues that the student can use to compensate for organization, memory, and motor deficits (Mateer, Kerns, & Eso, 1997). Assistive devices can include technical equipment and materials such as tape recorders, calculators, electronic spellers, computers or word processors, augmentative communication devices, timers, alarms, and beepers or equipment for mobility (e.g., wheelchair, walker, electric scooter). Other external cues used to remind students include labels, maps checklists, pictures or icons, photograph cues, post-it-notes, calendars, planners, and journals. A memory notebook is one such compensatory aid that has been used to assist in memory

Table 1 Compensatory Aids and Strategies for Students with Traumatic Brain Injury (TBI)

Cognitive Impairment	External Aids	Teaching/Learning Strategies
Attention	Use FM unit or earplugs. Use a timer or alare to focus attention. Place symbol or sign in an obvious location to remind student to attend.	Keep assignments and instructions simple and direct. Provide rest periods, breaks, or physical activity. Minimize distractions. Divide work into small sections. Use verbal, gestural, or visual cues to remind student to attend. Ask student to repeat or summarize instructions. Slow pace of instruction.
Memory	Use checklists, post-it notes, 3 × 5 cards. Keep appointment calendars, planners, electronic organizers, or dry-erase boards. Use memory log or card with personal information, map, schedule, etc. Set a timer or alarm to remind when a task needs to be done. Keep items in one designated location. Use tape recorders to review information. Provide photocopies of textbook pages for student to practice highlighting skills.	Ask student to repeat new information several times. Teach the use of visual imagery. Teach the use of mnemonic strategies. Simplify information to be remembered. Break each task into steps and teach each step separately. Teach study skills, note-taking techniques, and self-questioning. Test using multiple-choice format. Use fact cards and cue sheets to help recall. Teach student to rehearse or review notes immediately (within 1 hr.) after class.
Organization	Display pictorial or visual schedule of activities. Provide checklist with steps for completing tasks, or written outline of class lectures. Use a binder with subject sections and homework pockets. Use daily planner to record homework assignments. Use colored lines, highlighting, color-coding as cues for organization. Use graphic organizers to sequence thinking (time lines, outlines, flow charts, etc.)	Review daily routines with student. Teach use of student planner and cue student to record assignments in planner. Designate specific locations to turn in assignments/homework, use picture cues, or labels to identify place. Assign a peer buddy to assist with routines.
Writing and information processing speed	Use of tape recorders to record answers Assign a peer note taker to take carbon paper notes. Use assistive devices such as a word processor, Dictaphone, or peer scribe.	Reduce amount of written work that is required. Allow extra time to complete work or to verbally respond. Provide alternative forms of test taking. Enlarge the print on worksheets. Provide a make-up period at the end of the day. Present visual or verbal information at a slower pace.

and organization following TBI. The memory notebook can be very flexible and may contain maps, checklists, feelings log, and other information (e.g., telephone numbers, names of contact people). Students should be trained to use the notebook (Tate, 1997).

Modifications to existing materials can assist students with TBI to learn and function in the classroom setting. Typical alterations that allow students to participate at their level include providing carbon paper notes, large print books, books on tape, and graphic organizers (visual displays to organize information). A similar approach involves altering the expectations for student participation. For example, allow more time on tests, reduce the amount of written work required, provide exams in multiple-choice format rather than recall format, and give pass–fail grades rather than letter grades (Mateer et al., 1997). It is important that students are not simply given aids or devices to use without adequate training to recognize when and where appropriate aids are useful, and how to use the strategy properly. Table 1 provides a sampling of external aids and interventions that can be used to assist students with attention, memory, organization, and processing speed deficits.

Available Resources and Services

School districts have a variety of options and resources to accommodate the particular learning needs of students returning to school following a TBI. Because of the extreme variability in outcome following brain injury, a wide range of services and accommodations may be needed and highly individualized planning is required. Many students with mild to moderate TBI can be integrated into existing school programs in regular education with some adaptations and modifications. Students with TBI who attend mainstream classes may also receive accommodations or related services under the Rehabilitation Act of 1973, Section 504. Section 504 covers all students who have a physical or mental impairment that substantially limits one or more major life activities, including learning. For students who do not require special education, but need some accommodations to participate in the regular school program, it is important to complete a 504 Plan and formalize suggested accommodations with parents and teachers. The 504 Plan documents the accommodations and designates persons involved. It must be reviewed annually and should be revised as students' needs change.

Students with significant impairments should be referred for special education evaluation to determine if specialized services are necessary to address any cognitive, communication, physical, or social limitations. Since 1990, students with TBI are eligible for services under the Individuals With Disabilities Education Act (IDEA) under the category of Traumatic Brain Injury (IDEA, 2005). To receive services, the brain injury must adversely affect students' educational performances and students must require specialized instruction. Special education programs are frequently selected as an intervention of choice for students with TBI because they can provide a lower adult–pupil ratio, individually designed curriculum and specialized instruction, and necessary therapies. In one follow-up study of children with head injuries, 30% required special education intervention at 1 year postinjury, and 78% of those with severe injuries were placed in special education (Greenspan & MacKenzie, 1994).

Within the special education program there are a variety of services available, ranging from least restrictive (i.e., one resource period per day) to more restrictive (i.e., self-contained program). In addition to resource services for academic or adaptive needs, students may receive services with a speech or language pathologist, occupational or physical therapist, psychologist, or other related services (i.e., adaptive physical education, vision specialist). As with a 504 Plan, an Individualized Educational Program (IEP) must be written, reviewed, and revised annually. However, because levels of functioning may change rapidly with TBI, it is recommended that IEP reviews occur more frequently. Although there may be one or several students with TBI attending a specialized program or class, a designated "TBI classroom" is not typically offered. Students with TBI may be placed in a noncategorical program, in which students are grouped by functional skills and ability levels, and provided appropriate curriculum content and teaching strategies based on these abilities (Cohen, 1991).

Specialized Teaching Strategies

Empirically supported teaching strategies that are effective with students with different types of learning difficulties also may prove useful for students with brain injury. Although teachers must find what works best with a particular student, these techniques are effective antecedent-based interventions that can prevent or significantly reduce challenging behaviors and teach students the active use of compensatory strategies.

The Direct Instruction (DI) model is based on the principles of applied behavior analysis (Engelmann & Carnine, 1982) that include pacing, frequent opportunity to respond, feedback, and reinforcement to maintain student engagement and ensure learning. These principles can be applied in designing an instructional program with students with a TBI (Glang, Singer, Cooley, & Tish, 1992). Some recommended steps in using a DI method include the following:

1. Select a meaningful goal or skill the student will need to learn and present it at the level of the student;
2. Provide a simple rationale to help the student understand the relevance of the skill;
3. Give clearly stated task directions (limit the number of steps) and ask the student to repeat or paraphrase the directions to ensure understanding;
4. Break tasks into small steps and demonstrate each step;
5. Provide opportunities for student response and practice at an appropriate pace;
6. Provide immediate feedback and error correction when necessary—feedback should be positive and systematic; and
7. Use verbal praise and encouragement frequently.

There are a variety of commercially produced DI materials available that include sequenced curricula and scripted wording; however, teachers may need to tailor these materials for students with TBI.

Another proactive teaching strategy that will facilitate compliance is use of effectively stated requests or precision commands (Rhode, Jensen, & Reavis, 1993). *Precision commands* consist of steps teachers can use to prevent escalation of behavior problems by giving clear instructions, allowing the student a chance to comply without interrupting, and reinforcing students who follow the request promptly. All teachers of students with TBI should consistently follow the same format for making requests. Some suggestions for giving effective requests include the following:

1. Use a direct statement telling the student to start (rather than stop) a behavior;
2. Look directly at the student as you give the request, move close, and use a soft, calm voice; speak clearly, slowly and concisely—do not shout.
3. Limit requests to only two or three at a time and give requests that the student is capable of following;
4. Allow enough time for the student to follow through; and
5. Recognize their effort with verbal praise and encouragement.

Students with severe cognitive and memory problems may benefit from a teaching approach referred to as *errorless learning* (Wilson & Evans, 1996). Errorless learning is based on a model of behavioral rehabilitation that involves discrimination training with early prompting and support that is systematically faded to ensure successful responding. In errorless learning, individuals are not allowed to guess on recall tasks, but are immediately provided with the correct response, instructed to read the response, and write it down (Mateer et al., 1997). If errors do occur they are followed by nonjudgmental corrective feedback (Ylvisaker et al., 2001).

Successful positive support for students with TBI must include interventions designed to teach functionally equivalent skills or behaviors to replace problematic ones. The primary goal is to teach students new skills that will help them achieve their needs (e.g., skills to verbally express needs and emotions). Skills training in communication, coping and relaxation, pragmatic social, problem-solving, study, and task-specific skills will help students obtain access to desired outcomes, rendering problem behaviors irrelevant. Functional communication training, for example, is a validated approach that can be used to reduce maladaptive behaviors in individuals with brain injury (Ducharme, 1999). It involves identifying the communication function of a challenging behavior, teaching a communication skill that serves the same function, and providing ready access to the outcome or reinforcer that was previously obtained by the problem behavior.

Providing specific training in self-management or self-monitoring strategies is another approach to helping children. *Self-management* involves teaching students to evaluate and monitor their own behavior and performance. One simple approach involves routine recording of behavior. For example, the teacher gives the students a piece of paper with 20 boxes. At random intervals, the teacher instructs the students to ask him or herself at random intervals, "Am I listening (working, behaving, etc.)?" The student then records a plus or a minus sign in the box (Rhode et al., 1993). Other forms of self-management include the use of a checklist of open-ended questions to guide students through an assignment, the use of assignment rubrics to allow students to self-evaluate their progress, and the use of emotion logs to allow students to self-monitor their emotions (e.g., rating anger levels and responses on an Anger Log; Bowen et al., 2004).

Many children who sustain severe TBI exhibit difficulty with social adjustment related to newly acquired language deficits in pragmatic (social conversation) communication (Jordan & Ashton, 1996). Programs designed for improving social skills have been successfully implemented in the school setting that include teaching specific skills (e.g., initiation, topic maintenance, turn taking, active listening), using repeated practice and constructive feedback, and granting the opportunity to practice in the natural setting with peers, staff, and parents (Wiseman-Hakes, Stewart, Wasserman, & Schuller, 1998). Self-modeling and self-monitoring procedures can be combined with skills training, by videotaping students during the practice and having students rate their performance on scoring sheets.

The use of positive reinforcement is a valuable strategy used to create a rewarding environment and successfully reintegrate children with brain injury into school settings (Gardner et al., 2003). Reinforcement can be both contingent and noncontingent and can include a combination of primary and secondary reinforcers. For students with extremely difficult behaviors, a differential reinforcement of other behaviors or alternative behaviors contingency may need to be implemented to reinforce the student for compliance and engaging in positive or alternative behaviors. Praise is an extremely effective form of positive reinforcement and should be given more frequently than reprimands or directives (at least a 4:1 ratio). Praise should describe specific behaviors that are meaningful to the student and should be delivered immediately following a behavior. It is often necessary to prompt and reinforce each attempt at a skill or behavior that successfully approximates the desired behavior to shape the appropriate behavior over time. Other forms of positive reinforcement include social reinforcement (e.g., smile, thumbs up, high five), token economies, and awarding special privileges or small tangible or edible reinforcers. Opportunity to engage in a preferred activity or gain access to more preferred activities may be offered contingent on engaging in or meeting criteria on a less preferred task (Slifer et al., 1997).

Behavioral momentum is another strategy that has been used to increase positive behaviors and compliance in brain injury rehabilitation (Slifer et al., 1997). *Behavior momentum* involves making requests with which the students have a high probability of compliance before making a low-probability request—similar to the momentum of objects in motion. A sequence of high-probability requests is used to establish a high rate of reinforcement for compliance that will increase the momentum and carry over to tasks that might have a lower probability of compliance. Positive reinforcement is delivered immediately after the student performs each request. Feeney and Ylvisaker (2003) used behavior momentum as part of a multicomponent intervention for students with TBI. As part of the intervention, staff included relatively easy tasks with guaranteed high rates of reinforcement before introducing difficult work and preceded undesirable tasks with preferred activities.

Although many of the antecedent-focused interventions are effective in modifying challenging behaviors, consequences are also important components of an intervention plan; however, consequences for children with TBI should be natural and related to the behavior (Ylvisaker, Jacobs, & Feeney, 2003). Individuals with frontal lobe injury often demonstrate an inefficiency of learning from aversive consequences; therefore, punishments such as school suspension or expulsion are usually ineffective (Gardner et al., 2003). Rather than delivery of negative consequences (e.g., threats, nagging) for noncompliance or failure to complete tasks, natural consequences that will help the person complete the task are more appropriate (e.g., constructive feedback, guided compliance). Extinction is an effective intervention that consists of withholding reinforcers that were previously delivered following a target behavior (Yody et al., 2000). For example, if an inappropriate behavior is maintained by teacher attention, this teacher attention should no longer follow the inappropriate behavior. Extinction strategies can include planned ignoring of an inappropriate behavior until the student demonstrates behavioral control, and then reinforcing alternative, appropriate behaviors. Educators should try to anticipate students' difficulties and offer verbal or physical prompts or cues to redirect behavior. Time-outs may be required to remove students from environmental events contributing to the behavior. Time-out might consist of going to a quiet area and remaining calm for 10 min before rejoining the activity. Student who become angry or explosive in reaction to academic demands, for example, could be taught an impulse control procedure to calm down and take a 5-minute break. Skills training might include identifying a cue that prompts them to "stop" or "take 5." The student is given the cue and reminded to "stop" at natural times and is reinforced for rehearsal and eventual use of the skill to deescalate before an angry outburst occurs (Clark, Russman, & Orme, 1999).

Case Study: Josh

Josh, an 11-year old, sixth-grade student was severely injured in a motor vehicle accident when the car in which he was riding swerved out of control and collided with another car. Josh was found unconscious at the scene. He was intubated and transported to a local hospital where a head computer tomography scan revealed a severe TBI, with multiple areas of hemorrhage in the right frontal and temporal regions. Josh also sustained facial fractures, as well as a right humerus fracture. He remained in a coma for 2 days and, after regaining consciousness, spent an additional 3 weeks in the hospital's rehabilitation unit. After discharge, he continued to receive outpatient physical and occupational therapies 2–3 hrs per week.

Shortly after the accident, the school principal contacted Josh's parents and continued to communicate with them throughout the hospital stay. Prior to Josh's return to school, his teachers, principal, and the school psychologist scheduled a meeting with the parents. The principal asked the school psychologist to serve as Josh's case manager. Prior to his injury, Josh had been an average student in regular education, but struggled somewhat in math. He was social, had many friends, and was active in sports. At the meeting, Josh's parents discussed his current levels of functioning and areas of impairment and the school team developed a plan to accommodate his needs. Six weeks after his injury, Josh continued to have some cognitive problems in the area of memory, information-processing speed, and executive functioning. His verbal skills and reading skills remained relatively strong. Josh had slowed motor speed and had a mild right-sided weakness. He had decreased endurance and fatigued easily.

On the basis of this information, the school team recommended and developed accommodations for his return to school at the meeting. It was decided that Josh would initially return to school on a modified basis, starting with 2 hr per day, in the mornings, gradually increasing his attendance to all day as his physical endurance improved. The team scheduled more difficult subjects during the morning to minimize fatigue. Although Josh was eligible for special education services, the parents and school team decided Josh could be successful in his regular classroom with accommodations, and formalized these accommodations by developing a 504 Plan. These accommodations included the following:

1. Allowing Josh to take breaks in the counseling area as needed and to check in with the psychologist at the beginning of the day for organizing sessions and to review his schedule.
2. Seating Josh near the front of the classsroom in a quiet location near a designated peer buddy who could provide carbon copy notes and assist with prompts.
3. Reducing written work requirements giving additional time to complete assignments, allowing him to dictate responses, and provide him with an extra set of books for home use.
4. Providing multiple-choice exams and avoiding time limits in testing.
5. Posting a schedule of daily activities in a visible place and training and prompting Josh to record his assignments in a daily planner.
6. Determining environmental factors and situations that caused agitation and frustration (e.g., sensory overload, changes in routine) and avoiding them as much as possible. (The teacher and Josh developed a plan for him to "take 5" [take a 5 min. break when he became frustrated], by looking at magazines, or running an office errand).
7. Meeting with the middle school team: Prior to his transition to middle school in the 7th grade, the school team, parents, and Josh met with the middle school team to discuss concerns and review the plan.

Summary

Returning to school following a brain injury presents a number of new challenges for children with TBI, as well as for those who work with them. Although some children with brain injury experience persistent cognitive and behavioral changes, when provided appropriate resources and strategies, all students can reach maximum potential. Teachers and educators play a key role in helping students with TBI succeed in their adjustment and reintegration into the school environment. To develop programs that will facilitate a successful school reentry, educators must work together to develop a comprehensive plan based on each child's individual strengths and weaknesses. With careful planning, making needed adaptations to the learning environment, and using effective instructional aids and strategies to help children acquire new skills, most children can fortunately overcome many of these challenges and can experience success in their academic and social endeavors.

References

Bowen, J., Jenson, W. R., & Clark, E. (2004). *School-based interventions for students with behavior problems.* New York: Kluwer.

Clark, E., Russman, S., & Orme, S. (1999). Traumatic brain injury: Effects on school functioning and intervention strategies. *School Psychology Review, 28,* 242–250.

Cohen, S. B. (1991). Adapting educational programs for students with head injuries. *Journal of Head Trauma Rehabilitation, 6,* 56–63.

Ducharme, J. M. (1999). Subject review: A conceptual model for treatment of externalizing behaviour in acquired brain injury. *Brain Injury, 13,* 645–668.

Engelmann, S., & Carnine, D. W. (1982). *Theory of instruction.* New York: Irvington.

Ewing-Cobbs, L., & Fletcher, J. M. (1990). Neuropsychological assessment of traumatic brain injury in children. In E. D. Bigler (Ed.), *Traumatic brain injury* (pp. 107–128). Austin, TX: Pro-Ed.

Farmer, J. E., & Peterson, L. (1995). Pediatric traumatic brain injury: Promoting successful school reentry. *School Psychology Review, 24,* 230–243.

Feeney, T. J., & Ylvisaker, M. (1995). Choice and routine: Antecedent behavioral interventions for adolescents with severe traumatic brain injury. *Journal of Head Trauma Rehabilitation, 10,* 67–86.

Feeney, T. J., & Ylvisaker, M. (2003). Context-sensitive behavioral supports for young children with TBI: Short-term effects and long-term outcome. *Journal of Head Trauma Rehabilitation, 18,* 33–51.

Fletcher, J., & Levin, H. (1988). Neurobehavioral effects of brain injury in children. In D. Routh (Ed.), *Handbook of pediatric psychology* (pp. 258–295). New York: Guilford.

Gardner, R. M., Bird, F. L., Maguire, H., Carreiro, R., & Abenaim, N. (2003). Intensive positive behavior supports for adolescents with acquired brain injury: Long-term outcomes in community settings. *Journal of Head Trauma Rehabilitation, 18,* 52–74.

Glang, A., Singer, G., Cooley, E., & Tish, N. (1992). Tailoring direct instruction techniques for use with elementary students with brain injury. *Journal of Head Ttrauma Rehabilitation, 7,* 93–108.

Greenspan, A. I., & MacKenzie, E. J. (1994). Functional outcome after pediatric head injury. *Pediatrics, 94,* 425–432.

Jordan, F. M., & Ashton, R. (1996). Language performance of severely closed head injured children. *Brain Injury, 10,* 91–98.

Klonoff, H., & Paris, R. (1974). Immediate, shortterm and residual effects of acute head injuries in children: Neuropsychological and neurological correlates. In R. M. Reitan & L. A. Davison (Eds.), *Clinical neuropsychology* (pp. 179–210). Washington, DC: Hemisphere.

Mateer, C. A., Kerns, K. A., & Eso, K. L. (1997). Management of attention and memory disorders following traumatic brain injury. In E. D. Bigler, E. Clark, & J. E. Farmer (Eds.), *Childhood traumatic brain injury* (pp. 153–176). Austin, TX: Pro-Ed.

Individuals With Disabilities Education Act, 70 Fed. Reg. 19356-16358 (April 13, 2005) (to be codified at 20 C. F. R. pt. 406, 416).

Rehabilitation Act of 1973, 29 U. S. C. § 794 (1974).

Rhode, G., Jenson, W. R., & Reavis, H. K. (1993). *The tough kid book.* Longmont, CO: Sopris West.

Rosen, C. D., & Gerring, J. P. (1986). *Head trauma: Educational reintegration.* San Diego, CA: College-Hill Press.

Slifer, K. J., Tucker, C. L., Gerson, A. C., Seviers, R. C., Kane, A. C., Amari, A., et al. (1997). Antecedent management and compliance training improve adolescents' participation in early brain injury rehabilitation. *Brain Injury, 11,* 877–889.

Tate, R. L. (1997). Beyond one-bun, two-shoe: Recent advances in the psychological rehabilitation of memory disorders after acquired brain injury. *Brain Injury, 11,* 907–918.

Wilkening, G. N. (1997). Long-term outcome after moderate to severe pediatric traumatic brain injury. In E. D. Bigler, E. Clark, & J. E. Farmer (Eds.), *Childhood traumatic brain injury* (pp. 79–99). Austin, TX: Pro-Ed.

Wilson, B. A., & Evans, J. J. (1996). Error-free learning in the rehabilitation of people with memory impairments. *Journal of Head Trauma Rehabilitation, 11,* 54–64.

Wiseman-Hakes, C., Stewart, M. L., Wasserman, R., & Schuller, R. (1998). Peer group training of pragmatic skills in adolescents with acquired brain injury. *Journal of Head Trauma Rehabilitation, 13,* 23–38.

Ylvisaker, M., Jacobs, H. E., & Feeney, T. (2003). Positive supports for people who experience behavioral and cognitive disability after brain injury: A review. *Journal of Head Trauma Rehabilitation, 18,* 7–32.

Ylvisaker, M., Todis, B., Glang, A., Urbanczyk, B., Franklin, C., DePompei, R., & et al. (2001). Educating students with TBI: Themes and recommendations. *Journal of Head Trauma Rehabilitation, 16,* 76–93.

Yody, B. B., Schaub, C., Conway, J., Peters, S., Strauss, D., & Helsinger, S. (2000). Applied behavior management and acquired brain injury: Approaches and assessment. *Journal of Head Trauma Rehabilitation, 15,* 1041–1060.

JULIE M. BOWEN is a psychologist at the Jordan School District, Salt Lake City, Utah.

From *Preventing School Failure*, Vol. 49, no. 4, Summer 2005, pp. 34–41. Reprinted by permission of the Helen Dwight Reid Educational Foundation. Published by Heldref Publications, 1319, Eighteenth St., NW, Washington, DC 20036-1802. Copyright © 2005. www.heldref.org

Empowering Students with Severe Disabilities to Actualize Communication Skills

Paul W. Cascella and Kevin M. McNamara

Jessica is an 11-year-old child who attends the sixth grade at a local middle school. Jessica has a history of severe mental retardation, secondary to childhood meningitis and seizures. Jessica is essentially nonverbal and nonambulatory, and she relies on her parents and caregivers for eating, dressing, toileting, and participation in typical home and school events. Jessica has normal hearing, and she wears eyeglasses.

Jessica participates in both an academic and functional life skills program at her school. During most mornings, Jessica participates in middle school academic subjects within the general education context. Her middle school has a rotating daily class schedule; and Jessica attends sixth-grade classes in math, science, social studies, language arts, and Spanish. She eats lunch with students from her academic classes.

After lunch, Jessica participates in her school's functional life skills program. This program is a multi-aged group of 8 to 10 students; and the curriculum is threefold: prevocational job exploration, community experience, and recreation. Prevocational job exploration includes opportunities to participate in basic maintenance tasks (e.g., cleaning the school's library), gardening (e.g., working in the school's greenhouse), delivering snacks (e.g., as a volunteer at a local nursing home), and kitchen work (e.g., using an industrial-size kitchen at a local restaurant on Mondays when the restaurant is closed).

Activities of daily living include opportunities to set a table for meals, do laundry, go grocery shopping, and practice hygiene skills in the school's locker room. Community experience opportunities occur when Jessica participates in visits to the local public library and browses at local shop window displays.

When a speech-language pathologist or a special education teacher meets a child like Jessica, he or she might wonder about what to do for speech-language therapy and communication goals. Jessica presents an interesting challenge, not only because

of her significant developmental disability, but also because she is enrolled in a general education curriculum.

Many questions come to mind: Is Jessica a candidate for speech-language therapy? What is her prognosis for communication improvement? What are some realistic communication outcomes for her? What specific skills should the educator target? Gestures? Speech? Augmentative communication? What instructional format should the educator use? Should therapy be direct or indirect? How can specialists and teachers implement goals within both general and special education activities? This article addresses these questions and provides some concrete steps for promoting effective communication.

Students with Severe Mental Retardation

Students with severe to profound mental retardation need an extensive and pervasive array of supports to fully participate in everyday learning situations, community events, adaptive skills, self-determination, and social relationships (American Association on Mental Retardation, 2002). Reports suggest that these students have rich and diverse communication abilities, including contact and distal gestures (i.e., actions that convey interest in something out of direct reach), vocalizations, verbalizations, sign language, aberrant behavior, concrete object use, and picture symbol use. These students communicate for many reasons; for example, to direct someone else's behavior, to repair a misunderstood message, to request desired activities and objects, and to protest disliked events (Mar & Sail, 1999; McLean, Brady, McLean, & Behrens, 1999; Romski, Sevcik, & Adamson, 1999).

Skill Actualization and Functional Communication

To address the questions raised previously, the speech-language pathologist and the special education teacher should consider realistic and functional outcomes. For students with severe mental retardation, educators need to establish functional communication goals that target social and learning interactions within daily school routines (Calculator, 1995; McCarthy et al., 1998). This model relies on communication partners who encourage and respect communication skills, even when the skills are nonverbal and require interpretation (Ferguson, 1994; Payne & Ogletree, 1995).

For people with severe mental retardation, a functional communication model includes modifications to the physical environment and the structure of the curriculum so as to embed communication goals into naturally occurring daily school and life routines (Cascella, 1999; National Joint Committee, 2002). A functional model depends on treatment decisions made by a transdisciplinary team and the development of a cumulative set of objectives to foster skills across multiple settings and partners (Ervin, 2003; Farrell & Pimentel, 1996). This approach is consistent with milieu teaching strategies often employed in early childhood education settings that integrate language skills into naturally occurring class activities (Horn, Lieber, Li, Sandall, & Schwartz, 2000).

A critical aspect of functional communication is that it emphasizes *skill actualization,* where teachers give students the opportunity to use their already developed (i.e., extant) communication skills across multiple everyday situations (McLean & McLean, 1993). Skill actualization goals are represented on the individualized education program (IEP), as statements such as, "The child will use (an already developed communication action) to (their reason for communicating) during (a particular class or social routine)."

Student with severe to profound mental retardation need many supports to participate in learning situations, community events, and social relationships.

This model matches the child's extant skill set to the classroom curriculum and the supports that are needed to enable the child's full participation in the general education classroom. This requires a careful analysis of the child's abilities and the communication expectations of teachers and peers, as well as class activities, materials, and natural opportunities for communication (Rowland & Schweigert, 1993).

For Jessica, these objectives shift from acquisition goals (i.e., developmental skills) to practical outcomes that enable her to actively participate in the school day (see Figure 1).

Steps in Creating Communication Actualization Outcomes

Step 1: Create a Communication Profile

The first step toward developing skill actualization goals for students with severe mental retardation is to create a communication profile. A communication profile is a comprehensive list of the child's communication forms and functions. Communication forms are the methods the child uses to communicate, and communication functions are the identified reasons why the child communicates (see Figures 2 and 3).

The child's communication profile includes not only obvious communication actions (e.g., pointing, head nods) and functions (e.g., requests, protests) but also communication behaviors unique to the child. For example, at a recent meeting, one teacher commented, "Sometimes when Jessica has had enough work, she pushes the work away with her hands, but other times I know when she's had enough because her head tilts like this" (teacher demonstrates the head tilt).

The members of the child's educational team create the communication profile during a team meeting that lasts for about 1 hour. At this meeting, one team member is assigned the role

Receptive Vocabulary

Developmental	Jessica will identify 5 common objects during speech therapy with 80% accuracy.
Functional	Jessica will get 5 objects that are needed to participate in art activities after a request by the teacher.

Articulation

Developmental	Jessica will produce the consonants /f/, /t/, and /s/ with 80% accuracy in word-initial position (e.g., fun, ton, sun).
Functional	Jessica will repeat herself when teacher asks for clarification of misunderstood messages during free play activities outside.

Speech

Developmental	Jessica will imitate consonant-vowel (CV) and vowel-consonant (VC) combinations in 8/10 trials.
Functional	Jessica will vocalize to indicate her presence during morning roll call.

Figure 1 Examples of developmental versus functional IEP communication goals.

Vocalizations and sounds

Real words and phrases

Sign language or modified signs

Leading gestures (e.g., pulling someone)

Pushing objects (toward and away)

Pointing gestures

Reaching gestures

Showing gestures

Eye gaze

Head nod or shake

Body orientation (standing near or away)

Pointing to or exchanging pictures

Holding or pointing to real objects

Facial expressions

Figure 2 Examples of communication forms.

of facilitator while another team member acts as a recorder. The facilitator directs the discussion by asking the team to think about all of the child's possible communication skills, ones that the child deliberately uses, and ones that team members interpret from the child's behavior. The facilitator can assist the team by asking form-specific questions, such as "How does she tell you she is upset?" and "Describe how she conveys interest in an activity."

The facilitator can also guide a discussion with function-specific questions like "What is she trying to tell us when she takes someone's hand to lead them?" and "Why does she vocalize first thing in the morning?" The facilitator can also ask situation-specific questions, such as "What and how does she communicate at lunch?" "During physical therapy?" or "At the end of the day?"

After the meeting, the recorder summarizes the discussion into a succinct chart of the child's communication forms and functions. When the list is completed, team members share it

Name objects, people, activities

Tell people what to do

Secure help

Convey social pleasantries ("Hi," "Bye")

Convey interest in an activity

Protest

Convey emotional or physical state

Ask for objects, people, activities

Make a choice

Request and/or report information

Figure 3 Examples of communication functions.

with all of the people who might interact with the child during the school day. These people include the core members of the child's educational team who developed the profile and many other people—the bus driver, the librarian, the school secretaries, the lunchroom workers, the school janitors, and a select peer group. The team shares the communication profile with all of these people to encourage incidental communicative support across daily routines. Two useful phrases that school staff and peers can use are "It looks like you're telling me _____" and "Am I right that you're telling me _____?"

If the educational team has too many conflicting schedules and cannot meet together, another option is for the speech-language pathologist to take a lead role in creating the communication profile. In this strategy, the speech-language pathologist actively seeks the input of all the vested parties and develops a profile that accurately reflects their input. The speech-language pathologist completes observations of the child across all school events and discusses the child's communication with each of the teachers who routinely have contact with the child. Such tasks may seem like yet another hard-to-manage expansion of the already burdensome role of the school speech-language pathologist. It is consistent, however, with shifting practice patterns away from exclusively providing direct service to engaging in collaborative consultation.

Step 2: Identify the Communication Patterns of Class Routines

The second step toward communication skill actualization is to integrate the child's communication skills into classroom events and curricula activities. To do this, members of the educational team must first know about the typical dialogues, communication expectations, and communication opportunities that occur within every class situation and school activity.

In Jessica's case, her academic and life skill curricula activities are observed, and her teachers are interviewed. The speech-language pathologist and/or the special education teacher note the communication expectations that teachers and peers make in her classes. For example, the math teacher might greet the students at the beginning of class and expect them to reply a particular way. Or, perhaps the science teacher uses cooperative learning groups, and students are expected to engage in group verbal problem-solving activities.

The observer identifies the communication agendas of the people in the room and the expectations made within any classroom situation. The observer also interviews the teachers and a select group of peers to confirm whether the observations were relatively typical to that class or school activity. These interviews require the observer to understand the child from the perspective of each classroom teacher and acknowledge the strategies each teacher might already use to support the child.

Afterward, the observer creates a record of the typical communication events of the child's class activities, a summary of the expected content of those communicative acts, and the natural supports already in place. This record requires at least 1 day of class observations and teacher interviews.

Step 3: Integrate the Communication Profile into School Routines and the Curriculum

The third step to facilitate communication actualization occurs when the educational team has a second hour-long meeting in which they brainstorm and build a communication support plan focused on enabling the child to use communication across daily routines. This integration occurs by specifically matching the child's communication abilities to the communication expectations of each of the classes and activities.

This process results in a communication plan that specifically identifies what the child can do (the communication form), the reason for the action (the communication function), and the specific setting or event in which communication takes place. For example, Jessica's IEP can include statements such as "Jessica will look up (form) to convey she wants to go home (function) during the afternoon dismissal time (setting)."

Step 4: Expand the Communication Profile

Another strategy that supports actualization is to create communication opportunities so that the child can expand and diversify his or her skill base by generalizing an already established skill.

Many people in school—the bus driver, the librarian, the school secretaries, the lunchroom workers, the school janitors, and a select peer group—can become involved in students' functional communication plans.

For example, if Jessica already uses pushing away gestures to protest during free time after lunch, her teachers can encourage her to expand her skills by using other communication forms, such as body orientation, modified signs, and a vocalization. The teacher can say something like "Oh, you're telling me you don't like that. Let's use a sign, too." The premise underlying the examples in Figure 4 is that Jessica is encouraged to expand her existing communicative repertoire, based on the skills she already possesses.

Step 5: Evaluate the Effectiveness of the Communication Support Plan

All members of Jessica's educational team must periodically review the effectiveness of her communication and the progress she is making toward functional communication outcomes. Using a dynamic assessment model, the team should periodically observe and measure the degree to which Jessica maintains her extant communication abilities over time and across different communication settings and partners. The educational team should continuously review their own ability to provide

---

1. Actualization by Communication Form

Jessica's Action	Function	The Setting
Modified sign	To protest	During free time after lunch
Body orientation		
Pushing away gesture		
Vocalization		

2. Actualization by Communication Function

Jessica's Action	Function	The Setting
Vocalization	To protest	Geography group projects
	To request help	
	To gain attention	
	To state a feeling	

3. Actualization Across Communication Setting

Jessica's Action	Function	The Setting
Vocalization	To gain attention	During math roll call
		During lunch group
		Passing a teacher in hallway

Figure 4   Individualized education program (IEP) goal content to support communication actualization.

meaningful opportunities for Jessica to use her communication skills to affect her surroundings.

Two published options are available to educational teams that want to self-evaluate their communication supports for students with severe mental retardation. One protocol is the *Communication Supports Checklist* (McCarthy et al., 1998). This instrument was specifically designed to enable school and human service personnel to evaluate their ability to serve the communication needs of people with severe disabilities. This 97-item checklist encourages self-evaluation of program supports for communication, assessment practices, goal setting practices, program implementation, and team competencies.

A second protocol. *Analyzing the Communication Environment (ACE),* contains 52 items to assess opportunities for communication, adult interaction, specific activities, group dynamics, the materials being used, and the child's communication system (Rowland & Schweigert, 1993).

The educational team should *continuously* provide meaningful opportunities for Jessica to use her communication skills.

Final Thoughts

Although children who have severe mental retardation may present unusual challenges to school personnel, the use of a communication profile integrated into daily class events helps to establish functional communication goals and realistic outcomes. A communication profile carefully documents the child's existing communication forms and functions, and it allows the educational team to create opportunities that encourage the use of existing as well as new skills across daily school routines and the child's curriculum.

References

American Association on Mental Retardation (AAMR). (2002). *Mental retardation: Definition, classification, and systems of supports* (10th ed.). Annapolis Junction, MD: AAMR Publications.

Calculator, S. N. (1995). Communication sciences. In O. C. Karan & S. Greenspan (Eds.), *Community rehabilitation services for people with disabilities,* (pp. 277–293). Stoneham, MA: Butterworth-Heineman.

Cascella, P. W. (1999). Communication disorders and children with mental retardation. *Child and Adolescent Psychiatric Clinics of North America, 8*(1), 61–75.

Ervin, M. (2003). Autism spectrum disorders: Interdisciplinary teaming in schools. *The ASHA Leader, 8*(7), 4–5, 14.

Farrell, S. E., & Pimentel, A. E. (1996). Interdisciplinary team process in developmental disabilities. In A. J. Capute & P. J. Accardo (Eds.), *Developmental disabilities in infancy and childhood: Vol. 2. The spectrum of developmental disabilities* (2nd ed., pp. 431–441). Baltimore: Paul H. Brookes.

Ferguson, D. L. (1994). Is communication really the point? Some thoughts on interventions and membership. *Mental Retardation, 32*(1), 7–18.

Horn, E., Lieber, J., Li, S., Sandall, S., & Schwartz, I. (2000). Supporting young children's IEP Goals in inclusive settings through embedded learning opportunities. *Topics in Early Childhood Special Education, 20*(4), 208–224.

Mar, H. H., & Sali, N. (1999). Profiles of the expressive communication skills of children and adolescents with severe cognitive disabilities. *Education and Training in Mental Retardation and Developmental Disabilities, 54*(1), 77–89.

McCarthy, C. F., McLean, L. K., Miller., J. F., Paul-Brown, D., Romski, M. A., Rourk, J. D., et al. (1998). *Communication supports checklist.* Baltimore: Paul H. Brookes.

McLean, L. K., Brady, N.C., McLean, J. E., & Behrens, G. A. (1999). Communication forms and functions of children and adults with severe mental retardation in community and institutional settings. *Journal of Speech, Language, and Hearing Research, 42,* 231–240.

McLean, L. K., & McLean. J. E. (1993). Communication intervention for adults with severe mental retardation. *Topics in Language Disorders, 13*(3), 47–60.

National Joint Committee on Persons with Severe Disabilities. (2002). Adults with learning disabilities: Concerns about the application of restrictive "eligibility policies." *Communication Disorders Quarterly, 23*(3), 145–153.

Payne, H. W., & Ogletree, B. T. (1995). Training team members to respond to the communicative behaviors of children with profound handicaps. *Focus on Autistic Behavior 10*(5), 1–15.

Romski, M. A., Sevcik, R. A., & Adamson, L. B. (1999). Communication patterns of youth with mental retardation with and without their speech-output communication devices. *American Journal on Mental Retardation, 104*(3), 249–259.

Rowland, C., & Schweigert, P. (1993). *Analyzing the communication environment.* Tucson, AZ: Communication Skill Builders.

PAUL W. CASCELLA (CEC Chapter #58), Associate Professor, and **KEVIN M. MCNAMARA,** Clinic Director, Department of Communication Disorders, Southern Connecticut State University, New Haven. Address correspondence to Paul W. Cascella, Department of Communication Disorders, Southern Connecticut State University, 501 Crescent Street, New Haven CT 06515 (e-mail: cascellapl@southemct.edu)

From *Teaching Exceptional Children,* by Paul W. Cascella and Kevin M. McNamara, Vol. 37, No. 3, January/February 2005, pp. 38–43. Copyright © 2005 by Council for Exceptional Children. Reprinted by permission.

UNIT 9

Orthopedic and Health Impairments

Unit Selections

Key Points to Consider

- What hope have biotechnology and the mapping of the human genome given to parents of children with orthopedic and/or health impairments?

- What kinds of accommodations are appropriate for students with health impairments (e.g., cancer, asthma, epilepsy)?

- How do students with ADHD differ from their non-ADHD special-education peers? Do they receive necessary and appropriate services?

Student Web Site

www.mhcls.com/online

Internet References

Further information regarding these Web sites may be found in this book's preface or online.

Association to Benefit Children (ABC)
  http://www.a-b-c.org
An Idea Whose Time Has Come
  http://www.boggscenter.org/mich3899.htm
Resources for VE Teachers
  http://www.cpt.fsu.edu/tree//ve/tofc.html

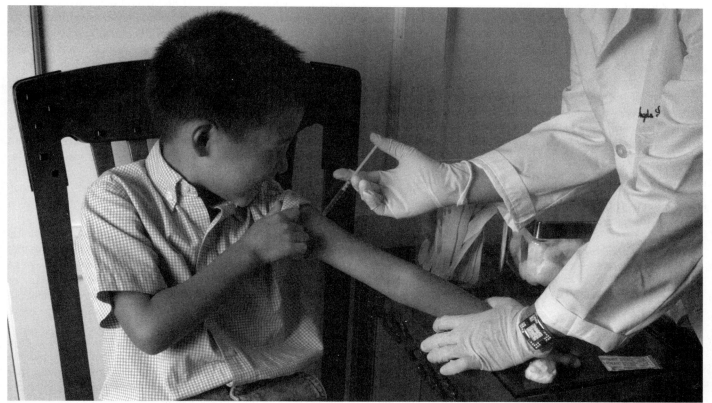

Two civil rights laws, the Americans with Disabilities Act (ADA) and section 504 of the Rehabilitation Act, prohibit discrimination against students with disabilities. They also mandate reasonable accommodations for them in education. Together with the Individuals with Disabilities Education Improvement Act (IDEIA) and the No Child Left Behind Act (NCLB), the United States has clearly articulated its desire that students with orthopedic and health impairments be given equal access to free and appropriate public education.

Children and youth with orthopedic and health impairments can be divided into classifications of mild, moderate, and profound. Within most impairments, the same diagnosis may not produce the same degree of disability. For example, children with cerebral palsy may be mildly, moderately, or profoundly impaired.

Orthopedic impairments are usually defined as those that hinder physical mobility or the ability to use one or more parts of the skeletomuscular system of the body. Orthopedic problems may be neurological (brain or spinal cord) or skeletomuscular (muscles or skeletal bones). Regardless of etiology, the child with an orthopedic impairment usually has a problem with mobility. He or she may need crutches or other aids in order to walk or may be in a wheelchair.

Health impairments are usually defined as those that affect stamina and predominantly one or more systems of the body: the cardiovascular, respiratory, gastrointestinal, endocrine, lymphatic, urinary, reproductive, sensory, or nervous systems. Children with health impairments usually have to take medicine or follow a medical regimen in order to attend school. The degree of impairment (mild, moderate, profound) is usually based on limitations to activity, duration of problem, and extent of other problems.

Attention-deficit hyperactive disorder (ADHD) is formally recognized as a health impairment. Often children with ADHD are also assessed as gifted or as emotionally-behaviorally disordered. It is possible for a child with ADHD to have characteristics of all of these categories.

Orthopedic and health impairments are not always mutually exclusive. Many times a child with an orthopedic impairment also has a concurrent or contributing health impairment, and vice versa. In addition, children with orthopedic and health impairments may also have concurrent conditions of educational exceptionality.

Some children with orthopedic and health impairments have only transitory impairments; some have permanent but non-worsening impairments; and some have progressive impairments that make their education more complicated as the years pass and may even result in death before the end of the developmental/educational period.

Each of the dimensions defined in the preceding paragraphs makes educational planning for children with orthopedic and health impairments very complicated.

The reauthorization of IDEIA mandated that schools must pay for all medical services required to allow orthopedically or health-impaired students to attend regular education classes. The only exceptions are the actual fees for physician-provided health services. Thus, if children need ambulances to transport them to and from school, the schools must pay the tab. Federal appropriations for special educational services only pay about 10 percent of the bills. Thus high-cost special needs students can quickly drain the funds of state and local education departments.

Teachers may resent the need to spend teacher time giving medications or providing quasi-medical services (suctioning, changing dressings, or diapers) for students with health impairments in the many U.S. schools that no longer have school nurses.

Resentment is common in parents of nondisabled students who feel that the education of high-cost disabled students robs their children of teacher time, curriculum, and supplies to which they should be entitled. More than 95 percent of special needs students attend regular schools today. About three percent attend separate schools and about two percent are served at home, in hospitals, or in residential facilities.

When orthopedic or health impairments are diagnosed in infancy or early childhood, an interdisciplinary team usually helps plan an individualized family service plan (IFSP) that includes working with parents, medical and/or surgical personnel, and preschool special-education providers.

When the orthopedic or health impairment is diagnosed in the school years, the school teachers collaborate with outside agencies, but more of the individualized educational planning (IEP) is in their hands. Children who have orthopedic or health impairments usually need psychological as well as academic support. Teachers need to help them in their peer interactions. Teachers should also work closely with parents to ensure a smooth transition toward a lifestyle that fosters independence and self-reliance. By middle school, individualized transition plans (ITPs) should be developed. They should be implemented throughout high school and until age 21 when the students move to adult living, and they must be updated every year. Schools are held accountable for their success in helping students with orthopedic and health impairments to make smooth transitions to maturity, independent living, and self-sufficiency.

The first article, "Savior Parents" emphasizes the importance of parental advocacy to insure that children with orthopedic and health impairments get the most up-to-date diagnoses and therapeutic assistance. New technologies are making remediation and/or cures possible that in the past were unthinkable. Educators must stay current of the ongoing progress and join parents in the role of "saviors" to students with such impairments.

The second selection for this unit suggests some of the accommodations that school systems must make to ensure that students with orthopedic and health impairments receive an appropriate education. It explains the 504 plans required under the Americans with Disabilities Act. MaryAnn Byrnes points out that the teaching profession is about allowing students to learn. Removing barriers will do that.

The third featured article in this unit addresses ADHD as a health impairment. A recent survey shows that many students with ADHD are also labeled as emotional behavior disorder (EBD) or other categories of disability. There are many problems associated with the diagnosis of ADHD. Important new research findings about ADHD are not well disseminated to the lay public or to educators. Better understanding about ADHD will result in better intervention strategies to improve their ability to achieve in regular education classes.

Savior Parents

Rescuing an ailing child can become a crusade and a career

ELIZABETH WEILL

Jannine and John Cody were packing to move from Sheppard Air Force Base in Wichita Falls, Texas, to Brooks Air Force Base in San Antonio in 1985 when a military doctor gave them some devastating news. Their 6-week-old daughter Elizabeth was missing part of her 18th chromosome. To explain what that meant, the doctor showed Jannine a textbook with a horrifying picture and caption that she still keeps in her files. It read, "They are probably the most seriously afflicted among carriers of chromosome abnormalities. They maintain the froglike position observed in infants and are reduced to an entirely bedridden and vegetative life." The young mother was incredulous. "That just didn't jibe with what I was seeing," Cody vividly recalls. "It had been raining for a week, everything was wet, the packers were angry. I had a 3-year-old, a 6-week-old and a mother-in-law to deal with. I was on total overload, so I said to myself, O.K., this doesn't quite fit; she doesn't seem like a vegetable. I'll deal with that later."

Elizabeth's first year included three surgeries to fix a cleft palate and a cleft lip. By age 2, she had slipped far behind on the growth charts. Her pediatrician seemed to think that was inevitable, but her mother demanded that Elizabeth's symptoms be treated, a radical notion at the time. She took her daughter to an endocrinologist, who put Elizabeth on daily injections of human growth hormone, a therapy that caused her to grow like a weed and blossom developmentally as well. When Elizabeth had difficulty learning to speak, Cody pushed for her to see a neurologist, who determined that the problem had more to do with the impairment of her hearing than with her intelligence. The 3-year-old was fitted with a hearing aid and began learning sign language.

The journey to save Elizabeth took both mother and daughter to unexpected places. Cody went back to college and earned a Ph.D. in human genetics at age 42. Her dissertation topic: syndromes of the 18th chromosome. Today this former homemaker and president of her local embroiderers' guild conducts genetic research at the University of Texas Health Science Center. Her work has helped raise Elizabeth's IQ into the normal range and has provided a model for helping the approximately 500 other kids in the U.S. with the same defect. Cody also set up the Chromosome 18 Registry and Research Society—a foundation that connects affected families with one another and funds research.

This month Cody will reap a huge personal reward for her efforts: Elizabeth will graduate from high school. A few years ago, Cody sat watching Elizabeth's pep squad perform at a football game, wearing red, white and blue, the school colors. "Suddenly I'm watching, and I realize I can't pick her out of the crowd. She wasn't so bad!" says Cody. "I just burst into tears. I never ever thought I would see the day when she'd just be one of the girls in high school, out there on the field with all the other kids. It was amazing."

Being a parent brings out the most extreme traits in all of us—capacities for love, fear, persistence you never knew you had—and those traits are only magnified when a kid is in danger. You stay up all night when your daughter spikes a 101° fever. You drive across town in five minutes flat when your son falls out of a tree. But parenting a child who has a serious genetic disease transcends that entirely, as movies like *Lorenzo's Oil* have shown. It turns Clark Kents into Supermen and former science-phobes into experts in molecular biology. "For a long time in the pediatric community, [the attitude was] if you have a major chromosomal abnormality, you're going to not grow well, you're going to be developmentally delayed, you're going to be mentally retarded, and there's not a darn thing we can do about it," says Dr. Daniel Hale, a pediatric endocrinologist who works closely with Cody. These days the situation is different. At the molecular level, genetic diseases are better understood, and new avenues are opening for dealing with them, thanks in part to the advocacy of parents like Cody who embrace the notion that kids with chromosomal abnormalities have a right to reach their fullest potential.

"I'm a person, NOT A DISEASE!" insists Sam Berns, age 7

Particular Clark Kents, of course, turn into particular superheroes because of varying talents and inclinations. Leslie Gordon and Scott Berns, for example, were both multidegree doctors—she has an M.D. and a Ph.D., he has an M.D. and a master's in public health—when a doctor friend diagnosed progeria in their 21-month-old son Sam, now 7 (the rare disease causes accelerated aging and often leads to death by early adolescence). The next day, Gordon took a leave from her training in pediatric ophthalmology. Within nine months, she created the Progeria Research Foundation to bring attention to and research funds for the disease, which affects just 1 in 4 million babies. "There was nothing out there. Zero," says Gordon from her home in Foxboro, Mass., her voice brimming with fierce enthusiasm. "I was surprised because as a doctor, you train, you train, you train, and when you get out there you realize there are holes."

Gordon and Berns are committed to the idea that Sam, who inhabits the body of a 70-year-old, should just be a kid. Currently he's obsessed with baseball, school and drums, and when a new friend informs him he has no hair, he says, "Tell me something I don't know. Let's go play." Gordon, in just over five years, has started a tissue bank, raised serious money and lured top scientists into studying her son's disease. In October 2002, she, along with an international team, succeeded in isolating the progeria gene. Progeria, it turns out, is caused by a tiny point mutation in a child's DNA, a one-letter typo in the chromosomal book. But even after that research triumph—the culmination of an 11-month, white-hot burn of constant phone and e-mail conversations—Gordon did not take a break. Sam, she reasons, has no time to waste. A stroke could hit at any time, and the same is true for the more than 50 other kids with progeria whom Gordon has come to know and love. "Somebody called me a barracuda once, and I said thank you," Gordon says. "You can't hand a child a paper saying we found the gene, and here, you're cured. Isolating the gene was the end of Chapter One. We now have a gene that leads to a protein defect that researchers can sink their teeth into. Fantastic labs can ask fantastic questions. We can pull in a lot more terrific researchers, ask better questions and start moving toward treatment."

Taking on the responsibility of finding a cure for your child's rare genetic disease can be both comforting and painful, like all parental obligations, except in this case the stakes aren't seeing a child's soccer game vs. working out, but seeing your child's future birthdays vs. (perhaps) not blaming yourself if you don't.

"You don't want to ever have to tell your kids someday that you didn't try your best," says Brad Margus, a Harvard M.B.A. and the former owner of a Florida shrimp-processing company who switched careers after discovering that two of his four boys had a rare, degenerative disease. "Being a dad, you're expected by your kids to be able to fix anything, right? So they're counting on you to do something about it," says Margus, who is now CEO of Perlegen Sciences, a Silicon Valley biotech firm.

Margus' nightmare started when he and his wife Vicki still had three boys in diapers, and his second eldest, Jarrett, then 18 months, developed difficulty walking and his speech slurred. At first doctors thought the cause was mild cerebral palsy. Then around his 18-month mark, Margus' next eldest boy, Quinn, started developing the same symptoms as Jarrett's, which suggested that the problem was genetic. The boys endured blood tests, spinal taps, muscle biopsies. After spending $60,000 and

turning up nothing, the Marguses took their sons to see Dr. Jean Aicardi, a world-famous French neurologist who happened to be visiting Miami Children's Hospital. "In the first five minutes, he saw our kids and said, 'It looks an awful lot like ataxia-telangiectasia,' which we couldn't even pronounce. 'I assume you've tested for this?' All it takes is a $20 blood test. The local doctors just looked at their feet." The Marguses recognized the name (it's pronounced ay-*tack*-see-uh teh-*lan*-jick-*tay*-sha), but all they knew was that A-T was really bad. At home that night they read that about 40% of kids with A-T get cancer by age 12; 100% deteriorate neurologically, so they're in wheelchairs as early as age 8; most die of lung problems or cancer by their late teens or early 20s. "You kind of go through a grief process," Margus says. "Your kids aren't dead, but the kids you thought you had are gone."

"You don't want to ever have to tell your kids that YOU DIDN'T try your best."

Like progeria, A-T is what might be called a superorphaned disease. It affects so few kids—just 400 in the U.S.—that scientists and drug companies don't bother with it. So Margus began applying his business brain to the problem of how to find a cure. He broke it down into smaller problems, assembling a list of things he needed to learn about: molecular biology, how the government funds research, how you capture the interest of top-notch scientists, what lobbying is all about. He decided his approach would be to pollinate as many excellent labs as possible, funding postdocs to work under superstars and hoping that whenever researchers discovered something relevant, they might at least ask themselves, Could this help Brad's kids? "Early on, you're naive enough that you don't know how challenging the problem really is, so you give it a shot." The result? Margus has raised more than $15 million to date, and he funded the research that isolated the A-T-mutated gene nine years ago.

Still, Margus sounds distinctly sad. Sure, he has raised a lot of money and even made a savvy career switch that puts him in regular contact with executives from five of the top 10 pharmaceutical companies. Yet, in his mind, "so far we haven't done squat." His kids, now 13 and 15, are deteriorating daily. This summer he hopes to move his family from Florida to California, where he spends most of his time, but first he will need to retrofit a house "for two teenagers in power wheelchairs who can't control their motor skills very well, so they take out huge chunks of drywall." When his boys ask their father about his work, Margus is honest. "Quinn is quite tough on me," Margus says. "He asks what those researchers are doing. And candidly, I have to say that we've failed. We've set up a center at Johns Hopkins, so at least there's one place in the world that's accumulating a lot of data on the kids. But as far as a treatment or cure or even slowing the progression of the disease, we still haven't done it."

The struggles of parents like Brad Margus and Leslie Gordon are less lonely than they were in the pre-Internet era. Numerous websites help such parents reach out and learn from one another; among them are sites created by the Genetic and Rare Diseases Information Center at the National Institutes of Health and the Genetic Alliance, an advocacy group. This June in San Antonio, Jannine Cody is convening the first World Congress on Chromosome Abnormalities. More than 1,000 parents, doctors and researchers are expected to attend. Sessions will range from "Neurological and Anatomical Imaging" to "Potty/Sleep Solutions." The event is the culmination of 15 years of work, with twin goals of building stronger advocacy groups for children with chromosomal abnormalities and establishing a nucleus of scientists dedicated to addressing their problems. "Somebody ought to give that lady a MacArthur," says Dr. Hale.

On a recent afternoon, Elizabeth Cody comes bounding down the stairs to greet her mother, who has just returned from work. There is nothing froglike or vegetative about the bright-eyed 19-year-old, who flops onto the sofa and expresses relief that her mother has remembered to bring home a chart showing exactly which part of her 18th chromosome is missing. "A boy at my school used to make fun of me, so I wanted to show him this," Elizabeth explains. After graduation in May, Elizabeth plans to attend a local community college, and then become a teacher's assistant in a hearing-impaired classroom and perhaps move out to California. One thing she can count on: her mother will be cheering all the way.

Accommodations for Students with Disabilities
Removing Barriers to Learning

Secondary school principals frequently encounter questions about educating students with disabilities. Sometimes the questions revolve around seeking a deeper understanding of the disability and the best way to meet student needs. Other times, the questions focus on all the changes that must be made to ensure students receive an appropriate education. What questions do teachers ask about accommodations for students with a disability?

MaryAnn Byrnes

Think about taking a driver's test without wearing glasses (if you do, that is). Not fair, you say; you need the glasses to see. You have just identified an accommodation that you need. Wearing glasses does not make a bad driver better or make driving easier; rather, wearing glasses makes driving possible. Glasses are so much a part of our lives that we do not even consider that they remove a barrier caused by a disability.

Secondary school teachers encounter students every day on an Individualized Education Plan (IEP) or 504 Plan, both of which address programs for students with disabilities. Most likely, the person charged with monitoring this plan has indicated that particular students need changes in teaching style, assignments, or testing strategies.

It is usually easy to understand the need for glasses or wheelchairs or hearing aids. These sound like changes the student must make. Other adjustments, modifications, or accommodations on these plans, such as extended time, may not be as clear.

What Is an Accommodation?

An accommodation is an adjustment, to an activity or setting, that removes a barrier presented by a disability so a person can have access equal to that of a person without a disability. An accommodation does not guarantee success or a specific level of performance. It should, however, provide the opportunity for a person with a disability to participate in a situation or activity.

Think of that pair of glasses, or the time you broke your leg and could not drive. Think of how your life was affected by these conditions. Your competence did not change. Your ability

to think and work did not change. Your ability to interact with (have access to) the reading material may be very limited without your glasses. Your ability to get to (have access to) work or the grocery store may be very limited without someone to transport you. The support provided by the glasses—or the driver—made it possible for you to use your abilities without the barrier presented by less than perfect vision or limited mobility.

An accommodation is an adjustment, to an activity or setting, that removes a barrier presented by a disability so a person can have access equal to that of a person without a disability.

The accommodations in IEPs or 504 Plans serve the same purpose. They identify ways to remove the barrier presented by a person's disability.

Why Do We Need to Provide Accommodations?

Accommodations are required under Section 504 of the Federal Rehabilitation Act of 1974 as well as the Americans with Disabilities Act. Both these federal laws prohibit discrimination against individuals who have a disability. Situations that limit access have been determined to be discriminatory.

Accommodations must be provided not just by teachers to students, but by employees for workers and governments for citizens. Curbs have been cut to provide access. Doors have been widened and door handles altered to provide access to people for whom the old designs posed a barrier. Employers provide computer adaptations or other adjustments in work schedules and circumstances.

For employers and schools, individuals with disabilities may have a document called a 504 Plan, which details the types of accommodations that are required. Students who have a 504 Plan will not require special education services, just changes to the environment or instructional situation.

Students who have a disability and require special education services in addition to accommodations will have this information contained in an IEP, which also details the types of direct services that need to be provided and the goals of these services. Accommodations will be listed within this IEP.

With the recent changes in IDEA '97, the federal law governing special education, you will be addressing accommodations that must be made so a student with a disability can participate in large-scale districtwide or statewide assessment systems as well as classwork and school life.

Who Needs Accommodations?

According to Section 504, an individual with a disability is any person who has "a physical or mental impairment that limits one or more major life activities." IDEA '97, the federal special education law, lists the following disabilities: autism, deaf-blindness, deafness, hearing impairment, mental retardation, multiple disabilities, orthopedic impairment, other health impairment, serious emotional disturbance, specific learning disability, speech or language impairment, traumatic brain injury, and visual impairment.

Students who have a 504 Plan will not require special education services, just changes to the environment or instructional situation.

Some conditions are covered by Section 504, but not special education. These can include attention deficit disorder—ADD, (also attention deficit hyperactivity disorder—ADHD); chronic medical conditions (such as cancer, Tourette Syndrome, asthma, or epilepsy); communicable diseases; some temporary medical conditions; physical impairments; and disorders of emotion or behavior. To qualify, there must be a demonstrated and substantial limitation of a major life activity.

Students (or adults) who have disabilities may require accommodations to have equal access to education. Not every student with a disability will require accommodations, and not every student with a disability requires the same accommodation all the time.

Think of Jim, a student who has limited mobility in his hands, affecting his ability to write. This disability will present a barrier in a class that requires the student to take notes quickly or write long essays in class. In a class that does not require either of these activities, no barrier may be present. Equal access is possible without accommodation. The student can learn and demonstrate what he knows and can do unaffected by his disability.

What Kind of Accommodations Are There?

Just as there is no limit to the range of disabilities, there is no limit to the range of accommodations. The point is to understand disability and determine if it presents a barrier to equal access. If so, decide whether an accommodation can be identified to remove the barrier—and make sure the accommodation is implemented.

Not every student with a disability will require accommodations, and not every student with a disability requires the same accommodation all the time.

Think of the student described above. The limited mobility in Jim's hands presents a barrier in a class that requires rapid note taking or the writing of long essays in class. There are several accommodations that can result in equal access. Jim might tape the lesson and take notes later. These notes could be written or dictated into a computer. Essays could be composed verbally at a computer workstation or dictated into a tape recorder or to a scribe. A computer might be adapted so typing becomes an effective way to record information on paper. In yet another type of accommodation, essays could be replaced by oral reports.

Are There Some Accommodations That Should Not Be Used?

Like many difficult questions, the answer depends on the context. An accommodation should not alter the essential purpose of the assignment. If the skill you want to measure is the ability to make multiple rapid hand movements, then there is probably no accommodation that is appropriate. Jim will not do well because of his disability. Alternately, if the purpose of a task is to see if someone has perfect vision without glasses, using those glasses is not an appropriate accommodation. If the purpose is to see if you can read, the glasses become a reasonable accommodation.

Who Decides about Accommodations?

The team that writes IEPs and 504 Plans reviews the disability and determines what accommodations, if any, are necessary. These are then written into the EIP or 504 Plan.

Once more, return to Jim. As you consider the requirements of your class, think of the most appropriate way to remove the barrier that is presented by the limited mobility Jim has in his hands.

If We Use Accommodations, How Will the Student Ever Be Prepared for Independent Life in College or the World of Work?

Some people are concerned that the supports provided in school will result in the student being unable to work productively when he or she leaves school. As a matter of fact, Section 504 applies to colleges and employers as well. Colleges offer support centers and provide accommodations upon documentation that a disability exists. Employers are required to provide reasonable accommodations to any person who is otherwise qualified to fulfill the elements of the job.

If companies remove barriers at the workplace, educators should be willing and able to take barriers out of the school activities that prepare a student for the workplace. Teachers can help a student identify the type of accommodation that will be the least cumbersome for everyone, and those that will permit the student to be most independent.

Don't Accommodations Just Make School Easier?

That depends on how you view the world. Does wearing glasses make driving easier? Not really—for a person with limited vision, wearing glasses makes driving *possible*. With or without glasses, you need to be able to drive to pass the test. The same is true of an academic accommodation; whether or not the accommodation is provided, the students still must demonstrate that they know required material.

An accommodation should not alter the essential purpose of the assignment.

Think about the important elements of your class: Is it more important that Jim take notes in class or understand the material? Is it more important that Jim demonstrate good handwriting or the ability to communicate thoughts in print? Often, when you identify the main purpose of your assignments and consider the skills and abilities of a student, you will see that an accommodation lets you determine more clearly what a student knows, understands, and can do.

Does a Student Need to Follow the IEP Accommodations in All Classes?

The IEP or 504 Plan needs to address any area in which the student's disability affects life in school. Sometimes this means in all classes, but not always. For example, a student who was blind would need to use Braille in all classes dealing with written material. Jim, our student with limited mobility in his hands, might not require accommodations in world languages or physical education.

Can We Make Accommodations Without Having Students on an IEP?

Many accommodations are just different ways of teaching or testing. You should be able to have this freedom in your classes. In some cases, the way in which a class is taught makes accommodations unnecessary. Accommodations change the situation, not the content of the instruction. However, accommodations on standardized tests must be connected to IEP's or 504 Plans.

May Teachers Give Different Assignments on the Same Content as a Way to Meet the Needs of Different Learning Styles without Lowering Standards?

Absolutely. The point is to remove the barrier of the disability; this is one way to accomplish that. Some teachers find they tap student knowledge best in active projects; others find that written work is best. Many secondary schools are using portfolios or performance activities to document student learning.

These assessment activities can be very compelling and they do tap different methods of expression. A student like Jim, for example, might communicate depth of understanding and analysis to a social studies debate with a disability in the area of speech or language might find barriers in the performance activities that do not exist on a paper-and-pencil task.

. . . educators should be willing and able to take barriers out of the school activities that prepare a student for the workplace.

What If Accommodations Are Not Implemented?

Since accommodations allow equal access, refusing to provide them can be viewed as discrimination. Individuals who knowingly refuse to implement accommodations make themselves personally liable for legal suit.

This sounds serious, and it is serious. Once the accommodations are found to be necessary, everyone must implement them in situations where the student's disability poses a barrier that prevents equal access.

If no barrier exists in your class, the accommodation is not necessary. No one has the option, however, of deciding not to implement a necessary accommodation. Telling students they could not wear glasses or use a hearing aid is unthinkable. Just as inappropriate is a decision not to allow Jim to use accommodations to remove the barrier posed by his disability, even though it means making some changes to your own work.

Questions about Specific Accommodations

Now that the issues underlying accommodations have been addressed, it is time to talk about frequently-encountered accommodations that raise questions and concern. All these questions have come from secondary school faculty members in a variety of school systems.

Why Is It Fair to Read Material Aloud to Some Students?

Some students have a learning disability that makes it difficult for them to decode print. They can understand the concepts; they can comprehend the material when they hear it; they can reason through the material. They just can't turn print into meaning. If the task is to determine if the student can read, you already know they will have difficulty. If the task is to determine if the student has content knowledge, reading material aloud removes the barrier of the learning disability. Reading material aloud to a student who does not understand the material will not result in a higher grade.

Why Is It Fair to Give Some Students Extra Time on Tests?

Some students have motor difficulties that make writing an enormous challenge. They may not be able to form the letters correctly. They may not be able to monitor their thoughts while they work on the physical act of writing. They understand the material, and they know what they want to respond; it just takes longer to write the answer. If the task is to determine how quickly the student can respond, you already know they will have difficulty. If the task is to determine if the student has the knowledge, providing extra time removes the barrier of the

motor disability. Providing extra time to a student who does not understand the material will not result in a higher grade.

Why Is It Fair to Permit Some Students to Respond Orally to Tests?

Think about the example above. For some students, responding orally would be a comparable accommodation. In this case, allowing an oral response will not result in a higher grade if the student does not know the material.

A student with a disability in the area of speech or language might find barriers in the performance activities that do not exist on a paper-and-pencil task.

The Bottom Line

It all comes down to deciding what is important. Think about your assignment and expectations. Think about the disability. If the disability provides a barrier, the accommodation removes it. The accommodation does not release a student from participating or demonstrating knowledge—it allows the student to be able to participate and demonstrate knowledge. And isn't that what school is all about?

References

Americans with Disabilities Act of 1990, P.L. 101–336, 2, 104 Stat. 328.1991.

Individuals with Disabilities Education Act Amendments of 1997, P.L. 105–17, 20 U.S. Code Sections 1401–1486.

Livovich, Michael P. *Section 504 of the Rehabilitation Act of 1973 and the Americans with Disabilities Act. Providing access to a free appropriate public education: a public school manual.* Indianapolis, Ind.: 1996.

Vocational Rehabilitation Act of 1973, 29 U.S.C. 794.

MARYANN BYRNES (byrnes@mediaone.net) is assistant professor at the Graduate College of Education, University of Massachusetts-Boston.

ADHD Among Students Receiving Special Education Services

A National Survey

Relatively little is known about attention deficit/hyperactivity disorder (ADHD) among students receiving special education in terms of their demographic characteristics, instructional settings, and programming, nor about how these factors differ from students with disabilities who do not have ADHD. Data from the Special Education Elementary Longitudinal Study (SEELS), a nationally representative study of students receiving special education, show that students with ADHD now constitute the majority of students in the categories of emotional disturbance and other health impairment. Hispanic students were underrepresented. Students with ADHD were more likely to receive accommodations and services than their non-ADHD special education peers.

CONNIE SCHNOES, ROBERT REID, MARY WAGNER, AND CAMILLE MARDER

Attention deficit/hyperactivity disorder (ADHD) is a chronic condition that is thought to affect from 3% to 5% of school-age children in the United States (American Psychiatric Association, 2000). Now one of the most commonly diagnosed childhood disorders (Barkley, 1998), ADHD is estimated to affect approximately 2 million school-age children (Forness & Kavale, 2002). These children experience difficulties in behaviors crucial to academic success, such as maintaining attention, modulating activity levels, inhibiting impulsive responses, and persisting with academic tasks (DuPaul & Stoner, 2003). Because of their large numbers and refractory behaviors, children with ADHD present a challenge for the school system.

Many children with ADHD qualify for accommodations and/or services under Section 504 of the Vocational Rehabilitation Act or the Individuals With Disabilities Education Act (IDEA; Reid & Katsiyannis, 1995). Estimates are that more than half of children with an ADHD diagnosis are school-identified as eligible for services under IDEA (Barkley, 1998; Reid, Maag, Vasa, & Wright, 1994). Most of these children are served under the categories of learning disability (LD), emotional disturbance (ED), or other health impairment (OHI). Some students with ADHD and a co-occurring cognitive impairment are served under the mental retardation (MR) category (Abikoff, 2002), and those with expressive and/or receptive language limitations are served in the speech-language impairment (SLI) category.

Although ADHD has been the subject of a tremendous amount of research attention (Reid, Maag, & Vasa, 1994), relatively little research has been conducted on ADHD among students receiving special education in the schools. Forness and Kavale (2002) have identified four major questions of interest regarding these students: (1) What is the prevalence of ADHD among students served in special education? (2) Under what categories are students with ADHD served by special education? (3) In what settings are these students served? (4) What services are they provided? The following sections summarize the current literature on these questions as background for presenting new findings related to each of them.

Prevalence of ADHD and Special Education Eligibility

Many studies have focused on the extent to which children with ADHD theoretically would meet diagnostic criteria for an IDEA disability category; however, this focus does not address the question of the number of children with ADHD who actually *are served* under IDEA. Further, data on the extent to which children with ADHD are served in various disability categories are sparse (Forness & Kavale, 2002). Gaining a clear picture of the prevalence and category distribution of students with ADHD receiving special education is further complicated by the fact that the diagnostic criteria for ADHD have changed three times since 1980, resulting in the use of slightly different definitions of ADHD over time.

Other Health Impairment

OHI is the main special education category under which students with ADHD who have no coexisting disabilities may be served. In 1991, the category was opened to children with ADHD based on the "limited alertness" language in the definition (Davila, Williams, & MacDonald, 1991). The intent was to provide a means for serving children with ADHD who would not otherwise qualify for special education services.

Because of their large numbers and refractory behaviors, children with ADHD present a challenge for the school system.

Few data have been available on the prevalence of children with ADHD in the OHI category because states do not report the specific disabilities of children in it. Forness and Kavale (2002) noted that the increase in children identified under the OHI category exceeds that for other categories of disability; they estimated that children with ADHD accounted for 68% of new students identified in the OHI category in the 4 years before their study.

Learning Disability

Estimates of the prevalence of ADHD among children with LD range from 10% to 92% (Du-Paul & Stoner, 2003). When appropriate diagnostic criteria are applied, estimates range from 10% to 25% (Barkley, 1998). Studies that have examined the extent of ADHD among students with LD are consistent with Barkley's estimates, ranging from a low of 16.2% (Bussing, Zima, Belin, & Forness, 1998) to a high of 31.1% (Lopez, Forness, MacMillan, Bocian, & Gresham, 1996), with other studies around 25% (McConaughy, Mattison, & Peterson, 1994). Reid, Maag, Vasa, and Wright (1994) examined the disability categories of students with ADHD, rather than the prevalence of ADHD among students in each category, and found that approximately 28% of them were served under the LD category.

Emotional Disturbance

ADHD appears to be slightly more prevalent among students with ED than among those with LD. Estimates range from 25% (Duncan, Forness, & Hartsough, 1995) to 44% (Mattison, Lynch, Kales, & Gamble, 1993; Mattison, Morales, & Bauer, 1993; McConaughy et al., 1994). Children with ADHD have a high likelihood of receiving special education services under the ED category because of the high rate of co-occurring psychiatric disorders. For example, research suggests that from 43% to 93% of children with ADHD exhibit conduct or oppositional defiant disorders, and estimates of the rate of anxiety or mood disorders range from 13% to 51% (Bird, Gould, & Steghezza-Jamarillo, 1994; Jensen, Martin, & Cantwell, 1997). Reid, Maag, Vasa, and Wright (1994) estimated that 51.9% of students with ADHD were served under the ED category.

Mental Retardation

Standardized IQ measures of children with ADHD are likely to be 7 to 15 points lower than their peers (Barkley, 1998). However, it is not clear whether these differences reflect teal deficits in intellectual functioning or whether they are due to the inattentive and impulsive nature of children with ADHD. Because researchers routinely exclude students with low intelligence scores from studies of ADHD, little is known about ADHD among children with MR. One estimate (Reid, Maag, Vasa, & Wright, 1994) suggested that 9.1% of children with ADHD were served in programs for students with MR.

Speech-Language Impairment

ADHD has been associated with an increased risk for delayed speech development (Hartsough & Lambert, 1985; Szatmari, Offord, & Boyle, 1989) and problems with expressive language (Barkley, DuPaul, & McMurray, 1990; Munir, Biederman, & knee, 1987). However, relatively few students with ADHD (7.8%) are identified in the SLI category (Reid, Maag, Vasa, & Wright, 1994).

Educational Settings

The settings in which children with ADHD are served have obvious implications for practice. If children with ADHD spend the majority of their time in general education classrooms (as do most children with special needs), then ADHD is both a general education and a special education issue, and teacher training programs should provide general education teachers with information about the characteristics of children with ADHD and effective methods for working with them. Unfortunately, we know relatively little about the instructional settings of children with ADHD. Reid and colleagues found that, among children with ADHD in special education programs, 73% were either in general education exclusively or in resource programs; 12% were in part-time self-contained classrooms; and 11% were in full-time, self-contained classrooms (Reid, Maag, Vasa, & Wright, 1994).

Service Provision

There are two main treatment approaches for ADHD: (1) behavioral interventions, classroom modifications, and accommodations; and (2) medication.

Behavioral Interventions, Modifications, and Accommodations

There is now good evidence available on effective interventions and accommodations for children with ADHD (e.g. DuPaul & Eckert, 1997; DuPaul & Stoner, 2003; Reid, 1999). They include strategic seating, modified assignments (e.g., shorter assignments, frequent breaks), individualized instruction, cooperative learning (e.g., peer tutoring), behavioral modification interventions, and specialized consultation for teachers and parents. The extent to which these techniques are implemented by special and general education teachers has not been well documented. Reid, Maag, Vasa, and Wright (1994) found that more than half of special education teachers reported using behavior modification, consultation, one-to-one teaching, and modified seating. With the exception of modified seating, special educators were significantly more likely than general educators to use these techniques.

Medication

Psychotropic medication is commonly used for treatment of ADHD (Barkley, 1998). Studies suggest that between 75% to 90% of children with medical diagnoses of ADHD are prescribed medication for at least some period (Angold, Erkanli, Egger, & Costello, 2000; LeFever, Dawson, & Morrow, 1999), and its use is increasing. For example. Safer and Zito (2000) analyzed state and regional data and reported that from 1990 to 1995, stimulant medication use increased by a factor of 2.5. Additionally, they noted that the use of poly-pharmacy (i.e., multiple prescriptions) also increased.

Unanswered Questions

The available data, though sparse, suggest that children with ADHD constitute a significant proportion of children with high-incidence disabilities and that some students with ADHD are served in each of the high-incidence categories. However, there are problems with extant data and important areas that are largely unexplored. First, although it is clear that students' individual and household characteristics (e.g., coming from a low-income household) can have important educational implications (Duncan & Brooks-Gunn, 1997), we have very little demographic information about children with ADHD in the schools. For example, we know very little about the extent to which various racial/ethnic groups are represented among children with ADHD. Low socioeconomic status (SES) is a possible risk factor for ADHD (Biederman et al., 1995; Szatmari, 1992), yet there is little or no available data about SES or other potential risk factors (e.g., parent mobility, school change) among special education students with ADHD. Second, most studies that have examined the rate of ADHD among special education populations used relatively small, local samples. No national estimates have been available (Forness & Kavale, 2002). Third, we were able to locate only one study that reported on educational settings and treatments of students with ADHD (Reid, Maag, Vasa, & Wright, 1994); it addressed a narrow range of accommodations and is now more than 10 years old.

The Office of Special Education Programs (OSEP) of the U.S. Department of Education is providing information to fill important gaps in the knowledge base regarding students with ADHD and other disabilities through the Special Education Elementary Longitudinal Study (SEELS). Data reported here include a nationally representative, stratified random sample of students receiving special education services who were identified by both their parents and schools as having ADHD. The purpose of this analysis is to provide (a) demographic information including race/ethnicity, SES, and parental factors; (b) an estimate of the extent to which children with ADHD are represented in special education disability categories; and (c) data on educational settings and reported use of services, interventions (both medical and nonmedical), and accommodations.

Method
Participants

Participants were drawn from the sample of the SEELS being conducted by SRI International as part of the national assessment of IDEA '97. (The SEELS sample and other design features are described in detail in Wagner, Kutash, Duchnowski, & Epstein, 2005; additional information is available on the SEELS Web site,

www.seels.net) Sampling was done in two stages: local education agencies (LEAs) and then students.

LEA Sample. First, a sample of 1,124 LEAs was selected randomly from the approximately 14,000 LEAs that serve students in Grades 1 through 7. Before selection, the sample was stratified by geographic region, district size, and district wealth. A power analysis revealed that enough students could be selected from 297 LEAs to provide the needed precision of estimates by the end of the 5-year data collection period; the 245 districts that agreed to participate were sufficient to generate the needed student sample, and subsequent analyses confirmed that the LEA sample was representative of the nation with regard to the stratification variables and the LEAs' metropolitan status and proportion of minority students.

Student Sample. Rosters containing the name, date of birth, and disability classification of all students who were ages 6 though 12 and receiving special education in first grade or higher in the 1999–2000 school year were requested from participating LEAs. Only students whose primary disability classification was LD, ED, SLI, MR, or OHI were eligible for the analyses reported here. These categories were selected because they were most likely to include students diagnosed with ADHD (Reid, Maag, Vasa, & Wright, 1994). A total of 5,205 SEELS students were eligible for these analyses because of their classification in these five disability categories.

Of these students, both school and parent reports of the presence or absence of ADHD were available for 1,950 students. Because an ADHD diagnosis requires that problems be manifested in two or more environments (e.g., school and home; APA, 2000), only students with both parent and school reports of the presence or absence of ADHD were selected. School staff were provided with a list of disabilities, including ADHD, and were asked to identify all of a student's disabilities. Parents were asked, "What are [child's name] physical, sensory, learning, or other disabilities or problems?" and then those who did not mention ADHD were asked specifically whether their child had ADHD. Similar identification procedures have been used by the United States Centers for Disease Control and Prevention (Pastor & Reuben, 2002) and other researchers (e.g., Redden, Forness, Ramey, Ramey, Brezausek, & Kavale, 2003). Parent and school staff reports regarding the presence or absence of ADHD were in agreement for 1,419 (73%) of the cases. Only these concordant cases were included in the analysis. Parents and school agreed that 467 (33%) students had ADHD and that 952 (67%) other students in special education did not have ADHD (the non-ADHD group).

Instrumentation

Parent Survey. Parent interviews were conducted between July and December of 2000. The interviews averaged about 40 min and gathered information about student and family characteristics and experiences. Parents were asked about the child's learning problems or disabilities, health and medication, and services received and about family demographics. Self-administered questionnaires, containing a subset of key items from the telephone interview, were mailed to parents who could not be reached by telephone. The parent interview/survey had a response rate of 85%.

Survey of Students' School Program. This 16-page instrument included items about students' instructional settings and programs, educational services, academic performance, and family support. It was completed between December 2000 and March 2001 by the school staff person best able to describe the overall school program of individual sample members; the response rate was 59%.

Analysis

Weighted data were used to describe the characteristics of the U.S. population of ADHD and non-ADHD students who receive special education services. Assigned weights correspond to the proportion of students in the population that are from each disability category in each cell of the LEA sampling frame, defined by district wealth, size, and geographic location. Thus, reported percentages are population estimates. Sample sizes shown in tables are the actual number of cases on which the weighted estimates are based. The ADHD and non-ADHD groups were compared on demographic characteristics, instructional settings, service provision, accommodations, representation in categories of disability, and medication use. Differences between groups were tested with two-tailed F tests; F statistics are reported only for statistically significant differences. Effects sizes (ES) using Cohen's d were computed for significant tests.

Disproportional representation in the ADHD group was analyzed for Caucasian, African American, and Hispanic students using procedures detailed by Artiles, Rueda, Salazar, and Higareda (2005). We computed a *composition index,* a *risk index,* and an *odds ratio* for each group. The composition index is calculated by dividing the total number of students in a target group (e.g., African American) with ADHD by the total number of students with ADHD in each of the five disability categories. This percentage is then compared with the percentage of the target group in the non-ADHD group. A group would be considered over- or underrepresented if the proportion in the ADHD group is equal to or greater than plus or minus 10% of the percentage observed in the non-ADHD group. The risk index is equal to the number of students with ADHD in a target group divided by the total number of students in the target group. Odds ratios are the odds of a child in a given target group also being in the ADHD group divided by the odds of a child in a comparison group being in the ADHD group. The Caucasian group was used as the comparison group (Artiles et al.). Thus, we computed odds ratios for African American/Caucasian and Hispanic/Caucasian.

Results
Demographic Characteristics

Special education students with and without ADHD were disproportionately male (see Table 1), although the ADHD group had a higher proportion of males (81.5%) than their non-ADHD counterparts (63.6%, $F = 17.32$, ES = .24). About two thirds (69.2%) of students with ADHD were reported by parents to be taking stimulant medication. Not surprisingly, this was a higher rate than the non-ADHD group (.5%, $F = 253.06$, ES = .89). Compared with the general population of students nationally, both the ADHD and non-ADHD special education groups were more likely to be in low-income households (36.4% and 35.6% in households with incomes of $25,000 or less compared with 23.3% in the general population, $F = 8.47$, ES = .17 and 22.38, ES = .27).

Disproportional Representation

Table 2 shows census data and the composition index (CI), risk index (RI), and odds ratios (OR) for the Caucasian, African American, and Hispanic groups. The CIs for the Caucasian and African

American groups are at or near the 10% range, and the RIs are comparable. The OR suggests that African Americans are not over-represented compared with the Caucasian group. However, the CI, RI, and OR for the Hispanic group suggest that they are under-represented in the ADHD group. Compared with the Caucasian group, Hispanic students are less than half as likely to be identified as ADHD.

ADHD Across Disability Categories

Table 3 shows the percentage of students with ADHD in each of the selected disability categories. Approximately two thirds of students in the OHI category had ADHD, as did almost 60% of students classified as ED. Approximately one fifth of students classified as MR or LD had ADHD. Only 4% of students classified as SLI had ADHD.

Another perspective on the prevalence of ADHD among students in various disability categories is provided by looking at the distribution of disability types within the population of students with ADHD. By far the most common disability category among special education students with and without ADHD was LD, with approximately half (49.7% and 48.7%) served under this category. Compared with special education students without ADHD, many more students with ADHD are classified as OHI (17.7% vs. 2.3%, $F = 19.44$, ES = .25) or ED (13.8% vs. 2.5%, $F = 12.46$, ES = .20), and fewer are classified as SLI (6.5% vs. 34.7%, $F = 71.71$, ES = .48). One in eight students with ADHD (12.4%) is classified as MR; this was not a significantly different rate than the 11.9% among non-ADHD students.

Educational Settings

The majority of both ADHD and non-ADHD special education students (63.1% and 69.4%, respectively) spent most of their time in the general education classroom (Table 4). The most notable difference in educational settings between the groups was that students with ADHD were less likely than non-ADHD peers to spend the large majority of their instructional time (i.e., 80% or more) in a general education classroom (28.3% vs. 44.1%, $F = 11.09$, ES = .18). Few students in either group spent less than 20% of their time in the general education classroom.

Services

Two thirds (67.5%) of students with ADHD received at least one type of nonacademic service, a rate that is virtually the same as non-ADHD special education students (66.3%). However, the types of services and supports provided the two groups differed markedly (Table 5). The following all were significantly more likely to be provided to students with ADHD than to students in the non-ADHD group: behavior management programs $F = 35.53$, ES = .34), mental health ($F = 18.18$, ES = .24), social work services ($F = 8.75$, ES = .17), family counseling ($F = 5.35$, ES = .13), and behavioral interventions ($F = 15.49$, ES = .22). On the one hand, these services were provided to only 8.3% (family counseling) to 37.1% (behavior management programs) of students with ADHD. On the other hand, students in the non-ADHD group were more likely to receive speech or language therapy (52.3% vs. 23%, $F = 36.35$, ES = .34).

Academic services were provided more commonly than non-academic services, as were supports td both the ADHD and non-ADHD groups, although students with ADHD received them significantly more often than non-ADHD peers (91% vs. 80%,

Table 1 Individual and Household Characteristics of Special Education Students with and without ADHD

Variable	ADHD (N = 467) %	ADHD (N = 467) SE	Non-ADHD (N = 952) %	Non-ADHD (N = 952) SE	General Population[a] %
Age (in years)					
6–9	35.9	4.3	44.3	2.6	
10–12	54.4	4.5	48.2	2.6	
13+	9.7	2.7	7.5	1.4	
Gender					
Male	81.5**	3.5	63.6	2.5	
Female	18.5*	3.5	36.4	2.5	
Takes stimulant medication	69.2	4.3	0.5	0.4	
Household income					
<$25,000	36.4	4.5	35.6	2.6	23.3
$25,001–50,000	28.8	4.2	32.1	2.5	27.6
>$50,000	34.8	4.5	32.3	2.5	49.1
Free/reduced-price lunch	42.6	4.5	44.2	2.9	
Two-parent household	62.5	4.5	72.4	2.5	68.7
Number of school changes					
0	57.9	4.6	61.9	2.7	
1	23.7	4.0	20.8	2.2	
2+	18.4	3.6	17.3	2.1	

Note. SE = standard error.
[a]Data on household income of the general population are household incomes of 6- to 17-year-olds and were drawn from the U.S. Census Bureau (2001b). Data on two-parent households for the general population are for children under 18 and were drawn from the U.S. Census Bureau (2001a).
*$p < .05$. **$p < .001$.

$F = 9.87$, ES = .18). Monitoring of their progress by a special education teacher was the most common academic support provided students with ADHD; 72% received it compared with 59.5% of the non-ADHD group ($F = 6.51$, ES = .14). Students with ADHD also were more likely than the non-ADHD group to have a classroom aide (45.2% vs. 33.1%, $F = 5.61$, ES = .13) and receive learning strategies/study skills instruction (40.8% vs. 28.5 %,$F = 6.12$, ES = .14). Both tutoring by a special education teacher and by an adult other than a teacher were more commonly provided to the ADHD than to the non-ADHD group (49.4% vs. 34.6%, $F = 6.96$, ES = .15;16.9% vs. 8.6%, $F = 5.24$, ES = .13).

Accommodations

On the whole, students in the ADHD group were more likely to receive educational accommodations (Table 6). For example, additional time for tests and to complete assignments were the most commonly provided accommodations for students with ADHD; 80.9% and 71.1% received them, respectively, compared with 65% and 57.7% of students in the non-ADHD group ($F = 13.30$, ES = .21 and 6.34, ES = .14, respectively). Additionally, students with ADHD were significantly more likely to receive computer-assisted instruction ($F = 4.32$, ES = .12) and shorter or different assignments ($F = 11.74$, ES = .19). There was no difference in the

Table 2 Composition, Risk Indices, and Odds Ratios for ADHD Representation among Caucasian, African American, and Hispanic Special Education Students

Group	Census Estimate[a]	ADHD CI	Non-ADHD CI	RI	OR
Caucasian	64.2	77.6	71.0	34.86	NA
African American	14.9	15.2	13.5	35.58	1.02
Hispanic	15.8	5.6	13.8	16.52	.47

Note. CI = Composition Index; RI = Risk Index; OR = Odds Ratio; NA = not applicable. Both CI and RI are expressed as perceiltages.
[a]Data for race/ethnicity distribution of the general population are for 5- to 13-year-olds, and were drawn from U.S. Census Bureau (2002).

Table 3 Prevalence of ADHD within Five Special Education Disability Categories

Disability Category	% ADHD	SE	N
Other health impairment	65.8	4.2	307
Emotional disturbance	57.9	4.6	204
Mental retardation	20.6	3.1	324
Learning disability	20.2	2.8	367
Speech/language impairment	4.5	1.9	217

Note. SE = standard error.

frequency of modified grading standards, tests read to students, alternative tests, and slower paced instruction.

Discussion

In this study we compared ADHD and non-DHD students receiving special education services in terms of demographics, disproportional representation, prevalence of ADHD in the various special edtication disability categories, educational setting, and services and accommodations. In this section we discuss each topic in turn.

Demographics

Compared with students in the general population nationally, income levels for both the ADHD and non-ADHD groups were somewhat lower. ADHD is found in all social classes; however, the relationship between ADHD and SES is not clear. There is some evidence that low SES is a risk factor for ADHD (Biederman et al., 1995; Szatmari, 1992), whereas some have contended that ADHD is a middle- to upper-middle-class disorder (Diller, 1998). Barkley (1998) suggested that when other factors are controlled (e.g., co-occurring conditions), there is no relationship between SES and ADHD. The results from the analyses reported here support Barkley's position. Among students in the special education categories of LD, SLI, MR, ED, and OHI, there were no SES differences

between ADHD and non-ADHD groups. The groups were equally likely to be in each income category, participate in free and reduced lunch programs, and live in two-parent households.

Disproportional Representation

Early concerns regarding the disproportionate representation of culturally different students focused on the possibility that African American students were overrepresented in ADHD groups (Penning, 1990). In contrast, our data for special education students are consistent with previous findings (e.g., Langsdorf, Anderson, Waechter, Madrigal, & Juarez, 1979; Reid, Maag, Vasa, & Wright, 1994) in suggesting that among students with ADHD, Hispanic students are noticeably underrepresented. Although the reason for this finding is unknown, several potential explanations exist. First, the incidence of ADHD among Hispanic students may actually be lower. Luk (1996) has suggested that cultural factors could serve to suppress the incidence of ADHD behaviors, and some evidence supports this theory (e.g., Weisz et al., 1989). Second, some research suggests that there may be different norms and perceptions of disordered behavior across cultural groups (Bussing, Schoenberg, & Perwien, 1998) or a different tolerance for the behaviors symptomatic of ADHD (Cuffe, Waller, Cuccaro, Pumariega, & Garrison, 1995). Finally, seeking an ADHD diagnosis may conflict with cultural values. Ultimately, further research is needed to better understand ADHD among Hispanic students.

Table 4 Percentage of Time Spent in General Education Classrooms by Special Education Students with and without ADHD

Time in General Education Classroom	ADHD (N = 467)		Non-ADHD (N = 952)	
	%	SE	%	SE
Mean percentage of time spent in general education classroom	63.1*	2.3	69.4	1.6
Students spending amounts of time in general education classrooms				
More than 80%	28.3**	3.9	44.1	2.7
61% to 80%	33.9*	4.1	24.5	2.3
21% to 60%	30.8	4.0	22.3	2.3
1% to 20%	2.9	1.5	4.5	1.1
None	4.2	1.8	4.7	1.1

Note. SE = standard error.
*$p < .05$. **$p < .001$

Table 5 Services Provided by or through Schools to Special Education Students with and without ADHD

Services Provided	ADHD (N = 464)		Non-ADHD (N = 932)	
	%	SE	%	SE
Nonacademic services				
Any of the following nonacademic services	67.5	4.4	66.3	2.8
Behavior management program	37.1***	4.2	10.1	1.7
Mental health services	21.2***	4.1	3.1	1.1
Behavior intervention	16.7***	3.7	1.8	0.8
Social work services	12.7**	3.3	2.5	1.0
Family counseling/training	8.3*	2.9	1.4	0.7
Speech/language therapy	23.0***	3.9	52.3	2.9
Occupational therapy	10.8	2.8	9.4	1.7
Self-advocacy training	5.5	2.0	4.4	1.1
Academic services				
Any of the following academic services	91.0**	2.6	80.3	2.2
Monitoring of progress by special education teacher	72.0*	3.9	59.9	2.7
Tutoring by:				
Special education teacher	49.4**	4.8	34.6	2.9
Peer	22.1	3.6	15.2	2.0
Adult other than student's teacher	16.9*	3.3	8.6	1.5
Teacher aide	45.2*	4.4	33.1	2.6
Learning strategies/study skills instruction	40.8*	4.3	28.5	2.5

Note. SE = standard error.

*$p < .05$. **$p < .01$. ***$p < .001$.

Prevalence of ADHD in the Various Special Education Disability Categories

The rates of ADHD in each disability category differed considerably—from 4.5% of students with SLI to 20% of students with LD or MR to almost 60% of students with ED and 66% of students with OHI. The high percentage of students with ADHD in the OHI category is not surprising given federal guidance that those with ADHD as their primary disability be included in the OHI category (Davila et al., 1991) and is consistent with Forness and Kavale's (2002) estimates. The high proportion of students with ADHD in the ED category suggests that special educators may need to give particular consideration to attention related problems among students in that category.

Approximately 50% of students in the ADHD group were eligible for services under the LD category. Whereas this proportion of ADHD students classified as LD was higher than that reported by Reid, Maag, Vasa, & Wright (1994), the proportion of ADHD students in the ED category (13.8%) was much lower than the 51.9% they reported. The high rate of ADHD students in the ED category could be due to the fact that oppositional defiant disorders and conduct disorders are common among children with ADHD (Barkley, 1998). Another dramatic change from past research has been among students included under the OHI category; 17.7% of students with ADHD were classified under OHI, second only to the LD category. The extent to which these changes are attributable to true changes in classification over time or to differences in the samples (past research did not use a nationally representative sample) is not clear.

The number of students with ADHD receiving special education services under the MR category also may have increased over time—from an estimate of 5% (Reid, Maag, Vasa, & Wright, 1994) to the 12.4% found in the present study. Although researchers have identified ADHD among children with MR (e.g., Aman, Armstrong, Buican, & Siiick, 2002), relatively little attention has been paid to these children. Very few students with ADHD received special education under the SLI classification. This is surprising, given the well-documented problems with language among children with ADHD (Barkley, 1998). Nevertheless, there does seem to be some recognition of these students' speech-language problems; 23% of students in the ADHD group received speech-language pathology services.

Educational Settings

Regardless of whether they have ADHD, most special education students in the LD, SLI, MR, ED, and OHI categories spent the majority of their time in general education classrooms. This is consistent with earlier work (Reid, Maag, Vasa, & Wright, 1994) and reflects the current emphasis on inclusion. It suggests the need for more extensive data about ADHD students in the general education classroom. If children with ADHD spend the majority of their time in the general education classroom, general education teachers' ability to understand them and intervene effectively may be crucial to their success.

Table 6 Educational Accommodations for Special Education Students with and without ADHD

Variable	ADHD (N = 464)		Non-ADHD (N = 932)	
	%	SE	%	SE
Modified grading standards	37.7	4.3	31.9	2.5
Testing				
More time for test taking	80.9***	3.5	65.0	2.6
Tests read to student	53.3	4.4	48.4	2.7
Modified tests	51.7*	4.4	38.7	2.7
Alternative tests	30.5	4.0	26.1	2.4
Instruction and assignments				
Extended time for assignments	71.1**	4.0	57.7	2.7
Shorter/different assignments	57.5***	4.3	40.1	2.7
Slower-paced instruction	49.3	4.4	42.0	2.7
More frequent feedback	45.3*	4.4	34.2	2.6
Computer-assisted activities	18.5*	3.4	10.6	1.7

Note. SE = standard error.
*$p < .05$. **$p < .01$. ***$p < .001$.

Services and Accommodations

In 1991, ADHD advocates expressed serious concerns as to whether children with ADHD received necessary and appropriate services. Our results suggest that, on the whole, children with ADHD are more likely than their non-ADHD special education peers to receive services and accommodations. Moreover, the types of supports provided are consistent with what are thought to be best practices for these students. Providing closer supervision, family support services, behavioral management, and learning and study skills are recommended practices for students with ADHD. Note that although the observed ESs were in the low to moderate range, these ESs, when applied to the ADHD population, translate into differences of thousand or tens of thousands receiving services or accommodations. However, despite being provided more often, only small fractions of students with ADHD received these services. The accommodations for students with ADHD (e.g., shorter assignments, more frequent feedback, extended time for tests) also are consistent with those generally recommended for these students (DuPaul & Stoner, 2003; Reid, 1999).

The high proportion of students with ADHD in the ED category suggests that special educators may need to give particular consideration to attention-related problems among students in that category.

Best-practice standards include medication management as a first line treatment of ADHD (Goldman, Genel, Bezman, & Slanetz, 1998). Thus, the high rate of medication use among the ADHD group was expected. The rate of medication among ADHD students was consistent with medication rates among students with a clinical diagnosis of ADHD, which range from 52% to 71% (Safer

& Zito, 2000). Moreover, given the increasing trend in medication use (Safer & Zito) and the emphasis on the medical model (Forness, Kavale, & Davanzo, 2002), the rate of medication may remain high or increase. Given the numbers of students with ADHD, their educational settings, and the high rate of medication use, both special and general education teachers should be knowledgeable about the effects and side effects of common medications. In addition, teachers could be helpful in monitoring the effectiveness of medication.

Limitations

There are four main limitations to the present study. First, because identification of the ADHD group was based on parent and school report, the clinical validity of the ADHD diagnoses is unknown. However, only students with concordant parent and teacher reports of ADHD were included in the analyses, and the demographics of the ADHD group are consistent with samples identified by research criteria (e.g., male to female ratio, medication rate; DuPaul & Stoner, 2003; Safer &C Zito, 2000). Moreover, these were the students who were considered to have ADHD by the schools and who were treated as such. Second, because the sample is a nationally stratified sample of students who received special education services, we are not able to report on students diagnosed with ADHD who do not receive such services. Students who were served under Section 504 or who did not receive services at all are not represented in SEELS. Third, all information about services and accommodations was based on reports from schools. We have no way of assessing the accuracy of the reports, or whether services and accommodations were administered correctly and consistently, nor can we determine whether they were appropriate to the individual students receiving them. Finally, because many in the ADHD group had a comorbid disability, the reader should remember that we were comparing children with multiple disabilities to a group that contained many children with a single disability.

Implications

The results of this study suggest a need to address teacher training and to investigate how effectively existing services are being delivered. The need for teacher training is obvious, particularly among general education teachers. Children with ADHD now constitute the majority of two special education categories (OHI and ED) and represent substantial proportions of two other categories: LD and MR. Children served under Section 504 further enlarge the population of students with ADHD who spend their day in general education classrooms. Thus, it is apparent that both general education and special education teachers will almost certainly work with children with ADHD regularly. It is important for teachers to have basic information about ADHD, including effective behavioral interventions, accommodations, and the effects and side effects of common medications. The extent to which teacher training programs educate preservice teachers on working with children with ADHD is uncertain, and there is very little information on the knowledge base of inservice teachers.

Further, how effectively and consistently schools deliver services should be the focus of future research. Research has identified barriers to working with children with ADHD in the classroom (Bussing, Gary, Leon, Garvan, & Reid, 2002; Reid, Vasa, Maag, & Wright, 1994). Yet there is little research on the realities of providing services for children with ADHD in the classroom. Our results suggest that children may be underserved in some area (e.g., only 37% of students with ADHD have behavior management plans). Nevertheless, results do suggest that service delivery has improved over the last 10 years. Identification of students from diverse cultural backgrounds also should be investigated. For example, if Hispanic students are truly underrepresented, they may not receive needed services.

References

Abikoff, H. (2002). Matching patients to treatments. In P. Jensen & J. Cooper (Eds.), *Attention deficit hyperactivity disorder: State of the science, best practices* (pp. 15–1 to 15–14). Kingston, NJ: Civic Research Institute.

Aman, M. G., Armstrong, S., Buican, B., & Silick, T. (2002). Four-year follow-up of children with low intelligence and ADHD: A replication. *Research in Devebpmental Disabilities, 23,* 119–134.

American Psychiatric Association. (2000). *Diagnostic and statistical manual of mental disorder* (4th ed., Text Revision). Washington, DC: Author.

Angold, A., Erkanli, A., Egger, H., & Costello, J. (2000). Stimulant treatment for children: A community perspective. *Journal of the American Academy of Child and Adolescent Psychiatry, 39,* 975–984.

Artiles, A., Rueda, R., Salazar, J., & Higareda, I. (2005). Within-group diversity in minority disproportionate representation: English language learners in urban school districts. *Exceptional Children, 71,* 283–300.

Barkley, R. A. (1998). *Attention deficit hyperactivity disorder: A handbook for diagnosis and treatment* (2nd ed.). New York: Guilford.

Barkley, R. A., DuPaul, G. J., & McMurray, M. B. (1990). A comprehensive evaluation of attention deficit disorder with and without hyperactivity defined by research criteria. *Journal of Consulting and Clinical Psychology, 58,* 580–588.

Biederman, J., Milberger, S., Faraone, S. V., Kiely, K., Guite, J., Mick, E., et al. (1995). Family—environment risk factors for attention-deficit hyperactivity disorder. *Archives of General Psychiatry, 52,* 464–470.

Bird, H. R., Gould, M. S., & Steghezza-Jamarillo, B. M. (1994). The comorbidity of ADHD in a community sample of children aged 6 through 16 years. *Journal of Child and Family Studies, 3,* 365–378.

Bussing, R., Gary, F. A., Leon, C. E., Garvan, C. W., & Reid, R. (2002). General classroom teachers' information and perceptions of attention deficit hyperactivity disorder. *Behavioral Disorders, 27,* 327–339.

Bussing, R., Schoenberg, N. E., & Perwien, A. R. (1998). Knowledge and information about ADHD: Evidence of cultural differences among African-American and White parents. *Social Science and Medicine, 46,* 919–928.

Bussing, R., Zima, B. T., Belin, T. R., & Forness, S. R. (1998). Children who qualify for LD and SED programs: Do they differ in level of ADHD symptoms and comorbid psychiatric conditions? *Behavioral Disorders, 23,* 85–97.

Cuffe, S. P., Waller, J. L., Cuccaro, M. L., Pumariega, A. J., & Garrison, C. Z. (1995). Race and gender differences in the treatment of pychiatric disorders in young adolescents. *Journal of the American Academy of Child and Adolescent Psychiatry, 34,* 1536–1543.

Davila, R., Williams, M. L., & MacDonald, J. T. (1991). *Clarification of policy to address the needs of children with attention deficit disorder within general and/or special education.* Washington, DC: U.S. Department of Education. Office of Special Education and Rehabilitative Services.

Diller, L. (1998). *Running on Ritalin.* New York: Bantam Books.

Duncan, B., Forness, S. R., & Hartsough, C. (1995). Students identified as seriously emotionally disturbed in day treatment classrooms: Cognitive, psychiatric, and special education characteristics. *Behavioral Disorders, 20,* 238–252.

Duncan, G. J., & Brooks-Gunn, J. (1997). *Consequences of growing up poor.* New York: Russell Sage Foundation.

DuPaul, G., & Eckert, T. (1997). The effects of school-based interventions for attention deficit hyperactivity disorder: A meta-analysis. *School Psychology Review, 26,* 5–27.

DuPaul, G., & Stoner, G. (2003). *ADHD in the schools: Assessment and practice.* New York: Guilford.

Forness, S., & Kavale, K. (2002). Impact of ADHD on school systems. In P. Jensen & J. Gooper (Eds.), *Attention deficit hyperactivity disorder: State ofthe science, best practices* (pp. 24–1 to 24–20). Kingston, NJ: Civic Research Institute.

Forness, S. R., Kavale, K. A., & Davanzo, P A. (2002). The new medical model: Interdisciplinary treatment and the limits of behaviorism. *Behavioral Disorders, 27,* 168–178.

Goldman, L. S., Genel, M., Bezman, R. J., & Slanetz, P. J. (1998). Diagnosis and treatment of attention deficit/ hyperactivity disorder in children and adolescents. *Journal of the American Medical Association, 279,* 1100–1107.

Hartsough, C. S., & Lambert, N. M. (1985). Medical factors in hyperactive and normal children: Prenatal, developmental, and health history findings. *American Journal of Orthopsychiatry, 55,* 190–210.

Jensen, P. S., Martin, D., & Cantwell, D. (1997). Comorbidity in ADHD: Implications for research, practice, and DSM-V. *Journal of the American Academy of Child and Adolescent Psychiatry, 36,* 1065–1079.

Langsdorf, R., Anderson, R. P., Waechter, D., Madrigal, J., & Juarez, L. (1979). Ethnicity, social class, and perception of hyperactivity. *Psychology in the Schools, 16,* 293–298.

LeFever, G., Dawson, K. V., Morrow, A. L. (1999). The extent of drug therapy for attention deficit-hyperactivity disorder among children in public schools. *American Journal of Public Health, 89,* 1359–1364.

Lopez, M., Forness, S. R., MacMillan, D. L., Bocian, K., & Gresham, F. M. (1996). Children with attention deficit hyperactivity disorder and emotional and behavioral disorders in the primary grades: Inappropriate placement in the LD category. *Education and Treatment of Children, 19,* 286–299.

Luk, S. L. (1996). Cross-cultural aspects. In S. Sandberg (Ed.), *Hyperactivity disorders of childhood* (pp. 350–381). Cambridge, UK: Cambridge University Press.

Mattison, R. E., Lynch, J. C., Kales, H., & Gamble, A. D. (1993). Checklist identification of elementary schoolboys for clinical referral or evaluation of eligibility for special education. *Behavioral Disorders, 18,* 218–227.

Mattison, R. E., Morales, J., & Bauer, M. A. (1993). Adolescent schoolboys in SED classes: Implications for child psychiatry. *Journal of the American Academy of Child and Adolescent Psychiatry, 32,* 1223–1228.

McConaughy, S. H., Mattison, R. E., & Peterson, R. (1994). Behavioral/emotional problems of children with serious emotional disturbance and learning disabilities. *School Psychology Review, 23,* 81—98.

Munir, K., Biederman, J., & Knee, D. (1987). Psychiatric comorbidity in patients with attention deficit disorder: A controlled study, *Journal of the American Academy of Child and Adolescent Psychiatry, 26,* 844–848.

Pastor, P. N., & Reuben, C. A. (2002). *Prevalence of attention deficit disorders and learning disability: United States, 1997–1998.* Vital Health Statistics, 10 (206). National Center for Health Statistics.

Penning, N. (1990). Definitions of handicapping conditions expands . . . almost! *School Administrator, 47,* 31–32.

Redden, S. C., Forness, S. R., Ramey, C., Ramey, S., Brezausek, C. M., & Kavale, K. (2003). Head Start children with a putative diagnosis of ADHD: A four-year follow-up of special education placement. *Education and Treatment of Children, 26,* 208–223.

Reid, R. (1999). Attention deficit hyperactivity disorder: Effective methods for the classroom. *Focus on Exceptional Children, 32,* 1–20.

Reid, R., & Katsiyannis, A. (1995). Attention deficithyperactivity disorder and Section 504. *Remedial and Special Education, 16,* 44–52.

Reid, R., Maag, J. W., & Vasa, S. F. (1994). Attention deficit hyperactivity disorder as a disability category: A critique. *Exceptional Children, 60,* 198–214.

Reid, R., Maag, J. W., Vasa, S. F., & Wright, G. (1994) Who are the children with ADHD: A school-based survey. *Journal of Special Education, 28,* 117—137.

Reid, R., Vasa, S. F., Maag, J. W., & Wright, G. (1994). An analysis of teachers' perceptions of ADHD. *Journal of Research and Development in Education, 27,* 195–202.

Safer, D. J., & Zito, J. M. (2000). Pharmacoepidemiology of methylphenidate and other stimulants for the treatment of attention deficit hyperactivity disorder. In L. Greenhill & B. Osman (Eds.), *Ritalin: Theory and practice* (2nd ed., pp. 7–26), Larchmont, NY: Liebert.

Szatmari, P. (1992). The epidemiology of attention deficit hyperactivity disorders. In G. Weiss (Ed.), *Child and adolescent psychiatry clinics of North America: Attention deficit disorder* (pp. 361–372). Philadelphia: Saunders.

Szatmari, P., Offord, D. R., & Boyle, M. H. (1989). Ontario child health study: Prevalence of attention deficit disorder with hyperactivity. *Journal of Child Psychology and Psychiatry, 30,* 219–230.

U.S. Census Bureau. (2001a). Table C2. Household relationship and living arrangements of children under 18 years, by age, sex, race, Hispanic origin, and metropolitan residence: March 2000. In *America's families and living arrangements March 2000: Detailed tables for current population report, P20-537.* Retrieved November 10, 2004, from http://www.census.gov/ population/ socdemo/hh-fam/p20-537/2000/tabC2.pdf

U.S. Census Bureau. (2001b). Table 23. Single years of age–Poverty status of people in 2000. In *Annual Demographic Survey, March Supplement.* Retrieved November 10, 2004, from http://ferret. bls.census.gov/macro/ 032001 /pov/new23_001.htm

U.S. Census Bureau. (2002). Table No. 16. Resident population by race and age, 1990 to 2000, and projections, 2005 and 2010. In *Statistical abstract of the United States: 2001.* Retrieved November 10, 2004, from http://www.census.gov/prod/ 2002pubs/01statab/ pop.pdf

Wagner, M., Kutash, K., Duchnowski, A., & Epstein, M. (2005). The Special Education Elementary Longitudinal Study and the National Longitudinal Transition Study-2: Study designs and implications for children and students with emotional disturbance. *Journal of Emotional and Behavioral Disorders, 13,* 25–41.

Weisz, J. R., Suwanlert, S., Chaiyasit, W., Weiss, B., Achenbach, T. M., & Trevathan, D. (1989). Epidemiology of behavioral and emotional problems among Thai and American children: Teacher reports for ages 6 to 11. *Journal of Child Psychology and Psychiatry, 30,* 471–484.

CONNIE SCHNOES, Research Assistant Professor, Center for At-Risk Children's Services; and **ROBERT REID,** Professor, Special Education and Communication Disorders, University of Nebraska–Lincoln, **MARY WAGNER,** Director of the Center for Education arid Human Services; and **CAMILLE MARDER,** Senior Social Science Researcher, SRI International, Menlo Park, California.

From *Exceptional Children,* Vol. 72, No. 4, Summer 2006, pp. 483–496. Copyright © 2006 by Council for Exceptional Children. Reprinted by permission.

Finding What Works

Medication helps many kids. But it's hard to know which drugs for which kids.

PEG TYRE

Hunter Walrath's parents were hopeful when a child psychiatrist prescribed Concerta for their 9-year-old son. A bright, highly verbal boy, Hunter has a laundry list of disabilities: he suffers from ADHD, faulty executive functioning, dyslexia and emotional problems that suggest Asperger's syndrome. His limited attention span and poor impulse control made him an outcast at school. But the Concerta, his parents say, had little effect. His doctor upped the dose, but still, Hunter struggled. A few months later, when the doctor switched Hunter to a cocktail of Ritalin and Strattera, their boy's behavior changed—but not for the better. He gained 25 pounds and his outbursts in class grew more intense. Back on Concerta, Hunter has improved and is starting a new school, but the Walraths are shaken. "Sometimes we wondered," says John Walrath. "Are the doctors making this up as they go along?"

The Walrath's aren't alone on the medication merry-go-round. In the last decade, the number of psychoactive medications available to children has more than tripled. And increasing numbers of children are taking the drugs, too. In a national study completed this February, the New York University's Child Study Center found that 15 percent of parents with children between the ages of 5 and 18 reported giving their kids psychoactive medication daily.

When they work, psychoactive medications can be a godsend. But John Walrath wonders if Hunter's medical team "had a solid understanding" of his son's complex interplay of issues. "Those doctors' visits are fleeting," he says. Experts share the concern. In the Child Study Center survey, about 28 percent of parents who gave their kids drugs deemed the treatment "somewhat unhelpful" or "extremely unhelpful." "We find this worrisome," says Dr. Harold S. Koplewicz, director of the center, because it suggests that many kids may be on the wrong meds. With only 7,000 child psychiatrists practicing in the United States and a growing wave of kids seeking treatment, "you have to wonder who is making the diagnosis," says Koplewicz. Most prescribing is done by a general practitioner or pediatrician, who may not have the time or expertise to do a thorough analysis.

The children who respond best to medication, experts say, are often the ones who fit snugly into widely recognized diagnostic categories like attention deficit or obsessive-compulsive disorders. For quirkier kids, whose symptoms are hard to classify or who seem to have several disorders at once, pinpointing the right treatment can depend more on clinical judgment than on hard science. For those kids, says Dr. Richard Gorman, chairman of the American Academy of Pediatrics' Committee on Drugs, "there is a lot more ambiguity and a lot less data about what works." Medicine aimed at one set of symptoms can exacerbate other symptoms. Susannah Budington says that by the time her daughter Allison Stoll was 5, she'd already been diagnosed with ADHD but was prescribed Prozac to help manage her hypersensitivity, anxiety and an extreme phobia about bugs. In first grade, though, Allison's teacher complained that while Allison was bright and kind, she was disruptive: she couldn't sit still and blurted out answers. So Stoll's psychiatrist added dexadrine to Allison's menu of meds. The next day, her mother noticed Allison was pulling out her eyebrows and her eyelashes. "The dexadrine overrode the Prozac," says Budington, who discontinued the dexadrine.

Even with the right drugs, determining the right dosage isn't easy. Children metabolize some drugs faster than adults—so pound for pound, they often require more. But too much medication has dangers, of course. Dr. Anne McBride, a pediatric psychopharmacologist at the Payne Whitney clinic in New York, has seen young patients suffering from agitation, sedation, cognitive dulling, abnormal liver and kidney function, and an impaired immune system. "They're toxic from too many drugs," she says. In those cases, McBride retains the medications that are appropriately prescribed and withdraws the questionable drugs one at a time. Another challenge: children can "outgrow" a drug's benefits. From third to sixth grade, Khristopher Royal used Ritalin to help him stay focused in class. But in sixth grade, it simply stopped working. His doctor tried Aderall, dexadrine and Wellbutrin. "Nothing worked," says his mother, Karran Harper Royal. "It was frustrating."

Prescribing drugs for kids can be an art and a science.

To help children get the most effective treatment, experts say that front-line physicians need better support. Pediatricians should be trained to treat simple cases and refer trickier kids to the specialists— child psychiatrists. Parents need to make sure that information flows between the child's prescribing physician and his teachers and therapist. And with a well-integrated program of behavioral therapy, says Dr. L. Eugene Arnold, an ADHD specialist at the Ohio State University Nisonger Center, "doctors can often reduce dosages of medication." Some can eliminate them altogether—giving parents and their quirky kids something to cheer about.

UNIT 10

Giftedness

Unit Selections

Key Points to Consider

- How can significant adults identify children with exceptional gifts and talents? What types of assessment are valid and reliable? What guidelines are important for their individualized education programs?

- What is hyperlexia? How can it be assessed and enriched?

- What types of instruction are most effective for students who have both giftedness and learning disabilities?

Student Web Site

www.mhcls.com/online

Internet Reference

Further information regarding this Web site may be found in this book's preface or online.

The Council for Exceptional Children
http://www.cec.sped.org/index.html

BananaStock/PunchStock

The individuals with Disabilities Education Improvement Act (IDEIA) mandates special services for children with disabilities, but not for children with exceptional gifts or talents. The monies spent to provide special services for three children with high-cost disabilities could pay for accelerated lessons for a classroom full of college-bound students with intellectual giftedness. Should schools in the twenty-first century be more egalitarian? IDEIA mandates appropriate education but not sameness of quantity or degree of knowledge for every child. Are we inclined to push compensatory education of students with shortcomings in learning, while leaving students with a gift for learning to cope for themselves to counterbalance the equation? Do we want educational parity?

Since many textbooks on exceptional children include children with special gifts and talents, and since these children are exceptional, they will be included in this volume. Instructors who deal only with the categories of disabilities covered by IDEIA may simply omit coverage of this unit.

The Omnibus Education Bill of 1987 provided modest support for gifted and talented identification and the education of students with giftedness in the United States. It required, however, that each state foot the bill for the development of special programs for children with exceptional gifts and talents. A few states have implemented accelerated or supplemental education for the gifted. Most states have not.

Giftedness can be viewed as both a blessing and a curse. Problems of jealousy, misunderstanding, indignation, exaspera-

tion, and even fear are often engendered in people who live with, work with, or get close to a child with superior intelligence. Are children with giftedness at a disadvantage in our society? Do their powerful abilities and potentialities in some area (or areas) leave them ridiculed or bored in a regular classroom? Children with special gifts and talents may be deprived of some of the opportunities with which less-exceptional children are routinely provided.

Students who are gifted tend to ask a lot of questions and pursue answers with still more questions. They can be incredibly persistent about gathering information about topics that engage them. They may, however, show no interest at all in learning about topics that do not. They may be very competitive in areas where they are especially skilled, competing even with teachers and other adults. They may seem arrogant about their skills, when, in their minds, they are only being honest.

Many children and youth with special gifts and talents have extraordinary sensitivity to how other people are reacting to them. As they are promoted through elementary school into middle school and high school, many such children learn to hide their accomplishments for the secondary gain of being more socially acceptable or more popular. Because they have not been challenged or have been discouraged from achieving at their highest potentialities, underachievement becomes a problem. They have poor study habits as a result of not needing to study. They may be unmotivated, intensely bored, and discouraged by the educational programs available to them.

Researchers who have studied creative genius have found that most accomplished high achievers share one childhood similarity. Their parents recognized their special abilities early and found tutors or mentors who would help them develop their skills. This is true not only of mathematicians and scientists but also of world-class sports players, musicians, artists, performers, writers, and other producers of note.

Educational programs that refuse to find tutors or mentors, to encourage original work, or to provide special education in the skill areas of students with gifts are depriving potential producers of the depth and breath of their talents.

The earlier that children with special gifts and talents are recognized, the better. The sooner they are provided with enriched education, the more valuable their future contributions will become. Children from all ethnic backgrounds, from all socioeconomic levels, and from both sexes can have exceptional gifts and talents. Researchers have reported that parents of gifted persons seldom have any special creative skills or talents of their own, by which to predict exceptionality.

The assessment of children with special gifts and talents, especially in the early childhood years, is fraught with difficulties. Should parents nominate their own children when they see extraordinary skills developing? How objective can parents be about their child's ability as it compares to the abilities of other same-aged children? Should measures of achievement be used (recitals, performances, art, reading levels, writings)? Many parents are embarrassed by their child's extraordinary aptitudes. They would rather have a popular child or a child more like his or her peers, than an exceptional child.

The first article in this unit suggests resources for parents and teachers of young gifted children. Guidelines are given for understanding the uniqueness of each preschooler with special gifts and talents. They are often described as "4 going on 40". In fact, each one has different areas of acceleration. Helping them understand themselves and their environments can be a challenging task. Many persons, unaccustomed to working with children with advanced talents, may misinterpret their unique behaviors. If unattended, they may learn to camouflage their giftedness in order to "fit in" with their peers. While peer tutoring can make children with advanced abilities feel needed, if used excessively it can lead to problems. Finding and reinforcing areas of giftedness, while attending to their social needs, and their self-esteem, are areas addressed in this article.

The second article, "Read All About It" discusses the unique gift of hyperlexia. Children with hyperlexia are very early readers. Using functional magnetic resonance imaging, scientists have discovered extraordinary temporal lobe activity in hyperlexics. How should these talented preschoolers be challenged to maximize their giftedness?

In the last article Mary Ruth Coleman describes students who are twice-exceptional: both exceptionally gifted and learning-disabled, a not uncommon phenomenon. They usually do not receive gifted education. Their school work may be patronizingly simple. Ms. Coleman cautions us not to take time away from their strengths. She suggests IEPs, which focus on time, structure, support and complexity. When gifted students with diverse learning styles really connect with new information, their education can have lasting effects for the greater good of all humanity. The ability of twice-exceptional students to self-monitor their progress cannot be underestimated or ignored.

Understanding the Young Gifted Child
Guidelines for Parents, Families, and Educators

Young children who are gifted or talented share special characteristics that impact on the way they learn and develop. Teachers and parents need to consider the unique needs of each child as they plan ways to nurture and educate these youngsters. Concerns such as uneven development, the need for acceleration and/or enrichment, appropriate socialization and peer interactions, and modification of the curriculum are some of the topics discussed. Suggestions for teachers and parents are included along with a variety of resources.

JENNIFER V. ROTIGEL

Introduction

Much has been written about the development of children, and it is generally agreed that early development has profound consequences for later development. However, the social, emotional, and intellectual development of young *gifted* children has received little attention outside of the journals that deal specifically with gifted and talented children. The net result is that teachers and parents are often uninformed or misinformed regarding the social and emotional development of young gifted children, particularly in relation to intellectual development and schooling. This article describes characteristics of young gifted children, focuses on typical concerns voiced by parents and teachers, and provides suggestions for appropriately meeting the needs of the young gifted child through curricular modification and enhanced understanding.

What Does It Mean to Be Gifted and Talented?

Gifted and talented children are usually identified by schools in the early grades when they are referred for evaluation by either the teacher or the parents. The child may be evaluated through the consideration of a constellation of factors, such as scores on an intelligence test, grades in school, classroom achievement, and teacher and parent input. For example, some schools require that the child demonstrate achievement of at least two grade levels above their current grade placement in reading or mathematics. The identification process varies from district to district and state to state, but the outcome should be that the gifted child receives necessary modifications to the school's curriculum so that she can be appropriately challenged in school.

It is important to realize that when a child is gifted and talented, all aspects of the child's experience are affected. Young gifted children are gifted all day, not just when they are in school or in a "pull-out" program. The cluster of traits that are characteristic of gifted and talented individuals encompasses intellectual, social, emotional, and physical aspects of the child's life. Not all gifted children demonstrate all traits, of course, but there is a commonality that allows for some description of the gifted individual. For example, gifted children often become deeply absorbed in a topic and need to know all there is to know about it, while high achieving children may be satisfied with a more superficial understanding and are then ready to move on. Gifted individuals are often perfectionists, and they grasp new information with little or no repetition. Many gifted children have advanced vocabularies and seek to understand and be involved in world events, even at a young age.

Research in the area of emotional and social adjustment of gifted children has produced overwhelmingly positive results. Children who are gifted are, in general, as well adjusted and emotionally mature as other students (Howley, Howley, & Pendarvis, 1995). As noted by Clark (1997), gifted children need to be given the opportunity to understand themselves and experience positive educational opportunities.

Helping young gifted children understand themselves and their world can be a challenging task for teachers and parents. Many gifted children strive to understand at an early age why they do not seem to fit in with their peers, and it is important that their questions be answered truthfully and carefully. Too many children misunderstand the interactions that they experience and draw conclusions that may be harmful to their development. For example, a young gifted child may be frustrated by his inability to guess the "right" answer that the kindergarten teacher is looking for. Often this is because he is thinking more deeply about a topic than the other children or than the teacher expects and therefore does not supply the simple answer to a simple question. Since he fails to have the answer that the teacher rewards, he may conclude that he is stupid or inadequate.

What Are Typical Concerns Regarding Gifted Young Children?

The information that a child has been identified as being gifted is not always welcomed by adults or even by the child. Teachers are sometimes intimidated by the news and fearful of the demands that may be made of them in terms of providing an appropriate education for the child. Teachers may lack specific information that would assist them in meeting the child's educational needs, and they may be uninformed regarding the social and emotional factors that must be considered in planning for the child. Teachers with little experience in educating gifted children may misinterpret a child's behavior. For example, at a meeting between the parents and the first-grade teacher of a gifted child, the teacher assured the parents that the child was being appropriately challenged in school. The parents reported that their daughter often complained that she was bored in school. The teacher countered with her observation that the child seldom participated in class, so she must not really know the material. When they got home, the parents asked their daughter about her reported lack of participation in class. She responded, "Well, I don't want the other kids to know that I know all of the answers. I do put up my hand when the teacher is really stuck, because I feel like I should help her out when no one else has the answer."

Schools that are already under fire for low performance in academic areas may not have the resources to devote to children who are already able to perform well on required state assessment tests. As school funding becomes increasingly problematic, programs for gifted children are among the first to go, thereby placing an increased burden on the classroom teacher.

Parents sometimes greet a diagnosis of giftedness with relief, as they may feel that there should be some explanation of their child's differences. Along with the information that the child is gifted, however, comes the expectation that somehow the child's educational experiences will improve. Unfortunately, this is not always the case, as school districts vary widely in their provisions for gifted children. This can lead to struggles between the school and the parents who advocate for their children. In many cases, the teachers and parents are in agreement regarding what would be best for the child, but the school administrators are unable to commit financial resources or are fearful of setting a precedent of service that they may not be able to provide for other gifted children.

Some parents, however, are upset by the news that their child is gifted, as they feel overwhelmed by the responsibility of raising a child who seems to be so different from anyone that they know. Many parents have little understanding of what giftedness really means and have heard some of the myths that surround giftedness. For example, on receiving the news of her 3-year-old child's high score on a screening test, a mother burst into tears because she believed that her child would grow up to be "weird" or "like Einstein." If parents are told that their child scored in the top 2% of the population, they may fear that they will need to send the child to a boarding school for very bright children.

Although to the uninitiated it might seem to be a blessing to be a gifted child, many children do not view their life experience as particularly lucky. Many will go to great lengths to camouflage their giftedness in order to "fit in" with their peers (Roedell, 1988). For example, one young gifted child who learned to read at an early age tried to hide this newfound skill from everyone. His mother overheard him confiding to his younger brother, saying, "It's not my fault that I can read, the words just keep jumping out at me!" This same child tried to conceal his reading abilities from his mother because he was afraid that she would stop reading aloud to him. He was, emotionally speaking, a young child who really enjoyed the closeness of the time that he spent each day sitting in his mother's lap as they shared books together.

How Do Young Gifted Children Develop?

Gifted children sometimes demonstrate uneven development that can be problematic (Tolan, 1989). For example, gifted children often have interests that are unusual for their age. A 4-year-old who is interested in the Civil War is unlikely to find someone among his age mates who is interested in exploring this topic with him. Unfortunately, it is sometimes difficult to find reading material that is suitable for such a child and similarly difficult to find an adult who wants to discuss Civil War events with a young child.

Because of their advanced vocabulary skills and unusual interests, gifted children sometimes seem to be more mature than their age mates. In fact, since they spend so much time conversing with adults about their shared interests, these young gifted children may seem to be 4 years old, going on 40. This can lead to difficulties, as often there is a gap between their emotional development and their intellectual development that is not as obvious as is the difference between their physical and intellectual development.

There are many ways to describe the differential that may occur between the physical, intellectual, social, and emotional development of gifted children. Researchers have called this differential "internal dyssynchrony" and use the term to describe areas of development that are not "in sync" with other areas within a particular child (Callahan, 1997; Roedell, 1988). Internal dyssynchrony may be a significant problem for some gifted children, yet it is poorly understood and seldom addressed by parents or teachers. A young gifted child may be able to function intellectually at a much higher level than her age mates and thus finds that sometimes she needs to discuss ideas with older children or adults who share her interests. But if a 6-year-old child is able to read at the fourth grade level, it may be very inappropriate to place her in a fourth-grade class because of physical, social, and emotional factors.

The level of dyssynchrony varies with each individual and is felt more severely by highly gifted children. For example, the 7-year-old child who is interested in the war on terrorism and how it relates to his understanding of religion is likely to have difficulty engaging a classmate in a conversation of this type. On the other hand, he may not have the emotional development that would allow him to participate in viewing the CNN reports on this subject, so his information must come from secondary sources. This child may be very concerned about what he hears adults discussing but lack the social development to understand that this is not a topic that can be adequately addressed in school. With no one to help him make sense of this, the child may become frightened and withdrawn, unable to explore ideas that have captured his imagination.

One of the most important aspects of socialization for gifted children is having peers who share similar interests. Because of the dyssynchrony they experience, many gifted children will need several different peer groups. One group may satisfy their intellectual needs and be able to discuss topics of mutual interest. Another group may fit better emotionally, and yet a third group may be the social solution that the child needs. The gifted child may have to hide her intellectual ability from the social group and her emotional development from the intellectual group. This role-playing can be difficult for the young child to understand, and she will need to talk with understanding adults who can help her to cope.

Gifted children are sometimes teased about their abilities and interests. One of the most common strategies is for someone to ask a very difficult question of the child. If the gifted child admits that they do not know the answer, the person may respond, "What's the matter, you should know since you are so smart!" Such exchanges are bound to cause the gifted child to resolve that they will no longer appear to know the answers to anything, if that would be the way to avoid such cruel teasing. In this way, abilities that cause very bright children to be so out of step with their classmates can come to be regarded by the child a poor gift, indeed.

What Are the Implications for Teaching and Curriculum?

Many people have criticized programs for gifted children on the grounds that providing programs for them is elitist, since the gifted and talented child already seems to have so much. Although it is certainly true that enrichment programs such as trips to the museum or the opera can and should be provided to all children who are interested in them and can benefit from them, it is equally true that gifted children deserve to learn something of value in school each and every day, just as we think all children should.

Gifted children are as different from the norm as are children with other special needs, and the range of abilities covered by the gifted label is wide. Gifted children are not necessarily gifted in all academic areas, either. The child who may absolutely zoom in math may be an average reader. Unfortunately, schools often attempt to treat gifted children as though they all possess the same strengths and weaknesses (Fiedler, 1993).

The curriculum in most schools is designed to meet the needs of the "average" student, so the assumption is made that most children benefit from that curriculum. However, many gifted children begin a school year having mastered most of the content that will be presented that year. Few schools provide routine pretesting of content mastery, so gifted children are expected to march in place for a large portion of their days, waiting for their classmates to grasp the material. This situation causes gifted children to waste much of their instructional time, unless their educational programs are modified to better meet their needs. Gifted children who are forced to waste much of their time in school sometimes resort to misbehavior in order to combat boredom. In addition, when schoolwork is always too easy, children do not learn how to study and are robbed of the opportunity to feel satisfaction in the accomplishment of a project that challenged them intellectually. Researchers have pointed out that when we reward children for doing tasks that are too easy, their self-esteem is not enhanced (Tomlinson, 1994).

For highly gifted children, the question of whether to provide acceleration or enrichment programs may come up very early in their schooling. Of course, the answer to this question is that both acceleration and enrichment should be provided as needed.

According to Boatman, Davis, and Benbow, "the goal of acceleration is curricular flexibility or curricular access without regard to age" (1995, p. 1085). An appropriate education for gifted children is one that allows the learners to make progress at their own pace. Since one of the hallmarks of giftedness is an increased rate of acquisition, this means that children who are gifted and talented naturally accelerate themselves. Allowing a kindergarten child to have access to third-grade materials is appropriate if he is reading on the third-grade level and comprehending the content well.

If a young gifted child needs to receive modifications in the school program, it is important to explain to the child why this is being done. One young 6-year-old whom I met was upset when he was told that he had been chosen to attend the special class. He concluded that he must have fallen far behind his classmates if he needed so much special help.

One of the surest ways to foster an unrealistic view of the world is to isolate a gifted child in a classroom where he has no intellectual peers. It is very important for gifted children to interact with each other so they can see that they are not the only ones with lots of answers, lots of questions, and perhaps some unusual hobbies and interests.

One difficulty that is sometimes ignored is the problem of providing reading material of an appropriate social and emotional level for a precocious reader (Halstead, 1990). For example, a third grader who reads on the college level cannot be expected to read only the third-grade text and elementary level chapter books. But finding college-level novels that have an appropriate theme and content for a young child can be a challenge to teachers and parents. Young children should not be exposed to the inappropriate language and adult content that are so often found in popular literature. It is also essential that the child have someone with whom to discuss his reading, and this can be problematic. Gifted children have lots of time to read and often can read faster than the adults who are trying to keep up. Local reading groups seldom welcome a young gifted child since they may indulge in gossip or adult conversation along with their discussion of the book of the week. If a child has no one to share his reading with, it can reinforce his feelings of isolation and limit his understanding of the content.

One of the inappropriate solutions that are sometimes employed is giving children three books to read while the other students are only expected to read one. This is referred to as "more of the same, piled higher" and often serves to make gifted children feel that they are being punished for their ability, especially if all of the books are at an inappropriately low level. The curriculum needs to be modified to meet a gifted child's needs, and this can only be done by assessing the child's needs and carefully planning strategies and content that will allow her to interact with challenging and appropriately difficult materials.

In school, group work may be assigned with a mixed-ability group. Unfortunately, the gifted child sometimes ends up "carrying" the group. Even when gifted children resent this, they are often trapped because they do not want to receive a bad grade or disappoint the teacher or the other group members. Gifted children are often asked to teach other children. Within reason, this can be beneficial to both parties, but if the strategy is used excessively, it can lead to problems. For example, when does the gifted child get a chance to learn something new if his time is spent tutoring his classmates? Additionally, simply because someone has ability in a particular area or understands a concept does not mean that he will

Table 1 How Can Teachers and Parents Help?

- View each gifted child as an individual. Make clear assessments of the child's social, emotional, physical, and educational needs.
- Group children according to ability, achievement, or interest. Flexible group strategies can be powerful tools in assisting children to find appropriate intellectual, social, and emotional peer groups.
- Guard against unrealistic and unfair expectations. Do not ignore the social and emotional development of the child when setting goals.
- Talk with children to discover their level of understanding regarding their giftedness. Children are not always able to articulate the reasons they do certain things.
- Ensure that the gifted child has intellectual peers who are also age mates.
- Encourage hobbies and interest. Mentors can be a wonderful help, as they can share their expertise in the area of interest.
- Remember that although children may interact with adults in a seemingly mature way, their emotional development may be more closely matched with that of their age mates.
- Make sure that the educational program is appropriate. Each gifted child needs to have an individual assessment and the curriculum needs to be modified in order to meet the child's needs.
- Do not expect the gifted child to spend too much time tutoring his classmates. All children need to be able to learn new things every day, not just repeat lessons already learned.
- Search out reading materials that are age appropriate as well as challenging, and make sure that the child has someone with whom to discuss his reading.

Conclusion

Parents and teachers need to develop a more complete understanding of the gifted child so that they can truly be helpful (Table 1). Nurturing young gifted children requires sensitivity to the special challenges that gifted children face and a willingness to work together with other adults who are involved with the child. Adults must clearly define giftedness, understand how it develops in children, and recognize the impact that it has on curriculum and instruction. When all of this is in place, a gifted and talented child is not likely to say, as one 8-year-old did, "school must be made for someone else, because it just doesn't work for me."

References

Boatman, T. A., Davis, K. G., & Benbow, C. P. (1995). Best practices in gifted education. In A. Thomas & J. Grimes (Eds.), *Best practices in school psychology-III* (pp. 1083–1095). Washington, DC: The National Association of School Psychologists.

Callahan, C. M. (1997). Giftedness. In G. Bear, K. Minke, & A. Thomas (Eds.), *Children's needs II* (pp. 431–448). Bethesda, MD: National Association of School Psychologists.

Clark, B. (1997). *Growing up gifted* (5th edition). Upper Saddle River, NJ: Merrill.

Fiedler, E. (1993). Square pegs in round holes: Gifted kids who don't fit in. *Understanding Our Gifted, 5*(5A), 1, 11–14.

Halstead, J. W. (1990). *Guiding the gifted reader.* Reston, VA: ERIC Clearinghouse on Handicapped and Gifted Children.

Howley, C. B., Howley, A., & Pendarvis, E. D. (1995). *Out of our minds: Anti-intellectualism and talent development in American schooling.* New York: Teachers College Press.

Roedell, W. C. (1988). "I just want my child to be happy." Social development and young gifted children. *Understanding Our Gifted, 1*(1), 1, 7–11.

Tolan, S. S. (1989). Helping your highly gifted child (ERIC Digest #477). Reston, VA: ERIC Clearinghouse on Handicapped and Gifted Children. (ERIC Document Reproduction Service No. ED321482 90)

Tomlinson, C. A. (1994). The easy lie and the role of gifted education in school excellence. *Roeper Review, 16*(4), 258–259.

be able to teach it to classmates. Some children do not want to be viewed as the teacher's aide, or worse, the teacher's pet. The child is often asked to tutor others in an area of content in which he excels. If the gifted child's progress is hampered by too much time spent tutoring others, he may lose interest in the subject completely.

JENNIFER V. ROTIGEL, Department of Professional Studies in Education, Indiana University of Pennsylvania. Correspondence should be directed to Jennifer V. Rotigel, D.Ed., Professional Studies in Education, 312 Davis Hall, Indiana University of Pennsylvania, Indiana, PA 15705; e-mail: jrotigel@iup.edu.

Read All About It

Kids take different neural paths to reach print mastery.

BRUCE BOWER

Ethan refused to play with the children who attended his first-birthday party. He ignored the presents that they brought for him. When Ethan's father tried to hold him in his lap, the boy wriggled free and returned to his true passion—scanning printed material. On this special day, Ethan plopped on the floor by his father's chair and intensely perused a pile of magazines. Although Ethan couldn't read, print riveted his attention with a power that neither brand-new toys nor gooey birthday cake could approach.

Ethan's romance with print blossomed with time. At age 1, he scrutinized each license plate in the supermarket parking lot. At 2½, he placed letter-emblazoned blocks in alphabetic order and corrected his mother, by moving her hand, when she pointed to the wrong line of text while reading to him. However, the boy was 3 before he uttered his first spoken word.

Now nearly 11 years old and attending fourth grade in a public school, Ethan reads words and spells as well as most high school seniors do, although his comprehension of written passages is only average for his age. He's also learning to read Hebrew. Ethan talks to other children awkwardly and has difficulty, maintaining conversations.

Scientists refer to Ethan's unusual condition, which afflicts roughly 1 in 5,000 people, as hyperlexia. Initially described in 1967, hyperlexia combines autismlike speech and social problems with a jump-start on reading. As the first precocious reader of this kind to submit to a brain-imaging analysis, Ethan stands at the forefront of scientific efforts to understand how the brain underwrites reading. In a report last year, a team at Georgetown University Medical Center in Washington, D.C., outlined the neural structures that foster Ethan's advanced grasp of printed words.

Since then, these and other researchers have accumulated evidence on neural regions that contribute to skilled reading of both Western-style alphabetic text and non-alphabetic systems, such as Chinese writing. These findings are beginning to show how learning to read triggers certain universal brain accommodations, no matter what the language. At the same time, other brain responses critical for effective reading vary with the nature of one's writing system.

Increased understanding of the neural building blocks of successful reading may inspire improved forms of reading

instruction. For now, brain research on Ethan and normal readers underscores the resilience and adaptability of each person's brain, so that there's more than one way to become a good reader, says G. Reid Lyon of the National Institute of Child Health and Human Development in Bethesda, Md.

Skilled Brains

When Ethan piqued the interest of Georgetown's Guinevere Eden, her team had already made headway in identifying how the brain develops in healthy kids who read well. Like professional musicians, Eden says, good readers learn a complex skill through nearly lifelong practice. At some point, playing musical notes or reading script becomes effortless, injecting newfound joy into the enterprise.

The brain makes accommodations to achieve such expertise. For instance, one research team has reported that in brain areas devoted to seeing, hearing, and coordinating muscle movements, professional musicians possess more neurons than either amateur musicians or nonmusicians do.

Reading invokes activity in a unique set of brain regions, according to Eden's group. The team used functional magnetic resonance imaging (fMRI) to measure the rate of blood flow, a marker of cell activity, in the brains of 41 young people, ages 6 to 22, who read well for their ages.

> **"One could envision this area as a dial that predicts a child's aptitude for reading."**
>
> —Guinevere Eden, Georgetown University

Reading skill in these people displayed a critical link to activity in a brain region known as the superior temporal cortex, which is located above the left ear. Rapid word reading ignited neural responses in this area for study participants of all ages.

In the fMRI test, each participant used handheld buttons to indicate whether a word briefly flashed on a computer screen contained a tall letter or not. The word *sauce,* for instance, contains no tall letter, but *alarm* has the tall letter *l*. Earlier studies had indicated that volunteers automatically read each word as they searched for tall letters.

The superior temporal cortex brokers an essential element of reading alphabetic text, Eden proposes. It assists in matching appropriate sounds to printed letters, so that words can be sounded out. "One could envision this area as a dial that predicts a child's aptitude for reading," she remarks.

At 9 years old, Ethan exhibited unusually intense activity in this brain region, even when compared with older children who read as well as he did.

Word reading also galvanizes two related parts of the frontal left brain, but only in experienced readers, Eden's team finds. Adults who performed particularly well on two phonies-related tests—using different-colored blocks to represent specific speech sounds and naming printed letters as fast as possible—exhibited the most activity in these neural locales while reading words.

In these frontal regions, Ethan displayed activity similar to that of adults. Eden suggests that these frontal-brain responses reflect an experienced reader's accumulated knowledge of spelling regularities and of the many exceptions to those rules.

Conversely, in budding readers, word reading evokes strong activity in right brain areas, at least for a few years. These regions, which exhibit much weaker activity in adult readers, were previously implicated in identifying objects by sight. Children often use visual patterns and cues in the early stages of learning to read, as in recognizing *dog* as a small word with a tail on its last letter, just as a real-life dog sports a tail on its end.

Intriguingly, Ethan displayed more such right brain activity than did the older volunteers who read at his level or children of his age who read at their age-appropriate levels. Right brain mechanisms may contribute to Ethan's intense focus on words, Eden says.

Word Hub

Neither Ethan nor the other good readers studied by Eden's team exhibited much activity in a brain area that receives considerable attention from other neuroseientists who study reading. Some argue that this small structure, situated at the back and bottom of the left brain, gradually specializes to recognize words instantly. Others suspect that this clump of tissue aids recognition of all sorts of objects, not just printed words.

Activity rises in this brain structure, called the left fusiform gyrus, as children become better readers, according to a group led by Sally Shaywitz and Bennett Shaywitz, both of Yale University School of Medicine. The team's findings suggest that the area specializes in identifying frequently encountered printed words, proposes Bruce D. McCandliss of Weill Medical College of Cornell University in New York City.

Cathy J. Price of University College London disagrees. People who suffer damage to the left fusiform gyrus experience difficulties in naming pictures of objects as well as in reading, she argues. Recent evidence suggests that this brain structure contributes to the identification of any item in the center of one's visual field, which includes a word being read, Price says.

This area was inactive in Eden's fMRI studies of young readers. However, her simple tests may not have called upon it. Conscious consideration of a word's spelling or pronunciation may rev up the left fusiform gyrus.

That and several other left brain areas respond to spelling and rhyming tasks with increasing vigor as good readers get older, according to James R. Booth of Northwestern University in Evanston, Ill. In the August 2004 *Journal of Cognitive Neuroscience,* he and his coworkers reported results of an fMRI study of 15 kids, ages 9 to 12, and 15 adults, ages 20 to 35.

In one series of trials, volunteers alternately read or listened to two words, such as *hold* and *plant,* and then indicated which word resembled the spelling of a third word, such as cold. In other tasks, participants read or heard two words, such as *myth* and *home,* and determined which one rhymed with a third word, such as *foam.*

Both the spelling task and the rhyming task evoked left fusiform gyrus activity in adults and children, Booth says. However, only adults exhibited strong responses in another left-brain structure, the angular gyrus. This tissue may foster experienced readers' ability to ladle out a stream of words from a stew of spelling regularities and exceptions, Booth proposes.

Chinese Universals

Just as the precocious Ethan offers an intriguing perspective on the brain's role in reading, so does a huge group of print consumers that has received surprisingly little scientific attention—the Chinese.

Recent investigations of Chinese readers suggest that people everywhere invoke core neural responses in order to read, but other types of brain activity are necessary to attain mastery of alphabetic or non-alphabetic writing systems, psycholinguist Charles A. Perfetti of the University of Pittsburgh explained last February in Washington, D.C., at the annual meeting of the American Association for the Advancement of Science.

Many investigators have assumed that, unlike alphabetic systems, written Chinese employs drawings that symbolize whole words.

Even if that were the ease with ancient Chinese pictographic symbols, those characters have transformed into much more abstract shapes that induce sounds of spoken syllables in modern readers' minds, Perfetti says. Chinese characters thus represent bigger chunks of spoken words than alphabetic letters do.

"All writing systems represent spoken language, but they have different design principles," Perfetti asserts.

Consider Mandarin Chinese. It currently includes 420 syllables. These syllables correspond to nearly 4,600 written characters, so an average of about 11 characters share a single pronunciation, which can be modified by using any of four tones.

In spoken Chinese, the meaning of the many different words that sound alike becomes apparent only in the context of conversation. People listening to English sometimes discern word meanings in this way—consider the words *guise* and *guys*—but need to do so much less often than Chinese listeners do.

Many Mandarin Chinese words consist of only one syllable, Perfetti adds. That has encouraged the false impression, at least among Westerners, that the language's written characters represent only words, he says.

Experiments show that Mandarin Chinese characters correspond to spoken Chinese rather than to the idea that the word represents, Perfetti says. For instance, if shown the written character for the word *red* printed in blue ink, volunteers name the ink color more slowly than if the same character is printed in red ink. Analogous results have been noted among English readers, whose writing system inarguably represents spoken sounds.

Response times for Chinese readers turn almost as sluggish if a different character with same pronunciation and tone as *red,* such as the character for *flood,* appears in blue ink. This effect indicates that written characters correspond to sounds in spoken Chinese, not to specific words. The pronunciation of *flood* calls to mind *red* and slows naming of the clashing ink color, Perfetti says. If the characters represented specific words, instead of sounds, this delay would not occur.

A smaller but still notable slowdown occurs when a character with the same pronunciation as *red* but a different vocal tone, such as character for *boom,* appears in blue ink. Again, the common pronunciation calls to mind *red,* causing readers to take a little longer to identify the different ink color.

Studies of blood flow and electric responses indicate that Chinese readers activate many of the same left brain areas that English readers do, Perfetti adds. Right brain regions involved in vision also contribute to reading Chinese but not to reading English. This finding is consistent with the possibility that learning to read Chinese stimulates spatial perception (*SN: 2/12/05, p. 99*).

Such results suggest that different neural disruptions may underlie severe problems in reading, depending on the writing system. For example, despite sharing some facets of disturbed brain function, kids with dyslexia in China and the United States display low activity in different parts of the frontal brain (*SN: 9/4/04, p. 148*). "The brain basis of dyslexia might not be universal," Perfetti says.

The neural roots of hyperlexia may also vary from one writing system to another. Someday, Ethan may pick up a magazine and read about how his brain compares with that of a precocious reader living halfway around the world.

Academic Strategies That Work for Gifted Students with Learning Disabilities

Mary Ruth Coleman

Gifted students who have learning difficulties are a puzzle and a paradox. Their areas of strengths and needs often interact, making academic success a hit-or-miss affair. The learning profiles of twice-exceptional students tend to be uneven: Sometimes these students shine, and sometimes they struggle (Coleman, 1992). When we think about ways to help them succeed in our classrooms, we can put in place basic strategies that maximize their strengths and that support them in their areas of need. This article discusses how students learn and addresses how we can apply learning theories to support gifted students who have learning disabilities.

Three Key Principles of Learning

The National Research Council's recent publication *How Students Learn* (2005) identifies three key principles of learning:

- Educators must build on the student's knowledge. Students come to the classroom with preconceptions about how the world works. If their initial understanding is not engaged, they may fail to grasp the new concepts and information, or they may learn the concepts for a test but revert to their preconceptions outside the classroom.
- Students must have a deep foundation of factual knowledge in order to develop competence in an area of inquiry; they must understand facts and ideas in the context of a conceptual framework, and they must organize knowledge in ways that facilitate retrieval and application.
- A metacognitive approach to instruction can help students learn to take control of their own learning by defining learning goals and monitoring their progress in achieving them. (pp. 1–2)

These three principles are essential for all learners if the information learned is to be useful, meaningful, and lasting. As early as 1929, Alfred North Whitehead identified what he called "inert knowledge" (Whitehead, 1929), which consists of information that we technically know but that we cannot activate and use for any meaningful purpose. A classic example of inert knowledge is logarithms—almost everyone encountered them in high school and again in college math classes, but a person who is not well versed in mathematical thinking probably does not remember how or when they might be useful. Even worse—perhaps we have no idea *why* we had to learn them. If we examine the three principles of learning, we can see that that these ideals were not part of our instruction when we learned logarithms. In other words, our prior knowledge and life experiences did not connect in a meaningful way with logarithms; we therefore did not organize the information on logarithms into a conceptual whole that we could

apply to new circumstances. In addition, we did not apply our own self-regulatory skills to mastering logarithms, thereby intentionally making them "ours." (If you really did learn logarithms—congratulations, and please replace the preceding example of logarithms with something else.)

This example may seem extreme, but for a student with a learning disability, much of what we teach may feel like logarithms. Even the most gifted student with a learning disability will struggle to make sense of instruction unless we explicitly do the following:

- Activate the students' prior knowledge.
- Help them build conceptual frameworks that organize fragmented ideas into meaningful wholes.
- Help them develop self-regulatory, intentional approaches to learning.

The question is: How can we incorporate these learning principles into instructional strategies that we can use in everyday learning?

Four Variables That Can Facilitate Success

Coleman (2003) identified four variables that can help students be successful. These variables are time, structure, support, and complexity. Each of these variables operates like a rheostat, with individual students requiring differing levels of intensity for each variable to enable them to be successful. We next examine each variable and the strategies that we can use with our students.

Time

Oddly enough, even though time is the most flexible of our educational resources, we rarely use it flexibly to optimize learning. We all know that individuals do not learn at the same rate. Furthermore, the differences among gifted students with learning difficulties mean that the amount of time required for success will vary depending on the task and the topic (see box, "Success in Testing Situations"). How can we begin to use time more flexibly and provide more time for students who need it while allowing others to progress more quickly?

The main strategy that we can apply as we begin to use time flexibly is to use dynamic assessments to identify where our students are in their learning process. These assessments allow us to "check in" with our students for three things:

- What they know.
- What they do not know.
- Where they have misconceptions.

Dynamic assessments are not something that we do *to* our students, but something that we do *with* our students. They often involve a brief conversation with the students to learn what and how they are thinking. This assessment method capitalizes on the third learning principle, the use of metacognitive strategies to help students monitor their understandings.

Dynamic assessments enable us to match students' instruction with their learning needs through tiering of assignments. We give some students time for additional practice so that they can master the basics (what they do not know) while allowing other students time to focus on enrichment or challenging activities after they have shown what they do know. Dynamic assessments also allow us to design specific learning activities to help students correct their misunderstandings. By engaging in dynamic assessments that lead to tiering of assignments, we can use students' time more effectively (Coleman, 1996). In this way, time is not the determining factor in our instruction—learning is.

Structure

The second variable for success is structure. The concept of structure involves three areas: the structure of our curriculum and content, the structure of our pedagogy, and the structure of our classrooms. We next look at each of these areas to learn how we can use them to help our students who are gifted and learning disabled (GLD) become successful.

Structure of Curriculum and Content. For the structure of the curriculum or content, we need to remember the second learning principle, the idea of teaching to conceptual frameworks. When we put this principle into operation, it means that less is more in many cases. If we can identify the big ideas that we want our students to master, we can reduce the fragmentation of the information that we present and our students can concentrate on the most important learning activities (Bulgren, Schumaker, & Deshler, 1988). For example, instead of 15 math problems that repeat the same basic skill, we can use 1 problem in a more complex way (see Figure 1, "Less Is More: A Second-Grade Math Problem"). With this strategy, we ask our students to process their problem- solving more deeply so that they can begin to build meaning. We can ask our students for a reflective analysis of the following:

- How and why they used this method to solve the problem (their thinking behind solving the problem).

Success in Testing Situations

Many gifted students with learning disabilities are more successful in testing situations if the teacher allows them extended time. These students need the extended time to process the information (i.e., to determine what is being asked, to retrieve the needed information from memory, and to put the answer on paper). For students without a learning disability, this processing happens very smoothly, so they do not need the extended time. In fact, some students actually do worse when given extended time because they go back and change their initial answers. Just giving students enough time to process the information will help them be more successful.

- Where this kind of math might be useful in real life.
- What they learned about solving this problem that they can apply to future problem-solving.

Although the less-is-more approach is helpful for all students, it is essential for students who are GLD. For these students, the fatigue of completing pages of rote computations often leads to numerous errors and to mindless inattentiveness, thereby reinforcing both poor work habits and incorrect mathematics. Again, we can see this approach to instruction in the words of Alfred North Whitehead (1929):

> Let the main ideas which are introduced into a child's education be few and important, and let them be thrown into every combination possible. The child should make them his own, and should understand their application here and now in the circumstances of his actual life.

The use of reflective questioning to deepen the learning experience also builds on the third learning principle, the metacognitive approach to learning that helps students monitor their understanding. The less-is-more strategy is key to helping us restructure our curriculum and content for student success.

Structure of Pedagogy. The second aspect of structure is how we present learning tasks. This is our pedagogical structure. All three learning principles apply to this aspect of instruction. The first principle, to build on prior knowledge, reminds us that unless we help students directly connect new information with their existing knowledge base, their learning is unlikely to have a lasting impact. Ellis (2001) noticed that middle school students with learning disabilities seemed to forget key information after they completed "the test." In fact, when he talked with them, they indicated that they intentionally forget, or erase, old information to make room for the next batch of material that they need to learn. This phenomenon may not come as a surprise to a middle school teacher, but it does make the accumulation of knowledge difficult.

Time is not the determining factor in our instruction—learning is.

The use of graphic organizers is a critical instructional strategy that helps students connect ideas with prior knowledge and with new information (Baxendell, 2003; Ellis, 2001). When our students create a "web of knowledge" at the beginning of a unit on the solar system, we can use it as an informal assessment to gauge the information that each student brings to the task. At various points during the unit, we can return these initial webs to our students and ask them to elaborate and refine their webs. If they use different colors of ink each time that they revisit the web, we can follow the progress of the student's understanding. The use of graphic organizers to explicitly show relationships across ideas is central to helping students make the connections needed to build conceptual understanding and to facilitate retrieval of information and, thus, learning. The process of reflecting on how our understanding changes as we learn, incorporates the third principle (metacognitive awareness) while we help students monitor their own learning.

Structure of Learning Environments. The third aspect of structure involves how we structure our classrooms and learning environments. When we use differentiated instruction to meet our students' needs, the learning environment should support this process (Kirk, Gallagher, Anastasiow, & Coleman, in press). We should have physical areas for quiet reflection, for small-group discussion, and for whole-group instruction. We should use varied lighting and sound to create comfortable zones for learning. At the very least, the environment should show respect for our students' ideas and work needs.

Support

"Support" includes three areas: emotional support, external scaffolding, and advocacy.

Emotional Support. Emotional support is the climate that we create to nurture our students. A very clear thread runs through the comments of twice-exceptional students concerning their need for emotional support (Coleman, 2001a). When we ask twice-exceptional students why they were successful in certain settings, what we hear again and again is, "The teacher liked me!" The students make this statement with some wonderment and a feeling of awe, and they often follow such a statement with, "and the teacher really believed I could do it." A student often cites the power of this connectedness with a teacher as the motivation behind her or his decision to work hard (Salend, Elhoweris, & Garderen, 2003; Turk & Campbell, 2002). Although the emotional climate is not directly linked to the three learning principles, it sets the tone for all our learning experiences.

External Scaffolding. The second aspect of support, external scaffolding, or bolstering, has to do with the amount of assistance that a student receives to ensure that he or she can be successful. Assistance can come in the form of direct instruction, modifications using technology (e.g., spell-checkers and calculators), tutorials in areas of need, and targeted remediation when specific background skills and knowledge are shaky (Hitchcock, Meyer, Rose, & Jackson, 2002). The main goal of this type of support is to minimize the impact of the disability area on learning. The major learning principle here is the third principle, the use of metacognitive instruction.

Unless we help students directly connect new information with their existing knowledge base, their learning is unlikely to have a lasting impact.

Advocacy. The third aspect of support is advocacy. It includes our role as an advocate for our students, as well as our role in encouraging our students to become self-advocates. In nurturing self-advocacy, we must ensure that students come to know their strengths and their needs with accuracy. We must also help them develop ways to share this information with teachers and others who need it. One strategy that we have used with twice-exceptional elementary children is to have them write a letter to their teachers for the following year. We encourage the students to share information about themselves in these letters and to express their hopes and concerns for the coming school year. Figure 2 is a letter from Andrew, a third-grade student, to his fourth-grade teacher. The main purposes of having the student write the letter are to help the student reflect on his or her strengths and needs and to help him or her develop enough confidence to share these with others.

The purpose of all types of supports is to build the student's confidence and foster his or her ability to operate independently with success. Thus, we must tailor this support to the student's needs and then gradually remove it as the student gains more independence. The ultimate goal of all aspects of support is to help the student become an autonomous learner.

Complexity

Complexity involves relationships across ideas. It is also the level of abstraction, that is, the guiding principles and generalizations that we use during instruction (Coleman, 2001b). Complexity is the sophistication in thinking in which we ask our students to engage, and they encounter it naturally as they learn more about any subject. Complexity is not something that we create to puzzle our students; it is something that we explore with our students to ensure that their learning is deep and that their understanding is solid. This is the second principle, the deep foundation of factual knowledge that has been organized into conceptual frameworks so that students can activate information and use it in meaningful ways.

When we think about how to help students with learning disabilities become more successful in school, we often jump to the conclusion that the work is too complex. In our attempts to be helpful, we may make things easier by reducing this complexity, but doing so only serves to undermine our students. Our goal should be to hold the complexity level as high as possible while we adjust the other three options—

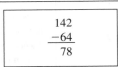

$$142$$
$$-64$$
$$78$$

(a) Show two ways you might solve this problem and tell which one works "best."
(b) When might someone need to solve a problem like this in their work or play?
(c) Is there anything "special" about solving these kinds of problems that you want to remember?
Student's answers:
(a) First method:
(a1) | | | | | | | | | | | | | | | | | | | | | | | | | | | | | | | | | | | | | | | | | | | | | | | | | | | | | | | | | | | | | | | | | | | | | | | | | | | | | | | | | | ++++++++++++
++—
Student says: You can draw out 142 and then mark out the ones you don't want.

(b) Second method:
(a2) 1³4¹2
   −6 4
   7 8
Student says: I fixed all the top numbers so they would be bigger. Then I did the take-a-ways.
(a3) I think that my second way is better because it was hard to count all the marks.
(b) Student says: You could have this problem if you were trying to buy candy bars that cost 64 cents. (Students can write their own word problems in this reflection.)
(c) Student says: What I think is that drawing pictures with big numbers is not good 'cause you make mistakes in counting.

Figure 1 Less is more: A second-grade math problem.

Dear Mrs. Johnsen,

My name is Andrew. I have red hair so you will probably recognize me when I get to school but just incase here is a picture of me with my dog hero. I am really looking forward to 4th grade but I'm also kind of nervous. I know we will have lot's of books to read and I read pretty slowly. I hope I have enough time. I also can't spell, but my mom sayes "that's what spell check is for!" So I guess that will be OK. I hope your summer was great and I will see you soon.

Your friend to be,
Andrew

P.S. Look for me on day one!

Figure 2 Andrew's letter.

giving more time, structuring the learning more explicitly, and offering additional support—to ensure that our students are successful.

Keeping the complexity level high does not mean making things artificially difficult or overwhelming our students with details. High levels of complexity encourage students to think deeply and to generalize meaning to new situations. To help twice-exceptional students achieve these goals, we must activate the other three variables. We must explicitly teach the relationships across ideas by using graphic organizers and other structures to show these relationships. We must encourage and support students while they develop their understanding, and we must give them time to reflect deeply on their learning.

By teaching to the highest level of complexity and through providing the necessary time, structure, and support to reach these levels, we are building a solid foundation for our students' success.

The major strategy for keeping the complexity level high is to use questions that promote high levels of thinking. We can select any of several questioning taxonomies. Bloom (Bloom, Engelhart, Hill, Furst, & Krathwohl, 1956), the new Bloom (Anderson, et al., 2001), and Marzano (2001) are all examples of taxonomies for thinking. They all work to help us design questions that promote students' thinking. When we teach for thinking, we must also incorporate the conceptual frameworks needed to address these high-level questions in our instruction and in our assessments of learning. By teaching to the highest level of complexity and through providing the necessary time, structure, and support to reach these levels, we are building a solid foundation for our students' success.

Final Thoughts

The ideas presented in this article are based on our knowledge about learning. We can apply them to all students, not just those who are both gifted and learning disabled. However, there is a crucial difference. Many students can succeed even if we are vague, disorganized, fragmented, and hurried; however, students with learning disabilities will not (Coleman, 2001a). Even our most gifted students with learning disabilities need us to teach with clarity, to make ideas explicit, and

to build the relationships across ideas to anchor learning. As we work to meet the needs of our twice-exceptional students, we increase our power to reach all our students.

References

Anderson, L. W., Krathwohl, D. R., Airasian, P. W., Cruikshank, K. A., Mayer, R. E., Pintrich, P. R., et al. (Eds.). (2001). *A taxonomy for learning, teaching, and assessing: A revision of Bloom's taxonomy of educational objectives.* New York: Longman.

Baxendell, B. W. (2003). Consistent, coherent, creative: The 3 C's of graphic organizers. *TEACHING Exceptional Children, 35(3),* 46–53.

Bloom, B. S., Engelhart, M. D., Hill, W. H., Furst, E. J., & Krathwohl, D. R. (Eds.). (1956). *Taxonomy of educational objectives: The classification of educational goals: Handbook I: Cognitive domain.* New York: David McKay.

Bulgren, J., Schumaker, J. B., & Deshler, D. D. (1988). Effectiveness of a concept teaching routine in enhancing the performance of LD students in secondary-level mainstream classes. *Learning Disability Quarterly, 11,* 3–17.

Coleman, M. R. (1992). A comparison of how gifted/LD and average/LD boys cope with school frustration. *Journal for the Education of the Gifted, 15(3),* 239–265.

Coleman, M. R. (1996). How to reward achievement: Creating individualized learning experiences. *Gifted Child Today, 19(5),* 48–49.

Coleman, M. R. (2001a). Striving or thriving? *Gifted Child Today, 24(3),* 56–63.

Coleman, M. R. (2001b). Curriculum differentiation: Sophistication. *Exploring Options, 24(2),* 24–25.

Coleman, M. R. (2003). Four variables for success. *Gifted Child Today, 26(1),* 22–24.

Ellis, E. S. (2001). *Make sense strategies: The works!* Tuscaloosa, AL: Masterminds.

Hitchcock, C., Meyer, A., Rose, D., & Jackson, R. (2002). Providing new access to the general curriculum: Universal design for learning. *TEACHING Exceptional Children, 35(2),* 8–17.

Kirk, S. A., Gallagher, J. J., Anastasiow, N. J., & Coleman, M. R. (in press). *Educating exceptional children.* Boston: Houghton Mifflin.

Marzano, R. J. (2001). *Designing a new taxonomy of educational objectives.* Thousand Oaks, CA: Corwin Press.

National Research Council. (2005). *How students learn: History, mathematics, and science in the classroom.* Washington, DC: National Academies Press.

Salend, S. J., Elhoweris, H., & Garderen, D. V. (2003). Educational interventions for students with ADD. *Intervention in School and Clinic, 38(5),* 280–288.

Turk, T. N., & Campbell, D. A. (2002). What's wrong with Doug: The academic struggles of a gifted student with ADHD from preschool to college. *Gifted Child Today, 25(4),* 48–65.

Whitehead, A. N. (1929). *The aims of education.* New York: MacMillan.

MARY RUTH COLEMAN (CEC NC Federation), Senior Scientist, Frank Porter Graham Institute, University of North Carolina at Chapel Hill. Address correspondence to Mary Ruth Coleman, FPG, CB #8185, University of North Carolina, Chapel Hill. NC 27514. (e-mail:mary-ruth-coleman@unc.edu)

UNIT 11
Transition

Unit Selections

Key Points to Consider

- Is there a timeline for assisting students with disabilities make the transition from elementary to middle school? What does it entail?

- What services are needed to make the transition smoother from middle school to high school for students with disabilities?

- What helps pave the way for students with disabilities to pursue college degrees?

- How do students with disabilities, who cannot achieve full participation, independent living, and self-sufficiency, fare in adulthood? Who cares for them after their parents/significant family members die?

Student Web Site
www.mhcls.com/online

Internet Reference
Further information regarding this Web site may be found in this book's preface or online.

National Center on Secondary Education and Transition
http://www.ncset.org

Transitional services help young children with disabilities who have been served by individualized family service programs (IFSPs) before school, make a smooth passage into the public school system. Transitional programs help modulate the next stages when students with special needs transfer from elementary to middle school, from middle school to high schools, from special classes into inclusionary classes, from one school district to another, or from high school to postsecondary academ-ics. The special services link the educational changes that take place.

Special educational services are required by law for students from the completion of their public school education through age 21 if they have a diagnosed condition of disability. The U.S. Individuals with Disabilities Education Improvement Act (IDEIA) has made terminal transitional services mandatory. Services are to help students transfer from their relatively protected life into the more aggressive world of work, driven by forces such as money and power.

The terminal services that the educational system needs to give to students with disabilities to help them prepare for the world of work start with an assessment of their interests, abilities, and aptitudes for different types of work. Career counseling about what they need to do to prepare for such employment, and its feasibility, comes next. Counselors must remember to allow students to dream, to think big, and to have optimistic visions of themselves. They also need to inculcate the idea that persistence pays: It takes a lot of little steps to achieve a goal.

The implementation of transitional services has been slow. The U.S. government defined transitional services as outcome-oriented, coordinated activities designed to move students with disabilities from school to activities such as college, vocational training, integrated employment, supported employment, adult education, adult services, independent living, and community participation. Choices are not either/or but rather multiple: to help students with disabilities move from school to successful adulthood. While some students may only be able to achieve partial independence and supported employment, others may achieve professional degrees and complete self-sufficiency.

Every student with a disability should have an individualized transition plan (ITP) added to his or her individualized education plan (IEP) by age 16, the upper limit for beginning transition planning. Transitional services are more difficult to design than educational plans because of the nearly unlimited possibilities for the rest of one's life compared to the defined academic subjects it is possible to learn while in school.

The first step is to determine what is an appropriate individualized transition plan (ITP) for each unique student. Many teachers, special educators, vocational counselors, and employment mentors (job coaches) are not sure what kind of vocational preparation should be given in the public schools. Should children with disabilities start planning for their futures in elementary school, in middle school, in high school, throughout their education, or just before they finish school? Should there be a trade-off between academic education and vocational education for these students? Should each student's vocational preparation be planned to meet the kind of needs and abilities of the individual, with no general rules about the wheres and whens of transitional services? Should students with disabilities be encouraged to seek out postsecondary education? The choices are legion. The need to rule out some possibilities and select others is frightening. Nobody on a team wants to make a mistake. Often the preferences of the student are quite different from the goals of parents, teachers, counselors, or significant others. Compromises are necessary but may not please everyone, or anyone.

The transition to the world of work may take the form of supported employment (mobile work crew, clustered or enclave placement, on-site training and supervision by a job coach, group providing a specific service product) or sheltered employment (in a workshop). Many students with disabilities can make a transition from school to competitive employment. If they will eventually work side-by-side with nondisabled coworkers, they may need transitional services such as assertiveness training, conflict resolution, negotiating skills, and personal empowerment counseling.

Just a few years ago, adults with disabilities were expected to live in institutions or with parents, siblings, or extended family members. This is no longer considered appropriate. Each individual with a disability should be encouraged to be as autonomous as possible in adulthood. Self-sufficiency is enhanced by providing education in life skills such as meal preparation and cleanup, home deliveries (for example, mail) and delivery pickups (for example, trash), using money and paying bills, making household repairs, and following home safety precautions.

The transition from noncommunity participant to fully participating member of society requires ITP modifications quite different from IEP academic goals. Students with exceptional conditions may need more than the usual amount of assistance in learning to drive a car or to use public transportation. They need to know how to read maps and schedules. They must be able to assert their right to vote in secret (for instance, ballot in braille or computerized for their software) and to marry, divorce, reproduce, sue, defend themselves, or even run for public office. They should know social conventions (greetings, conversation skills, manners), grooming fashions, and clothing styles. They deserve to have the same access to health settings, religious locales, social activities, and information services (telephone, television, computer networks) as do persons without disabilities.

In the first article, Theresa Letrello and Dorothy Miles address the problems that occur when students with disabilities change school programs and schools, while also undergoing the vast physical transitions of puberty. The article gives suggestions for making this period of time less traumatic.

The second article in this transition unit deals with postsecondary academics. It describes the steps involved in preparing qualified students with exceptionalities for college.

The last choice of reading to complete this compendium asks, "What Happens When They Grow Up?" People who cannot outgrow their disabilities, nor achieve self-sufficiency, are usually supported and protected by family members. What happens when they outlive their parents and/or have no significant family to care for them. The authors report on efforts by disability advocates to find solutions to this ongoing dilemma.

The Transition from Middle School to High School

Students with and without Learning Disabilities Share Their Perceptions

Theresa M. Letrello and Dorothy D. Miles

The move to high school by eighth grade students can be a traumatic experience, especially for students with learning disabilities. Because this transition can have an impact on students' success in high school, we felt that it was an important subject to investigate. We explored how students perceived this transition period and whether there was a difference in the perceptions of students with learning disabilities and those without.

As students in eighth grade prepare to enter ninth grade, they are experiencing significant physical growth and change. Wiles and Bondi (2001) said that the middle school years for ten to fourteen-year-olds are characterized by emotional instability. Erratic and inconsistent behavior is present; anxiety and fear are also common and contrast with reassuring false security. Dealing with physical changes, striving for independence from family, and acquiring new methods of intellectual functioning are all emotional issues for emerging adolescents. "Students have many fears real and imagined. At no other time in development is a student likely to encounter such a diverse number of problems simultaneously" (Wiles and Bondi 2001, 35). Students experience a transition in their physical environment in the move from one school to another, as well as different academic requirements, larger school size, and new social interactions.

Although for some the transition from middle school to high school can be easy, many young adolescents experience a decline in grades and attendance (Barone, Aguirre-Deandreis, and Trickett 1991); they begin to view themselves more negatively and experience an increased need for friendships (Hertzog et al. 1996). The change can overwhelm the coping skills of some students, lower self-esteem, and decrease motivation to learn (Mac Iver 1990). For some students, the singular and unsettling act of changing from one school in eighth grade to a new school in high school may be a precipitating factor in dropping out (Roderick 1993).

Students with learning disabilities making the move to high school face even more challenges (Smith and Diller 1999). A crisis often develops when the student enters high school because the students' compensating efforts are no longer adequate (Smith and Diller 1999). Wagner (1993), in a report from the National Longitudinal Transition Study of Special Education Students (NLTS) (which studied a nationally representative sample of 8,000 students aged 15 to 23 in secondary special education classes), found that the school programs for students with disabilities in the ninth and tenth grades were strenuous. Because of the heavy load of academic requirements, students with disabilities were more likely to experience problems in these years.

With the heavy academic focus in high school, the predominance of regular education placements, and the lower level of support services provided, it is not surprising that ninth and tenth grade students were more likely to receive failing grades than were students in the upper grades. By failing classes, students with disabilities may fall behind their peers in progress toward graduation. Marder (1992) reported that students with learning disabilities had a dropout rate of 30 percent, one of the highest for students with disabilities.

Students in eighth grade usually begin to prepare for the move to the high school during their last semester. To do so, most students experience transition activities that acquaint them with the high school. Transition programs should address all aspects of the transition—academic and social—so that the students have the greatest opportunity to succeed (Hertzog and Morgan 1998). Typical transition activities consist of registration, high school principal talks, peer panels, high school visits, and pairing with upperclassmen. Students with learning disabilities experience these activities also, but often more is involved in their transition process. According to their Individual Education Programs (IEPs), learning-disabled students are usually followed more closely by parents and special educators. These special educators track the progress of learning disabled students and make sure they are placed in classes where they will receive needed assistance.

Interviews

The first researcher did individual interviews of twelve ninth grade students—six with learning disabilities and six without learning disabilities—about their transition to high school. All students attended the same Midwestern high school at the time of the interviews. The school, located in a suburban district, had a total of 1,200 students in grades 9–12. In the eighth grade, all students had attended the local middle school with a total population of 1,150 students in grades 6–8. All interviews took place at the high school in a private room. To assure confidentiality, all participating students were identified by codes and not names. After all interviews were completed, we divided the interview data into two groups for study: students with learning disabilities and students without learning disabilities. We then analyzed the data for emerging themes or concepts.

The major research question was, "What transition activities did the students find helpful, and were there differences between the experiences of those with learning disabilities and those without?" We used the following interview questions:

1. What were some of your fears about going to high school when you were in eighth grade?
2. As an eighth grader, what were some of your expectations of high school?
3. What major differences between middle school and high school have you observed?
4. What do you feel was the most difficult aspect of moving to high school?
5. What do you feel was the easiest aspect of moving to high school?
6. What activities have you been involved in at high school?
7. While in eighth grade, you were introduced to the high school with various activities, such as counselor and principal visits. What activities helped you get acquainted with the high school?
8. If you had a chance to talk to current eighth graders, what advice would you give them as they prepare for the move to ninth grade?

Results

When we analyzed the interviews, it was apparent that both groups gave extremely similar responses to the questions. Both groups expressed that as eighth graders they were fearful of high school, especially of the size of the school, of older students, of not having enough friends, and of not being able to find all their classes. Students in both groups expected that high school would be "hard," that they wouldn't see their friends, that they would have difficult classes and difficult and demanding

teachers, and that high school students would be more mature than those in middle school.

Major differences that students in both groups described were that the high school was bigger, that they had more freedom in high school, that they participated in more extracurricular activities, and that high school students were more accepting of student differences. The students said that the most difficult aspects of moving to high school included getting accustomed to the block schedule, high expectations of the teachers, managing time, and lack of time for social activities because of the demands of homework. Students with learning disabilities indicated that they relied more heavily on help from peers and teachers to be successful in the ninth grade year than did students without learning disabilities.

The easiest aspect of moving to the high school, expressed by students in both groups, included making friends, getting involved in extracurricular activities, and having more fun and freedom. All of the students were involved in extracurricular activities such as sports, band, drama productions, and student council, but students with learning disabilities were involved in fewer such activities than students without. Activities that helped both groups get acquainted with the high school as eighth graders included talking to their academic counselors and friends. Many students in both groups felt that just talking to older friends and siblings helped them understand life in high school. Some students in both groups also said they learned about the high school by visiting the school on their own and attending athletic events. Students in both groups said they would advise future ninth graders to use good study habits, to get involved in extracurricular activities, complete homework, and be prepared to meet new and different people.

The interview data revealed two major recurring themes—social interaction and activity involvement. Students in both groups talked frequently about interaction with friends and other students. This demonstrates that social interaction, particularly with peers, was important for them in their transition to high school. Moreover, even though students with learning disabilities engaged in fewer activities, participation was important for students in both groups during the transition.

Recommendations

From this study, we have produced the following recommendations to enhance the transition from eighth grade to ninth grade:

1. Middle schools should have as many activities as possible to prepare students for the change to high school. These activities should include high school visits and explanation of activities as well as curricula.
2. Transition teams should be formed at the middle school and the high school to plan activities for the transition to ninth grade. These teams should work together with planned activities starting in eighth grade.
3. Students' needs and fears regarding the move to high school should be assessed and addressed in eighth grade.

4. Because social interaction proved to be an important facet of satisfaction with high school, high school students should be trained to facilitate groups at the middle school to discuss concerns with eighth graders and should also become peer mentors to the students when they move to the high school.

5. Students with learning disabilities should have continuous support from teachers and staff during the transition and after they have entered high school.

6. Students entering ninth grade should be encouraged to get involved in extracurricular activities.

References

Barone, C., A. J. Aguirre-Deandreis, and E. J. Trickett. 1991. Means-end problem solving—solving skills, life stress, and social support as mediators of adjustment in the normative transition to high school. *American Journal of Community Psychology* 19:207–25.

Hertzog, C. J., and P. L. Morgan. 1998. Breaking the barriers between middle school and high school: Developing a transition team for student success. *National Association of Secondary School Principals Bulletin* 82:94–98.

Hertzog, C., P. L. Morgan, P. A. Diamond, and M. J Walker. 1996. Making the transition from middle level to high school. *The High School Magazine* 3(1): 28–30.

Mac Iver, D. J. 1990. Meeting the needs of young adolescents: Advisory groups, interdisciplinary teaching teams, and school transition programs. *Phi Delta Kappan* 71:458–64.

Marder, C. 1992. Education after secondary school. In Wagner, M., *next? Trends in post school outcomes of youth with disabilities. The second comprehensive report from the National Longitudinal Transition Study of Special Education Students.* Menlo Park, CA: SRI International.

Milligan, P. 1995. The fast lane to high school: Transitions from middle school/junior high school to high school. Salt Lake City, UT: *Systematic transition of Utah's disabled youth.* ERIC, ED 389105.

Roderick, M. 1993. *The path to dropping out. Evidence for intervention.* Westport, CT: Auburn House.

Smith, J., and H. Diller. 1999. *Unmotivated adolescents.* Dallas, TX: Apodixis Press.

Wagner, M. (Ed) 1993. *The secondary school programs of students with learning disabilities: A report from the National Longitudinal Transition Study of Special Education Students.* Menlo Park, CA: SRI International.

Wiles, J., and J. Bondi. 2001. *The new American middle school: Educating preadolescents in an era of change* (3rd ed.). Upper Saddle River, NJ: Prentice-Hall, Inc.

THERESA M. LETRELLO is a language arts and history teacher at Parkway West Middle School, in Chesterfield, Missouri. Dorothy D. Miles is an associate professor of educational psychology, disabilities studies, and research and statistics at Saint Louis University, in Missouri.

From *The Clearing House,* March/April 2003, pp. 212–214. Reprinted by permission of the Helen Dwight Reid Educational Foundation. Published by Heldref Publications, 1319, Eighteenth St., NW, Washington, DC 20036-1802. Copyright © 2003. www.heldref.org

Postsecondary Academies
Helping Students with Disabilities Transition to College

Postsecondary education within the reach of all? Even students with disabilities? Is this such a revolutionary idea? Could this be possible for our students? How can educators make such an exemplary goal happen?

MARY MCGRATH KATO, BRENDA NULTY, BRANDON T. OLSZEWSKI, JENNIFER DOOLITTLE, AND K. BRIGID FLANNERY

Despite many barriers (see box, "What Does the Literature Say?"), a group of Oregon educators began to discuss ideas about bow they could provide information that would build skills to improve the entry and success rate for high school students with disabilities in postsecondary education. These educators included high school, community college, and university staff. The Postsecondary Academies are the result of these efforts.

What Is a Postsecondary Academy?

Postsecondary Academies are 1-day conference-type events for high school juniors and seniors with a wide range of disabilities. Their parents, teachers, transition specialists, and other high school staff are also welcome to attend. Breakout sessions cover specific topics and resemble college classes. In addition, tours of campuses familiarize students with various departments; college recreational programs; the disability services offices; and where to find tutoring, counseling, and advising services.

The first Postsecondary Academy was held in April of 2002 at Lane Community College, which serves a suburban-rural area. Thirty-five students, teachers, and parents were in attendance at that Academy. Since that time, two more community college regions of the state have added Academies: Clackamas Community College, in a larger, more urban area, and Rogue Community College, which serves two rural counties. The number of participants has increased each year with the 2005 Academies ranging from 110 to 250 participants per event. Table 1 shows the total number of participants and range of disabilities represented at the 2005 Postsecondary Academies.

What Does the Literature Say about Postsecondary Transition?

The provision of transition services for students with disabilities has for many years been a focus of policymakers and practitioners. Transition services for these students includes planning and preparing for employment, postsecondary education, or a combination of the two (Brinckerhoff, McGuire, & Shaw, 2002). Even with these transition services, there remains a significant disparity between students' goals for the future and their actual outcomes (Horn, Berktold, & Bobbitt, 1999). Research shows that students with disabilities reach college settings at a significantly lower rate than their peers without disabilities (Wagner, Newman, Cameto, Garza, & Levine, 2005). In a National Organization on Disability study (1998), one third of people with disabilities report encountering key barriers to obtaining the education and training they desire. These barriers include the following:

- A lack of awareness by students, families, and school staff of postsecondary education opportunities and requirements.
- A lack of support to meet postsecondary education requirements.
- The inability of students to identify their own disabilities, recognize accommodation needs, and use self-advocacy skills necessary to access these accommodations (National Council on Disability, 2000; Smith, 1992).

Table 1 Number of Postsecondary Academy Participants per College Site for 2005 and Participant Disability Information

Participants	Community College			
	Lane	**Rogue**	**Clackamas**	**Total**
High school students	206	118	109	433
Teachers and transition specialists	21	7	13	41
Parents	60	3	8	71
Total	287	128	130	545
Student Disabilities				
Learning disabilities	159	96	71	326
	(77%)	(81%)	(65%)	(75%)
ADD/ADHD	16	14	30	60
	(6%)	(12%)	(27%)	(13%)
Mobility impairment	6	5	0	11
	(2%)	(4%)		(2%)
Visual impairment	3	4	0	7
	(1%)	(3%)		(2%)
Autism	13	10	3	26
	(6%)	(8%)	(3%)	(6%)
Hearing impairment	7	1	0	8
	(3%)	(>1%)		(2%)
Emotional disturbance	2	4	2	8
	(>1%)	(3%)	(2%)	(2%)
Traumatic brain injury	0	2	0	2
		(2%)		(>1%)
Total	206	136	106	448

Note: ADD/ADHD = Attention deficit disorder; attention deficit/hyperactivity disorder.

How to Host an Academy: Key Steps

Four steps were critical to the success of these events: establish a planning committee, identify content and format, market and implement the Academy, and evaluate the results.

Step 1: Establish a Planning Committee

A key aspect of the Academies was the participation and dedication of the planning committees. The members came from community colleges and universities (e.g., disability services and academic learning services), K–12 education (e.g., special education directors, teachers, and transition staff), and state agencies (e.g., vocational rehabilitation). Researchers have shown that such collaboration across multiple stakeholders improves student outcomes in the transition to postsecondary education (Johnson, Stodden, Emanuel, Luecking, & Mack, 2002; Mull, Sitlington, & Alper, 2001; Skinner & Lindstrom, 2003).

Each of the planning committees discussed how to improve transitions for students with disabilities. Individual planning committee members provided information about (a) funding the event, (b) locating where the Academy could take place, (c) planning presentations, and (d) recruiting presenters and panel members.

Step 2: Identify Funding, Content, and Format

Wide representation in the planning committee members helped make available a variety of funding sources. For example, colleges donated meeting rooms, volunteered faculty time, and provided accommodations; and high school districts provided transportation for students to the event, as well as food.

The content presented at the Academies was determined by the planning committees. In the beginning, each committee generated a list of knowledge and skills important for students with disabilities transitioning to postsecondary education. From this initial list, each committee then identified five key areas that were barriers for their students. These key areas were the overall goals of the Academies, so it was important that they were (a) broad enough to effect change for a wide number of students and (b) attainable. Table 2 lists these local goals and demonstrates their alignment with the three national needs and the key program components delivered by the Academies.

With content areas identified, the local planning committees next decided on the format in which this content would be delivered. The committees believed that it was important to keep activities and presenters varied using both hand-on activities and lectures to help students stay engaged. Presentation formats included large- and small-group sessions, tours, panel discussions, and small-group activities (see Figure 1 for a sample agenda).

Table 2 Alignment of Nationally Identified Needs, Locally Identified Needs, and Academy Key Components to Meet Those Needs

Nationally Identified Needs	Locally Identified Needs	How Needs Were Met: Academies Key Components
Lack of awareness of postsecondary education opportunities and requirements (Brinckerhoff, 1996; Janiga & Costenbader, 2002; Mull et al., 2001; Sitlington, 2003; Skinner & Lindstrom, 2003)	Lack of information about the differences between high school and college	• Student panel • Disability services office (DSO) orientation • Breakout sessions • Disability accommodations provided at the Academy
	Lack of awareness about college options	• Specific tours • Handout/materials • Parent/teacher panel • Student panel
	Lack of familiarity with college campus	• Tours (college services) • College services panel • Handouts/materials • Breakout sessions • DSO orientation • Disability accommodations
Lack of education and support to meet postsecondary education requirements (Hicks-Coolick & Kurtz, 1997; Hitchings, Retish, & Horvath, 2005; Janiga & Costenbader, 2002; Vogel 1993; Vogel & Adelman, 1992)	Lack of information regarding accessing college resources	• Tours • Lunch • Student participants with disabilities • Overall college setting
Lack of self advocacy, ability to identify disability and accommodation needs (Goldhammer & Brinckerhoff, 1992; Hicks-Coolick & Kurtz, 1997; Janiga & Costenbader, 2002; Vogel 1993; Vogel & Adelman, 1992)	Lack of self-awareness/advocacy skills	• Student disability panel • DSO orientation • Breakout sessions

Presenters at the Academies were college students with disabilities, instructors, department representatives, vocational rehabilitation counselors, and other postsecondary staff. Although some aspects of the agenda differed by site, several components, such as student panels, were critical at every Academy.

Student Panels

At each Academy the disability services representative facilitated a student panel of four to five college students with disabilities who shared their personal stories about accessing postsecondary education and the essential aspects of college success. The panel speakers shared information about planning for college, differences between high school and college, understanding different college options (such as associate degree programs and occupational skills training programs), and the importance of self-awareness and self-advocacy.

Through these students' stories, participants at each Academy learned about documentation requirements, how to apply

for services, and other important information, such as recreation and extracurricular college activities.

Tours

Campus tours took students to locations such as the disability services office, campus tutoring center, library, cafeteria, and the counseling and advising office. Some tours also introduced students to specific campus facilities, such as culinary arts, welding, and auto body. Limiting tour groups to 10 participants provided the opportunities for one-on-one communication with the tour guides. These guides were usually college students or staff from the host college.

Specific Sessions

Informational sessions took place in college classrooms covering subjects such as improving study skills, determining learning styles, and choosing college courses. All sessions emphasized specific skills for success in college, as well as the need to understand the effect of one's disability so as to access

8:15–9:00	Registration with refreshments
9:00–9:15	Guest Speaker—President of college
9:15–9:20	Overview of the agenda and map of campus
9:20–10:20	Panel of college students with disabilities
10:20–10:30	Break and move to sessions
10:30–11:00	Concurrent Sessions

       a) Explore your career options

       b) Improve your note-taking and test-taking skills

       c) Learn about today's technology for disability accommodations

       d) What is your learning style?

       e) Thrive (not just survive) in college!—Panel of college staff

       f) Thinking about attending a University?

       g) Tours of campus—Three guides, only 12 people per guide

11:00–11:10	Break and move to sessions
11:10–11:40	Concurrent Sessions (See previous sessions)
11:40–12:40	Lunch in the college cafeteria
12:50–1:20	Concurrent Sessions (See previous sessions)
1:30–2:00	Summarize the day and evaluations

Figure 1 Sample academy agenda.

appropriate accommodations. Also, because these sessions were held in campus classrooms, students had an opportunity to experience learning in a college environment.

Researchers have shown that such collaboration across multiple stakeholders improves student outcomes in the transition to postsecondary education.

Handouts

Each student's registration folder included handouts; the break-out sessions also provided handouts. These documents included information about the college programs, presentation materials, and helpful transition reminders for students, parents, and teachers. Alternate formats (e.g., Spanish, CD-ROM, large print, Braille) of the handouts were also available.

Specific Sessions for Parents and Teachers

Additional sessions for parents and teachers presented key information about how to support students as they transitioned to postsecondary education. These parent and teacher panels represented college and university staff from financial aid, disability services, tutoring, short-term and certificate training programs, and other support resources. They all emphasized the need for students to advocate for themselves, to understand the

changes regarding the roles of their parents, and to be aware of the confidentiality requirements associated with colleges and universities. Parent and teacher availability was taken into account when planning these sessions and thus held near the lunch hour or the evening before an Academy.

Step 3: Market and Implement

To market the Academies to diverse stakeholders statewide, planning committee members presented Academy information at local teacher and transition specialist meetings, sent flyers and e-mails to special education teachers and high school counselors, and phoned specific high school staff notifying them about the local Academy. The committee members also sent announcements to state and local educational newsletters, posted information on related Web sites, and provided radio and print news releases.

Each Academy was scheduled for 1 full school day. Starting and ending times for the events depended on high school class and bus schedules. For example, some schools in rural areas had late start times; and other schools needed their students to be back at the high school by a specific time to ensure that students met their busses for their commute home. The dates of the Academies were coordinated with the high school and college schedules, teacher training days, finals and midterms, and holidays.

As for the location of these Academies, students said that just "being there, at college" was one of the most effective aspects of the event. Being on campus provided more than just the opportunity for a tour: it helped students "warm up" to the campus and realize this was a place where they could study and learn. Not all Academies, however, were held on a college campus. One Academy for a rural area was held in the city library across the street from the college, using free large conference rooms and providing easy access to the college for tours.

Because the Academies were full-day events, food was an important consideration in planning. Unless there was a concurrent activity planned at lunch, such as a college fair or college program presentations, lunch was 30 minutes, allowing ample time for the students to eat and socialize. Some Academies also arranged and paid for lunch. While students at these events consistently loved the "free food," other Academies scheduled students to be on their own for lunch in the student union or cafeteria areas. This type of lunch also helped to familiarize students with more of the campus amenities.

Step 4: Evaluate the Results

Participants' feedback provided important information for planning future events. Each participant completed Academy evaluations at the end of the event; these evaluations have helped to clarify the most effective and popular activities. During the 2003 Academies, additional information was also obtained through follow-up interviews with students who provided consent.

The tours were consistently the most popular activities, and around half of the students mentioned tours as something they liked. Students were excited about seeing the layout of the campus and, in addition, they enjoyed the chance to move

Student and Teacher Quotes

Quotes from students who attended the Academy:

"I will need to self-advocate more than in high school."

"Help is available at college."

"I am not alone in having a disability."

"Students can advocate for themselves."

"You need to be more self-directed in college than in high school."

Teacher quote:

"The information provided at the Academy helped reinforce transition lesson plans with students and hopefully will help the students speak up for themselves . . . as they discuss their transition goals."

these quotes, disability services presenters emphasized self-awareness and self-advocacy for the students as they navigate college. In fact, of the 2003 Academy participants who enrolled in classes at Clackamas Community College, 77% had accessed disability services by spring 2005.

The tours were consistently the most popular activities, and around half of the students mentioned tours as something they liked.

The breakout sessions provided instruction on specific skills for navigating academic barriers. The students stated that in the study skills sessions they learned tips to help them retain information and take effective notes. While these skills may be presented in the high school setting, students reported that learning about such skills in "real college classrooms" from "real college staff" helped to emphasize the ways in which college learning was more challenging, and also what resources were available to help them.

around. The students contacted in the 2003 follow-up phone interviews were able to recall visiting specific resource areas and talked about how the tours exposed them to new college options.

The follow-up phone interview data reaffirmed the effectiveness of the panel of college students with disabilities and the importance of having them relate their stories at these Academies. The student panel described how they had experienced new opportunities in college and faced some unexpected challenges. Participants reported that personal stories from successful students informed them about the importance of self-advocacy and self-awareness. In addition, panel members described how they overcame barriers and offered "survival strategies" for students with disabilities negotiating college for the first time. These presenters helped give students a clear picture of barriers that may be encountered, as well as some ideas for working through those barriers. They also emphasized to students the need to advocate for themselves and actively seek assistance from college staff to access college information and services.

Participants also enjoyed the student panel presenters' description of their journeys through college and how they chose their particular degree pathways. During this presentation, Academy participants gained information about degree choices such as certificate programs, hands-on learning programs, and transfer degrees. Although students may have heard about such programs previously, reiteration by the panel presenters helped students remember this important information.

In the follow-up phone interviews, many students commented about how they learned important things regarding disability services from the student panel presentation (see box "Student and Teacher Quotes"). Students said that this session taught them "you have to ask for help," "help is available," "talking first about your disability can help your learning," and to "go talk to the disability services coordinator." As is evident from

Final Thoughts

As seen by the increase in the number of participants every year, the need for the Academies continues to be great. The Academies were instrumental in developing an awareness of college services and support programs for the high school students, teachers, and parents who participated in these events.

For high school students, the Academies helped build skills and awareness and improved students' abilities to make informed choices regarding postsecondary education. For parents and teachers, the Academies provided an exciting opportunity to learn about postsecondary opportunities and how to help their students navigate these programs. Because it can be difficult to find appropriate transition activities for high school students relating to postsecondary education, the Academies were a perfect fit as a transition activity for the students.

High school teachers and transition specialists enthusiastically refer their students and parents to the Postsecondary Academy year after year. In the evaluation of the Academies, all participants stated they would recommend this event to a friend or colleague. Through careful planning by varied stakeholders, the Academies have had a positive influence on students, parents, and teachers, opening doors to postsecondary educational opportunities for high school students with disabilities.

References

Brinckerhoff, L. C. (1996). Making the transition to higher education: Opportunities for student empowerment. *Journal of Learning Disabilities, 29*(2), 118–136.

Brinckerhoff, L. C., McGuire, J. M., & Shaw, S. F. (2002). *Postsecondary education and transition for students with learning disabilities.* Austin, TX: PRO-ED.

Goldhammer, R., & Brinckerhoff, L. C. (1992). Self advocacy for college students. *Their World,* 94–97.

Hicks-Coolick, A., & Kurtz, D. P. (1997). Preparing students with learning disabilities for success in postsecondary education: Needs and services. *Social Work in Education, 19*(1), 31–43.

Hitchings, W. E., Retish, P., & Horvath, M. (2005). Academic preparation of adolescents with disabilities for postsecondary education. *Career Development for Exceptional Individuals, 28*(2), 26–35.

Horn, L., Berktold, J., & Bobbitt, L. (1999). *Students with disabilities in postsecondary education: A profile of preparation, participation, and outcomes.* U.S. Department of Education: National Center for Education Statistics.

Janiga, S. J., & Costenbader, V. (2002). The transition from high school to postsecondary education for students with LD: A survey of college service coordinators. *Journal of Learning Disabilities, 25*(5), 462–468, 479.

Johnson, D. R, Stodden, R. A, Emanuel, E. J., Luecking, R., & Mack, M. (2002). Current challenges facing secondary education and transition services: What research tells us. *Exceptional Children, 68,* 519–531.

Mull, C., Sitlington, P. L., & Alper, S. (2001). Postsecondary education for students with learning disabilities. *Exceptional Children, 68,* 97–118.

National Council on Disability. (2000). *Transition and post-school outcomes for youth with disabilities: Closing the gaps to post-secondary education and employment.* Washington, DC: Author.

National Organization on Disability. (1998). *The 1998 N.O.D./Harris Survey of Americans with Disabilities.* New York: Louis Harris & Associates.

Sitlington, P. L. (2003). Postsecondary education: The other transition *Exceptionality, 11*(2), 103–113.

Skinner, M. E., & Lindstrom, B. D. (2003). Bridging the gap between high school and college: Strategies for the successful transition of students with learning disabilities. *Preventing School Failure, 47*(3), 132–137.

Smith, J. O. (1992). Falling through the cracks: Rehabilitation services for adults with learning disabilities. *Exceptional Children, 58,* 451–460.

Vogel, S. A. (1993). Educational and psychological factors in successful and unsuccessful college students with learning disabilities. *Learning Disability Research and Practice, 8*(1), 35–43.

Vogel, S. A., & Adelman, P. B. (1992). The success of college students with learning disabilities: Factors related to educational attainment. *Journal of Learning Disabilities, 25*(7), 430–441.

Wagner, M., Newman, L., Cameto, R., Garza, N., & Levine, P. (2005), *After high school: A first look at the postschool experiences of youth with disabilities.* (A report from the National Longitudinal Transition Study-2, NLTS2). Menlo Park, CA: SRI International.

MARY MCGRATH KATO, Research Assistant; **BRENDA NULTY,** Research Assistant; **BRANDON T. OLSZEWSKI,** Doctoral Candidate; **JENNIFER DOOLITTLE** (CEC OR Federation). Doctoral Candidate; and **K. BRIGID FLANNERY** (CEC OR Federation). Senior Research Associate, Assistant Professor. College of Education, University of Oregon, Eugene. Address correspondence to Mary McGrath Kato, Educational and Community Supports, University of Oregon, 1761 Alder St., Eugene, OR 97403 (e-mail: Mmcgratl@uoregon.edu).

From *Teaching Exceptional Children,* by Mary McGrath Kato, Brenda Nulty, Brandon T. Olszewski, Jennifer Doolittle, K. Brigid Flannery, Vol. 39, no. 1, September/October 2006, pp. 18–23. Copyright © 2006 by Council for Exceptional Children. Reprinted by permission.

What Happens When They Grow Up

Teenagers and young adults are the emerging face of autism as the disorder continues to challenge science and unite determined families.

BARBARA KANTROWITZ AND JULIE SCELFO

Chicken and potatoes. Chicken and potatoes. Danny Boronat wants chicken and potatoes. He asks for it once, twice . . . 10 times. In the kitchen of the family's suburban New Jersey home, Danny's mother, Loretta, chops garlic for spaghetti sauce. No chicken and potatoes, she tells Danny. We're having spaghetti. But Danny wants chicken and potatoes. Chicken and potatoes. His 12-year-old sister, Rosalinda, wanders in to remind her mother about upcoming basketball tryouts. His brother Alex, 22, grabs some tortilla chips and then leaves to check scores on ESPN. His other brother Matthew, 17, talks about an upcoming gig with his band. Danny seems not to notice any of this. "Mom," he asks in a monotone, "why can't we have chicken and potatoes?" If Danny were a toddler, his behavior would be nothing unusual. But Danny Boronat is 20 years old. "That's really what life with autism is like," says Loretta. "I have to keep laughing. Otherwise, I would cry."

Autism strikes in childhood, but as thousands of families like the Boronats have learned—and thousands more are destined to learn—autism is not simply a childhood disorder. Two decades into the surge of diagnoses that has made autism a major public health issue, a generation of teenagers and young adults is facing a new crisis: what happens next?

As daunting as that question may be, it's just the latest in the endless chain of challenges that is life for the dedicated parents of children with autism. Twenty years ago, they banded together—largely out of desperation—to raise awareness of a once rarely diagnosed, often overlooked disease. They are united by the frustration of dealing with a condition that has no known cause and no cure. They have lobbied passionately to get better education for their kids and more money for research into autism, a neurological disorder characterized by language problems, repetitive behaviors and difficulty with social interaction. At the same time, more sophisticated epidemiology has revealed the true magnitude of the problem. Autism is now estimated to affect from one in 500 to one in 166 children—or as many as 500,000 Americans under 21, most male. That includes individuals with a wide range of abilities—from socially awkward math whizzes to teens who aren't toilet trained—but who all fit on what scientists now consider a spectrum of autism disorders.

The culmination of much of this parental activism is the Combating Autism Act, which was pushed by a collection of advocacy groups like Cure Autism Now, led by Hollywood producer Jon Shestack and his wife, Portia Iverson; Autism Speaks, started by Bob Wright, CEO and chairman of NBC Universal, and the Deirdre Imus Environmental Center for Pediatric Oncology. The bill unanimously passed the U.S. Senate in August but was blocked in the House by Texas Republican Joe Barton, chair of the House Committee on Energy and Commerce. In a September meeting, Barton told autism activists that he would continue to oppose their legislation, which earmarks $945 million for research over the next five years, because it conflicted with his own proposal to reform the National Institutes of Health. As a result, autism advocates began inundating him with faxes and phone calls and lambasting him in the press. To advance the cause of research, radio host Don Imus joined in and pressured Barton on the air, calling the congressman, among other things, "a lying, fat little skunk from Texas."

Now that the Democrats have won the House, Barton will lose his chairmanship in January and NEWSWEEK has learned that he is attempting to pass a compromise version of the bill before then. If passed, the House bill would fund a new push for early diagnosis, which is critical to starting therapy as soon as possible. In a particular victory for parents, the legislation specifies that the research oversight committee should include at least one person with autism and a parent of a child with autism.

The House bill authorizes money for research into many questions, including whether environmental factors may trigger autism. One point of contention: the Senate bill mandated a specific amount of money for the NIH to research the role environmental factors might play in causing autism. But Barton resisted, and now the specificity about how much should be spent and where has been lost in the compromise version. Still, a Barton bill could come up for a vote as early as the first week in December and the legislation, says Alison Singer, the mother of a daughter with autism and an executive at the advocacy group Autism Speaks, "is probably the single most important thing that could happen besides the cure."

196

A win in Washington may lift their spirits, but a legislative victory won't really change much for the Boronats and others like them. Some kids have made dramatic progress after intensive physical and behavioral therapy; many others still struggle with basic activities. Often, when lower-functioning young people reach 18, their parents will establish legal guardianship to protect them. But no matter what level they've reached, many will need help for the rest of their lives. Most government-sponsored educational and therapeutic services stop at the age of 21, and there are few residential facilities and work programs geared to the needs of adults with autism. "Once they lose the education entitlement and become adults, it's like they fall off the face of the earth" as far as government services are concerned, says Lee Grossman, president and CEO of the Autism Society of America, a major national-advocacy group.

Adolescence is never easy, but autism transforms even routine activities into potential minefields.

According to the Harvard School of Public Health, it can cost about $3.2 million to care for a person with autism over a lifetime. Caring for all persons with autism costs an estimated $35 billion per year, the same study says. Families with limited financial resources are particularly hard hit. Other chronic diseases like diabetes are covered by insurance. But parents of youngsters with autism "have to navigate a maze and, if they find providers, then they have to figure out how to pay for it," says Singer. Grossman's early wish for the Combating Autism Act was that it would address the dire needs of autistic adults, and he drafted 30 pages of service-related issues. But that part was never introduced because a consortium of activists working on the bill concluded, for the sake of political expediency, that the bill shouldn't try to take on too much. In this light, restraint seems especially critical now, when the Iraq war has siphoned off so much federal money. "It's like a forest fire running through science and it burns a lot of trees down," says Dan Geschwind, a UCLA neurogeneticist. However, advocacy groups vow that the moment the bill passes, government funding for adult services will become their next priority. Wright believes there is substantial congressional support for this, possibly from Sen. Hillary Clinton.

Moving through adolescence to adulthood is never easy, but autism transforms even the most routine activities into potential minefields. Recognizing the norms of teen behavior can be a Sisyphean task. Helen Motokane's daughter, Christine, 14, has Asperger's syndrome, a high-functioning form of the disorder. She struggles to fit in at her Los Angeles public school—and that means hiding parts of her true self. One secret: she loves Barbie. "She knows it's not cool to wear clothes with Barbie logos, so she tries to keep that at home," says Helen, who gently prods her daughter into developing more mature interests. "She says, 'You're trying to make me grow up, aren't you? You want me to do all these things right away.' I go, 'No, no, no.' I

reassure her that we're not trying to push her." But an hour or two later, her mother says, Christine will ask, "Is it OK if I like Disney Princess even though other kids my age don't like it?"

Keri Bowers of Thousand Oaks, Calif., says her son, Taylor Cross, 17, seems perfectly normal at first. But sometimes he'll just blurt out what he's thinking without any internal censorship. Passing a stranger on the street, he might say, "You're in a wheelchair!" "When you're socially odd, people are afraid," Bowers says. "They want to get away from you and cross to the other side of the street." Not surprisingly, Taylor had no friends at all in the public school he attends until he began to meet other teens with autism—young people his mother describes as equally "quirky."

In one way, he's not quirky at all. "He's attracted to girls," Bowers says, "but he's shy. He doesn't really know how to talk to them." A few months ago, he asked out a girl from his school who does not have autism but who had been friendly to him. Bowers had a psychologist friend shadow the couple at the movies. "Taylor only spoke about subjects he was interested in," Bowers says. "He wouldn't do a reciprocal back-and-forth conversation on topics about her." Still, when Bowers later asked if he wanted to kiss the girl, Taylor surprised his mother with his sensitivity. "He said, 'Yes, but she's very religious and I would never do that'."

As young people with autism approach adulthood, some parents can't help but feel the huge gaps between their child's lives and others the same age. "It's very hard, especially in our competitive society where people strive for perfection," says Chantal Sicile-Kira, whose son, Jeremy, 17, can communicate only by pointing to letters on an alphabet board. The San Diego resident hosts "The Real World of Autism With Chantal" on the Autism One Radio Internet station and wrote "Adolescents on the Autism Spectrum" (*Penguin, 2006*). Like many youngsters with autism, Jeremy finds new environments difficult. "If he walks into a new store," his mother says, "and there's horrendous fluorescent lighting, within 10 minutes I'll look down and he's starting to wet himself." Despite such challenges, Sicile-Kira plans to help Jeremy live on his own when he's an adult—perhaps rooming with another young person with autism.

Independent living is a major goal of many families and, with the help of therapy, thousands of youngsters who in earlier generations would have been consigned to institutions are now going to college and looking forward to a normal life with a job. But for every one who makes it, there are many more young people like Danny Boronat, who has come so far and yet still faces much uncertainty. Once unable to utter a sentence, Danny now reads at a second-grade level, competes in the Special Olympics and willingly takes on household chores like loading the dishwasher. But he also can spend hours playing with water. He picks obsessively at his cuticles, and sometimes cuts himself (his mother tries to hide any scissors in the house). He has no close friends. Next year he'll turn 21 and will no longer be eligible for the workshop where he does simple assembly-line work three days a week. After that? No one knows, not even his parents. "It's terrifying," says his mother, who started her own charity called DannysHouse to focus on adults.

Unlocking the Secrets of Autism

Autism is a neurological disorder that appears during the first three years of life. It affects social and communication skills in as many as 1.5 million people in the U.S. An overview:

The Growing Brain

The brain of a child with autism is, on average, about 10 percent larger than an normal brain. Growth varies by region and age and has been linked to behavior.

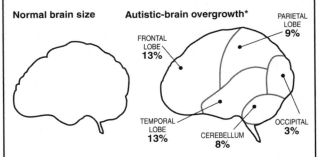

Normal brain size | **Autistic-brain overgrowth***

PARIETAL LOBE **9%**
FRONTAL LOBE **13%**
TEMPORAL LOBE **13%**
CEREBELLUM **8%**
OCCIPITAL **3%**

THE DIFFERENCES: The average volume of a healthy young child's brain is about 1,180ml. An autistic brain can be closer to 1,300ml. Unlike the brain of a child with autism, that of a healthy child continues to grow until adolescence. The autistic brain can grow to its full size roughly eight to 10 years prematurely, which may influence the generation of neural circuitry and the child's behavior patterns.

WHEN BRAIN SIZE CHANGES:
At birth, the autistic brain is similar in size to a healthy child's brain. Between birth and 2 years it grows to be abnormally large, reaching its maximum size between 3 and 6 years of age.

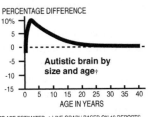

PERCENTAGE DIFFERENCE

Autistic brain by size and age†

AGE IN YEARS

*LOBE PERCENTAGES ARE ESTIMATED. † LINE GRAPH BASED ON 19 REPORTS.

Autism Sprectrum Disorders

A RANGE OF CONDITIONS: The disorders on the spectrum are characterized by severe impairment in certain areas of development, including social and communication skills. Autism is the best known of the group.

Higher functioning | **Lower functioning**

| ASPERGER'S SYNDROME | PDD-NOS | AUTISM | CHILDHOOD DISINTEGRATIVE DISORDER | RETT'S DISORDER |

Possible Causes

- **Genetics:** Few theories maintain that a single gene causes autism. Multiple genes, possibly ranging in number from five to 15, or gene networks, are now thought responsible.
- **Environmental factors:** Chemicals such as pesticides or PCBs, as well as infections, may play a role.
- **Gene-environment interaction:** Genetic variations—the MET gene, for instance—could increase susceptibility to environmental factors.
- **Hormone Imbalance:** About four times as many boys as girls have autism, leading some experts to believe that hormone

Areas Implicated in Autism

Studies have shown that there are several parts of the brain linked to the disorder. A look at some areas affected in autism:

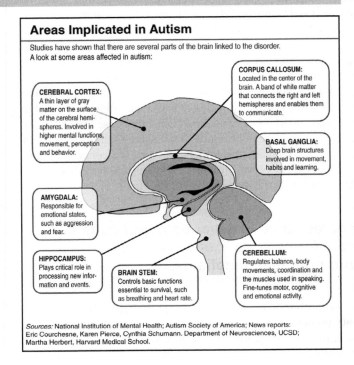

CEREBRAL CORTEX: A thin layer of gray matter on the surface of the cerebral hemispheres. Involved in higher mental functions, movement, perception and behavior.

CORPUS CALLOSUM: Located in the center of the brain. A band of white matter that connects the right and left hemispheres and enables them to communicate.

BASAL GANGLIA: Deep brain structures involved in movement, habits and learning.

AMYGDALA: Responsible for emotional states, such as aggression and fear.

HIPPOCAMPUS: Plays critical role in processing new information and events.

BRAIN STEM: Controls basic functions essential to survival, such as breathing and heart rate.

CEREBELLUM: Regulates balance, body movements, coordination and the muscles used in speaking. Fine-tunes motor, cognitive and emotional activity.

Sources: National Institution of Mental Health; Autism Society of America; News reports: Eric Courchesne, Karen Pierce, Cynthia Schumann. Department of Neurosciences, UCSD; Martha Herbert, Harvard Medical School.

imbalances during development could play a role in determining who develops the disorder.

Warning Signs

- Does not babble or coo by 12 mos.
- Does not gesture (point, wave, grasp) by 12 mos.
- Poor eye contact
- Delayed in learning speech
- Does not say two-word phrases on his or her own by 24 mos.
- Doesn't know how to play with toys
- Excessively lines up toys or objects
- Doesn't respond to name

Treatments

- **Learning approaches:** These strategies address language, sensory and behavioral difficulties. Among the most accepted forms of treatment is applied behavior analysis, which teaches skills (like getting dressed) in a series of simple steps. ABA also helps reduce inappropriate behavior patterns and provides regular reinforcement of appropriate behavior.
- **Biomedical and dietary approaches:** Medication is used to treat behavioral problems like aggression, not the underlying condition. The type of medication will differ based on the behavior a doctor is attempting to address. Research has also found that gluten and casein are not property proccessed in the bodies of some children with autism; incomplete breakdown and excess absorption may disrupt brain functions. A gluten-free, casein-free diet is thought to address this problem. Some consider vitamins helpful. A common supplement used in autism is vitamin B, which plays a role in creating enzymes needed by the brain. Essential fatty acids have also been shown to improve behavior.

—Jessica Ramirez and Marc Bain

'Parents fight this all their lives, and then they don't have a place for their child after they die.'

A few states like California and Connecticut, newly aware of the crisis, have launched efforts to meet adult needs. But until programs are widely available, families are left to cobble together a patchwork of solutions—from informal day care to hourly caretakers to private residential programs. But these are stopgap measures. Parents worry that they will run out of money to pay for these services—and that they won't be around forever to arrange them for their children.

It's understandable that these parents would feel distraught. Many adults with autism require so much special care that it's hard to imagine anyone but a loving family member willing to provide it. "My wife and I are concerned about what's going to happen to our son when we pass on," says Lee Jorwic, whose son Christopher, 17, is unable to speak even though he's been in therapy since childhood. At 6 feet 4 inches and 290 pounds, Christopher is "our gentle giant," his father says. But because of his disabilities, even the most routine tasks require extraordinary preparations. Two years ago, for example, Christopher got an eye infection. He couldn't sit still long enough for the doctor to perform an exam so he had to go under anesthesia twice "just so the guy could look in his eye," his father says. Grossman says the Autism Society gets hundreds of calls every day from families like the Jorwics. "The most distressing, most disheartening, are from parents of older kids, parents who are at the end of life," he says. "They've been fighting this all their life, and they don't have a place for the kid after they die."

The natural successors to parents as caretakers would be siblings. Some families feel that's too much of a burden; others say that's a natural part of life in a family with autism. When one sibling has autism, the needs of so-called neurotypical children may seem to come second. Beth Eisman of Potomac, Md., recently sent her oldest daughter, Melanie, 18, off to college. Her goal for her younger daughter, Dana, 16, is more basic: independence. Dana's tantrums limited the family's participation in Melanie's school activities. "The old days were pretty bad," Eisman says. "Melanie often took the brunt of it." Now that Melanie is gone, Dana feels the loss. Eisman says Dana often goes into her sister's room and says, "I want Melanie."

Many families are sustained knowing that, by raising awareness of autism, they have already given their children the gift of a meaningful identity. "If this was 10 years ago, my daughter's classmates might say she's the one who talks to herself all the time and flaps her hands," says Roy Richard Grinker, an anthropologist at George Washington University and father of Isabel, 15. "But if you ask these kids in 2006 about Isabel, they say she's the one who plays the cello and who's smart about animals." Inspired by his daughter, Grinker explored autism in different cultures for his book "Unstrange Minds: Remapping the World of Autism" (*Basic Books, 2007*). "The more peers of the same age group understand about autism, the more likely they are to be kind, caring and integrate them into community life."

Twenty years ago, that kind of acceptance was inconceivable. Autism was considered rare and few physicians understood it or were able to help. The disorder was first identified by Leo Kanner of Johns Hopkins in 1943. About the same time a German scientist, Hans Asperger, described a less severe form of the condition. But with the ascendancy of psychoanalysis in the postwar years, the predominant view was that autism was a psychological disorder caused by a lack of love from "refrigerator mothers," a term introduced by the controversial psychologist Bruno Bettelheim. In the 1970s, parents started pushing back against this theory and encouraging researchers to look for neurological causes. It wasn't until 1980 that autism became an official clinical diagnosis, separate from childhood schizophrenia or retardation. Since that time, as scientists have learned more, they have broadened the diagnosis to include a spectrum of disabilities. Now, they are re-evaluting it even further, considering the idea that there may be multiple "autisms."

As knowledge about autism spread in the 1990s, families began to get more accurate diagnoses for children who might in the past have been labeled mentally retarded or emotionally disturbed, and the number of cases skyrocketed. Because of the Internet and extensive networking, parents around the country found allies and became powerful and articulate advocates. Even longtime autism researchers say families have really led the way. "Beyond raising awareness," says Dr. Thomas Insel, director of the National Institute of Mental Health, "families have become the real experts on this disorder. They have to figure out how to cope with a child who becomes explosive, disruptive, who could have a meltdown at any moment. They become highly skilled at knowing what helps."

Autism has set all these families on a unique journey and, while the road ahead is still unclear, they cherish small triumphs along the way. Grinker has a Ph.D. from Harvard and, in his community, many parents dream of sending their children to the Ivy League. He and his wife, Joyce, a psychiatrist, know that Isabel will never join them. But raising Isabel has its own rewards. Isabel's sister, Olivia, 13, is "like a third parent," says Grinker. The family judges Isabel not by the standards of others but by how far she has come. "When Isabel achieves something, I feel like we're a team, like we all did it, and I feel incredibly rewarded," he says. For now, that is enough.

With Karen Springen and Mary Carmichael

Test Your Knowledge Form

We encourage you to photocopy and use this page as a tool to assess how the articles in *Annual Editions* expand on the information in your textbook. By reflecting on the articles you will gain enhanced text information. You can also access this useful form on a product's book support Web site at *http://www.mhcls.com/online/*.

NAME:

DATE:

TITLE AND NUMBER OF ARTICLE:

BRIEFLY STATE THE MAIN IDEA OF THIS ARTICLE:

LIST THREE IMPORTANT FACTS THAT THE AUTHOR USES TO SUPPORT THE MAIN IDEA:

WHAT INFORMATION OR IDEAS DISCUSSED IN THIS ARTICLE ARE ALSO DISCUSSED IN YOUR TEXTBOOK OR OTHER READINGS THAT YOU HAVE DONE? LIST THE TEXTBOOK CHAPTERS AND PAGE NUMBERS:

LIST ANY EXAMPLES OF BIAS OR FAULTY REASONING THAT YOU FOUND IN THE ARTICLE:

LIST ANY NEW TERMS/CONCEPTS THAT WERE DISCUSSED IN THE ARTICLE, AND WRITE A SHORT DEFINITION:

We Want Your Advice

ANNUAL EDITIONS revisions depend on two major opinion sources: one is our Advisory Board, listed in the front of this volume, which works with us in scanning the thousands of articles published in the public press each year; the other is you—the person actually using the book. Please help us and the users of the next edition by completing the prepaid article rating form on this page and returning it to us. Thank you for your help!

ANNUAL EDITIONS: Educating Children with Exceptionalities 08/09

ARTICLE RATING FORM

Here is an opportunity for you to have direct input into the next revision of this volume.
We would like you to rate each of the articles listed below, using the following scale:

1. **Excellent: should definitely be retained**
2. **Above average: should probably be retained**
3. **Below average: should probably be deleted**
4. **Poor: should definitely be deleted**

Your ratings will play a vital part in the next revision.
Please mail this prepaid form to us as soon as possible.
Thanks for your help!

RATING	ARTICLE
	1. Learn about Your New Students
	2. Using Technology to Teach about Individual Differences Related to Disabilities
	3. Large-Scale Assessments
	4. Use Authentic Assessment Techniques to Fulfill the Promise of No Child Left Behind
	5. Making the Case for Early Identification and Intervention for Young Children at Risk for Learning Disabilities
	6. Collaborative Steps
	7. Building Relationships with Challenging Children
	8. Build Organizational Skills in Students with Learning Disabilities
	9. No More Friday Spelling Tests?
	10. Addressing the Social and Emotional Needs of Twice-Exceptional Students
	11. Assessment and Intervention for Bilingual Children with Phonological Disorders
	12. A Speech-Language Approach to Early Reading Success
	13. Filling the Potholes in the Road to Inclusion
	14. Service-Learning Opportunities That Include Students with Moderate and Severe Disabilities
	15. Fitting In
	16. Psychiatric Disorders and Treatments: A Primer for Teachers

RATING	ARTICLE
	17. I Want to Go Back to Jail
	18. Classroom Behavior Management
	19. Students with Emotional and Behavioral Disorders *Can* Manage Their Own Behavior
	20. The Debate over Deaf Education
	21. Using Tactile Strategies with Students Who Are Blind and Have Severe Disabilities
	22. Making Inclusion a Reality for Students with Severe Disabilities
	23. Classroom Interventions for Students with Traumatic Brain Injuries
	24. Empowering Students with Severe Disabilities to Actualize Communication Skills
	25. Savior Parents
	26. Accommodations for Students with Disabilities
	27. ADHD Among Students Receiving Special Education Services
	28. Finding What Works
	29. Understanding the Young Gifted Child
	30. Read All About It
	31. Academic Strategies That Work for Gifted Students with Learning Disabilities
	32. The Transition from Middle School to High School
	33. Postsecondary Academies
	34. What Happens When They Grow Up

ANNUAL EDITIONS: EDUCATING CHILDREN WITH EXCEPTIONALITIES

ABOUT YOU

Name   Date

Are you a teacher? ☐ A student? ☐
Your school's name

Department

Address   City   State   Zip

School telephone #

YOUR COMMENTS ARE IMPORTANT TO US!

Please fill in the following information:
For which course did you use this book?

Did you use a text with this ANNUAL EDITION? ☐ yes ☐ no
What was the title of the text?

What are your general reactions to the Annual Editions concept?

Have you read any pertinent articles recently that you think should be included in the next edition? Explain.

Are there any articles that you feel should be replaced in the next edition? Why?

Are there any World Wide Web sites that you feel should be included in the next edition? Please annotate.

May we contact you for editorial input? ☐ yes ☐ no
May we quote your comments? ☐ yes ☐ no